Interaction Between

Brāhmaṇical and Buddhist Art

Interaction Between
Brāhmaṇical and Buddhist Art

Editor
R.C. Sharma

Associate Editor
Pranati Ghosal

Acharya Narendra Dev
International Research Institute
of Buddhist Studies
Lucknow

Jñāna-Pravāha
Centre for Cultural Studies
Varanasi

D.K. Printworld (P) Ltd.
New Delhi

Cataloging in Publication Data — DK
[Courtesy : D.K. Agencies (P) Ltd. <information@dkagencies. com>]

International Seminar on Interaction Between Brāhmaṇical and Buddhist Art (2003: Varanasi, India)
Interaction between Buddhism and Brāhmaṇical art / editor, R.C. Sharma; associate editor, Pranati Ghosal.
p., 25 cm.
Proceedings of the International Seminar on Interaction Between Brāhmaṇical and Buddhist Art, held at Varanasi during 14-17 February 2003.
Includes bibliographical references.
Includes index.
ISBN 8124602646

1. Art, Hindu — India — Congresses. 2. Art, Buddhist — India — Congresses. 3. Art, Hindu — Influence — Congresses. 4. Art, Buddhist — Influence — Congresses. I. Sharma R.C. (Ramesh Chandra), 1936- II. Ghosal, Pranati, 1956- III. Title.

DDC 704.948 945 095 4 21

Proceedings of the **International Seminar on Interaction Between Brāhmaṇical and Buddhist Art** held during 14-17 February, 2003 at Jñāna Pravāha, Centre for Cultural Studies, Varanasi (UP) in collaboration with Archarya Narendra Dev International Research Institute of Buddhist Studies, Lucknow.

First Published in India in 2004

ISBN 81-246-0264-6

Publishers

Jñāna-Pravāha
Centre for Cultural Studies
South of Samne Ghat
Varanasi – 221005
Phone : (0542) 2366326 Fax : 2366971
e-mail : jpvns@satyam.net.in
website : www.jnanapravaha.org

Acharya Narendra Dev International Research Institute of Buddhist Studies
Vipin Khand,
Gomti Nagar
Lucknow
(Uttar Pradesh)
Phone : (0522) 2300504

D.K. Printworld (P) Ltd.
'Srikunj,' F-52, Bali Nagar
New Delhi – 110015
Phone : (011) 2545 3975, 2546 6019 Fax : (011) 2546 5926
E-mail : dkprintworld@vsnl.net
www. dkprintworld.com

Printed by : D.K. Printworld (P) Ltd., New Delhi.

Contents

Dedicated to

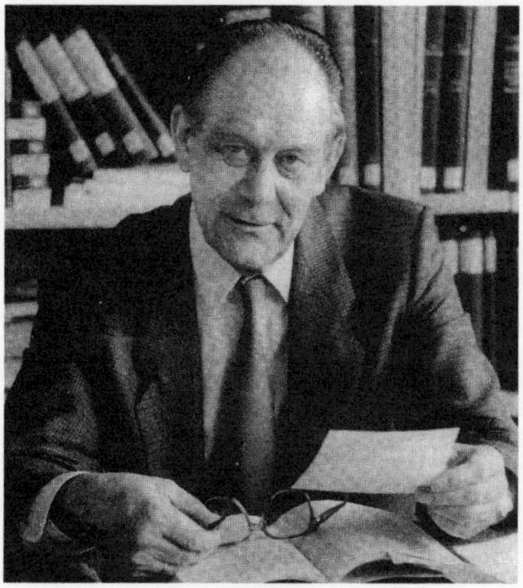

Professor Herbert Härtel

(b. 1921, Founder-Director of the Museum für Indische Kunst
and Professor of Indian Art History at the Freie Universität, Berlin)

&

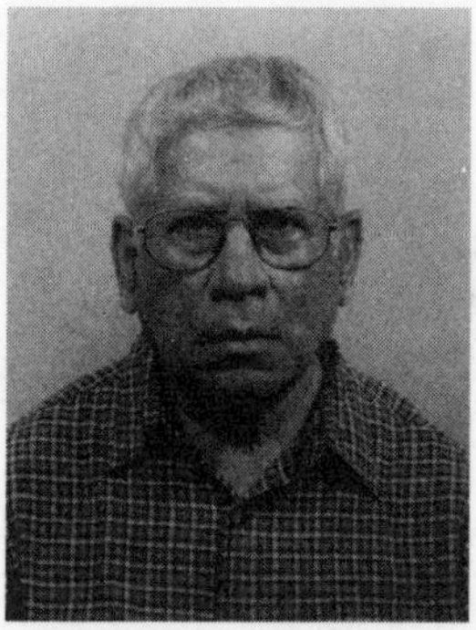

Dr. Gouriswar Bhattacharya

(b. 1924, Former Scientific Scholar in the Museum of Indian Art, Berlin
and teaching in Freie Universität, Berlin)

Preface

It is a great pleasure to place before the scholars and researchers, the proceedings of an International Seminar held at Jñāna-Pravāha, Varanasi in February 2003 on *Interaction Between Brāhmaṇical and Buddhist Art.*

With the exchange of thought process of two religions, artistic traits were interwoven, mostly happily and sometimes forcefully and malignantly. The seed of interaction was sown in the Kuṣāṇa period and this continued to grow for more than a millennium and half. We, thus, find the fusion of Brāhmaṇical and Buddhist deities in different parts of the country, either in the forms of symbols and motifs or through iconographic representation. It was, therefore, deemed proper to elucidate this important theme in some important academic forum. Consequently, a good number of aspects has been covered by the scholars who presented their papers; they deserve our heartfelt gratitude.

The seminar was organized in collaboration with Acharya Narendra Dev International Research Institute of Buddhist Studies, Lucknow — an organization, which is deeply involved in the dissemination of Buddhist theme and culture at higher level. Besides Dr. Yogendra Singh, Director of the Institute, we are much indebted to Sri Sailesh Krishna, the then Secretary of Culture, Government of Uttar Pradesh for his benevolent attitude and release of grant not only for Seminar, but also for the publication of this volume. Similarly, Smt. Bimla Poddar, Founder Trustee of Jñāna-Pravāha lent her tremendous support at every stage of Conference and in bringing out the proceedings. Dr. Gouriswar Bhattacharya deserves our special thanks for his multiple cooperation.

Shri Chandraneel Sharma and Dr. Neeraj Kumar Pandey have assisted in different ways in preparation of the press copy of the book.

The book is dedicated to Prof. Herbert Härtel, and Dr. Gourishwar Bhattacharya, two eminent German scholars, who have seen eighty springs of life and whose contribution in the field of Indology is laudable. We wish them जीवतां शरद: शतम्।

List of Illustrations

Plates

Figures

Transliteration Chart

अ *a* (but)
आ *ā* (palm)
इ *i* (it)
ई *ī* (beet)
उ *u* (put)
ऊ *ū* (pool)
ऋ *ṛ* (rhythm)
ए *e* (play)
ऐ *ai* (high)
ओ *o* (toe)
औ *au* (loud)
क *ka* (skate)[1]
ख* *kha* (blockhead)[1]
ग *ga* (gate)[1]
घ *gha* (loghut)[1]

ङ *ṅa* (sing)[1]
च *ca* (chunk)[2]
छ* *cha* (catch him)[2]
ज *ja* (john)[2]
झ *jha* (hedgehog)[2]
ञ *ña* (bunch)[2]
ट *ṭa* (start)[3]
ठ* *ṭha* (anthill)[3]
ड *ḍa* (dart)[3]
ढ* *ḍha* (godhead)[3]
ण* *ṇa* (under)[3]
त *ta* (path)[4]
थ *tha* (thunder)[4]
द *da* (that)[4]
ध* *dha* (breathe)[4]

न *na* (numb)[4]
प *pa* (spin)[5]
फ* *pha* (loophole)[5]
ब *ba* (bin)[5]
भ *bha* (abhor)[5]
म *ma* (much)[5]
य *ya* (young)
र *ra* (drama)
ल *la* (luck)
व *va* (vile)
श *śa* (shove)
ष *ṣa* (bushel)
स *sa* (so)
ह *ha* (hum)

ं *ṁ anusvāra* (nasalisation of preceding vowel)
: *ḥ visarga* (aspiration of preceding vowel)

* No exact English equivalents for these letters.

[1] guttural [2] palatal [3] lingual [4] dental
[5] labial

1

*Introduction**

R.C. Sharma

INTERACTION is a natural phenomenon, particularly between man and man, community and community, races and races, civilization and civilization or between one stock of people and the other stock. Those who know or want to know each other, the interaction is sure and frequent, but even between the unknown people the interaction takes place and it depends on numerous factors. The process and progress of interaction may be unfolded through multiple layers.

Coming closer or together is the fundamental principle of interaction. This may be through conversation, exchange of thoughts or philosophy, exchange of goods, different types of alliances including the matrimonial ones. All these are friendly interactions. But there are some other or critical circumstances when the interaction is activated or the two groups are forced to interact. There is some type of interaction in war and battlefield between the two armies nowadays; the network of communication plays a vital role to decide the fate of an event such as war.

Thus, the interaction is of willing and unwilling nature. The willing interaction leads to harmony and the unwilling or forced interaction ends into disharmony. Annihilation, destruction, surrender, submission, animosity, and imposition continue to widen the gap despite a visible interaction at the surface level and hence the conflict erupts like a volcano.

---

* This is the Keynote Address delivered by the author at the International Seminar held at Jñāna Pravāha, Varanasi from 14th to 17th Feb. 2003.

If we consider these different channels of interaction, we find that in the case of Brāhmaṇical and Buddhist art, iconography and architecture mainly projects the mutual goodwill and harmony, although the rigid and sectarian champions in both the camps have been undermining this cordiality from time to time. There are more than one reasons to believe that an in-built consentience is the basic characteristics of Brāhmaṇism and Buddhism. Both have evolved in the same land, both have almost the same background, both have the same society or people, both had the same audience, both believed in the same social order basically following the theory of *karma*, both followed the similar methodology and both used almost the same language. This may be submitted here that beside Pāli, Prākṛta or Māgadhī, there exists a large number of important Buddhist texts in Sanskrit. The other uniting force has been the adoption of image worship, which reflects a great deal of harmony at thought and its implementation level. At the same time, the occasional rivalry and sectarian competition can also not be overlooked.

If one cares to go into depth, the differences seen between the two at the surface, vanish soon. Both Brāhmaṇism and Buddhism are progenies of the same mother culture. In the case of other religions, the distinction may be clear and sharp, but in these two such a dividing line cannot be incised. The same can be said about Jainism and Sikhism. All these are the branches of the great banyan tree, which we call religion or culture. These are not contradictory to each other, but essentially supplementary.

Since the Medieval Age, the Buddha has been called as *nāstika* because he did not accept the Vedas as authority and supposed to have denounced them. This presumption is not wholly correct. The fact is that the Master did not discuss God as the Creator and the later Buddhist exponents just discarded the idea. There are some schools of thought in the Brāhmaṇic or Hindu tradition, which do not depend on God who plays almost nil or scanty role. These are Mīmāṁsā, Vaiśeṣika, Sāṁkhya, etc., yet these are not branded as *nāstika*.

With regard to the rejection of the Vedas, this may be pointed out here that the Buddha denounced only the rituals of Vedas, and particularly those portions, which advocated for the sacrifice of animals. Poet Jayadeva, in his famous lyric *Gītagovinda*, puts the fact convincingly

> निन्दसि यज्ञविधेरहह श्रुतिजातं सदय हृदय दर्शित पशुघातम् केशव धृत बुद्ध शरीर — **1.13**

> O Lord! After seeing the slaughter of animals your heart was filled with compassion and you had denounced such Vedic sacrifices and rituals. (For this reason) Keśava assumed the body of the Buddha.

In another verse, the Buddha has been called as embodiment of compassion — कारुण्यमातन्वते ।

This means that the criticism of Vedas was confined to the ritual part — *karma-kāṇḍa* only and the other two vital parts, i.e., *jñāna* (knowledge) and *upāsanā* (devotion) were not attacked. The *Brāhmaṇadhammīya-sutta* of *Suttanipāta* informs that the Buddha was shocked to watch the killing of animals but at the same place he pays respect to the Brāhmaṇic traditions and also the Vedic *yajña*s, which are devoid of animal killing.

The views of Jayadeva have been upheld and further elaborated by the nineteenth-century Buddhist poet Sambudhāgama Cakravartī Rāmacandra in his *Buddhaśataka-stotra:*

> यत्रच्छाग तुरङ्ग मारण विधिर्वेदेऽपि तं निन्दसि
> प्रेम्णा प्राणभूतामत: सकरुणस्त्वत्तो महान् नापर:।
> एवं ते गुणसम्पदो न विषया बुद्धेरसूयात्मनां
> ते मूढा: प्रलपन्ति हन्त सुगतो यद्वेद निन्दतीत्ययम्।।
>
> — *Buddhabhaktiśataka*, 96

> You condemn only those parts of the Vedas, which narrate the process of killing of goat and horse. You are full of mercy and none can surpass you in compassion. The wealth of your virtues is beyond the grasp of those who feel envious of you and such foolish fellows absurdly say that Sugata (Buddha) opposes Vedas.

Of course, there are some occasions (Canki of *Majjhimanikāya* and *Tebijjasutta* of *Dīghanikāya*, etc.) when the Vedic conventions have been criticized, but such statements do not aim at humiliating the Vedas. We come across a number of passages in the highly esteemed Brāhmaṇic literature where the sacrificial Vedic rituals have been rejected but the other parts have been respected. The verses of the *Gītā* are well known in this regard:

> यामिमां पुष्पितां वाचं प्रवदन्त्यविपश्चित:।
> वेद वादरता: पार्थ नान्यदस्तीति वादिन:।।
> कामात्मन: स्वर्गपरा जन्मकर्मफलप्रदाम्।
> क्रियाविशेषबहुलां भोगैश्वर्य गतिं प्रति।। — **2.42-43**

> Only the unwise persons, who cling to the multiple rituals of the Vedas, speak the flowering language that there is nothing more meritorious than the gaining of wealth, worldly pleasures and heaven.

But such practices result in the bondage of birth and rebirth. Like *Gītā*, the Upanisadic wisdom did not favour the Vedic sacrifices, which have been seen with disfavour and termed as a weak boat:

प्लवा ह्येते ह्यदृढा यज्ञरूपा: अष्टादशोक्तमवरं येषुकर्म।

— मुण्डक, 1.2.7

> This *yajña* boat is weak and the eighteen forms of their deeds are of lower nature.

There were some contemporary philosophers, such as Ajita Keśakambalin, who did not believe either in this world nor the other, birth or rebirth and also negated the merits and vices of deeds. They are known as *ucchedavādin*s and are the *nāstika*s in the true sense. The *Majjhimanikāya* explains their line of thought, but the Buddha never agreed with them.

In the *Doṇasutta* of *Aṅguttaranikāya,* the Buddha refers to the four categories of Brāhmaṇas, viz., Brahmā, Devasama, Maryādā and Sambhinna-maryāda or Brāhmaṇa-cāṇḍāla. This *sūtra* also suggests his respect for the good conduct and criticism for the low character brāhmaṇas. *Aśoka* held brāhmaṇas and śramaṇas in equal regard — ब्राह्मण समणानं साधु दाने.... Numerous references of Buddhist literature suggest the birth of Buddha either in brāhmaṇa or in the kṣatriya family and not in the lower cast — बुद्धो लोके उप्पज्जन्ता खत्तियकुलेवा ब्राह्मणकुले (*सुत्तनिपात*)

It was on the foundation of this philosophical thought that the castle of Brāhmaṇical and Buddhist art and iconography evolved, developed and flourished for more than a millennium of years. In the beginning, the important gods, like Brahmā, Indra and his companion Pañcaśikha Gandharva and a few nymphs appear to request the Buddha to preach the Law to gods in heaven. This was an amicable interaction and the request was granted. Earlier, before *bodhi*, the gods he had a hostile attitude and deputed Kāma (cupid) to disturb the penance of *Bodhisattva* Siddhārtha, who took the vow not to leave the seat until the Enlightenment was obtained. The episode of *Māravijaya* (victory over cupid) provided a high pedestal to the Prince emerging into the Buddha, and the artists in the early sculptural schools, like Mathurā, Amarāvatī, Nāgārjunakoṇḍa and especially of Gāndhāra, illustrated this event vividly and repeatedly. The glory of the Master through *Jātaka* narrations and preachings specially spread and a good number of folk deities became the part of the pantheon of Buddhism. These include Kubera, sometimes known as Jambhala, *yakṣa*s, *yakṣī*s, *nāga*s, *nāgī*s, etc. Some came willingly and others, like Apalāla, were forced to surrender. Their position remained inferior or subordinate. The future Buddha Maitreya supports the theory of incarnation in the early Kuṣāṇa age.

The conflict with Devadatta or with some *yakṣa*s and *nāga*s, probably necessitated for providing an escort and Vajrapāṇi holding the thunderbolt, like Indra, appears on the scene. In the Gupta period, the attending figures or the subordinate deities almost disappear and the *Bodhisattva* in the form of Avalokiteśvara wearing a crown resembles Viṣṇu with distinction of a *dhyānī* Buddha on the forehead. This was a process of subtle interaction. The Gupta period witnessed the aesthetic zenith, although the number of production was restricted.

With the passage of time, new horizons of interaction were explored through art. Tārā combined at least two aspects, e.g., Sarasvatī and Lakṣmī symbolizing learning and prosperity. Similarly, the goddess of dawn Uṣā was transformed into the Marīcī, who was provided a chariot of pigs instead of horses. The process of interaction is conspicuously reflected in the sculptures of Kārttikeya as Manjuśrī, Sūryalokeśvara, Śivalokeśvara, Viṣṇulokeśvara, Umāmaheśvara, Akṣobhya with Gaṇeśa below. We do notice sometimes the warring deities, like Aparājitā, trampling Brāhmaṇical deities. On the other hand, Siṁhanādalokeśvara represents a complete and harmonious fusion between the Brāhmaṇical and Buddhist art. At the thought process, the Buddha was ultimately conceived as one of the incarnations and the artists soon gave him the place in a panel above or on the side of the Viṣṇu images.

The following verse of Mānatuṅgācārya is an excellent citation of harmonious Interaction between Brāhmaṇism and Buddhism:

बुद्धस्त्वमेव विबुधार्चित! बुद्धिबोधात्
त्वं शङ्करोऽसि भुवनत्रय शंकरत्वात्।
धातासि धीर! शिव मार्ग विधेर्विधानात्
व्यक्तं त्वमेव भगवन्! पुरूषोत्तमोऽसि।।

— *Bhaktāmara Stotra,* 25

2

Buddha in Brāhmaṇical Art and Architecture

N.P. Joshi

In the Brāhmaṇical sculptures we do come across Buddha but his images are hardly intended for worship. Buddha was well accepted as the ninth incarnation of Viṣṇu by most of the authorities, so much so that even in the *saṅkalpa* text, which is daily recited, the word *Bauddhāvatāre* is there to mark the time sequence. In spite of this, worshipping him in image or symbolic form was prohibited; obviously because the very aim of this incarnation, as the Purāṇas inform was to mislead people by advocating false doctrines (*māyāmoha-śāstra*) and dissuade them from following the right path advocated by the Vedas, that is Śrutis and Smṛtis. This position of controversial nature was a hard pill to swallow. On one side the Buddha was to be accepted as *avatāra* of Viṣṇu, but on the other his preachings were not to be venerated and followed. It is interesting to see how the Brāhmaṇical sculptors and artists did face this paradoxical situation.

Among the ten incarnations of Viṣṇu the independent figures of Varāha, Narasiṁha and Kṛṣṇa as Vāsudeva, that is the four-handed form, appeared right from the early centuries of the Christian era. Trivikrama that is Vāmana, Paraśurāma and Rāma came to be added later. No images of Matsya and Kūrma *avatāras* assignable to the early age have yet been reported. Images of Buddha and Ṛṣabha too were there, but that was in the Buddhist and Jaina context. Appearance of all the ten incarnations together either on a slab (*daśāvatāra-paṭṭa*) or on the back-slab of the images of Viṣṇu, Śeṣaśāyī (Bhopal Museum, no. 156), Hari-Hara (Khajuraho Museum, no. 558), Varāha (State Museum, Lucknow, no. O.84), Sūrya (Mathura Museum, 88.19), etc., are post-Gupta features. Earliest *daśāvatāra-paṭṭa* from Paṭhārī in Madhya Pradesh has been attributed to late Gupta age. Another slab of tenth century AD is there in the Bharatpur Museum (21/117) in Rajasthan. Daśāvatāra representations on the back-slab, even with Buddha as the ninth one, served as the decorative elements. A number of Viṣṇu figures from eastern and central India, and some from south (e.g., Kolhapur Museum, no. 63 — Viṣṇu from Bay Bag — Maharashtra; Archaeological Museum, Goa, no. 320 — Viṣṇu from Sawāī-verā) show Buddha in the following poses as the ninth *avatāra* :

(i) Standing with right hand in *abhaya-mudrā* (SML. 57.73) — seventh century AD.

(ii) Seated in *lalitāsana* (SML. 59.34) — seventh-eighth century.

(iii) Standing with right hand in *vara* and the left holding hem of the garment (SML. 42.189) — eighth century.

(iv) Standing as above, but the right hand has been brought near the chest in *abhaya-mudrā* (SML. 51.73) — eighth-ninth century.

(v) Seated in *padmāsana* with right hand placed near the navel, left holding hem of the garment (SML. H.115) — tenth century.

(vi) Seated in *bhūmisparśa-mudrā* (SML. 41.55) — eleventh century.

(vii) Seated in meditation (SML. O.239) — twelfth century.

(viii) Seated in *padmāsana* with both hands in *abhaya-mudrā* (SML. O.275) — twelfth-thirteenth century.

Besides these *avatāra* depictions, the sculptors of the Eastern school sometimes carved syncretistic images such as Hari-Hara-Sūrya-Buddha, Sūrya-Lokeśvara, Viṣṇu-Lokeśvara, etc., where in Buddha or Lokeśvara also appeared in subordinate position.

Independent figures of the Buddha in the Brāhmaṇical context is a rare phenomena, but not totally absent. One comes from Orissa and the other from Karnataka.[1] On the rear wall of the sanctum of the Jagannātha temple at Purī there appears independent depiction of Buddha assignable to *c.* twelfth century. He is seated in meditation with an uprising long stemmed lotus on both sides and surrounded by small Buddha figures, apparently his disciples or perhaps other

1. B.V. Shetti, "An Image of Buddhāvatāra Viṣṇu at Badami," *Nirgrantha*, vol. 1, Ahmedabad, 1995, pp. 89-91.

Buddhas. The other case is more interesting. Near Bādāmī (ancient Vātāpī, the capital of the Western Cāḷukyas) there is a large lake called Agastya-tīrtha. Near this lake upon the cliff, a large enthroned male image has been carved, which is locally known as *koṣṭhī-rāya* or the "laper king." The bejewelled person depicted here is seated in *padmāsana* on a lion-throne under heavy foliage of a tree. His right hand raised in *abhaya-mudrā* carries a rosary and the left rests on the lap. His head bears no *uṣṇīṣa,* that is the top knot, but knobby curves are there. The circular halo behind his head suggests the divine character of the figure. He is flanked by well dressed and crowned chowrie (flywhisk) bearers. The most interesting is the appearance of miniature *cakra* and *śaṅkha* on the terminals of the throne-back, which further add to the divine nature of the main figure. Though the local tradition takes him to be a king originally suffering from leprosy, but got cured after bathing in the Agastya-*tīrtha,* it is in fact something more than that. Delineation of the image of the Buddha seated on *vajrāsana* under the *bodhi*-tree, halo behind, *abhaya* pose and appearance of *śaṅkha* and *cakra* in the composition call for deeper probe. Working on these lines B.V. Shetti has identified the figure as Buddhāvatāra or Māyāmoha-Viṣṇu. Viṣṇu was the family deity of the Cāḷukyas of Bādāmī, and therefore, his depiction as Māyāmoha in a secluded cave is not a surprise.

In spite of all what has been said above, the depiction of Gautama Buddha as the scion of the Śākya clan and the preceptor of a heretic sect as an *avatāra* of Viṣṇu was not readily accepted by all. The persons of this school of thought took recourse to the following ways for depiction of the ninth incarnation :

(A) Some in the name of the Buddha preferred to substitute Viṣṇu himself in some form. For example, the *Matsya Purāṇa*[2] describing *nakṣatra-puruṣa-vrata* recommends worship of Vāsudeva figure specially his forehead, on Citrā *nakṣatra* in the name of Buddha. Similarly, the *Varāha Purāṇa*[3] prescribes worship of the gold figure of Dāmodara in connection with the celebration of Buddha-dvādaśī.

(B) In Maharashtra, the figure of Viṭṭhala or Pāṇḍuraṅga was sometimes used as the substitute of the Buddha.

(C) In Orissa, Jagannātha served the same purpose, a fact which can clearly

2. *Matsya Purāṇa*, Mor Edition, Calcutta, 47.244, p. 123.
3. *Varāha Purāṇa*, 47, 1-5.

be noticed in the sets of Daśāvatāra *gañjiffās*[4] or playing cards current in Orissa. Here one can see the God standing with upraised hands and nine conches or lotuses or any other symbols indicating the serial number of *avatāra*. The type from other regions is also interesting.

In the Sāvantawāḍī set[5] from Maharashtra, the Buddha has been shown as four-handed God seated cross-legged and carrying lotuses in the upraised extra hands. His normal hands have been brought near the navel.

In the Rājasthānī *gañjiffa*[6] sets, the Buddha is again four armed richly dressed seated on throne flanked by two devotees on right, and two attendants carrying chowrie (flywhisk) and *morchala* on the left side.

The symbolic and colour representations of the ninth incarnation in the Daśāvatāra *gañjiffa* sets is no less interesting. It, is being tablized below[7] :

Region	*Deity*	*Colour*	*Symbol*
Rajasthan	Buddha	Yellow	Five-petalled flower or lotus
Deccan (Nirmal)	Buddha	Ochre Yellow	Turbaned male head
Deccan (Karnool)	Buddha	Red	Turbaned male head
Deccan (Cuḍḍapah)	Kṛṣṇa	Gold	Seated male in profile
Mysore	Kṛṣṇa	Brown	Cow
Sāvantawāḍī I	Buddha	White	Conch
Orissa	Jagannātha	Green-brown	Lotus bud
Orissa	Jagannātha	Dark grey	Three-petalled lotus
Orissa	Jagannātha	Yellow	Three-petalled lotus bud

Buddha in the Purāṇas[8]

Since Buddhism and Jainism commanded wide popularity in spite of their being totally adverse to the Purāṇic doctrines, the Purāṇas could not afford to neglect them altogether. Though some like the *Viṣṇu*, *Vāyu* and *Brahma Purāṇa* omit mentioning Buddha as an incarnation, others like the *Matsya*, *Varāha*, *Agni*, *Padma*,

4. Rudolf von Leydon, *Indische Spielkarten Leinfelden*, Echterdingen, 1977, inv.-Nr. B. 994, Kat. No. 80, p. 99.
5. Rudolf von Leydon, *Indische Spielkarten Leinfelden*, Echterdingen, 1977, inv.-Nr. B. 994, Kat. No. 80, p. 95.
6. Rudolf von Leydon, *Indische Spielkarten Leinfelden*, Echterdingen, 1977, p. 83.
7. *Ibid.*, p. 21.
8. N.P. Joshi, "Teachers of the Heterodox Sects — Buddhism and Jainism in the Eyes of the Purāṇas (Viṣṇu, Śiva and Bṛhaspati)," *Nirgrantha*, vol. 1, 1995, pp. 50-68.

Skanda, Bhāgavata, Bhaviṣya do accept him as the ninth *avatāra* of Viṣṇu, but portray him altogether in a different colour. He has been described as one produced by Viṣṇu from his own body to mislead the invincible demons by teaching them false doctrines. The idea was to make them quit the "right path" laid down by the Vedas and Smṛtis, embrace the foul principles (*pākhaṇḍa, māyāmoha śāstra*), and thus making them weak easily to be defeated by the gods. The *Viṣṇu Purāṇa*[9] describes this form, not *avatāra*, as *māyāmoha*, or *nagna*, who was naked (*digambara*), had his head shaven (*muṇḍī*), and carried peacock feathers in his hands (*barhi-piccha-dharaḥ*). This fellow, later on wore red garments (*raktāmbara-dharaḥ*), talked of *nirvāṇa* in sweet tone, kept on murmuring "know" and "understand" (*buddhyatā, buddhyatva*) and asked the *asuras* to refrain from killing the animals (*paśughāta*). This episode of Māyāmoha finds mention in the *Agni Purāṇa*[10] also. It is said that Viṣṇu in the form of Māyāmoha became son of king Śuddhodana and His followers became the Bauddhas. Later on He became *arhat* and converted other group of the *daityas*. Some other Purāṇas like the *liṅga*[11] and Śiva[12] state that Māyāmoha created by Viṣṇu was the author of voluminous Māyāmoha-śāstra in *apabhraṁśa* language. He dissuaded Tripurāsura and his people by preaching the Buddhist texts (*bauddhāgamas*). As per *Padma Purāṇa*[13] this Mayāmoha was Buddha himself. The *Bhaviṣya Purāṇa*[14] makes mention of Buddha in a very confusing way. As per this work Kāśyapa produced god Gautama, who ruled and preached at Paṭṭaṇa-nagara. His successors were Śākyamuni, Śuddhodana, Śākyasiṁha, Buddhasiṁha, Candragupta, Bindusāra and Aśoka.

As per other Purāṇic versions, the role of dissuading people from the right path was played by Bṛhaspati, the priest of the gods and Śiva also. Bṛhaspati approached the demons as imposter of Śukrācārya, who had then left the camp of the demons for practising penance, and preached them Jaina doctrines. The *Varāha Purāṇa* refers to the creation of *moha-śāstra* by Śiva under the name of *Niśvāsa-saṁhitā* of the Pāśupatas for the *veda-bāhya* brāhmaṇas of *kaliyuga*. The

9. *Viṣṇu Purāṇa*, III, *adhyāya* 18, Gita Press, Gorakhapur.
10. *Agni Purāṇa*, 16, 1-4, p. 27, Mor Edition.
11. *Liṅga Purāṇa*, 71, 73-94, p. 211, Mor Edition.
12. *Śiva Purāṇa*, Rudra, V, Yuddha Kāṇḍa II, 5-4, 1-3.
13. *Padma Purāṇa*, VI, 252, 19-20, p. 917, Mor Edition.
14. *Bhaviṣya Purāṇa, Bhaviṣya, pratisarga parva* I.6, cited by Saṁkṣipta Bhaviṣya — *purāṇāṅka, Kalyāṇa*, Gorakhapur.

Mahābhārata calls Śiva as Ṛṣabha among the holy people. Iconographically, there are a number of similarities between the images of Śiva and the first *tīrthaṅkara* Ṛṣabhanātha.

For our present purpose the most interesting information comes from the Kāśī-Khaṇḍa of the *Skanda Purāṇa,*[15] which talks about the Buddhist activities in the regions of Vārāṇasī. The account in brief runs as follows :

> Once there were no rains for sixty long years. Thereupon Brahmā requested Ripuñjaya, a scion of Manu's family, who was practising penance at Vārāṇasī to accept the throne and save the dying prosperity. The prince accepted the offer under condition that then the Devas would quit the earth, and he would be the sole monarch. Brahmā agreed to this and Ripuñjaya under the name Divodāsa successfully started his mission. As settled before along with the other gods, Śiva too had to quit his favourite seat at Vārāṇasī. He was very eager to come back, but this was never possible in the regime of Divodāsa, and ousting of Divodāsa depended on finding faults in his dealings and administration. Several people from Śiva's side tried in vain, but Gaṇapati impressed the King and his ladies and did prepare good ground for further action. He told the King, who had approached him to seek solace, that on 18th day from the day of the event a brāhmaṇa would appear from North before the king and that the king should follow the new comer's advice without any hesitation.

Next role was to be played by Viṣṇu. He assumed the garb of a Buddhist *bhikṣu* (*saugata rūpa*), Puṇyakīrti by name and found a sacred place (*dharmakṣetra*) for himself in the north of Vārāṇasī. Garuḍa became his disciple under the name Vinayakīrti, and Lakṣmī too joined the party as Vijñāna-Kaumudī holding a manuscript in her hand. *Bhikṣu* Puṇyakīrti had mastered religion (*dharma*), polity (*arthaśāstra*) and different sciences (*jñāna-vijñāna*) and had great power of sweet, tender and distinct speech. He had also mastered several practices of black magic like *stambhana, uccāsana, ākṛṣṭi, vaśīkaraṇa*, etc. His discourses were heard with deep interest by birds and the entire flock of deer around remained spell bound and paid reverence. The Purāṇa devotes thirty verses for describing the teachings of Puṇyakīrti, which very much reflect the Buddhist ways of thinking. Vijñāna-Kaumudī preached the ladies of the town, but her teachings and activities were more akin to the Cārvāka and Tāntric doctrines like achievement of happiness at every cost, use of *añjana, yantra, tilakauṣadha, vaśīkaraṇa*, etc. This group of the Buddhists successfully disturbed the subjects of Vārāṇasī.

15. *Skanda Purāṇa*, Kāśī-Khaṇḍa, IV, 58, 71-229, pp. 403-12, Mor Edition.

On the 18th day, as predicted by Gaṇapati, *bhikṣu* Puṇyakīrti from *dharma-kṣetra* assumed the form of a brāhmaṇa and appeared before Divodāsa. There is no indication that the king himself had embraced the Buddhist faith, but his superior and strong position was certainly torpedoed and Śiva's return to Vārāṇasī was thus facilitated.

The Buddhist activities referred to in the Purāṇa suggest the following points:

(A) The *dharma-kṣetra* or the seat of Puṇyakīrti in the north of Vārāṇasī with flocks of deer is the present day Sāranāth, old Mṛgadāva or Ṛṣipaṭṭana. Near the present Sāranāth there is a locality called Saraṅgā or Sāraṅga, which has got something to do with words Sāraṅga (a deer) and Śārṅga-pāṇi (Viṣṇu). Sāranāth, we all know was a famous Buddhist seat for a very long time.

(B) The description suggests a period, when the Buddhist church had come under the Tāntric influence and a number of evil practices had crept in.

(C) SML — State Museum, Lucknow.

3

Interactive Ultimate in the Brāhmaṇical and Buddhist Art

G.B. Deglurkar

I

Both of the same soil Buddhism and Brāhmaṇism were bound by the cultural ethos. The interaction between the Buddhist and Brāhmaṇical art is only the obvious visual form of this common cultural heritage. But even here the interaction between the two can be visualized in two regions (1) religion and philosophy and (2) art and architecture. In other words the syncretism in philosophy and religious thought was responsible to some extent for interaction in art. The religion of the Buddha is for *avidyānivṛtti* (eradication of ignorance) which leads to the *nirvāṇapurogāminām advayapatham* (the only path to attain *nirvāṇa*). This exactly is the outlook of the Upaniṣads also. Ādiśaṅkara has expressed the same in the words *yāvad avidyā na nivartate tāvat jīvasya jīvatvam* (unless and until there is no eradication of ignorance, emancipation of soul is not possible). Śrī Rāmakṛṣṇa too accepted the divinity of Buddha and pointed out the similarities of his teachings to those of the Upaniṣads (*Rāmakṛṣṇa — Prophet of New India*, 1947 Introduction: 29). The interaction in the realm of philosophy and the religious thoughts between Buddhism and Brāhmaṇism influenced various other aspects, especially the religious art and architecture as these fields were more proned to such influences since they make man's mind visual. To sustantiate this statement a brief reference may be made to two Brāhmaṇical icon types and an architectural edifice where distinct traces of Buddhist motifs are discernible and vice versa and to a Buddhist icon type where an influence of Brāhmaṇical icon is clearly implied.

The two Brāhmaṇic images which are referred to above are (1) Lakulīśa and (2) Vyākhyāna Dakṣiṇāmūrti Śiva. Students of iconography know well that there is a great similarity in the depiction of these two images. Lakulīśa was the reviver or organizer of an old religious system as was the Buddha. Obviously, he was looked upon as a preacher and Śiva in his Vyākhyāna Dakṣiṇāmūrti represents very much the same aspect. Thus Lakulīśa with hair arranged in *kapardin* fashion and in *dharma-cakra-mudrā* surrounded by his four disciples reminds one the Buddha delivering his sermon in the Mṛgaśikhāvana at Sāranāth. To simulate with this aspect of the Buddha, occasionally Lakulīśa is also shown with the *dharma-cakra* flanked by two deers carved on the pedestal.

As on the images the influence is perceptible on architecture also. The Buddhist *caityagṛha* with apsidal end and keel-vaulted roof has influenced the Brāhmaṇical temples in the sixth-eighth centuries AD, e.g., the Trivikrama temple at Ṭer in Osmānābād district of Maharashtra, Durgā temple at Aihoḷe in Bījāpur district of Karnataka, the Sahadeva temple at Māmallapuram in Tamil Nadu are tailored on the plan of the *caityagṛha*s. They have apsidal-ended rectangular halls and keel-vaulted roofs unlike the usual Brāhmaṇical temple plans. Moreover, the *kudu*-motif seen on the various parts of the temples is directly borrowed from the Buddhist *caitya gavākṣa*.

II

Let us now turn to an image of the Buddha, which seemingly reflects the Brāhmaṇical philosophy. After all, the images are not only to be admired as works of art which, however, may be a mere *bahiraṅga parīkṣā* but to be read, so to say, as a literary text. Instead of looking at the images in the esoteric way it is always meaningful to read them in an esoteric way which allows the devotee who has been initiated to the inner meaning of the doctrine to understand the image in its full significance or in its spiritual *tattva* (Guiseppe Tucci 1988, Foreword). We are aware that there are two categories of Buddha images classified in Buddhist iconography as (1) symbolic representation and (2) representation in human form. Since the symbolic images were made to fulfil religious needs they are called *dhammakāya*, the form suited to further the *dhamma*. While those which are in human form are designated as *rūpakāya*. After the *nirvāṇa* of Buddha, since there was nothing concrete to concentrate upon, there might have arisen a lot of discussion as to how should he be made visible. Hence, the *stūpa*s were erected at various places symbolizing the Lord's *nirvāṇa*. Likewise, other important events of the Master's life were also symbolized. These symbolic representations are in the form of the footprints, the *bo*-tree, the empty throne, the wheel of law and the parasol. The footprints indicate that He is worthy of following. The *bodhi* tree commemorates his Enlightenment underneath it, while the parasol announces the triumphant march of the Buddha in the field of religion akin to a *cakravartin*, the Wheel of Law reminds all of His maiden sermon delivered in the Deer Park at Sārnāth.

There was nothing besides these to remind the devotee of the events and the important deeds in the life of the Buddha. Later when the Buddhist *saṁgha* split into the Hīnayāna and the Mahāyāna sects, the latter thought of giving human form to the aforementioned symbols so far used by the Hīnayānists. The formless Buddha was now given human form and his images replaced the symbolic representations. The foot-steps were transformed into the person of the Buddha himself, the symbol *dhammacakka* took the shape of an icon in which the Tathāgata is shown with His hands in *dhammacakka pavattana muddā*. Such images are called *rūpakāya*. This emergence of the images of the Buddha also have been the result of the great impact of the *bhakti* movement which was becoming more and more popular in and around Mathurā during the first-second centuries AD.

Images are expected besides other things to personify the cardinal principles of a religious sect and enable the *bhakta* to have an intimate personal dialogue with his deity appearing before him in the human form. The Greeks and the Gāndhārans (Kuṣāṇas in India) could not achieve this desired effect in the icons they sculpted, for their emphasis was on physical beauty and proportion. They were able to create physically very proportionate and attractive images of alluring beauty but failed to inject godliness in them. The *Samādhirāja* says that a devotee should be attracted more towards the god's limitless greatness than his physical proportion and sharp attractive features. It were the Indian artists who presented the Buddha's images with half closed eyes suggestive of his contemplative mood, compassionate soul and spiritual fervour. They, thus could portray the desired emotion on the face of the Master by supplementing them with hand gestures, i.e., *mudrās*.

The *rūpakāya* images were in great demand in the first few centuries of the Christian era and became very popular. But in course of time the devotees and the monks could not derive enough satisfaction from these images since they longed for higher solace. And for this they have ready models through Brāhmaṇical images before them. These are the Ultimate in iconography, since they personify formulae of the Sāṁkhya, the Śaiva Siddhānta and the Pāñcarātra. They can be called *bimba-brahma*. One example of this type of image from the Brāhmaṇical pantheon would be enough to bring our point home.

Iconography is as often, at one and the same time, the artistic expression of religious fervour, as well as the search for the metaphysical ultimate. The search in this regard continued assuming diverse metaphysical expressions, the elusive ultimate within the reach of only an intuitive experience. As the devotional theism of the *bhakti* school gained momentum a new pathway was thrown open for the realization of the formless ultimate. The *nirguṇa* became *saguṇa*, the *nirākāra* assumed vibrant *ākāra* (unqualitative became qualitative, formless assumed form), the metaphysical transformed into the physical. The iconic expression of the metaphysical ultimate not only took diverse form — but forms, which were pregnant with beautiful suggestivity. These fantasies in sculptural stone came to personify in concrete form the dogmas and tenets of the various schools of philosophy, struggling to give expression to the ultimate that pervades the universe. What the words could express through endless discourses appeared in visual stone in compact suggestion.

The image of the Ardhanārīśvara provides an apt example of this. It combines the physical form of a man and woman. *Prima facie,* the image, for any lay devotee would symbolize a synchronic representation of Śiva and his Śakti. The visual impact of the mighty god and his female counterpart in perfect physical harmony, however aesthetic, can also be emotionally disturbing a symbol of perfect union, the androgyne, nevertheless by its very nature that is anti-erotic and barren. The earliest known images belong to the Kuṣāṇa school at Mathurā. The chronological sequence pre-dates the Purāṇic myths which are lame attempts at exploring the mystery of the image, superficially explanatory but not able to reach out to the inner depths of the icon. The chrono-logical origins of the image are also a strong pointer to the true source of inspiration, the eternal duality of the ultimate principle, the *puruṣa* and *prakṛti* of the Sāṁkhyas. The distancing of the *puruṣa* from *prakṛti,* the unconscious matter, was for the Sāṁkhyas the final liberation, the everlasting bliss of unfettered consciousness. The Sāṁkhya doctrine came to be epitomized in *Sāṁkhya-Kārikā* of Īśvarakṛṣṇa around the medieval period, but was only the final blossoming forth of a long process of metaphysical enquiry going back to the pre-Buddhist phase of intellectual ferment. The Sāṁkhya influence went deep permitting the *Mahābhārata* and the *Bhagavad-Gītā,* the Sāṁkhya *jñāna,* the Sāṁkhya path of knowledge forming the foundation for the edifice of *bhakti.* The devotional current, however, transformed the inactive Puruṣa into the active Puruṣottama, the Īśvara who knows everything, who is conscious of everything. The Sāṁkhya duality was no longer simply a play of the conscious and the unconscious; it was not superimposed by a watchful caring *īśvara.* The *Śeṣāvaratā* of the Sāṁkhya sent vibrant currents of creativity into the artistic outpourings of the early centuries AD, the Ardhanārīśvara being one of the manifestations. The two eternal existents, *puruṣa* and the *prakṛti* found an unparalleled form, an imposing and aesthetic blend whose visual impact transports the devotee into the realm of intuitive experience of the primeaval forces of creation.

This and other such images personifying the philosophy might have inspired the Buddhists to prepare an image of the Buddha, which embodies his philosophy. And the outcome of this is the image of the Buddha in preaching attitude.

The Buddhist philosophers amongst the sculptors, thus started to shape an icon, which would emanate the glow of inner peace and knowledge. The icon which emerged out of this intense urge can be designated as *ajjatika rūpa,* i.e., *ādhyātmika rūpa.* The *Vinayapiṭaka* states *ajjati rupe mocceti,* i.e., form that makes man free from all the worldly clinging, vol. iii, p. 113. The *Dhammasaṅgani* describes it as a form (*rūpa*) which reveals an impermanence (*annatto*) of the *rūpa* but arouses wisdom (*panna*). The *ajjatika rūpa* is the form through which one can achieve salvation or *nirvāṇa.* It is thus a form which transports you into another world, rid of all worldly cravings and unfettering the self. How to prepare an image embodying the philosophy leading to *nirvāṇa* might have been hotly discussed. Lengthy deliberations over this matter might have been responsible for many sleepless nights for the thinkers and sculptors. Finally, an image which incorporates the suggestions of the philosophers was prepared successfully by the artists, rightly recognized as the *ādhyātmikakāya.* This is an image of the Buddha in the preaching attitude which was prepared in the fifth century AD. This is the ultimate image.

III

The Buddha in this particular image form is shown seated on a throne on the lower part of which is carved the Wheel of Law flanked by two deer, one on each side indicating the place where the delivery of the first sermon took place. It is also flanked by his five disciples who listened to the first sermon. The Buddha is depicted with half-closed eyes in a deeply contemplative mood, his hands in a preaching attitude. This image is intended to exert the devotees to dwell upon the path which was preached by the Lord and to follow it zealously. The impact of the image was meant to personify the Buddha's doctrine enabling one through its worship to realize the ultimate *jñāna* leading to salvation, i.e., *nirvāṇa*. In other words, it is the personified formula of Buddha's life and philosophy, and hence such images can be called *bimba-brahma* — the ultimate and the fully evolved image in the Buddhist iconography. This is the reflection of the icons like that of the Ardhanārīśvara, the *vilakṣaṇa catuṣpāda sadāśiva* and the *vaikuṇṭha* in which one can see the personification of the Sāṁkhya, the Śaiva-Siddhānta and the Pāñcarātra doctrines enabling the devotees to realize the ultimate knowledge or the *brahma-jñāna* which leads to salvation. These images represent in a visual package, the quintessence of the doctrine and its ultimate goal and are the products of a long and deep search for the ultimate form that would symbolize the Ultimate Truth. These images, therefore, present the best examples of the interaction between the two underlining the outlook of the Indians towards art which conveys some message for better life and not mere art for art sake.

Bibliography

Brown, Percy, 1965, *Indian Architecture*, vol. I, Taraporevala, Mumbai.

Deglurkar, G.B., 1997, *Bimba-Brahma-Vāstu-Brahma*, Nagpur.

Dhammasaṅgani, 1885, Pāli Text Series.

Tucci, Guisseppe, 1988, Foreword to *Iconography of Sadāśiva*, N. Delhi.

Ramakṛṣna — Prophet of New India.

Rhys, Davids, *et al* (ed.), 1931, *Sumangala Vilasini*, Pāli Text Series.

Talim, M.V., 1991, *Primordial Philosophy in the Buddhist Art*, Seminar Papers, Department of Sanskrit, Mumbai University.

Vinaya Piṭaka, vol. III.

4

Common Heritage of an Interaction between Buddhist and Brāhmaṇical Art and Iconography

K.K. Thaplyal

SYMBOLS and motifs are essential ingredients of religious art. Being in circulation for centuries, they acquired meaning, purpose and sanctity, and were deeply ingrained in the minds of the people. Various sects — Brāhmaṇical, Buddhist, Jaina and others, had to resort to older tradition and "were not reluctant to adopt and adapt the existing pattern and formulae of their crafts to their requirement."[1] Symbols stand for deities or serve the designation emphasizing the idea underlying the icon. Because of the use of common symbols by the followers of different sects, sectarian character of religious art in India is not prominent, and often such art can be labelled as Indian rather than Brāhmaṇical or Buddhist. Further, as Coomaraswamy says, in ancient times there was a common Asiatic art in the region from Mediterranean to Ganges, characterized by common symbols and motifs.[2]

Buddhism, Brāhmaṇism and other religious sects were part of the same cultural ethos, and the worship of the *caityas*, relics, and the sacredness and auspiciousness of certain symbols, like *svastika*,[3] *śrīvatsa*, *triratna* (or *nandyāvartta*), etc., have been a common feature. Before the introduction of the Buddha image, the Buddha

1. H. Zimmer, *The Art of Indian Asia*, I, p. 163. See also the evidence of *Mahāvastu*, as cited by P. Banerjee, "Birth of Buddha and its Vedic Parallel" in *Buddhist Iconography*, published by Tibet House, New Delhi, 1989, p. 2.
2. A.K. Coomaraswamy, *History of Indian and Indonesian Art*, pp. 11-14.
3. *Svastika* is met with in Hindu, Buddhist and Jaina art — sculpture, architecture, painting, coins, seals, etc. Besides India, it was considered auspicious in Bactria, Iran, Assyria, Cyprus, Greece, Egypt, China, Japan, Combodia, and several other countries.

was worshipped in the form of *stūpas*, Buddhist relics and various symbols related to the Buddha.[4] The very fact that the Buddha enjoined his followers that after his death, *stūpas* should be erected for him on the cross-roads as is done for the *cakravartī* kings,[5] shows that the Buddhists adopted the practice of erecting *stūpas* from the Vedic tradition. The introduction of the image of the Buddha was due to the pressing demand of the laity as the atmosphere in general was charged with the idea of *bhakti*.[6]

It is believed that the body of the great men (*mahāpuruṣas*) bear several auspicious marks (*lakṣaṇas*)[7] and that such features as hands extending up to the knee (*ājānu-lamba-bāhu*) or halo (*prabhā-maṇḍala*) around head were characteristic of great men.

Yoga is common to Brāhmaṇism, Buddhism and Jainism. Its origin goes at least as back as the Indus Civilization in which "Śiva-Paśupati"[8] (*Pl.* 4.1) and some other figures on seals and in terracotta are shown in yogic postures. In historical period, some Brāhmaṇical deities, particularly Śiva, are shown in this posture. The Buddha and the Jaina *tīrthaṅkaras* attained Enlightenment meditating in yogic posture and yogic practices remained important part in the life of Buddhist and Jaina monks. Several *mudrās*, like *dhyāna, abhaya* and *varada,* are common with the Brāhmaṇical and Buddhist deities. The *dharma-cakra-mudrā,* which is a combination of *cin-mudrā* and *vyākhyāna-mudrā,* and of which the most artistic and famous example is the Buddha image of Gupta period from Sārnāth (*Pl.* 4.4),[9] is also met with in the icons of Lakulīśa, the founder of Śaiva Pāśupata sect.[10] Worship of the feet of Viṣṇu and those of the Buddha is a common feature, and Buddha's feet in early art, as seen at Bharhut and Sāñcī, often represent the Buddha himself.

4. For different symbols symbolizing the Buddha, see A.K. Coomaraswamy, *History of Indian and Indonesian Art*, p. 31.
5. *Mahāparinibbana-sutta, Buddhist Suttas*, SBE, XI, pp. 92-93.
6. The Buddha said that the cause of the bondage of his body has extinguished, and as such, men and gods could not see it in that form (*Dīgha-nikāya, Brahmajāla-sutta,* II. 3. 23).
7. For *mahāpuruṣa-lakṣaṇas*, see *Lakkhana-suttanta, Dīgha-nikāya*, translated as *Dialogues of the Buddha* (PTS), III, p. 142ff.
8. J. Marshall, *Mohenjo-daro and the Indus Civilization*, pt. I, pl. XII, figure 17, pp. 52-56.
9. A.K. Coomaraswamy, *History of Indian and Indonesian Art*, pl. XLI.
10. J.N. Banerjea, *Development of Hindu Iconography*, pl. XXXI, 1.

Certain animals were highly venerated and even worshipped since remote antiquity, and were deemed so by the followers of Brāhmaṇical, Buddhist and other sects. The representation of elephant, bull (or buffalo), rhinoceros and tiger on the "Śiva-Paśupati" seal from Mohenjo-Dāro[11] must have been because of their religious significance. In the historical period, lion, elephant, bull and horse are given importance and find depiction in various art objects. All these four find representation on the famous Sārnāth lion capital of Aśoka.[12] These animals symbolize power, vigour and majesty and were held sacred. In the Buddhist context, the elephant symbolizes Conception, the bull Nativity, the horse Renunciation and the lion represents the Buddha himself (Śākyasiṁha).[13] In the Brāhmaṇical context, elephant is the *vāhana* of Indra, lion of Durgā, horse of Sun and bull of Śiva. The four animals have also been found represented together in the different media of art.[14]

Folk deities like *yakṣa*s and *nāga*s were not only tolerated but also adopted by the followers of the Buddhist, Brāhmaṇical and Jaina religions with a view to making their religion more acceptable to the people, as these deities were quite popular with the masses. *Yakṣa* cult is of pre-Buddhist origin. The Śākyas, it is said, used to present newborn child before the tutelary deity *yakṣa* Śākyavardhana.[15] *Yakṣa* Kubera is associated with Śiva. *Yakṣa* statues of Maurya-Śuṅga period, characterized by their robust and sturdy physical features, are known from Parkham, Pawaya, Patna, etc.[16] Several *yakṣiṇī* images have been found, of which the one from Dīdārgañj is known for its voluptuous figure.[17] The *yakṣa* figures (*Pl.* 4.2) provided prototypes for the early Buddha and *Bodhisattva* images. So close is the resemblance between them that the *Bodhisattva* image at Sārnāth, installed by *bhikṣu* Bala (*Pl.* 4.3)[18] could very well be identified as a *yakṣa* figure,

11. See J. Marshall, *op. cit.*, pt. I, pl. XII, figure 17.
12. See K.K. Thaplyal, "The Symbolism of Sārnāth Lion Capital and its Purpose," *Journal of the UP Historical Society* (New Series), VIII, (1960), pp. 11-19, and plates.
13. N.G. Majumdar, *Guide to Sārnāth*, p. 46; A. Foucher, *On the Iconography of Buddha's Nativity*, tr. from French by H. Hargreaves as *Memoir of the Archaeological Survey of India*, no. 46, p. 2.
14. See K.K. Thaplyal, *Studies in Ancient Indian Seals*, p. 267.
15. A.K. Coomaraswamy, *The Art Bulletin*, 1879, p. 298.
16. For some *yakṣa* statues, see A.K. Coomaraswamy, *Yaksas*, 2 parts; J.N. Banerjea, *The Development of Hindu Iconography*, pp. 337ff.
17. For Dīdārgañj *yakṣī*, see A.K. Coomaraswamy, *History of Indian and Indonesian Art*, pl. XXII, figure 83.
18. *Ibid.*, pl. XXII.

if the inscription on it would not have mentioned it as a *Bodhisattva*.[19]

Nāga cult is also of quite ancient origin and was quite popular. *Nāga*s came to be associated with various religious cults. *Nāga* Mucalinda protected the penancing Buddha against rain and storm, by keeping its hoods over his head.[20] *Nāga* Elāpatra and some other *nāga*s are closely associated with the life-story of the Buddha.[21] *Nāga* Dharaṇendra sheltered *Tīrthaṅkara* Pārśvanātha in the same way and in similar circumstances as Mucalinda did for the Buddha.[22] The icons of the seventh *Tīrthaṅkara* Supārśvanātha[23] and the twenty-third *Tīrthaṅkara* Pārśvanātha,[24] bear serpenthoods over their heads. According to the *Bhāgavata Purāṇa*, child Kṛṣṇa was protected by a *nāga* when, after his birth, he was being carried to the house of Nanda across the Yamunā. Balarāma, considered as an *avatāra* of Śeṣanāga and Viṣṇu, as Śeṣaśāyī, is shown as reclining over the bed of serpent Śeṣa with its hood over his head.[25] The legend relating to Kṛṣṇa's punishing the serpent Kāliya (Kāliyadamana)[26] is symbolic of the triumph of Kṛṣṇa cult over the *nāga* cult. Some *nāga* statues, like the *yakṣa* ones, might have served as models for some Buddha-*Bodhisattva* statues. Besides *yakṣa*s and *nāga*s, there were other folk deities — *gandharva*s, *apsarās*, *vidyādhara*s, etc., which find place in both Brāhmaṇical and Buddhist art.

Lakṣmī, the goddess of wealth and prosperity, was a deity popular with the followers of different sects. The female figure with the label inscription *ṣirimā-devatā* at Bharhut[27] is to be taken as the representation of Śrī-Lakṣmī. Female deity, seated or standing on lotus, being anointed by two elephants, as Abhiṣeka-Lakṣmī, is a popular motif in Brāhmaṇcial, Buddhist and Jaina art. In the Śrī-sūkta of the *Ṛgveda*, the deity Śrī is mentioned as seated on lotus (*padma-sthitā*), born of lotus (*padma-sambhavā*), lotus-coloured (*padma-varṇā*), with lotus-thigh

19. For Dīdārgañj *yakṣī*, see A.K. Coomaraswamy, *History of Indian and Indonesian Art*, pl. XXII, figure 83, p. 68.
20. See J. Ph. Vogel, *Indian Serpent Lore*, p. 10.
21. See J. Ph. Vogel, *Indian Serpent Lore*, p. 10.
22. See M.P. Tiwari, *Jaina Pratima Vijñāna*, p. 125.
23. *Ibid.*, p. 101.
24. *Ibid.*, p. 125.
25. For Śeṣaśāyī Viṣṇu at Deogarh, see J.N. Banerjea, *The Development of Hindu Iconography*, pl. XXII, figure 2.
26. For Kāliyadamana, see H. Zimmer, *The Art of Indian Asia*, II, pls. 407, 423.
27. See Siri-mā-devatā, see B.M. Barua, *Bharhut*, pl. LXV, figure 78.

(*padma-uru*), lotus-eyed (*padmākṣī*) and as delighted by the trumpeting of elephants (*hasti-nāda-pramodinī*).[28] In the Buddhist art of Bharhut, Sāñcī and Bodha-Gayā, female figure being anointed by two elephants has been interpreted by A. Foucher as Māyādevī, mother of the Buddha, being bathed by two elephants[29] (the word in the text in this context is *nāga*, one of the meanings of which is "elephant"). Only a few scholars accept this interpretation, while most of them identify it as Abhiṣeka-Lakṣmī. Foucher's view that the Gaja-Lakṣmī motif has its prototype in Māyādevī figures[30] has not been accepted by scholars, as the antiquity of the motif in Brāhmaṇical context goes to an earlier period than its representation in the Buddhist context.

The worship of trees, the givers of shade, flowers, fruits and wood, has been the universal phenomenon in ancient times. On the basis of the representation of trees on seals,[31] pottery, etc., of the Harappan period, scholars are of the opinion that they were held sacred and even worshipped. In historical times, several trees like *aśvattha*, *vaṭa*, *bilva*, etc., are considered as particularly sacred. There has been a concept of wish-fulfilling tree (*kalpa-vṛkṣa*), which could grant all kinds of foods, drinks and also wealth. Of so many representations of this tree in the Buddhist and Brāhmaṇical art, that from Besnagar[32] is most significant. In the *Gītā*, Kṛṣṇa compares himself with the *aśvattha* tree[33] and it is this tree under which the Buddha attained Enlightenment. The primordial *aśvattha* tree has been described as with roots above and branches downwards (*ūrdhva-mūlamadhaś śākhamaśvattham*).[34] Worship of *caitya-vṛkṣa*, each village having at least one, was quite common and all the villagers, irrespective of their religious leanings, worshipped them. Trees could be conceived in human form. In the *Nidāna-kathā*, it is said that Sujātā, a village girl, took the penancing Buddha for a tree-god.[35] Trees were considered as a source of knowledge and also of vitality of life. Each Buddha and each *Tīrthaṅkara* is said to have attained the highest knowledge after penancing under a tree. Significantly, the Buddha's Birth, Enlightenment

28. *Ṛgveda*, II. 3 (*khila*).
29. A. Foucher, *op. cit.*, pp. 12ff.
30. A. Foucher, *op. cit.*, p. 21.
31. J. Marshall, *op. cit.*, p. 63.
32. For Besnagar *kalpa-vṛkṣa*, see A.K. Coomaraswamy, *Yakṣas*, II, pl. I, figure 23.
33. *Bhagavad-Gītā*, X.26.
34. *Ibid.*, XV.1.
35. G.P. Malalasekera, *Dictionary of Pali Proper Names*, II, p. 1186.

and Decease took place under trees. He was born in Lumbinī garden under a *śāla* tree;[36] he obtained Enlightenment at Bodha-Gayā under *aśvattha* tree[37] and he died at Kuśīnagara under a *śāla* tree.[38] He is said to have preached his mother in the *trayastriṁśaka-loka* under a tree.[39]

Buddhists (and also Jainas) included several Brāhmaṇical deities in their pantheons. In the Brāhmaṇical religion, Indra is the Lord of gods and Brahmā is the Creator. They, however, were given much lower position than the Buddha in the Buddhist pantheon. Both these deities request the Buddha to preach, attend his sermons and act as his attendants.[40] Some Vajrayānic Buddhist icons show Brāhmaṇical deities being trampled by the Buddhist deities.[41]

As seen above, lotus is closely associated with Lakṣmī in various ways, and also with Brahmā who is "lotus-born." It is held in one of the hands of Viṣṇu, and invariably in that of *Bodhisattva* Padmapāṇi. The wheel, which in secular context could represent such things as potter's wheel, or cart-wheel, or spinning-wheel, when in the hands of Viṣṇu, represents *sudarśana-cakra*, and in the Buddhist context, the *dharma-cakra*. The *tri-ratna*, in Buddhist context, could be taken for the Buddha, the *dharma* and the *saṁgha;* in the Jaina context, *samyak-śraddhā, samyak-jñāna* and *samyak-ācāra;* and the symbol is very near to the Śaiva *triśūla*.[42] Some Brāhmaṇical and a few Buddhist deities are characterized by multi-heads and multi-arms, reflecting their manifold power.

The Buddha, like Vāsudeva-Kṛṣṇa, was a kṣatriya prince. He is said to have borne thirty-two major and eighty minor marks of great men (*mahāpuruṣa*),[43] and as such, was destined to become a *cakravartī* — *rāja-cakravartī* or *dharma-cakravartī*. It is in the fitness of things that the Buddha's life-story should have been modelled, at least partly, on that of Indra, the king of gods, and there are "striking similarities between Indra and the Buddha in respect of their births and

36. G.P. Malalasekera, *Dictionary of Pali Proper Names*, I, p. 788.
37. *Ibid.*, I, p. 793.
38. *Ibid.*, I, p. 653.
39. *Ibid.*, I, p. 609.
40. *Vinaya-piṭaka*, translated as *The Book of Discipline* (PTS), IV, p. 51.
41. B. Bhattacharya, *The Indian Buddhist Iconography*, p. 344.
42. For significance and various interpretations of *tri-ratna*, see A.L. Srivastava, *Nandyāvarta — An Auspicious Symbol in Indian Art* (Allahabad), 1991.
43. For 32 major signs of great men, see *Lakkhana-suttanta, Dīgha-nikāya*, translated as *Dialogues of the Buddha* (PTS), III, pp. 142ff.

their aims and assertions."[44] It was an old concept that great men or supermen are born from the side of the mother.[45] In the *Ṛgveda*,[46] Indra has been mentioned as born from the side of his mother, and in the *Nidāna-kathā*,[47] the Buddha has been mentioned as born similarly. Immediately after birth, Indra is said to have become quite prominent,[48] and the Buddha is also known to have declared himself as the best shortly after his birth.[49] On the birth of Indra,[50] and on that of the Buddha,[51] mountains became agitated. Indra is said to have "tore the sun's wheel off,"[52] which reminds us of the Buddha's turning the Wheel of Law (*dharma-cakra-pravartana*),[53] as the First Sermon is known. Indra is said to be leader of men and gods,[54] and so also the Buddha.[55]

Indra defeated Vṛtra[56] and Namuci.[57] Buddha defeated Māra[58] who was bent upon creating hurdles against his attaining Supreme Knowledge. Significantly, the name of Māra is also Namuci.[59] Māra attacks in two ways — his army hurling deadly weapons[60] and his charming women enticing a person or a deity;[61] and in the case of the Buddha, he used both of them. In Brāhmaṇical literature, Kāmadeva also acts like Māra. He, however, used only the powerful arrows of love, which

---

44. P. Banerjee, *op. cit.*, p. 3.
45. H. Zimmer, *The Art of Indian Asia*, p. 80.
46. IV. 18. 1-2.
47. *Nidāna-kathā*, as referred to by P. Banerjee, *op. cit.*, pp. 1-2.
48. *Ṛgveda*, I.61.14.
49. *Majjhima-nikāya*, III. 118, vide P. Banerjee, *op. cit.*, p. 1.
50. *Ṛgveda*, I.61.14.
51. *Majjhima-nikāya*, III, 118, vide P. Banerjee, *op. cit.*, p. 1.
52. *Ṛgveda*, I.130.9.
53. *Dhamma-cakka-pavattana-sutta, Buddhist Sutta*s (SBE, XI), pp. 149-50.
54. *Ṛgveda*, III.34.2.
55. See *Saṁyutta-nikāya*, as referred to by P. Banerjee, *op. cit.*, pp. 4-5.
56. For Indra's defeating Vṛtra, see *Ṛgveda*, VII.19.5; I.32.5; etc.
57. For Indra's defeating Namuci, see *Ṛgveda*, VIII.14.13; X.73.7; VII.19.5; etc. P. Banerjee (*op. cit.*, p. 4) takes Namuci as one of the names of Vṛtra. Namuci, like Vṛtra, is a demon, but is different from him. Macdonnell, *Vedic Mythology*, pp.158-59; 161-62; and A. Hillebrandt, *Vedic Mythology*, pp. 101-24 and 148-50). This was brought to my notice by Dr. Prashant Srivastava.
58. For the Buddha's defeating Māra, see G.P. Malalasekera, *op. cit.*, II, p. 614.
59. For Namuci as another name of Māra, G.P. Malalasekera, *op. cit.*, II, p. 131.
60. *Ibid.*, p. 614.
61. *Ibid.*, p. 616.

made him successful against such great *yogīs*, like Viśvāmitra who, as a consequence, fell in love with the nymph Menakā; and Śiva, who agreed to marry Pārvatī. Interestingly, Aśvaghoṣa says that Māra, whose arrows had succeeded in arousing passion even in Śiva, failed in doing so in the case of the Buddha.[62] This shows that the Buddhist poet took Māra and Kāmadeva as identical[63] and this would have been the general view of the people.

It may be noted that the elephant Airāvata is the *vāhana* of Indra, and in some cases, could even represent that deity in the animal form. Elephant is deeply associated with the Buddha, as it is said that the *Bodhisattva* entered the womb of Māyādevī in the form of a white elephant.[64]

The Buddha's taking seven steps immediately after birth reminds of the three steps taken by Viṣṇu as mentioned in the *Ṛgveda* (*idaṁ viṣṇur vicakrame tredhā nidadhe padam*).[65] The Buddha's saying to Namuci that he would even prefer to die than to be defeated by his (Namuci's) army[66] reminds one of Kṛṣṇa's telling Arjuna that it is better to die fighting than face disgrace for not giving a fight.[67]

It is doubtful whether Vedic people worshipped icons; though such references, as one asking who would purchase his Indra for ten cows,[68] shows that icons of Indra in some form do existed.

On the basis of archaeological evidence at Lauriya Nandangarh indicating the existence of a free-standing pillar erected before the *stūpa*, and from the literary evidence of the *Divyāvadāna*, which mentioned *yūpa-yaṣṭi* at the centre of the *stūpa*, J. Irvin concludes that the earliest *stūpa*s had a monumental axial pillar based on the tradition of Vedic *yūpa* as their central component.[69]

The wheel-and-deer device is also significant. The deer on the seat (which is described as the low Indian throne) of the "Śiva-Paśupati" figure on a Harappan

---

62. Aśvaghoṣa, *Buddhacarita*, verse 16, vide Ratan Parimoo, "Buddha's Enlightenment," in *Buddhist Iconography*, p. 106.
63. Ratan Parimoo, *op. cit.*, p. 106.
64. *Majjhima-nikāya*, III, 118, vide P. Banerjee, *op. cit.*, p. 1.
65. *Ṛgveda*, I.22.17.
66. E. Thomas, *The Life of Buddha as Legend and History*, p. 73, vide P. Banerjee, *op. cit.*, p. 4.
67. *Bhagavad-Gītā*, II.33-34.
68. *Ṛgveda*, IV.24.10.
69. J. Irvin, p. 253.

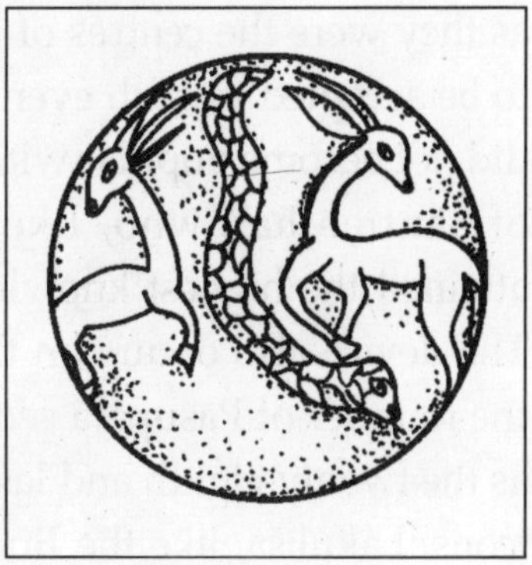

fig. 4.1

seal from Mohenjo-Dāro (*Pl.* 4.1),[70] anticipates the two deer flanking a wheel on the pedestal of the Buddha's icons. The symbolism seems to have had a wider distribution in this early age. A seal of Persian Gulf origin found at the Harappan site, Lothal (Gujarat), shows two deer flanking a dragon, which looks like a wheel kept sideways (*fig.* 4.1).[71] For representing a Deer Park, even one deer would have been enough. But two deer were chosen because the tradition of depicting two deer was of hoary antiquity and also because of the aesthetic considerations. As regards the wheel, nothing could represent momentum so well as the wheel. *Cakra* is associated with *cakravartī* and Buddha was a *dharma-cakravartī*. The representation of the two deer flanking a dragon, shown on the Persian Gulf seal, shows that Coomaraswamy was justified in saying that ancient Indian symbols form part of large repertoire of symbols of ancient Orient.[72]

The Buddhist adopted this wheel-and-deer symbol as it very much suited to symbolize the turning of the Wheel of Law (as the First Sermon of the Buddha is termed) at the Deer Park (Mṛgadāva) of Sārnāth (Ṛṣipaṭṭana) (*Pl.* 4.4).[73] It is not known if the symbolism of two deer had similar connotation in the Harappan context, though it can be said that in the historical period, Śiva is known as a great teacher.

The wheel-and-deer motif, symbolizing the First Sermon, came to denote any sermon of the Buddha, and still later, to symbolize the imparting of knowledge, and was chosen as the device of seal of several Buddhist monastic establishments[74]

70. J. Marshall, *op. cit.*, pl. XLI, figure 17. For the genesis and transformation of the wheel-and-deer device, see K.K. Thaplyal, "Genesis of the Wheel-and-deer Device," in B.M. Pande and B. Chattopadhyaya (eds), *Archaeology and History, Essays in Memory of Shri A. Ghosh*, I, pp. 467-70, and "Transformation of Symbols : A Case Study of Wheel-and-deer Device," in *Buddhist Iconography*, pp. 47-51, respectively.
71. S.R. Rao, "A Persian Gulf Seal from Lothal," *Antiquity*, vol. 37, pp. 96-99.
72. A.K. Coomaraswamy, *History of Indian and Indonesian Art*, pp. 11-14.
73. D.R. Sahni, *Catalogue of the Museum of Archaeology at Sārnāth*, pl. XX.
74. For wheel-and-deer device on seals of Sārnāth monastery, D.R. Sahni, *op. cit.*, pp. 307-08; K.K. Thaplyal, *Studies in Ancient Indian Seals*, pp. 207-08, pl. XXIII, figure 1; on seals of Kuśīnagara monastery, J. Ph. Vogel, "Excavations at Kāśī," *ASIAR*, 1905-06, p. 83; and on seals from Nālandā, Hirananda Sastri, *MASI*, 66, p. 38, pl. IIc.

as they were the centres of teaching and learning. It came to be accepted as such even by the other sects, although it did not become popular with them. It occurs on the images of Śāntinātha[75] who, like any other *Tīrthaṅkara*, had attained the highest knowledge and was a great teacher. The device also occurs on the icons of Lakulīśa, who was the founder of Pāśupata sect of Śaivism and is considered as the twenty-eighth and last incarnation of Śiva. On some icons, Lakulīśa, like the Buddha, is shown in the *dharma-cakra-mudrā* with four disciples shown on the pedestal, reminding us of the Buddha with his first five disciples (*fig*. 4.2).[76]

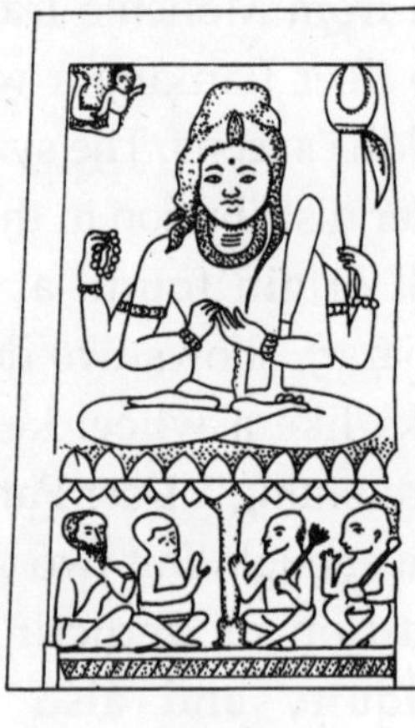

fig. 4.2

In some images, Lakulīśa is shown in double-petalled lotus raised by two *nāga* kings,[77] which resembles the representation of the Buddha showing him in "Great Śrāvastī Miracle" scene.[78] It appears that while the Vaiṣṇavas, with a view to establishing rapprochement with the Buddhists and winning them to their own fold, gave place to the Buddha in the galaxy of the *avatāras* of Viṣṇu; the Śaivas, with a view to establishing Śaiva-Buddhist harmony, modelled the iconography of Lakulīśa, who is considered as an incarnation of Śiva, after that of the Buddha.

75. The device is met with on the inscribed pedestal giving the name of Śāntinātha, in State Museum, Lucknow.

76. For the Buddha in the *dharma-cakra-pravartana-mudrā* with disciples, see A.K. Coomaraswamy, *History of Indian and Indonesian Art*, figure 161.

77. J.N. Banerjea, *The Development of Hindu Iconography*, pl. XXXIX, figure 1. The *Vāyu* and the *Liṅga* Purāṇas refer to the four disciples of Lakulīśa, viz., Kuśika, Garga, Mitra and Kauruseya. See D.R. Bhandarkar, *Epigraphia Indica*, XI, p. 5.

78. J.N. Banerjea, *The Development of Hindu Iconography*, p. 6.

5

Influence of Nāga-Worship in Buddhist Art

Yogendra Singh

THE antiquity of *nāga*-worship goes back to the remote past. Various references found in the literature of the *nāga* festival (*nāgamaha*), fairs and procession made in their honour (*nāgayātrā*) show the popularity of *nāga*-worship in ancient India.[1] The *nāgas* were serpent deities of folk-cult. The offering to a *nāga* deity was called the *nāgabali* or *sarpabali*, the purpose of which was to get rid off snakes.[2] We have a long tradition of *nāga*-worship in India. Vedic literature refers the famous battle between Indra and Vṛtra. Here Vṛtra signifies as the Dragon of the Deep (Ahir-budhnya) and also identified with Ananta, the cosmic serpent.[3] Marshall refers to two seals found at Mohenjo-Dāro, which bear figures of a god seated in *yoga* posture, on whose either side is represented a half human, half-animal form of a *nāga* with hands uplifted in prayers.[4] These seals suggest that *nāga*s were also considered sacred and personified by the Harappans. Many other depictions of the *nāga*s in the art of Indus Valley Civilization are also the evidence of the popularity of *nāga* cult during that period.[5]

The *nāga*s are said to have been born of Kaśyapa and Kadru, the latter being mentioned as the mother of all the snakes in the *Mahābhārata*.[6] In the *Rāmāyaṇa*,

1. V.S. Agrawala, *Prācīna Bhāratīya Lokadharma*, Ahmedabad, 1964, p. 68.
2. J.N. Banerjea, *Development of Hindu Iconography*, New Delhi, 1974, p. 346.
3. V.S. Agrawala, *Indian Art*, Varanasi, 1965, p. 48.
4. J.H. Marshall, *Mohenjodaro and the Indus Civilization*, 1, London, 1931, p. 68.
5. Heinrich Zimmer, *The Art of Indian Asia*, vol. 1, New York, 1964, pp. 25-26.
6. *Mahābhārata*, Ādiparvan, 16.

it is Surasā who is said to be the mother of the snakes.[7] These *nāga*s reside in the depths of the water and their abode is in the *pātālaloka* (*nāgaloka*) from where they rule.[8] The *nāga*s are also regarded as the guardians of the treasures.

The epic and the Purāṇas have exhaustive lists of the *nāga*s, the most common amongst them are Śeṣa, Vāsuki, Takṣaka, Karkoṭaka, Dhanañjaya, etc.[9] In the *Bhagavad-Gītā*, Vāsuki is mentioned first among the snakes and Śeṣa as the chief of the *nāgas*.[10] Śeṣa is also known as the bearer of the earth. He supports Lord Viṣṇu on the coils while He sleeps in the water of the ocean. *Nāga*s occupy an important place as these are associated with Śiva who uses them as his ornaments. We find that a large snake protected the newly born Kṛṣṇa when he was carried in a basket through the Yamunā in flood with heavy rains.[11] In Brāhmaṇism, though not worshiped as principal divinities. *Nāga*s have played a significant role in the religious life and art.

The association of *nāga*s also appears with Jaina *Tīrthaṅkaras*. The seventh *Tīrthaṅkara* Supārśvanātha and twenty-third *Tīrthaṅkara* Pārśvanātha are distinguished by a serpant canopy over their heads.

The Buddha is also associated with snake. In Buddhism *nāga*s who play important role in several events in the life of the Buddha are Elāpatra, Nanda and Upananda, Kālikā and Mucalinda. While, Elāpatra waited for the appearance of the Buddha in this world Nanda and Upananda gave a miraculous bath when he was born.[12] The *nāgarāja* Kālikā offered prayers and *nāgī*s presented flowers in the honour of the Buddha.[13] Mucalinda protected him during a storm.[14]

The story about Mucalinda has some interesting parallels with a snake protecting Kṛṣṇa from the rain. It is said that after achieving the Enlightenment, once Buddha sat cross-legged under the Mucalinda tree for seven days enjoying the bliss of Enlightenment. At that time a huge cloud appeared and for seven days rain and cold wind continued. Mucalinda, the serpent king, enveloping the

7. *Rāmāyaṇa*, Sundara-Kāṇḍa, 137.

8. *Mahābhārata*, Ādiparvan, 21, 6; 25, 4; *Viṣṇu Purāṇa*, 204.

9. B. Sahai, *Iconography of Some Important Monor Hindu and Buddhist Deities*, New Delhi, 1975, p. 74.

10. *Bhagavad-Gītā*, X, 28-29.

11. *Bhāgavata Purāṇa*.

12. *Lalitavistara*, pp. 78 and 85; *Buddhacarita*, I, 27, 35 and 38.

13. Handy, *Manual of Buddhism*, pp. 269-71.

14. *Ibid*, p. 182.

body of the Blessed One seven times with his coils, kept his long hood spread over the Master's head protecting for all the seven days.[15] The story of Mucalinda is also given in later texts like *Nidāna-kathā, Lalitavistara* and *Mahāvastu* with a slightly changed version.[16]

In the Buddhist art, three forms of *nāga*s are illustrated, first mere animal form, second human form with serpenthood shown depicted over the head and third both the human and the animal combined in such a way that the human bust is shown attached with lower animal part as coils. Generally, *nāga*s in human form with their female counterparts are represented worshipping the Buddha.

Images of the Buddha with serpenthoods over the head are known from the sites like Bharhut, Sāñcī, Amarāvatī, Nāgārjunakoṇḍa, etc. At Bharhut the scene of Elāpatra Nāgarājə's visit to the Buddha is represented (*Pl.* 5.1). At first Elāpatra is shown in his serpent form and at another place in the anthropomorphic form with snakehoods attached behind his head. Elāpatra (Erāpata) Nāgarāja is shown worshipping the *bodhi* tree with his family.[17] On a pillar, now housed in Allahabad Museum in the central medallion is the five-hooded Mucalinda Nāgarāja below a Banyan Tree and footprints of the Buddha are also depicted.[18] Mucalinda is said to have protected the Buddha during a storm. This story is carved at Sāñcī (*Pls.* 5.2 & 5.3), Amarāvatī (*Pl.* 5.4) and Nāgārjunakoṇḍa *stūpa*s also.[19] A typical *nāga* figure named Nāgarāja Cakravāka (*cakravāko nāga rājo*) on a railing pillar, which stood in the corner of the south gate at Bharhut, is represented in human form with a canopy of five snake-hoods attached behind his head.[20]

At Sāñcī Mucalinda, the king of the *nāga*s has been shown on the western and small gateways. Another five-hooded *nāga* king along with his four *nāgī* queens and *nāga* attendants has been depicted on a pillar of the southern gateway. On the middle architrave of the same gateway, the *nāga*s and *nāgī*s children are coming out of a pond and seen worshipping a *stūpa*.[21] In Gāndhāra art Nāgarāja

---

15. *Mahāvagga, Vinayapiṭaka*, vol. I, p. 3; J. Ph. Vogel, *Indian Serpent Lore*, pp. 102.
16. *Lalitavistara*, vol. I, pp. 379; *Mahāvastu* (ed. Senart) vol. III, pp. 300f.; *Buddhacarita*, XV, 49-53; *Jātaka*, vol. I, 80; Rhys Davids, *Buddhist Birth Stories*, p. 109.
17. V.S. Agrawala, *Indian Art*, p. 135.
18. *Ibid.*
19. *Ibid.*, p. 135.
20. A.L. Srivastava, *Life in Sanchi Sculpture*, New Delhi, 1983, p. 125, plates XIX, XX, XXXIII.
21. J. Ph. Vogel, *Indian Serpent Lore*, p. 38.

Apalāla, struck by Vajrapāṇi, appears with his consort before the Buddha with hands in adoration (*Pl.* 5.5).

Thus, the *nāga*s have played a significant role in the history of religion and art. These being folk divinities were worshipped among the common people as the guardian deities of water and tṛeasures. Their shrines have also been mentioned in literature. Many temples dedicated to the *nāga*s were built. One such temple belonging to the Kuṣāṇa period was excavated at Sonkh near Mathurā. This region was once a great centre of *nāga*-worship, and this worship continue even today in the form of Nāgapañcamī *pūjā* throughout India. Though their status was raised to the rank of *devatā*s in Brāhmaṇical cults, but in Buddhism and Jainism, these were regarded as tutelary gods and considered to be the subordinate and attend on the Buddha, Pārśvanātha, Mahāvīra, Kṛṣṇa and Śiva.

6

Some Glimpses of Interaction between Brāhmaṇical and Buddhist Art

Amar Singh

ARCHITECTURE and sculpture in India are closely related with religion and show a kind of continuity and changes throughout in the history of art. The architectural forms and their decorative motifs including gods and goddesses on the *stūpas*, rock-cut *caityas* and temples have greater affinity due to their interactions and influences. From sixth century BC onwards Brāhmaṇism, Buddhism, Jainism and other minor sects flourished together. The monuments belonging to these religions have their old traditions. The earliest forms of the *stūpas* and *caityas* were already existing in bricks and wood which were later on copied in stone. The living examples of the early Buddhist art in stone are the product of Śuṅga-Sātavāhana period.[1]

There was an ancient and long tradition of *stūpa* architecture before the great *stūpas* like those at Bharhut, Sāñcī and Amarāvatī were raised.[2] Many literary, epigraphical, architectural and sculptural sources have revealed that various Brāhmaṇical cults and sects existed side by side with Buddhism and Jainism during the second-first centuries BC.[3] Besides, Brāhmaṇical gods and goddesses like Indra, Brahmā, Sūrya, Lakṣmī, Kāmadeva and numerous other folk deities in the form of *nāgas*, *yakṣas*, *vṛkṣas*, *apsarās*, *gandharvas*, *kumbhāṇḍas* and *kinnaras*, etc., were

1. Percy Brown, *Indian Architecture* (*Buddhist and Hindu Periods*), Bombay, 1995, p. 15.
2. V.S. Agrawala, *Indian Art*, Varanasi, 1965, pp. 119-24.
3. V.S. Agrawala, "Religious conditions in the Ashtadhyayi," *Journal of UP Historical Society*, vol. XIX, p. 14; J.N. Banerjea, *The Development of Hindu Iconography*, New Delhi, 1974, pp. 75-77; 90-107.

also worshipped during this period.[4] Since Buddha never denied the existence of these gods, his followers felt no hesitation in adopting, associating and assimilating with the popular deities of Brāhmaṇical order. Thus, we see that the early Buddhist art was a reflection of popular Brāhmaṇical religion and art of that period, which was adopted to the requirements of Buddhism.

The seeds of *bhakti* (devotional worship) are already found in the Vedas, originated in the Upaniṣads, developed in the epics and Purāṇas and became perfect philosophy by thought and actions in the *Bhagavad-Gītā*.[5] Worship of Buddha was a result of *bhakti* movement. In the beginning he was regarded as a historical being but later on due to the advent of Mahāsāṁghikas, Buddha was deified and people started worshipping him even earlier than the Mauryan period.[6]

Thus, *bhakti* movement which already prevailed in the Brāhmaṇical society largely affected the later Buddhism and all the traits of worship like the devotional prayer (*stuti*), offering (*bhoga*), the sprinkling of the sacred water (*jalābhiṣeka*), the garlanding (*mālyārpaṇa*), touching feet (*caraṇa-sparśa*) and the circumambulation (*pradakṣiṇā*) were adopted as mode of worship in Buddhism also.[7] The widespread different forms of worship are illustrated in the early Buddhist art of Bharhut Sāñcī, Bodha-Gayā, Amarāvatī and Mathurā where Lord Buddha represented by various symbols is seen generally decorated with garlands (*Pls.* 6.1, 6.2, & 6.3). In few cases *kinnaras*, *vidyādharas*, *gandharvas* and human devotees are depicted with garlands in their hands offering to the Buddha (*Pl.* 6.1). Scenes of *pradakṣiṇā*, devotional prayer with folded hands (*Pl.* 6.3), ladies kneeling down before the deity and touching the symbol by their hands (*Pl.* 6.2), offering made by the monkeys (*Pls.* 6.4 & 6.5), *nāgas* and elephants worshipping the Buddha, are also noticed.[8]

Many Brāhmaṇical gods and goddesses such as Indra, Brahmā, Śrī-Lakṣmī and Kāmadeva were associated with Gautama Buddha and got a place in early Buddhist art. Indra or Śakra (Inda or Sakka in Pāli), a Vedic god, is represented attending *bodhisattva* Gautama during his birth and again when he cut-off his

4. A.L. Srivastava, *Life in Sanchi Sculpture*, New Delhi, 1983, p. 116.
5. J.N. Banerjea, *op.cit.*, pp. 72-75; R.G. Bhandarkar, *Vaishnavism, Śaivism and other minor Sects*, p. 9.
6. S.R. Goyal, *A Religious History of Ancient India*, vol. I, Meerut, 1984, pp. 320-21.
7. A.L. Srivastava, *op.cit.*, pp. 112-13.
8. *Ibid*, pp. 119-20.

hairs after *mahābhiniṣkramaṇa*, Indra taking them deposited in the *cūlamaṇi caitya*. Indra is also presented in the scene of Māra (Kāmadeva) when he attempted to prevent Buddha from reaching Enlightenment. He is again depicted on the reliefs of *stūpa*s along with Brahmā in the scene of Buddha *avataraṇa* at Saṅkisa from Trayastriṁśa heaven. Thus Indra, the supreme god of the Vedic period and Brahmā one of the Trinity god of the Purāṇas were placed in a subordinate position in the Buddhist pantheon.

Śrī-Lakṣmī or Gaja-Lakṣmī (*Pls*. 6.6 & 6.7) has been represented on the panels of Bharhut, Sāñcī and Bodha-Gayā. In the several panels on the gateways of the *stūpa*s at Sāñcī, there is a female figure either seated or standing on a full blown lotus coming out of a pot, holding lotus or its stalk in one of her hands and in some cases water is being poured out of two jars held by two flanking elephants over the head of the goddess.[9] At least three representations of the goddess Śrī-Lakṣmī standing and seated on full blown lotus springing from a *pūrṇa-ghaṭa* and bathed by elephants are depicted at Bharhut.[10] The cult of Śrī-Devatā or Śrī-Lakṣmī was already in existence before she was executed in the Buddhist art, as Śrī-Lakṣmī, the ancient Mother Goddess is referred in the Vedas.[11] In the Brāhmaṇical literature she is mentioned as the consort of Viṣṇu and her origin is attributed to the ocean.[12]

Kāma, the love god of Hindus in the name of Māra, along with his wives, daughters and attendants have been represented on the western and northern gateways of Sāñcī.[13] Besides, Indra, Brahmā, Śrī-Lakṣmī and Māra, many other divinities like *yakṣa-yakṣīs*, *dvārapālas*, *gandharvas*, *apsarās*, *kumbhāṇḍas*, *nāgas* and *nāgīs*, *vidyādharas*, *kinnaras* and various symbols such as *cakra, kalaśa, kalpa-vṛkṣa, mithuna, śrīvatsa*, etc., are also executed in the early Buddhist art. The *gandharvas* and the *apsarās* are popular tutelary divinities in the Brāhmaṇical mythology and also found full acceptance in Buddhist religion and art which are placed in the numerous scenes of music and dance at Bharhut and Sāñcī.[14] On the other hand, as mentioned in some of the Purāṇas and Pāñcarātra Saṁhitās, the Buddha

9. A.L. Srivastava, "Identification of a Female Motif in Sanchi Sculpture," *Journal of Indian History*, vol. L, pt. I, pp. 129-32.
10. V.S. Agrawala, *op.cit.*, p. 135, fig. 65.
11. J.N. Banerjea, *op.cit.*, pp. 370-72.
12. *Ibid.*, V.S. Agrawala, *op.cit.*, p. 328-29.
13. A.L. Srivastava, *op.cit.*, p. 122.
14. *Ibid.*, pp. 123-44; V.S. Agrawala, *op.cit.*, pp. 138-47.

was assimilated among the incarnations of Viṣṇu and also shown depicted in the *daśāvatāra* panels either seated cross-legged in *abhaya* or *bhūmisparśa-mudrā* or standing with right hand in *abhaya-mudrā* mainly in the sculptures of medieval period.[15]

Some decorative motifs depicted on the *stūpa*s have also influenced the art of later period. The *toraṇa*s at Bharhut are remarkable for the earliest carvings of open mouthed *makara* (crocodile) figures having curved tails on both projecting ends of the architraves represented on the superstructure of the gateways.[16] Later on this motif is variously repeated at Mathurā and in due course of time became an essential feature of the *toraṇa* architecture attached with temples.[17] The Mathurā artists inherited the structural traditions of Bharhut and Sāñcī. The remains of horizontal beams, excavated at Sonkh near Mathurā, were parts of a *toraṇa* attached to a *nāga* temple of Kuṣāṇa period. Here we have a western end of a top lintel depicting an elephant with a *makara* who carries a lotus-stalk in his trunk.

The other piece which is the western end of the bottom lintel shows a *nāga-puruṣa* stepping out from the open mouth of a *makara*. Several other *toraṇa* fragments from Mathurā also show the spiral *makara*s as represented at Bharhut.[18]

Though the forms and shapes along with the decorations of later *toraṇa*s are greatly changed but the illustrations of *makara-mukha* (crocodile) not only continued rather it gained popularity as being essentially represented in most of the examples, on both the sides of each *toraṇa*, projecting *maṇḍala* (loops) or other kind of figures from the mouth of the crocodile. Numerous such *toraṇa*s are found from medieval temples of north India. The entrance porch of the Lakṣmaṇa temple (*c.* tenth century), the Kandarīya Mahādeva temple (*c.* eleventh century) and the Javari temple (late eleventh century) at Khajurāho (district Chhatarpur, M.P.) is entered through an ornate *makara-toraṇa*, where loops (*maṇḍala*) are shown coming out from the mouth of a flanking crocodile, which has been forced open by a bearded gladiator carrying a sword in the right hand and a scarf-like object in

---

15. J.N. Banerjea, *op.cit.*, pp. 391-93; N.P. Joshi, *Brāhmaṇical sculptures in the State Museum, Lucknow*, part II, vol. I, Lucknow, 1989, pp. 141-42.
16. V.S. Agrawala, *ibid*, p. 130, Plate XXII, fig. 59.
17. *Ibid*, pp. 219-21.
18. Amar Singh, "On Torana Architecture," *Prāgdhārā, Journal of the UP State Archaeology Department* No. 10. (1999-2000); "Gupta Architecture of Mathurā," *Prāgdhārā*, no. 11, p. 198.

the left in the Lakṣmaṇa temple.[19]

The Ghaṭeśvara temple (*c.* AD 925) at Baroli, district Koṭā, the Sāsa-Bahu temples at Nāgdā, district Udaipur and the later temples of Dilwārā group in Rajasthan and the Solaṅkī temples of Kumbhāriā (district Banaskaṇṭhā) in Gujarat also represent *makara-toraṇa* hanging between two pillars in their *sabhā-maṇḍapas* and *raṅga-maṇḍapas*.[20]

Architecture of the rock-cut Buddhist *caitya* halls at Bhājā, Kondane, Pītalkhora, Ajantā, Kārle and other places located around Nāsik in Maharashtra, consisted of an apsidal half with wagon vaulted roof and a large *caitya*-window on the façade above doorway, has also influenced later temples in their structural form and decoration. The *caitya* window, literary known as *kīrttimukha* or *gavākṣa* was to provide light and air in the *caitya* hall. Besides its functional role, the shape of *caitya*-windows in their miniature forms were also used to decorate the cornice mouldings on the facade of *caitya* halls, sometimes depicting human faces too. In due course of time this artistic design was gradually adopted in the temple architecture and became a favourite motif of the artists during the Gupta period and onwards. The functional *caitya*-window or the large circular opening of the *caitya*-hall was perhaps retained as the principal decorative element on the facade of the temple *śikhara* in the name of *śukanāsā* in its sublimated form. Besides this, the miniature form of *caitya* window also became one of the principal decorative motifs on the temples called as *candraśālā, thakarika surasenaka* or *kudu* embellished on *kapota* cornices and *śikhara*. The tradition is marked by the findings of many *candraśālā*s of various sizes bearing figures of gods and goddesses from Mukundara, Bhūmara, Mathurā, Vārāṇasī and some other places belonging to the temples of Gupta period. Some of them which are comparatively bigger in size were certainly used as a *śukanāsikā* of the temples. Later on this *caitya* window motif became an essential part of decoration in the early medieval and medieval temples which is not only used as a *śukanāsā* represented in the lower half facade of the *śikhara* above the roof of *kapili* but also adorned on the *kapota* mouldings, *udgama*s and on the *latā-jāla* of the *śikhara* in the Pratihāra, Candella and other temples of north India.[21]

19. Amar Singh, "On Torana Architecture," *Prāgdhārā, Journal of the UP State Archaeology Department*, no. 10, pp. 204-5.
20. *Ibid.*
21. Amar Singh, "Evolution of Sukanasa in the Temples of Central India," *Prāgdhārā, Journal of the UP State Archaeology Department*, No. 7, pp. 203-6, plates 112-18.

The other influence of the rock-cut Buddhist *caityas* is marked in the Valabhī temples of north India and in the temples having *śālā śikhara* and *gopuramas* of the south India. The semi-cylindrical or wagon vaulted roof above the apsidal *caitya* hall was modified and copied in the superstructure of *valabhī* (*gajapṛṣṭhākṛti* or *khākharāmuṇḍī*) temples, as noted in the Telī-kā-Mandira at Gwalior Fort (mid-eighth century AD) and Vetal Deul (ninth century AD) at Bhubaneśvara in Orissa.[22] The *Bhīma-ratha*, *Nakula-Sahadeva ratha* and *Gaṇeśa-ratha* at Mahābalipuram and *gopurams* in the south Indian temples are inspired by the models of the Buddhist *caitya*-halls.[23]

---

22. Amar Singh, "Some observations on the Valabhi Temples," *Kalā, The Journal of Indian Art History Congress*, vol. IV (1997-98) Guwahati (India), pp. 117-23.
23. Krishna Deva, *Temples of India*, New Delhi, 1995, p. 235.

7

Some Common Symbols and Motifs in Buddhist and Brāhmaṇical Art

Sheo Bahadur Singh

THE Indian symbols of art bespeak the same truth in the Brāhmaṇic as well as the Buddhist philosophy and myths. They are the signals of the same pilgrim's progress to understand the ultimate truth revealed through the means of art. We have to understand their abstract nature, concept and philosophical thoughts. The symbols are the pictorial script of India's real wisdom. The ancient tradition of India preserves and conserves the meanings of those very symbols found in the Buddhism, Brāhmaṇism and Jainism. It is noteworthy that these symbols are the common heritage and source of vital energy with almost similar meanings and concept since time immemorial.

Lotus

Lotus is the important symbol in Indian art and religion. It symbolizes the life floating on the surface of creative waters. It is a flower of life blossoming on earth; it is the visible sign of consciousness in matter. V.S. Agrawala aptly remarks:

> A gamut of meaning is associated with the lotus. It symbolizes the principle of growth, rising from the immortal Navel of Viṣṇu, or the cosmic deity whose awakening throws up the lotus as the seat of Brahmā, the genius of emanation. The lotus-leaf typifies the womb of creation. Lotus is also the cosmic mind and of the center of energy in the individual.[1]

The womb of the individual and the universal mother giving birth to the child is

1. V.S. Agrawala, *Indian Art*, p. 53.

symbolized as the lotus growing in water. The cosmic lotus is called the highest form of earth. Śrī-Lakṣmī is associated in every possible way with the symbol of lotus. She is praised as "lotus-born," "standing on a lotus," "lotus coloured," "lotus eyed," "abounding in lotuses," "decked with lotus garlands." Lotus Goddess is honey-like, and is said to grant gold, cows, houses and slaves. She bestows health, long life prosperity, offspring and fame. The Goddess Padmā is seated or standing over a lotus. Padmapriyā is among the principal figures sculptured on the richly decorated gates and railing of Sāñcī and Bharhut *stūpas*. An image of lotus goddess is found on the terracotta plaque from Basārh dating from about the third century BC. She stands on a lotus pedestal with two lotuses and two buds at her side. The deity is shown with wings, a rare feature in India. Wings are common in Western tradition but the Indian figures betray connection with that tradition.[2]

Prajñāpāramitā is the highest feminine personification in Mahāyāna Buddhism.[3] She is the female aspect of universal Buddha, similar to Lakṣmī as the consort of Viṣṇu and symbolizes the supreme wisdom that guides and enlightens. She is invariably characterized by the lotus-seat. The lotus is the symbol of enlightenment that dispels the darkness of ignorance, inherent in all living beings according to the Buddhist philosophy. "The lotus symbol, which originally gave birth to beings and existences in unending succession, now carries the powerful wisdom of *nirvāṇa;* the word that puts an end to all individual existence, whether in heaven or on earth."

The *Śatapatha Brāhmaṇa* records "The lotus means the waters, and this earth is a leaf thereof, even as the lotus leaf here lies spread on the waters, so this earth lies spread on waters." The earth is conceived of as resting on the back of the waters. This symbolism sufficiently accounts for the use of the expanded lotus flower in iconography and architecture as the typical support of a figure and building. Moreover, the lotus is represented as a direct source of wealth, as in the case of *padma-nidhi* of Kubera. Furthermore, the more edifying symbolism of purity is drawn from the fact that the lotus leaf is not wetted by the water that rests on it, nor is the flower soiled by the mud from which it springs. Moreover, Coomaraswamy also records it. Thus the lotus represents the Tree of life and this Cosmic Tree which sprang originally from the navel of Varuṇa, leaving the deities

2. H. Zimmer, *Myths and Symbols in Indian Art and Civilization*, p. 93.
3. VII, 4, 1, 8.

within its branches, is later represented as rising from the navel of Nārāyaṇa or Viṣṇu and bearing Brahmā.[4]

Padmākāravedikās in the Śuṅga Kuṣāṇa art at Mathurā represent lotus designs or the ornamental railings. The pillars and cross-bars are profusely decorated with motifs and designs showing great originality and richness in depicting floral and animal motifs. The lotus-garland ornating *vedikā* consisted of thousand of flowers interwoven with many varieties of floral wealth and foliage. F.D.K. Bosch[5] records:

> The notion of the lotus as the very symbol of life risen from the waters lands a new aspect to the relation between this plant and other living creature, particularly its fellow plants.

He further remarks:

> If we now proceed to enquire into the nature and meaning of the mystic lotus we should concentrate on the fact that according to the products of art we discussed above, the whole creation represented by lotus plant has its beginning and origin in the primeval lotus which feeds and supports it just as the primeval waters are the foundation of all things created and are identified with *dharma*, so the primeval lotus, the symbol of these waters, is the foundation, their *pratiṣṭhāna* and at the same time the supporter of the universe, for *dharma* means supporter.[6]

Pūrṇa-kumbha

Pūrṇa-kumbha is the auspicious symbol in the Indian art employed equally by all religious sects, and occurring not only in India proper, but also farther India and Indonesia.[7]

The earliest examples in art are found in the Śuṅga period at Sāñcī and Bharhut associated with Lakṣmī. In these representations, the goddess is standing or seated on a lotus which rises from a *pūrṇa-kumbha*, or the *ghaṭa* is shown alone with efflorescence of lotus flowers and leaves rising from it. In the Jaina art, the *pūrṇa-kumbha* is one of the eight auspicious symbols and also are of the 14 lucky dreams of Triśalā. The *pūrṇa-ghaṭa* is carried as a symbol by *nāga*s and river-goddesses. It is still in vogue on any auspicious occasion, festival decoration and on shrines.

4. Coomaraswamy, *Yakshas* II, p. 57.
5. *The Golden Germ*, p. 82.
6. *Ibid*, p. 63.
7. *Indian Art*, p. 51.

Coomaraswamy records:

> The *pūrṇa-kumbha* is plainly thought of as inexhaustible vessel, but the actual form is associated with vegetation. The *pūrṇa-kalaśa* is generally a globular vessel with a foot and a constricted neck, the body of the vessel is invariably encircled by a ribbon or other band, tied with knots and serving the purpose of a magical fence, from the mouth there rises a spray or bunch of lotus flowers or leaves hang over symmetrically on each side of the mouth like the volutes of palmette.

This form is essentially that of flower base, combining a never failing source of water with an ever living vegetation. This type is of the widest distribution in later art. The *pūrṇa-kumbha* is a symbol of life with plenty. It symbolizes the expression of a wish that the recipient enjoys health, wealth and long life.

He further records:

> As the motif has a continuous history from the Śuṅga period onwards, and there is not the slightest reason to suppose that it was either invented or borrowed precisely at the moment when stone came into use as a building material, we must infer an antecedent history of the motif on Indian soil.[8]

V.S. Agrawala[9] observes:

> *Pūrṇakumbha*, pot and foliage, full vase was the symbol of plenty and creativity. The water in the jar is the sap or humidas radicle and the over-flowing leaves and flowers typify life itself with its manifold blessings and joys. The human body is the *pūrṇaghata* and so is the created cosmos.

The *pūrṇa-kalaśa* of the *Ṛgveda* is filled with immortal sap of *soma*, while the *pūrṇa-kumbha* of the *Atharvaveda* is filled with streams of *ghṛta* and *amṛta*. Further *pūrṇa-kumbha nārī* is mentioned in the *Atharvaveda*, *pūrṇa-ghaṭa kanyā* walks in the Lumbinī procession of Māyādevī. In Jaina manuscripts, it is given an anthropomorphic form and in religious worship it is regarded as the symbol of Trinity.

Pūrṇa-kumbha also represents as the womb in the rituals of *navapatrikā-praveśa* during Durgā-Pujā. A Tāntric diagram *sarvatobhadramaṇḍala* is drawn upon the ground depicting pictures of female generative organ. A *pūrṇa-kumbha* is to be placed on this diagram with full of water. It symbolizes a female womb. The figure of a baby is drawn on the vessel. Five kinds of leaves, coconut, smeared with vermillion are placed on the open mouth of jar. It is a simple fertility rite by

8. D.P. Chattopadhyaya, *Lokāyata*, p. 294.
9. V.S. Agrawala, *Indian Art*, 1965, p. 51.

which the plants are brought into contact with the female reproductive organ, evidently to ensure multiplication. N.N. Bhattacharya suggests:

> That the main purpose of the *yantra* and the *pūrṇaghaṭa*, referred to above, is to identify natural fertility with human fertility, so that the productivity of nature becomes increased by the imitation of female reproductivity.

The *Śatapatha Brāhmaṇa* also equates *pūrṇa-kumbha* with the womb of Mother Goddess, whereas the *kalaśa visarjana* identifies *kumbha* with uterus. The *pūrṇa-kumbha* as representation of Mother-Goddess still survives in many festivals. It is profusely represented in the early-medieval art.

Cakra

Cakra is the symbol of the Sun, time or rotation of the world. It is also identified with the supreme moral order in the form of *dharma-cakra* or *sudarśana-cakra*, both having a thousand spokes. The worship of the *cakra* represents the supreme ideals underlying the cosmic manifestation on the one hand and of the individual life on the other. V.S. Agrawala observes:

> The cosmos is known as *brahmāṇḍa-cakra*, the World order as *saṁsāra-cakra*, Human life as *bhava-cakra*, the flux of Men's action as *karma-cakra*, the Revolving wheel of time as *kāla-cakra*, the Moral order which governs the universal and the individual ordinances as *dharma-cakra*. The *cakra* stands for the perfect cycle of life which is at once beautiful and accessible to all and therefore called *sudarśana-cakra*, the wheel of the Divine Preserver of world and life, Bhagavān Viṣṇu. The Divine is transcendent creator but His immanent presence becomes manifest as the dynamic *cakra* or revolving Wheel.[10]

The *cakra* bearing a centre and the circumference represents the law of unity in diversity. The *cakra* begins from the time immemorial in the Indian tradition. The *Ṛgveda* records the ageless wheel that revolves round the heaven of cosmic order. The basic feature of the *cakra* is its cyclic movement in a rhythmic order which brings blessings and happiness. Thus, its meaning has an universal appeal. It stands for the supreme law of the cosmos and human life. The *cakra* is a frequently repeated motif in the railings and gateways of the *stūpa*s at Sāñcī. The *cakra*-worship is forcefully demonstrated in early Indian art at Bharhut, Sāñcī, Bodha-Gayā, Amarāvatī and Mathurā.

10. V.S. Agrawala, *Chakradhvaja*, 1964, Preface, p. 1; and *Ṛgveda*, I.164, 11.

A regular worship of the *cakra* can be seen from the earliest times in Jainism. The Jaina *stūpa* at Kaṅkālī Ṭīlā bear witness to the deification of the *cakra*. The motif of the *cakra-stambha* framing a *Tīrthaṅkara* image together with an *aṣṭamāṅgalika mālā* is represented on the *āyāgapaṭṭas*. Sometimes, the whole *āyāgapaṭṭa* is conceived in the form of a *cakra* supported on the arms of eight maidens of space. Furthermore, the depiction of a *cakra-paṭṭa* on a tablet of homage in the ancient Jaina art is notable. These facts indicate that the Jainas had a deep feeling of reverence for the *cakra* symbol. The Buddhists also had a great reverence for the *cakra* symbol right from the earliest times following the age old Vedic tradition.

The conception of the *cakra* was perfected in the Vedas as the symbol of creation and of time. The *Ṛgveda* conceives of it as the black and the white *rājasa* forces.

> Both space and time are the outcome of movement and both are symbolized as *cakra*. In temporal aspect past, present and future form a *cakra*, and in the spatial the earth, sky and heaven. Both of these are symbolized in nature as Sun and therefore Mārtaṇḍa or Sūrya is conceived of as the Great Wheel.[11]

The number of spokes in *kāla-cakra* can be 3, 5, 6, 12, 50 and even a thousand. The *cakra* in the *Ṛgveda* has been described as *sanemi* (circumference) and *sanābhi* (centre of the wheel). Buddhists borrowed this description of *cakra* almost verbatim from the *dharma-cakra*. The Buddhist *cakra* is supposed to be of one thousand spokes, emitting rays of light from a centre, a full vase and a *svastika* mark, the symbol of the Sun. In fact, the symbol of *cakra* equated with Cosmos, Time, Supreme Law and finally the Divine Will as expressing itself through Man and society, was the common heritage of the entire Indian people. V.S. Agrawala aptly remarks "There is hardly any other cult of such universal hold as *cakra*-worship."

The devotees of Viṣṇu in the Gupta period regarded the *cakra* as the *sudarśana-cakra*, whereas the Buddhists revered it as the *dharma-cakra* of the Buddha. In the polity, the theory of a *cakravartī* king paying homage to the *dharma-cakra* was personified as the *cakra-puruṣa* as represented on the *cakra-vikrama* coin of Candragupta II, the Gupta ruler.

The Bhāgavata teachers included the entire field of knowledge, and of the scriptural texts as the two forms of *sudarśana-cakra*. They defined this *cakra* as the

11. V.S. Agrawala, *Chakradhvaja*, p. 54.

principle of life, Divine Power, Activity, Energy, Emotions, Ideals, Exertion and Will. Whatever may have been the reason of this, it is certain that as a *brahmamūla* symbol, the *cakra* had to play a no less important part when it appeared as the top piece of the cosmic column, identified with the stem of the tree, and so occupies the place which Sūrya usually takes on reaching the zenith of its orbit and forming the *stambha* — top.[12] Bosch further observes "So it is little wonder that amongst the *brahma-mūla* symbol *cakra* ranks foremost and as a *stambha*-top occurs more frequently than any emblem." This is shown by many Borobudūr relief pictures of topped standards big *cakra*.

The *triśūla-cakra* symbol is particularly known in the Buddhist art though it is also found in Jainas and Hindu sects. It depicts a wheel topped by a trident. This symbol has been used in many ways on the monuments of Bharhut, Sāñcī and Amarāvatī, often as a top for *stambhas*, thrones and *toraṇa* — architraves and also as decorative motif on railing. Bosch[13] observes:

> Since the *triśūla-cakra* emblem appears to belong to the vast group of representations reducible to Tree-symbolism, it is easily understood that the emblem, being pre-Buddhist, pre-Jaina and pre-Hindu, became the common property of all religious sects and more particularly became closely related to Buddhism.

The whole emblem came to be regarded as *triratna* symbol. Thus, the various motifs as symbols were the common heritage of the Brāhmaṇism, Buddhism and Jainism since the time immemorial.

12. F.D.K. Bosch, *op.cit.*, p. 159.
13. F.D.K. Bosch, *op.cit.*, p. 163.

8

A Brāhmaṇical Episode of Buddhist Art in Mathurā

S.D. Trivedi

IRRESPECTIVE of time and distance, humans have always interacted, influenced, competed with and inspired each other. This give and take, when applied to artists and donors of art, flowered into a rare synthesis of creativity. The result was a similarity and proximity of certain traits and motifs in Brāhmaṇical and Buddhist art. A few examples are cited to support the viewpoint.

Take, for example, the traditional Brāhmaṇical practice of performing *tapas* or physical austerities by holy men. This became an interesting subject of portrayal in art. In Buddhist tradition, Māra, the god of love, along with his retinue, is depicted as trying to interrupt Buddha's meditative efforts in the way of acquiring Supreme Knowledge. In Jaina art, Sambar, the evil one, is shown attacking the twenty-third *Tīrthaṅkara* Pārśvanātha when the latter is engaged in *tapas*. This idea originates from Śiva's *tapas* being disturbed by Kāmadeva, the Brāhmaṇical god of love; the latter proving ineffectual and being burnt to cinders in the bargain.

Depiction of *ūrṇā*, a circular mark or a pronounced, slightly raised, dot on the forehead of deities is a motif common to the protagonists of Brāhmaṇic, Buddhist and Jaina faiths. *Ūrṇā* or *ṭīkā* is considered an auspicious mark in the Bhāgavata sect. This special mark can be seen displayed on the icons of Buddha and is also found on some of the Jaina heads of Kuṣāṇa period at Mathurā.

Certain Hindu deities find place in the Buddhist art of various centres. Gaja-Lakṣmī, an essentially a Brāhmaṇical goddess[1] is depicted in the early Buddhist

1. *Śatapatha Brāhmaṇa*, 12.4.1.11

art[2] at Bharhut,[3] Sañcī[4] and Bodha-Gayā.[5] Sūrya images of Bhājā and Bodha-Gayā are actually associated with Buddhism.[6] The depiction of Sūrya is also found on a carved stone slab[7] from Mathurā wherein the important events of Buddha's life are prominently shown on a Kuṣāṇa exhibit of the State Museum, Lucknow. Jambhala and Hārīti, prototype of Hindu deities, are frequently sculpted in the Buddhist art. Similarly, the assimilation of Brāhmaṇical gods — Indra and Brahmā in Buddhist literature and art is a beautiful example of interaction. The concept of Lokapālas, adopted in Buddhism, has roots in Vedic literature. There are several other similarities born out of the interaction of various Indian faiths. This paper deals with a particular Brāhmaṇical episode, which became popular in Buddhist art of Mathurā in the Śuṅga-Kuṣāṇa age.

The legend of Ṛsyaśṛṅga attracted the stone carvers of Śuṅga and Kuṣāṇa period and this attests the popularity of the legend as well as the state of maturity in their story-telling aspect of plastic creativity. The story is narrated in the great Epics and Buddhist books with different captions. Some slight variation is found in the contents of each account; otherwise the essence is same to lure the young ascetic to a new world for the good cause. A brief summary of the tale[8] would be helpful to understand the full context.

Once upon a time, Lomapāda was the king of Aṅgadeśa. When he was performing manifold religious acts to redress the sufferings of people from the awesome drought but with no consequences, his priests told him to bring the young ascetic Ṛsyaśṛṅga to his State. The young man, son of Maharṣi Vibhāṇḍaka, was living in *puṇya āśrama* in the forest. This mission was entrusted to an old woman prostitute who took her daughter and other young women to lure the young ascetic. As per plans, the maidens in the guise of *brahmacārins* aroused the amorous emotions in the innocent boy who never having known even about the

2. A.K. Coomaraswamy refers to this representation as of Māyādevī with elephants, assuming the nativity of Buddha. In Hindu art, this is Gaja-Lakṣmī. This opinion is now no more tenable in the scholarly world. *History of Indian and Indonesian Art* (*HIIA*), p. 38.
3. R.C. Sharma, *Bharhut Sculptures*, p. 28 & fig.
4. Marshall *et al.*, *Monuments of Sañcī*, pl. 74, 83, 87, 88 & 90.
5. *HIIA*, fig. 61.
6. J.N. Banerjea, *Development of Hindu Iconography*, p. 432; V.C. Srivastva, *Sun-Worship in Ancient India*, pp. 292-94.
7. State Museum, Lucknow, Accn. No. B.208; Sharma, *Buddhist* . . . ., p. 201, fig. 115.
8. This is mainly based on *Mahābhārata*, which gives most elaborate account of the legend.

existence of woman before this maiden pleasure. An interesting account of young man's wondrous experiences of joyful romance is given in *Mahābhārata.* Ultimately, the young ascetic was brought to the drought-ridden kingdom and on his arrival it began to rain heavily. The king's daughter, Śāntā was also married to Ṛṣyaśṛṅga.

According to *Nalinī* or *Nalinika Jātaka,*[9] the father of Ṛṣyaśṛṅga was no other person than the Buddha himself in his previous birth and Śṛṅgī was a monk. Here Nalinī, daughter of Brahmadatta, the king of Benāras, accomplished the mission.

Alambuṣā Jātaka[10] says that she was an *apsarā* named Alambuṣā who was assigned to corrupt the purity of the sage by Śakra, god of heaven who was afraid of getting dethroned from his *śakratva* by the extraordinary religious merits and pious practices of *ṛṣi* Śṛṅga. He was born from a Dove who became pregnant having grazed over the spot where *ṛṣi* had made water. Consequently, a male child was born with a horn on his head. All the works agreed on the presence of a horn on his head, a biological phenomenon. The poet Kṣemendra also describes him as Ekaśṛṅga in his *Bodhisattvāvadāna-Kalpalatā.*

The legend of Ekaśṛṅga was depicted in Bharhut[11] under the caption ISI-SINGA JĀTAKA. The birth of a rather famous *ṛṣi* Ekaśṛṅga from the womb of a deer is shown in detail. The father, who is himself a sage, is shown receiving the boy. The deer is shown again with the *ṛṣi* after the delivery of the child. At Sañcī,[12] the scene is portrayed on the projecting end of the lower lintel of the northern gateway. The baby is easily identifiable due to the protuberance or horn on his forehead. The child is shown being lustrated in a lotus pond immediately after his birth. He can be seen on the left side as if he was presenting himself before the anchorite.

In Mathurā, the one-horned sage is found at least on four sculptures. A railing pillar[13] shows the figure (*Pl.* 8.1) of an ascetic with a single, rhinoceros-like horn on his forehead, standing under a mango tree in blossom with his right hand

9. *Jātaka* No. 526, *Jātaka,* Volume V.

10. *Jātaka* No. 523, *Jātaka,* Volume V.

11. A. Cunningham, *Stupa of Bharhut,* p. 64, pl. XXVI, 7.

12. Sir John Marshall & Alfred Foucher, *The Monuments of Sāñcī,* vol. 2, pl. XXVII.

13. Government Museum, Mathurā (hereafter denoted as GMM), Accession No. J.7.

raised to his lips, and the left akimbo. The most important feature of this sculpture is the unique gesture and the expressive face of the figure. The index and middle fingers of his right hand are placed on the lower part of his chin, giving a beautiful rendition of "astonishment" *vismaya* that is further reinforced by the expression of the face. The reverse of the upper panel shows worship of *bodhi* tree, a sure indication that this upright pillar must have been part of a Buddhist *stūpa* railing.

Another pillar[14] (*Pl.* 8.2) in the Mathurā Museum is also carved with scenes depicting the Ekaśṛṅga episode. The front of the pillar has the figure of a lady[15] and the reverse shows the Ekaśṛṅga story.[16] The uppermost compartment shows some women in a boat, probably the princess and her friends going to the hermitage of Ṛṣyaśṛṅga. The middle portion of the pillar is carved with the figure of the youthful sage enjoying a musical soiree, and the lowest compartment shows him in the company of some ladies. The continuity of the scenes indicates a story in progress. The horn on the forehead of the youth clearly marks him out as Ekaśṛṅga.

A fragment of a door-jamb[17] (*Pl.* 8.3) sculpted on two opposite faces has several scenes in separate sunken panels. The upper compartment shows a youth sitting under a central tree and a lady sitting in his lap. The youth is easily identifiable because of the horn on him. Interestingly, a four-line inscription[18] in Brāhmī script of about first century BC is incised on the relief.

Yet another rail-post[19] (*Pl.* 8.4) was found from Govindnagar, Mathurā, in 1976. It has four sunken panels with carvings. The top depicts a haloed royal turban, which is a symbolic representation of Buddha/*Bodhisattva*. The other three compartments separated with railing motif sport the scenes from Ekaśṛṅga story. These are:

1. Intimate meeting of a sage and a deer, the old sage displaying a kind of romance.[20]

---

14. GMM, Accession No. 11.151.
15. A lady is holding a bunch of grapes in her right hand and a jar of wine covered with a glass in the left hand.
16. R.C. Sharma, *The Splendour of Mathurā Art & Museum*, pp. 127-28.
17. State Museum, Lucknow, Accession No. J.532.
18. Bühler, *Epigraphia Indica*, vol. 1, p. 390 ; Luder's no. 108.
19. GMM, Accn. No. 76.40; R.C. Sharma, *Buddhist Art of Mathurā*, p. 101.
20. *Ibid*, p. 101.

2. Birth of a baby and the sage receiving the newly born child.
3. The marriage of the youth Ekaśṛṅga as the culmination of his romance.

The presence of the typically Buddhist symbol of the haloed turban makes it obvious that the artefact belonged to a Buddhist monastery.

Let us now examine certain factual details of this relief:

i. The personage and the scenes relating to the episode in question are depicted on upright pillars only.
ii. They have been found at different sites, viz., Caubārā mound, Bhūteśvar,[21] Kaṅkālī mound,[22] and Govindnagar,[23] all sites of Mathurā city.
iii. Out of the four, two are certainly from a Buddhist *stūpa.*[24] One does not offer decisive[25] clues and the fourth one has Jaina[26] inscription of the same age.
iv. In none of the scenes did the master craftsmen forget to depict the horny protuberance on the forehead of the young sage, leaving no margin for erroneous identification.
v. The sculptures of this episode were found at different places at different dates. The popularity of the tale and the Mathurā artists' fascination with it throws up the possibility that there may be some more sculptural renditions of the story that are still lying buried under the earth.

It is a well-known fact that the stories of many *Jātaka*s were taken from the Epics, *Pañcatantra* and some other Hindu scriptures. Obviously, the narrative contents of popular stories were borrowed, changed a little bit and morphed in Buddhist mythology making suitable additions to fit the framework of the new faith. *Daśaratha Jātaka* proves the point admirably. As it has been stated that the story of the one-horned Sage is elaborately narrated in the *Rāmāyaṇa,*[27] and in the *Mahābhārata,*[28] Buddhist writers of edificatory tales found it interesting and

21. *The Splendour of Mathurā Art and Museum,* pp. 127-28.
22. V.A. Smith, *The Jain Stupa and other Antiquities of Mathurā*, pl. XXVIII.
23. R.C. Sharma, *op. cit.*, p. 101.
24. The upright pillars have one or two Buddhist subjects either on front or on the back.
25. Some Bhūteśvar railing pillars depict Buddhist scenes. It may also be a part of Buddhist *stūpa.*
26. The inscription begins with *namo arhatanams sramana sravikaye.*
27. *Rāmāyaṇa*, Bālakāṇḍa, Sarga 10.
28. *Mahābhārata*, Vanaparva, Adhyāya 110-13.

included it in the *Jātaka* book under the name *Isi-Singa Jātaka.* In the Ceylonese version of the *Jātaka* book[29] it is neared under the name *Nailinī Jātaka* and in *Mahāvastu,*[30] an important Buddhist chronicle, it is mentioned as *Alambuṣā Jātaka.*

At Bharhut the episode has been carved on a railing medallion and labelled *Isi-Singa Jātaka*, showing only a part of the story. At Sañcī the story does not find much importance. The character forms only a small part of a very crowded scene in which the emphasis is mainly on the decorative aspect. Marshall and Foucher[31] rightly observed that here the only purpose of the artist was to fill in the landscape.

The episode found no space in the Gāndhāra art.[32] In contrast to other places, the story seems to have held the Mathurā artist in thrall who carried out varied representations on upright pillars. But the portrayal is not as per the *Jātaka* story. It is more in line with the tale as it appears in the epics. In support of this view, certain points are given below for due consideration.

Mathurā artists were cognisant to the special characteristics and way of presenting *Jātaka* stories, as evident at Bharhut and Sañcī. They executed the fables in a summary form that was short but fully illustrative of the events as they unfolded in the original story. They executed with elan the basic purpose of acquainting the worshippers and visitors to the religious shrines with a much loved and popular story already in circulation. However, the case with the Ekaśṛṅga story is somewhat different. This was a highly popular subject given a rather different treatment. All the important events of the story were not only grouped in the same frame but were also illustrated exhaustively. Some *Jātaka* stories like *Kuśala-mānava Jātaka*, *Ulūka Jātaka* and *Kacchapa Jātaka*[33] are a little difficult to identify because they do not have any special mark to help us identify them. On the other hand, by the addition of a protuberance on the head of the young sage as a representative horn, the sculptor made sure that the story could be identified with ease.

More significant for our consideration is the independent image[34] of a horned

29. Bhadant Anand Kausalyayan, *Jātaka*, fifth vol., *Jātaka* No. 526.

30. *Mahāvastu*, Jones, p. 78 H.

31. *Op.cit.*, p. 225.

32. The identification of a relief as the illustration of the legend of sage Ekaśṛṅga by its excavator, Aurel Stein was ruled out by Ingholt Harold, *Gandharan Art in Pakistan*, p. 144

33. N.P. Joshi, *Mathurā Sculptures*, pp. 50-56.

34. V.S. Agrawal, *A Relief of Rishya Sringa Studies in Indian Art*, pp. 160-61.

young man, the hero of the episode carved on a railing pillar from Mathurā. No personage of any *Jātaka* story has got separate independent portrayal except Ekaśṛṅga.[35]

It is worth mentioning that a sunken panel of Govindnagar rail-post even goes into the graphic details of showing the sensuous feelings of the sage for the beautiful female deer. Apart from this, the marriage of an ascetic with the daughter of the king is also clearly shown at the niche of bottom. This version is part of the Brāhmaṇical story narrated at length in the *Mahābhārata.*

About the identification of this theme, the scholars express a mixed opinion. They mention the *Jātaka* story as well as refer to the episode as given in the *Mahābhārata.* Dr. N.P. Joshi, while documenting the various Brāhmaṇical stories of Mathurā art,[36] did count Ṛṣyaśṛṅga legend among them. Probably he endorses our viewpoint.

It is possible that the Jainas were also attracted to the popularity of this theme and they too conceived a story relating to a horned man.[37] It may be presumed that the original story was taken from the Epics and the sculptors of Mathurā freely transposed the scenes on the upright pillars of Buddhist railing in full

35. During the presentation of this paper in the Conference, a noted Indologist, Dr. Gouriswar Bhattacharya suggested that the sculpture in question does not represent Ekaśṛṅga but it is a figure of an eunuch. Later the author discussed in very brief about the basis of his new identification. The image has a one-line inscription in Kuṣāṇa Brāhmī. It reads: *abhyamtaro pastayakasa kathikas danam* which can be freely translated as "gift of Kathika, the servant of the interior." According to him, the word "Kathika" occurs in some other inscription, which indicates him a castrated man, working in the royal harem. Apart from this inference, his other point of argument is that the figure has a feminine look.

The short inscriptions engraved on Mathurā sculptures are not meant for identifying labels. It may be interpreted that the image was gifted by one named Kathika (who was a servant of inner court) to be set-up in the Buddhist monastery at Mathurā. The figure does not have a tender look at all. He has a pleasant and engrossed gesture. He recalls the pleasurable moments and lost in bewildering thoughts. The posture of the figure is so well treated that it indicates everything going in his mind. The physiognomy of the figure, his ornaments and turban — all features resemble with the masculine character. It is true that the horn is projected from the turban with little decoration but the leafy background is given to enforce the symbol.

We can conclude that it is a matter of opinion. The author just joins the galaxy of scholars and agrees with them who propose the identification as Ṛṣyaśṛṅga. The author wishes to emphasize that the description of *Rāmāyaṇa* and *Mahābhārata* about the state of mind of the young ascetic can be viewed in this relief.

36. N.P. Joshi, *Mathurā Kī Mūrtikalā*, pp. 51-54.

37. Shailendra Kumar Rastogi, *Lucknow Saṅgrahālaya Kī Jaina Pratimāyen*, p. 36.

awareness of the fact that the subject was also known by way of *Isi-Singa Jātaka* in Buddhist lore. The author, therefore, concludes that this is one of the best examples of interaction and syncretism between the Brāhmaṇical and Buddhist sects.

9

Interaction between Buddhist and Brāhmaṇical Images in the Sārnāth Museum

Niharika & Ajay Srivastava

SĀRNĀTH is one of the four most important Buddhist pilgrimage centres, which were advised to visit by the Buddha himself. He delivered the First Sermon *dharma-cakra-pravartana* at this place, previously known as Ṛṣipatana — Mṛgadāya or Mṛgadāva. It flourished as a main Buddhist centre during the reigns of different dynasties as Maurya, Śuṅga, Kuṣāṇa, Gupta and Gahaḍavāla; and produced beautiful and elegant images of gods and goddesses of different cults and sects. These images can be categorized as Buddhist or Brāhmaṇical gods and goddesses. But a few of these can well be connected with Hinduism or they show few prominent similarities with its predatory religion. A careful study will indicate that these icons are in adaptation of Brāhmaṇical cult into Buddhist icons. According to Grunwedel, with the spread of Buddhism, "the converts naturally carried into their new religion much of their reverence for the old Hindu gods." The Hīnayāna sect changed a little in the nomenclature and iconography of Hindu deities like Viṣṇu, Śiva, Brahmā, etc., but they were mostly represented as acolytes or attendants of Buddha.[1] But in Mahāyāna, these gods received a new nomenclature and a place in the Buddhist mythology. Many Buddhist gods and goddesses can be compared with Hindu gods and goddesses as Vajrapāṇi with Indra (*Pl.* 9.1), Avalokiteśvara with Viṣṇu, Nīlakaṇṭha with Śiva, Vasudhārā with Lakṣmī, Mārīci with Sūrya, Jambhala with Kubera, Yamāntaka with Yama, Mañjuśrī

1. J.N. Banerjea, *The Development of Hindu Iconography*, 1956, p. 558.

with Brahmā, Vajraśāradā with Sarasvatī, etc. Images of Heruka and Hārīti also show one or the other interaction with the Brāhmaṇical deities.

Such figurines are displayed in the Archaeological Museum, Sārṇāth, Vārāṇasī or kept in the reserve collection. This is the oldest site museum of Archaeological Survey of India, going to celebrate its century in AD 2010. It is adjacent to the excavated area at Sārnāth. The building forms half of a monastery *saṅghārāma* in plan.

A few images of this Museum, showing Brāhmaṇical and Buddhist significances are being discussed in the following pages.

Nīlakaṇṭha Avalokiteśvara

Among such images, Nīlakaṇṭha Avalokiteśvara can be seen in the museum. These are made of Chunar sandstone. The *Bodhisattva* is seated cross-legged with a large bowl against his chest on the flat top of the base. On the head of the *Bodhisattva* a headless figure of Buddha Amitābha in meditation can be seen (*Pl.* 9.2). This feature identifies the main statue as that of Avalokiteśvara who is wearing a simple cloth in the lower part of the body, the hem of which is visible below the knee in one image; while in the other image, it wears a garment covering the left shoulder and chest. One male and a female figure with the same bowl are standing on either side of the main statue. There are two more images of Nīlakaṇṭha Avalokiteśvara, but are so weathered that much cannot be studied.

According to Hindu mythology, Nīlakaṇṭha is a name of Lord Śiva who quaffed off the poison obtained by *deva*s and *asura*s after churning the ocean of milk *kṣīrodasamudra-manthana* to obtain immortality by tasting the Elixir (*amṛta*). In this process, they procured the deadly poison (*kālakūṭa*) and nectar (*amṛta*).[2] The former was cheerfully taken by Lord Śiva who didn't allow this liquid to pass down the neck, which turned his neck (*kaṇṭha*) in blue (*nīla*). Thus, Śiva got the name of Nīlakaṇṭha. Other literary evidences also prove this name of Śiva:

ब्रह्मावादीत्तदानीं शृणुत हर कुलं वेदकण्ठौग्रकण्ठौ,
श्रीकण्ठान्नीलकठ प्रहसितवदनः पातु वश्चन्द्रचूडः।[3]

Heruka

Two images of Heruka are stored in the Museum. One of these is noteworthy. It

---

2. B. Majumdar, *A Guide to Sārnāth*, p. 100.
3. *Subhāṣitaratnabhāṇḍāgāram*, p. 8, 98.

is an unfinished image of dancing Heruka on a demon lying full length on the base. He is wearing a garland of human skulls *muṇḍa-mālā* and holds probably a club with an unfinished human head *khaṭvāṅga* in his left hand. He has two long tusks. The dot on his forehead is meant for third eye.

Heruka can be compared with the images of dancing Śiva, as he is also known as Naṭarāja.

Mārīci

There are more than ten images of Mārīci in the Museum. They are made of Chunar sandstone of green, grey, buff and reddish colours. The images show different emblems of the goddess in one hand, like *vajra*, *aśoka*-flower or leaf, *śara*, *cāpa* and the other hand is in the attitude of menace. Her body is in *pratyālīḍhapāda-mudrā* that is of an archer. Thus, the images are identified as that of Mārīci, the Goddess of rising Sun.[4] They are all dated to medieval period.

Two of these images are very noteworthy. It shows an archer Mārīci wearing a garment fastened with a plain girdle (*kāñcī*) on the waist. The upper half of the body is naked, though a scarf (*uttarīya*) can be seen over two of her arms. The central face is bigger and the left one is that of a pig. The uppermost right hand is broken, but by comparing with other images, it can be presumed that she was holding a thunderbolt in this hand. The second and third hands of this side hold an arrow (slightly damaged) and an elephant goad (*aṅkuśa*), respectively. The uppermost left hand is also broken but again it can be assumed that it might have been holding an *aśoka*-flower. The second hand is raised in a menacing attitude *tarjanīdhara-mudrā* against the breast. The *dhyānī* Buddha Vairocana, expounding the law, can be seen on the head of the central figure.

Seven boars in a row can be seen on the front of the base. The central one is facing to the front while the remaining are running in opposite directions. The seven boars are pulling the chariot of Mārīci; hence, she is known as *sapta-śūkararathārūḍhā*. Though the chariot is not evidently carved, but the female (?) figure riding astride on the central boar is evidently the charioteer. The male and female figures at the base are probably of the donor and his wife. This figure is comparable to the three other images of Mārīci, with a few differences; one kept in the Lucknow Museum and the rest in the Indian Museum, Kolkata.

4. Daya Ram Sahni, *Catalogue of Museum of Archaeology*, Sārnāth, p. 156.

In another fragmentary sculpture, the main image of Mārīci is missing, but her chariot is intact. Its wheels are carved on both sides of the base. The female charioteer is sitting astride on the demon with a thunderbolt in her right hand. Its head and breast are broken off. Two figures are visible on either side of the chariot. The right one is broken but the left one shows only one face, which is of a boar. She holds a bow (*cāpa*) in the left hand, and with the right hand, she is drawing an arrow out of a quiver.

According to D.R. Sahni,[5] these are mere repetition of the goddess herself. The seven pigs depicted are so immature that it looks like mice. One of the remaining images is draped in a *dhotī* and accompanied by a female attendant who might have been holding an umbrella over her head; but the head, right hand and feet are missing. She is standing in the position of an archer with her left hand disposed before her breast in menace and may be identified as Mārīci or Vajravārāhī.[6] It is pale buff in colour.

Other image is a companion of the main image of Tārā. It is seated cross-legged on a lotus. It holds a thunderbolt (*vajra*) in the right hand and left hand is holding *aśoka*-flower. It also shows marks of probably a third eye. A standing figure, in association with the figure of Tārā, is also secured in the Museum. It is buff in colour and holds a *vajra* in her right hand.

A three-faced head is noteworthy; the left one being of a boar, which must have belonged to a statue of Mārīci. All the three heads are heavily ornamented. A votive *stūpa* of Chunar sandstone has a big niche with trefoil arch in the front. It contains a three-faced goddess with six arms, standing as an archer. It is identified as Mārīci, the goddess of dawn. Her left face is that of a boar. She is holding a thunderbolt (*vajra*) and an arrow (*śara*) in the upper two right hands. The lowest right hand is resting on the thigh. The lowest left hand is in menacing attitude on the breast. The upper two have a leaf (*aśoka-pallava*) and a *cāpa*. The seven pigs are not carved, but we can see a figure of a driver between the goddess's legs.

Maitreya, Mañjuśrī and Avalokiteśvara can be seen on the remaining three sides in smaller niches.

Another is a part of pediment with a double-storeyed *caitya* in the middle. It

5. Daya Ram Sahni, *Catalogue of Museum of Archaeology*, Sārnāth, p. 150.
6. Daya Ram Sahni, *op. cit.*, pp. 152-53.

shows Mārīci and other figures of a goddess, a dancing figure and a figure sitting in Indian style. A grey coloured hand of a goddess is also stored in the Museum, which is finely executed and adorned with finger-rings. It holds an object resembling a thunderbolt (*vajra*) and hence, it is presumed that this hand belonged to a figure of Mārīci.

Two more images show a bust of three-faced Mārīci and Mārīci with her chariot of seven boars.

Mārīci, according to *Sādhanamālā*, is a goddess emanated from Vairocana, the *dhyānī* Buddha, which is mostly depicted on the head of Mārīci. All deities emanated from Vairocana are female, which are considered to be the presiding spirits. Mārīci is most important of them and is considered to be the wife of Vairocana and the goddess of dawn. She is still worshipped in Tibet in the early morning at the rising sun. The word Mārīci has some significance with Mārīci, meaning "the solar rays" in Sanskrit. Thus, Mārīci means the emanation from "Sunlight" or "born of the sun." According to Lexicon, Mārīci is one of the many names of Māyādevī or Vajrakālikā. So, it can be compared philosophically with the Śakti emanated from the effulgence of Higher Wisdom *śūnyajñānam*, which is symbolized as the *dhyānī* Buddha. So the conception of Mārīci may have been inspired by the Purāṇic Sun with his chariot of seven horses.

सप्ताश्वं चैक चक्रं च रथं तस्य प्रकल्पयेत्।

— *मत्स्य पुराण* **261.2**

अरुण: सारथिश्चास्य पद्मिनी पत्रसंभव:

— *मत्स्य पुराण* **261.7**

Probably, the seven horses are symbolic to seven rays or the colours of seven rays. The three faces of this goddess are suggested to be the personification of three sentiments (*rasa*), i.e., *śṛṅgāra* (amour), *vīra* (heroic) and *harṣa* (joy). The seven pigs are supposed to be the seven major planets and the many figurines lying under the wheel are personified diseases that befall on mankind. The sun is also worshipped as the repressive of diseases as described in Dīnājpur inscription.[7]

सूर्यसमस्त रोगानामाहर्त्ता विश्वप्रकाशक:।

The bodiless figurine of charioteer is probably *Rāhu*[8] (*Agni Purāṇa*) referred as Aruṇa, the feetless charioteer of Sun.

7. *JAS*, I, 26, p. 147.
8. Majumdar, *op. cit.*, pp. 110-11.

Vasudhārā

There are eight images of Vasudhārā, the goddess of plenty, sometimes named as Vasundharā.[9] She is depicted individually or with her male counterpart Jambhala (*Pl.* 9.3 left), the Buddhist god of wealth. She is very often associated with other gods and goddesses too; as a slab of pale grey colour of Chunar stone shows Vasudhārā, Jambhala, Kubera, Hārīti, a man and the donor couple. Here, Vasudhārā is carved with many ornaments and a long garland. Her left hand is gone, while the right hand's object is missing. In comparison to other figures of this goddess, it is presumed that she might be holding an ear of corn (*dhānyamañjarī*) and a fruit (?). Beneath the goddess is carved a pair of vases (*ratna-ghaṭa*) a symbol of abundance over which she presides. According to *Sādhanamālā*, ear of corn and vase of treasure are the main emblems of goddess Vasudhārā (*dhānyamañjarīnānā-ratnavarṣāghaṭa-vāmahastā*).

Another is a fragmentary sculpture of pale buff colour of Chunar stone. It shows three figures, which are the repetition of goddess Vasudhārā. The main figure is in the middle, but the head and the forearms are missing. It is wearing a lower cloth and a scarf with lots of ornaments. The upper half of the body wears nothing. The right hand is in the gift-bestowing attitude (*varada-mudrā*) and left was probably holding an ear of corn. The vases of treasures are kept under her both feet. The other two smaller figurines are the repetition of the same goddess. The right hand in gift-bestowing attitude and left hand holding ear of corn, is also visible in other image of red sandstone.

There are three more fragmentary sculptures, which show seated Vasudhārā in an easy attitude (*lalitāsana*) on a lotus throne. The right foot is placed on an inverted vase (*ratnaghaṭa*), which rests on a lotus flower. Seven, seven and five vases respectively are lying upside down in these sculptures, probably to indicate goddess's total command on wealth.

Another image of Vasudhārā displayed in the Museum in Gallery No. 2 is unique due to its depiction of Gaṇeśa's miniature image. The four-armed goddess is sitting cross-legged on a jar guarded by a snake on either side. Only the upper left hand is intact, which is holding a vase of treasure. In the upper proper left corner, there is probably an ear of corn. Both of these emblems indicate towards the goddess being Vasudhārā. There are four snake hoods at the proper left side and they were probably at the other side too.

9. Daya Ram Sahni, *op. cit.*, pp. 135-47. Majumdar, *op. cit.*, p.

Vasudhārā can be compared with the Vedic Lakṣmī, goddess of fortune and wealth.[10] One who seeks for treasure and wealth worships Lakṣmī who bestows happiness, prosperity and riches to him.

Jambhala

A few images of Jambhala, the Buddhist god of wealth with his female counterpart Vasudhārā is noteworthy (*Pl.* 9.3). The characteristics of Vasudhārā are described earlier. Jambhala is also carved in association with Vasudhārā and Hārīti. The god is dwarfish with a prominent belly (*lambodara*) and with disproportionately short legs, the feet is broken off. The god is depicted nude and he wears cobras as bracelets, armlets and anklets. He is also wearing a snake in the manner of *yajñopavīta* (Brāhmaṇical thread), his teeth are visible between his lips and from the corners of the lips protrude crooked tusks, a characteristic of *yakṣa*s. But a *dhyānī* Buddha, surrounded by a flaming halo of oval shape,[11] differentiates it from a statue of *yakṣa* and identifies as Jambhala. He is holding a bowl against his chest as in the Mathurā sculpture. This bowl is compared with a skull (*kapāla*) by Sri B. Majumdar.[12] The left hand is broken; but with the traces of a tail, it can be presumed that he was holding a mongoose in his left hand. He is standing in a *pratyālīḍha-mudrā* on Dhanada lying at full length on a lotus and wearing a high diadem and ornaments. There are two more images, which look like that of Jambhala.

Jambhala's similar deity in Indian Mythology is Kubera who is the god of wealth, prosperity and good luck. He has a big belly (*lambodara*) and is adorned with beautiful ornaments and a crown. He holds a moneybag and a mongoose in his hands. Mongoose is supposed to eject jewels (*maṇi*) from his mouth while pressing his stomach. Brāhmaṇical art shows his wife "prosperity" on his left thigh, who is depicted as Vasudhārā in Buddhist art. *Matsya Purāṇa* describes Kubera in following words:

कुबेरं च प्रवक्ष्यामि कुण्डलाभ्यामलंकृतम् ।
हारकेयूररचितं सिताम्बरधरं सदा ।।

— *Mat. Pur.* 261.20-21

10. Vasudeva Upadhyaya, *Prācīna Bhārtīya Mūrti Vijñāna*, p. 139.
11. Daya Ram Sahni, *op. cit.*, p. 135.
12. Majumdar, *op. cit.*, p. 111.

Hārīti

There is one image of Hārīti (?) in which she holds a child in her arm. Its head is broken off. Hārīti is compared with Hindu goddess Śītalā or with Ṣaṣṭhī. It is dated to fourth-fifth century AD.[13]

Yamāntaka

Two images of Yamāri or Yamāntaka are noteworthy. One of these is a part of sculpture depicting Mañjuśrī, whose left hand attendant is called Yamāri or Yamāntaka. He is holding a skull filled with blood (*raktapūrṇa-kapālam*) in his left hand, and in the right hand, a staff with human head (*muṇḍāṅkita sitadaṇḍa-dharam*). An other image shows Yamāntaka with head tied with a band of skull and snakes can also be seen.

To conclude, the seventh century AD indicates towards a change in art and its soul. According to Vasudeva Upadhyaya, it was due to the enlightenment of Vajrayāna (Tantrayāna) sect. It is quite clear that Buddhism was a reincarnation of Upaniṣadic principles. The pessimistic view of worldly life, the ignorance and attachment as the prime cause of all bondage (*bandhana*) and sufferings (*duḥkha*) of mankind are the soul of Vedic doctrines. The word *nirvāṇa* was also taken from the Upaniṣads. The influence of Brāhmaṇical religion changed symbol worship of Buddhism into image worship. Before the reign of Kuṣāṇa rulers, Buddha was worshipped as symbols, like *bodhivṛkṣa*, *cakra* and *stūpa*, etc.; due to the advent of Mahāyāna, Buddha was worshipped as a human being, and with the beginning of Pāla dynasty when Vajrayāna came into light they imagined *ādi* Buddha and Prajñāpārmitā who are compared with Brahmā and Māyā of Brāhmaṇical religion, responsible for the birth of Universe. *Pañcadhyānī* Buddha and his counterpart Tārā become the soul reason of Universe. Each of them has their own family. Thus, for about 600 years (AD 700-1300) art was mainly affected with Vajrayāna sect. Buddhist literature of medieval period *Sādhanamālā* refers towards such differences and similarities between the two sects, and is evident in the icons also. Thus, the theoretical rivalry of Hindu and Buddhist cult showed its impact on the art of medieval period. Religious differences, debate and bad criticism forced the artists to depict such images that show these feelings in their art.

10

Buddhist and Hindu Art — A Comparison

R. Nagaswamy

sarvjñaṁ jñānakāyaṁ dinakara vapuṣaṁ padmapatrāyatākṣam
buddhaṁ siṁhāsanasthaṁ suravara namitaṁ mastakeṇa praṇamyaṁ ।
pṛcchet rāja sucandraḥ karakamala pūtaṁ sthāpayitvā uttmāṅge
yogaṁ śrī kālacakre kaliyuga samaye mukti hetoḥ narāṇām ॥

THIS is the invocatory verse of the Buddhist text *Kālacakra-Tantra-Rāja,* a verse that seems to sum up the theme of this seminar. Buddha is described in this verse as *jñāna-kāya,* knowledge, constituting his body. It is clear from the context that we are not dealing with the historic Buddha with a human body, but divine Buddha whose body is knowledge; not the acquired knowledge, but the Supreme Knowledge. So he is called *sarvajña,* All knowing God. In the Śaivite temples worship is offered to Śiva in the form of *liṅga*. The texts tell us that there are two types of imagery in worship; one is called *bimba-mūrti,* the physical image, and the other *mantra-mūrti,* hymnal image. The *bimba-mūrti* — physical image is only an aid and not the end. In daily ritual, the *bimba-mūrti* is psychologically transformed into a divine body called *vidyā-deha* and the worship is offered to that knowledge. When Śiva is invoked in the sacrificial altar daily, he is invoked as Vāgīśvara and the Goddess as Vāgīśvarī. In both the Buddhist and Hindu systems, the ultimate identity behind the visual image, is pure knowledge. So Buddha is *jñana-kāya.*

The second point that deserve attention in the verse of *Kālacakra-Tantra-Rāja* cited above is that the Buddha appears in the form of *sūrya-dinakara-vapuṣaḥ.* The Sun, rising and setting in regular cycles is the creator of Time which is Kālacakra. Sūrya is supreme in this Kālacakra system and so Sūrya is identified with Buddha which is of utmost importance.

The verse also says that the foremost gods (*suravara-namita*) adore Buddha. And finally the system is mentioned as Kālacakra Yoga, the unity of physical and mental image.

In this connection an important passage in the *Vālmīki Rāmāyaṇa*, which I call as the *Rāmāyaṇa Gītā*, needs close study. Sage Agastya advises Rāma in the battlefield to worship Sūrya for victory over Rāvaṇa. It is called *Āditya Hṛdayam.* "Adore Rāma Vivasvān-Bhāskara the Lord of the world, who is the body of all the Gods *Sarvadevātmaka*. He is Brahmā, Viṣṇu, Śiva, Indra and all other gods. Sūrya is the creator of Time." Kṛṣṇa says in the *Bhagavad Gītā*, that "I am Viṣṇu among Ādityas" — *ādityānāmahaṁ viṣṇuḥ; kālaḥ kalayatamaham*. Sūrya is identified in all Hindu texts as the personification of all Gods. Sūrya is therefore the Supreme Kālacakra according to all systems.

Before elaborating this concept, I would like to draw attention to the *Kālacakra-Tantra-Rāja,* which speaks of Meru, its form, the surrounding peaks, the circling islands (*dvīpas*), the gardens, and also the oceans and the lives in them. It also speaks of the galaxy of stars, 27 *nakṣatras*, the nine planets, etc.

> *pravara bhūmitala cakravālasya samyak.*
>
> Mention is also made of Jinavaras adored by great gods in the Cakaravāla.
>
> *brahmāṇḍaṁ kālacakraṁ jinavara sahitaṁ saṁstutaṁ devabṛndaiḥ.*

The *dikpālas* like Indra, Agni, Yama Nirṛti, Varuṇa, Vāyu, Kubera, Īśāna, Brahmā and Viṣṇu are thus mentioned by name in the text. Īśāna is mentioned as Hara. Thus the central object of worship is adored by Brahmā, Viṣṇu and other gods, who form the *maṇḍala*. Compare this with the statement in *Āditya Hṛdayam: brahma īśāna acyuta īśāya sūryāya āditya varcase.* Āditya Sūrya is the supreme lord of Brahmā, Acyuta and Īśāna. According to this verse of *Kālacakra-Tantra-Rāja,* Brahmā, Viṣṇu, Īśāna remain with their weapons and retinues, around Kālacakra who is the creator of *jinavaras*.

The Early Tamil Buddhist epic *Maṇimekhalai,* speaks of a temple of Cakravāla. It consisted of the high Meru surrounded by the other peaks, the islands, oceans, and the living beings. This corresponds to the Cakravāla mentioned in *Kālacakra Tantra.* It also speaks of *arūpa Brahman, rūpa Brahman,* the two celestial Fires, and the *devagaṇas*. This was a temple built of brick and images made of stucco, a beautiful artistic creation by Maya, as per tradition.

pankura mannittal panbura vakuttu
mikka mayanal izhaikkappatta cakravalkottam

The Cakravāla-koṭṭam includes temple structure and sculptures. The great *stūpa* of Mahāsthān — eighth century — still retains some of the stucco sculptures like Gaṇeśa, Subrahmaṇya, Brahmā, Durgā and other *parivāras* still *in situ*.

Regarding *arūpa* and *sarūpa Brahman*, the following deserves attention. The Supreme is called *Brahman* in Buddhist context in *Maṇimekhalai*. Also the descend of the Supreme from *arūpa* stage to *rūpa* stage is also known in Śaiva tradition. The supreme Śiva — Paraśiva — who is beyond form, colour, taste, etc., manifests as first as *nāda-Brahman*, identified with *oṁkāra*. The first physical brāhmaṇas are called *pañca* brāhmaṇas — Tatpuruṣa, Aghora, Sadyojāta, Vāmadeva and Īśāna, the last who is on the top is said to be of the nature of all knowledge *īśānaḥ sarva vidyānām*, similar to the *jñānakāya* of the Buddha.

Lokesh Chandra has done yeomen service by publishing the Chinese version of the thousand armed Avalokiteśvara, whom he rightly points out as Harihara. This may further be pointed out that the Harihara form arises from the inseparable nature of Agni, especially the celestial Agni Sūrya. This is a Vedic concept extolling the destructive power of Agni by its terrific heat and the other life-giving and protective power by its benign heat. It is extolled in the *Kṛṣṇa Yajurveda* as Agnā — Viṣṇū — Agni standing for Rudra *rūdro vā eṣa yad agni*. This is known to us as Harihara and also as Ardhanara. Sūrya is both Rudra, Agni and Viṣṇu. In Vaiṣṇavaite parlance he is Sūryanārāyaṇa and in the Śaivite parlance he is called Śiva Sūrya. Sūrya has thousand legs, thousand hands, and thousand eyes, which are his rays, *sahasrākṣaḥ, sahasranayanaḥ,* and *sahasrapāt*. The thousand-armed Avalokiteśvara is Harihara and also *dinakaravapuḥ* — Sūrya, the Kālacakra.

Finally, one word, when Brahmā, Viṣṇu and Śiva are extolled as occupying secondary position, it was not intended to denigrate the Hindu gods but is to be understood in the contextual sense, as rightly mentioned in several Purāṇic texts. If one holds one form as inferior to other, he knows neither of them.

11

Interaction between Buddhist and Brāhmaṇical Art in Orissa — A General Survey

H.C. Das

CULTURAL interaction, assimilation, integration, diffusion, etc., have been the process of history from the dawn of civilization. The interactive cultural force is more conspicuous in the heterogeneous religious system of India and in multi-dimensional art forms. It may be pertinent to note here that no religious faith or a school of art in the Indian context can claim to have its own independent evolution and development in all phases without any interaction or interchange with other schools of thought or art. Thus, the cultural interactions between the two systems have been but inevitable. Traits of a cultural group are assimilated or integrated in each other through interaction. The interactive process may either be constructive or destructive, otherwise positive or negative. Once a god or goddess is conceived and manifested in an individual religious faith having wide celebrity and acceptability in the society, it creeps into other system through interaction in some other form having different nomenclature and iconography but losing its own identity. How such an interaction took place over the ages between the Buddhist and Brāhmaṇical art in the context of Orissa, is our concern here.

This paper aims at highlighting the interaction between the Buddhist and Brāhmaṇical art in Orissa. The present state of Orissa, formed with the territorial units of ancient Oḍra, Utkala, Kaliṅga and Kośala, had embraced in the past the mainspring of Indian religions and developed religious art pertaining to the major faiths under the royal patronage and peoples' support. Orissa had its own school of art and architecture and Śilpaśāstras. It was one of the seven temple-building zones of India. The artistic endeavour started here from the time of Aśoka in the third century BC and continued unabated till the sixteenth century AD. Untold number of monuments built during different cultural epochs relating to Buddhist, Jaina and Brāhmaṇical faiths were erected. Many a magnificent extant monuments, like the temples of Mukteśvara, Rājarānī, Brahmeśvara, Liṅgarāja at Bhubaneśvar, the great Jagannātha temle at Purī. The stupendous Sun Temple at Koṇārk, the gigantic Buddhist monastic establishments at Ratnagiri, Lalitagiri, Udayagiri, Ayodhyā, etc., bear the testimony of the state's art and architecture heritage.

Buddha never visited Kaliṅga, but his humanitarian teachings were echoed here during his lifetime. The *Aṅguttara Nikāya* and the *Jātakas* relate that Tapassu and Bhallika, two merchants of Utkala, while moving in the Madhyadeśa with their cartloads of merchandize happened to see the Buddha just after his Enlightenment. They offered him home-made cakes and honey; the Blessed One, out of compassion, offered them a handful of shaven hair and cut nails, which are stated by some scholars to have been enshrined in the *stūpa*s in Kaliṅga. They are supposed to be the first lay disciples of the Buddha. According to the *Aṅguttara Nikāya*, the Vassa and the Vanna tribes of Utkala accepted the teachings of the Blessed One.[1] The *Buddha Vaṁsa* made us believe that after the *mahāparinirvāṇa* of the Buddha, his tooth relic was brought to Kaliṅga and enshrined in its capital Dantapura.[2] In this way, we get several references in the Pāli literature regarding the spread of early Buddhism in Kaliṅga and Utkala.

The Kaliṅga War, which was fought between the Kaliṅgans and Aśoka in 261 BC in the vicinity of Dhauli hill near Bhubaneśvar, was a great landmark in the history of Buddhism. The horror of the devastating war causing havoc, bloodshed and indescribable human misery awakened, in the heart of the Emperor Aśoka, the feelings of repentance and sorrow. The horror of the Kaliṅga War, described in Rock Edict XIII found at Sahabazgarhi in Pakistan, turned Caṇḍāśoka to a Dharmāśoka.

1. अठ वसाभिसितेन देवनं प्रियस प्रिअद्रशिस रञो कलिंग विजित दिअढ मत्रे प्रणशत सहसे ये ततो अपबुढे शत सहस मत्रे तत्र हते बहुतवत के वमुटे ।

---

1. N.K. Sahu, *Buddhism in Orissa*, Utkal University, 1959, p. 13.
2. *Ibid.*

2. ततो प च अधुन लधेषु कलिगेषु तिब्रेध्रम शिलन ध्रम क्रमत ध्रमनुशस्ति देवनं प्रियस सो अस्ति अनुसोचन देवन प्रिअस विजनति कलिगनि।

In the war, Kaliṅga lost its independence and was included in the Mauryan Empire, forming a separate province with its capital at Toṣali (identified with present Śiśupalgarh at Bhubaneśvar). Simultaneously, Dhauli, about 6 km to the south-west as the crow flies, rose to eminence as the earliest known Buddhist centre of Kaliṅga. From this time onwards, a systematic propagation was carried on by the protagonists of different schools, and Buddhism made considerable headway here. The Emperor built here the Bhojakgiri *vihāra* for his brother Tissa who spent here his last days. Dharmarakṣita came to this monastery and stayed here with his disciple Tissa.[3] The Mahāsāṁghika *ācārya* Mahādeva visited Kaliṅga and drew a large followers by his impressive preaching. In course of their whirlwind wanderings, *ācārya*s, like Dhītika and Upagupta came to Kaliṅga and preached the Mādhyantika School of Buddhism.

> Thus, Buddhism in Kaliṅga received a new spirit and vigour since the rule of the Piyadasi Aśoka and it very soon assumed a position of pre-eminence among other religions/creeds of this territory. The resurgence of Kaliṅgan Buddhism must, however, be regarded as a part of the great Buddhist movement in India, which was the result of the phenomenal missionary activities of a large number of celebrated *Ācāryas*.[4]

One of the greatest contributions of Aśoka to Indian art was the use of stone as the medium of building structures and carving of sculptures. It may also be noted here that Aśoka laid the foundation of stone sculptures and the fortress in Orissa and obviously justified the statement of scholars that Buddhist art is the earliest art in India.

Stone sculptures in Orissa date from Aśoka's times. After the conquest of Kaliṅga, Aśoka engraved separate Rock Edicts at Dhauli. Above the Edicts was carved, from the rock forepart, an elephant figure. It is a freestanding sculpture carved in the round. This is the single example of Aśoka's time of an elephant being carved out of the living rock.[5] All other animal figures of Aśoka's time were hewn from blocks of stone. This rock-cut elephant, is a remarkable piece of art in form and contents and not inferior to other Aśokan animal figures, though it

3. H.K. Mahtab, *History of Orissa*, vol. I, Cuttack, 1959, pp. 40-41.
4. N.K. Sahu, *op. cit.*, p. 24.
5. C.L. Fabri, *History of the Art of Orissa*, Calcutta, 1974, p. 5.

lacks the Mauryan polish, which is due to the rough and coarse-grained sandstone used for the purpose. Elephant has a special significance in Buddhism, as it is connected with the birth of the Buddha. The Buddhist literature allude the prominence of white elephant. In pursuance of the textual description, Aśoka caused carving of the elephant figures over his Rock Edicts in other places. The elephant figure over the Rock Edict XIV at Kalasī in Uttar Pradesh, contains a small inscription which read as *gajatame*. Similar elephant figure is found over a Rock Edict on Girnār mountain in Gujarat containing an inscription that read as *śvetahasti sarvaloka sukha hetu nāma*.[6]

Once the elephant appeared in sculptural art, other pantheons accepted it and carved it in different fashions. The elephant, which symbolizes majesty, dignity, strength, vigour, sacredness, etc., was profusely carved in the Brāhmaṇical art as the vehicle of deities and formed an important segment of motifs. It acted as the royal insignia of the medieval monarchs. Almost all the temples are lavishly decorated with elephants in procession, in war, in the illustrated scenes, etc. This is an example to show how the elephant first sculpted in the Buddhist art came to be profusely used in the Brāhmaṇical and Jaina art.

The other early monuments and sculptures of Aśokan period, were the two *stūpa*s on the Dhauli hill and in the adjoining region, an Aśokan pillar, some rock-cut caves, Bhojakagiri *vihāra* and several colossal sculptures of *nāga-nāgī* and *yakṣa-yakṣī*. The eminent archaeologist J.D. Beglar visited Dhauli in 1838 and found the ruins of the two *stūpa*s.[7] A. Cunningham visited Dhauli in 1868 and wrote on the relics of the hillock.[8] Parts of the Aśokan pillar, enshrined as Bhāskareśvara *śiva-liṅga* (*Pl.* 11.1), are the matter of discussion. In accordance with the size of *liṅgam* (9' high and 12' 8" in circumference at the bottom), the extant temple by the same name was built over it by the Somavaṁśī rulers in the eleventh century AD. This *liṅgam* was recovered from the vicinity of the temple and chiselled to suit as a *liṅgam*. The Aśokan origin of the pillar is attested by the discovery of a number of railing pillars from the area in the twentieth century. Some of them are preserved in the Orissa State Museum, Bhubaneśvar. Prof. K.C. Panigrahi[9] brought to light in 1948, a lion figure from the neighbourhood of the

6. K.N. Mahapatra, *Dhaulika Itihasa* (Oriyā), 1992, 2nd edn., Bhubaneśvar, p. 46.
7. H.C. Das (ed.), *Jainism & Buddhism*, Cuttack, 1976, p. 100.
8. *Ibid.*
9. K.C. Panigrahi, *Archaeological Remains at Bhubaneśvar*, 2nd edn., Cuttack, 1991, p. 180.

Bhāskareśvara Temple. This is an imposing figure (3' 7" high and girth of 8' 7") of the fifth century AD and it contains a small inscription that read as *śrīsiṁhabandha*. Dr. Panigrahi[10] created a sensation by discovering a huge bell-capital (height 5' and circumference of 15'5") from the eastern edge of the Aśokjhar tank attached to the Rāmeśvara Temple, Bhubaneśvar. Both lion and the bell-capital are kept in the Orissa State Museum. The circular socket of the bell-capital suggests that it was originally set in a circular pillar. The frieze of the capital is decorated, from left to right, with the full-blown lotuses, geese, lotus bud with stem, winged tiger, a galloping winged horse, etc. The motifs are Aśokan in character and execution; and as such, the bell-capital can safely be ascribed to the reign of Aśoka.

Destruction of the earliest monuments, particularly the monolithic Aśokan pillar took place during the Gupta and post-Gupta period, when vigorous attempts were made to revive the Brāhmaṇical religion, especially Śaivism. The earliest Saivite temples of Orissa are assigned to this age. However, the destruction of Buddhist monuments by the Śaivas reflect sectarial rivalry and antagonism. The rivalry led to the emergence of Śaiva monuments in place of Buddhist ones.

Thus, the sectarial rivalry, interchange, interaction between the three well-developed faiths (Buddhism, Jainism and Hinduism) have been a regular process since their inception. Hence, a proper recognition of images, which in some cases are similar in all these pantheons, is really a very difficult task for scholars. In this context, Benoytosh Bhattacharya has rightly stated,

> The difficulties of the investigator are again increased by the fact that free and frequent interchange of deities took place among the three religious systems. Hindu deities Pārvatī and Indra are to be found among the Jainas; the latter as well as Gaṇapati, Sarasvatī, Mahākāla, Nīlakaṇṭha and the like, are famous in the Buddhist Pantheon. The Hindus are indebted to the Buddhists for borrowing gods, like Mahācīnatārā, Jaṅguli and Vajrayoginī under the names of Tārā, Manasā and Chinnamastā, respectively. Thus, we have evidence that free interchange of gods actually did take place first at the very outset of Buddhism and Jainism, as well as in the more promiscuous Tantric Age. The Jainas and the Buddhists alike borrowed Hindu gods in the earlier stage, but in the Tantric Age, the Buddhist gods were commonly exploited.[11]

10. K.C. Panigrahi, *Archaeological Remains at Bhubaneśvar*, 2nd edn., Cuttack, 1991, p. 181.
11. Benoytosh Bhattacharyya, *The Indian Buddhist Iconography*, 1924, Calcutta, p. i.

Free interchange of gods and goddesses between the pantheons was more conspicuous when Tantrism crept into Śaivism, Śaktism and Buddhism. It was in the eighth century AD that the Mahāyāna Buddhism was connected to the Tāntric Buddhism, popularly known as Vajrayāna, which spread sporadically in India attracting the general mass to attain an easy salvation. The priests, the *guru*s and *vajrācārya*s held high esteem in the society. The general illiterate people, being unable to understand the unintelligible *mantra*s, texts, *dhārīṇī*s and the elaborate and esoteric rituals, resorted to the *guru*s for *siddhi*. The *tantra*s gave a paramount position to *śakti* or female principle. The union of male and female energy is the essence of *Tantra*. "...... The feminine elements in the doctrine attracted a large number of followers and made it extremely popular and the most exquisite art ... made it doubly attractive."[12]

"Whatever might be the fault of the Vajrayanists, it is to them we owe the legacy of a rich, varied and extensive pantheon."[13] The Tāntric gods were invariably associated with their *śakti*s in art. The goddesses were represented jointly or in separate seats, sometimes on the lap of gods and sometimes in embrace.

Spread of Tantrism was coincided with the illustrious rule of the Pālas (from the eighth to the eleventh century AD) of Bengal and Bihar and the Bhaumakaras (AD 736-940) of Orissa. It was during this period that the Śaktism first made its appearance in Bhubaneśvar. The Vetal Temple, the first Śakti shrine shown in its sculptural representation, is a strange amalgam of Śaktism, Śāivism and Buddhism. Eight-armed Cāmuṇḍā is the presiding goddess associated with Saptamātṛkās and Yoginīs in the sanctum. The exterior wall shows the representation of Śaiva-Śākta sculptures and an image of Amoghasiddhi, one of the *dhyānī* Buddhas.[14] One spectacular feature during this period is the development of a peculiar form of temple, known in the Orissan Śilpaśāstra as the *khākharā* assigned to a form of Hindu Śākta-Tāntric goddess. This period is also marked for the sporadic spread of Mahāyāna and Vajrayāna Buddhism in Orissa. The great Buddhist monastic establishments at Ratnagiri, Lalitagiri, Udayagiri, Lāṅguḍī, Kaima, Kuruma, Ajodhyā, etc., are assigned to the Buddhist monarchs, Bhaumakaras.[15] These monasteries exhibit myriads of sculptures both

12. Benoytosh Bhattacharyya, *The Indian Buddhist Iconography*, 1924, Calcutta, p. xviii.
13. *Ibid.*
14. K.C. Panigrahi, *op. cit.*, p. 232.
15. H.C. Das (ed. jointly), *The Cultural Heritage of Khurda*, Bhubaneśvar, 2003, pp. 121-22.

of Mahāyāna and Vajrayāna pantheons. Some of the Buddhist gods and goddesses, which have close approximation with the Hindu images, will be discussed in the succeeding pages. It may not be out of place to mention that the sculptures of Kaliṅgan School are undoubtedly the remarkable specimens of Indian art.

Vajrayāna created incalculable number of gods and goddesses, deified the regional tribal godlings, important preachers, and saints, and even invented *yantras* (magic diagrams) and *maṇḍalas* (magic circles). *Mantras*, and *bīja-mantras* were assigned to the individual deities. The Vajrayānic pantheon had thus increased astonishingly and the faith developed at a marvellously rapid degree.

Vajrayāna first created the five *dhyānī* Buddhas — Vairocana, Akṣobhya, Ratnasambhava, Amitābha and Amoghasiddhi. To fortify the faith, many texts were composed which greatly enlarged the horizon of religious literature. Vajrayāna was first propounded by Indrabhūti, the king of Uḍḍīyāna (Orissa). The term Vajrayāna first occurred in his famous work *Jñānasiddhi* composed in the 1st half of eighth century AD. A chapter of the work, *Pañcakara,* deals with the forms of the *dhyānī* Buddhas. The theory of *mahāsukha* appears for the first time in the work with many manifestations. There was a controversy in regard to the identification of *Uḍḍīyāna Pīṭha*, one of the four *mahāpīṭhas* (the other three being Kāmākhyā, Śrīhaṭṭa and Pūrṇagiri) of India. On the basis of the numerous Tāntric-Buddhist images and *pīṭhas*, B. Bhattacharyya,[16] Prof. N.K. Sahu,[17] Dr. H.C. Das,[18] K.N. Mahapatra, etc., have rightly identified Oḍa, Oḍra, Uḍra, Oḍivisa and Uḍḍīyāna with Orissa. The *Kālikā Purāṇa* represents this *pīṭha* clearly as *Oḍra Pīṭha.*

उड्राक्षं प्रथमं पीठं द्वितीयं जालशोलकम् ।
तृतीयं पूर्णपीठन्तु कामरूपं चतुर्थकम् । ।[19]

In the *Sādhanamālā,* there is a *sādhana* for the *Uḍḍīyāna Kurukulla* (*Pl.* 11.2) which will be discussed in the subsequent pages. N.N. Vasu, in his book *Mayurbhanj Archaeological Survey,* has rightly observed that images of Kurukulla are extremely rare and only one image of this variety has been discovered in Orissa. It is pertinent

16. B. Bhattacharyya, *op. cit.*, pp. xxvi-xxvii.
17. N.K. Sahu, *op. cit.*, pp. 143-44.
18. H.C. Das, *Śākta Pīṭhas — A Study*, Bhubaneśvar, 1999.
19. Panchanan Tarkaratna (ed.), *Kālikā Purāṇa*, Vangavasi Edition, p. 410.

to mention that several images of Kurukulla (including a bronze image) have been brought to light during the recent years.

I have indicated earlier that the interaction between the Buddhist and the Brāhmaṇical art became more perceptible when Tantrism crept into these two pantheons. How the cultural integration, assimilation, borrowing, and interaction took place in art and architecture of both the pantheons, will be discussed, of course, citing examples of some images and structural forms. It may also be indicated that the sectarial rivalry, antagonism, as well as interaction in between the Śaiva-Śākta sects and Tāntric Buddhist sects, will be shown as far as possible.

Stūpa and Circular Yoginī Temple

Stūpa, derived from the root term *thūpa* (heap or mound), has funerary connection containing the corporeal remains. To the Buddhist, the *stūpa* has a special significance. The Buddha himself revealed to his disciples that after his demise, the charred bones and other corporeal remains should be enshrined in the *stūpa*s. This particular form of structure was regarded by the Buddhists as a shrine of supreme veneration and sanctity. In the earliest stage, *stūpa* was the only structural shrine for worship. In course of time, a regular form of worship was introduced to satisfy the religious emotions of the *bhikṣus*. The worship of *stūpa* became a practice even after the images of the Buddha and the *bodhisattva*s were introduced.[20]

In the early medieval times, numerous *stūpa*s, including the votive ones, were erected at the centres of Buddhist importance. As for instance, the *mahāstūpa*s, one each at Ratnagiri, Lalitagiri and Udayagiri monasteries (now in the present Jaipur district) are of striking importance. These *mahāstūpa*s circular in appearance are built of bricks. In course of excavation in the last chamber of the *mahāstūpa* at Lalitagiri, three stone caskets containing three pieces of bone wrapped in silver and gold were found. Similar caskets were discovered at Nālandā. The bone pieces are the relics of the three chief disciples of the Buddha.

The impressive main *stūpa* is noticed on the highest point of the Ratnagiri hillock to the north-western side (*Pl.* 11.3). The superstructure existing upon a solid podium or base (14' high) is fine brickwork with the plaster of shell-lime. The *stūpa* is a *tri-ratha* on the plane and has six projections, each separated from

20. Debala Mitra, *Buddhist Monuments*, Calcutta, 1971, p. 21.

one another by recesses. The drum above the podium is in the form of a wheel. The main *stūpa* (eighth century AD) is upon an earlier *stūpa* of the Gupta period to which belonged a few slabs having inscriptions from with the Buddhist text *Pratītyasamutpādasūtra.*[21]

To the east of the main *stūpa,* there is another *stūpa* on *tri-ratha* design measuring 31'9". The extant height of the base above the *upāna* is 7'7". It has three chambers inside, one bringing to light the terracotta plaques inscribed with *dhāraṇī*s. In the precincts of the main *stūpa,* are seen a large number of miniature *stūpa*s of different dimensions — circular, square, octagonal, etc., made either of bricks or of Khondalite stone. The stone *stūpa*s are decorated with the images of Buddha, *dhyānī* Buddhas, Tārā, Lokeśvara and also the figures of Vajrayāna pantheon — Aparājitā, Tārā, Vajra-Tārā, etc.

Here, it is attempted to correlate the *stūpa* with the circular Yoginī temple of Śaiva-Śākta sects. The Śilpaśāstras of Orissa deal in detail with *rekhā, pīḍhā* and *khākharā* types of temple, but not a single word about the circular architecture. While writing a book entitled *Tantricism: A Study of Yogini Cult,* the present author referred to some other Śilpa texts, but nowhere came across any reference about the circular cloister. In the absence of any relevant text it was interpreted as hypaethral structure on the basis of the circular *cakra, yantra* and *maṇḍala.* When Tantricism was in extreme form, Śakti in one was multiplied into 64 manifestations, and to enshrine so many goddesses in one apartment, a circular structure was considered suitable. In the 64 Yoginī temple, Bhairava, the malevolent form of Śiva is the central figure seated on a square open *maṇḍapa* around whom the malevolent goddesses Yoginīs are enshrined in the respective niches.[22]

The hypaethral 64 Yoginī temples have no porch hall or *śikhara,* no *garbhagṛha,* no central presiding deity. The general structure is totally different from the other extant temples. It appears that the protagonists of the Śaiva-Śākta sects might have borrowed the structural appearance from the *stūpa* concept.

Art Interaction in Some Images

Benoytosh Bhattacharyya[23] has remarked that the Vajrayānists displayed a great

21. Debala Mitra, *Buddhist Monuments,* Calcutta, 1971, p. 227.
22. H.C. Das, *Tantricism: A Study of Yogini Cult,* New Delhi, 1981, pp. 17-20.
23. B. Bhattacharyya, *Sādhanamālā,* vol. 2, Gaekward Oriental Series, no. 41, 1968, p. CXXX.

hatred towards the gods of the Hindu religion. His remark is based on the textual evidence reflected in the *Sādhanamālā*. Conversely, the same view of hatred is expressed by the Hindus towards the heterodox Vajrayānists and their gods. In fact, this antagonism is nothing but the expression of sentiments and feeling. Whatever might be the situations leading to rivalry, animosity, hatred, etc., the religious art is greatly benefited not only in the enlargement of the pantheons but also in style, form and content. How these feelings are expressed in art is being discussed through some cult images.

MĀRĪCI

Emanated from the *dhyānī* Buddha Vairocana, Mārīci occupies a very prominent position in the Vajrayānic pantheon. The goddess is believed to be the consort of Vairocana[24] and reside in the interior of the *caitya*. The concept of the goddess seems to have been borrowed from the Brāhmaṇic god Sūrya. Similar to the Sun god, Mārīci has a chariot drawn by seven pigs. Sūrya's charioteer is Aruṇa and that of Mārīci is Rāhu or sometimes a female figure. Here, an attempt has been made to depict her as powerful and refulgent as the Sun god. Animosity of the Vajrayānists against the Hindu god is expressed by co-opting Rāhu, the enemy of Sun and Moon as the charioteer. Her connection with Sūrya is also known from the fact that the Lāmās invoke the goddess at the time of sunrise.[25] She is the goddess of dawn.[26]

The *Sādhanamālā* records as many as 16 *sādhanas* mentioning six forms of Mārīci — Aśokakāntā, Āryā-Mārīci, Saṅkṣipta-Mārīci, Ubhayavarānanā-Mārīci, Daśabhujāsita-Mārīci, Vajradhātvīśvarī-Mārīci. The translation of the appropriate *dhyāna* of Saṅkṣipta-Mārīci:

> The worshipper should conceive himself as Mārīci (Pisuva), who displays the sentiments of *śṛṅgāra*, *vīra* and *harṣa* in one of her faces, which is of the colour of Jambunada (gold); in the middle face, which is of the colour of *Indranīla* gem, the sentiments of *bhaya, bībhatsa* and *raudra* are displayed and in the third face of crystal colour, the sentiments of *karuṇā, adbhuta* and *śānta* appear. She has three eyes in all the three faces, which give freedom from the three great evils. Her essence is made up of the *dharmakāya* and *sambhogakāya*. She is clad in garments of yellow colour and resides happily in the mass of

24. B. Bhattacharyya, *op. cit.*, p. 93.
25. B. Sahai, *Iconography of Minor Hindu and Buddhist Deities*, Delhi, 1975, p. 243.
26. N.K. Bhaṭṭaśāli, *Iconography of Buddhist and Brāhmaṇical Sculptures in the Dacca Museum*, Dacca, 1929, p. 43.

> rays. She sews up the eyes and the mouths of the wicked by the needle and sews them with string. She strikes their hearts with the *aṅkuśa*, draws them by the neck with the noose, pierces them by the bow and the arrow, and by rending their heart to pieces with the *vajra*, sprinkles water with the leaves of Aśoka . . . she tramples under her feet Prajñā and Upāya.[27]

We have in Orissa, 11 images of Mārīci, most of whom approximate to the category of Saṅkṣipta-Mārīci. She is three-faced, three-eyed, eight-armed standing in *pratyālīḍha* pose on a chariot drawn by seven pigs. Her first face of golden colour displays *śṛṅgāra*, second one like sow-face displays wrath and looks terrible with fangs and protruding lips. The third face to the right of deep red colour shines in resplendent splendour and displayed the feeling of *śānta*. Rāhu or a female figure is the charioteer. She is flanked by four attendant goddesses — Varttalī, Vadalī, Varalī and Varāhamukhī. Varttalī is sow-faced, four-armed, and carries in her hands — noose, *aśoka* branch, *vajrāṅkuśa* and needle. She is decked with all ornaments. Vadalī is similarly ornamented having the noose, the *vajra*, *aśoka* and needle. In many respects, Varalī is similar to Vadalī, but she has a needle and a *vajra* in her right hands and *aśoka* and the noose in the left ones. Varāhamukhī has the same ornaments as others. She is red in complexion and carries the *vajra* and the arrow in the right hands and the *aśoka* and bow in the left.

It is interesting that most of the images of Mārīci in Orissa belong to this variety. An excellent image of eight-armed and three-faced Mārīci (3'6") is worshipped in the village Ajodhyā, which was a prominent centre of Tāntric Buddhism yielding a large number of Buddhist images with exquisite workmanship. She stands in *ālīḍha* pose. The left face is of a sow and all the three faces express *śṛṅgāra*, *vīra* and *śānta* sentiments, respectively. This is in good state of preservation and the *āyudha*s in hands are discernible. The first pair of hands, holds the thread and the needle, the second pair shows *tarjanī* and the goad. The third pair holds the bow and the arrow. In the fourth pair, one hand is broken, but it holds Aśoka branch and the right one, probably a *vajra*. The *dhyānī* Buddha Vairocana is depicted on her crown and is flanked by attendant figures. The *dhāraṇī* is inscribed on the slab in the character of the tenth century AD. The charioteer here is a female figure.[28] Another image of this variety in excellent workmanship from *caudvār* (now in the Indian Museum, Calcutta), is of striking

27. B. Bhattacharyya, *The Indian Buddhist Iconography*, 1924, Calcutta, p. 96.
28. N.K. Sahu, *op. cit.*, pp. 209-10.

importance. The other images of Mārīci of bold workmanship are found in Khicing and Bārīpāḍā Museums, at Aṣṭaraṅga and Rāmcaṇḍī in Purī district. The images of the museums belong to the Aśokakāntā variety and are not associated with the attendant goddesses.

JAMBHALA

This god is emanated from the earliest *dhyānī* Buddha, Akṣobhya, who manifested the largest number of deities. The gods and goddesses emanated from him are — Candrāsana, Heruka, Buddha Kapāla, Hayagrīvā, Raktayamāri, Kṛṣṇayamarāja, Jambhala, Ucchuṣma-Jambhala, etc.[29] Except Jambhala, all other emanated deities are in terrific appearance having distorted face, protruding tongue, bare gangs, three eyes, garland of human heads and skulls, tiger-skin in the waist and snake-ornaments, etc.

B. Bhattacharyya[30] has traced the antiquity of Jambhala from the Kuṣāṇa times. As a result, he has an independent origin like Mañjuśrī. He may have Ratnasambhava, Akṣobhya, the five *dhyānī* Buddha or Vajrasattva. Images of Jambhala have been found in the hoards of sculpture at Gāndhāra, Mathurā, Magadha, etc. He is the Vajrayānic god of wealth. The *Sādhanamālā* specifies the following *dhyāna*s of the god (*Pl.* 11.4):

> The figure presents an easily excitable temperament with a flabby, phlegmatic constitution and a bulging belly, but it is well-decorated with jewellery and costly ornaments and dress. The figure is one-faced and two-armed and holds very peculiar symbols in the hands, namely, the citron in the right and the mongoose in the left; the mongoose vomits jewels as the result of the pressure exerted by the hands of the master.[31]

The text runs:

भगवन्तं जम्भलं ध्यायेत सुवर्णवर्णा लम्बोदरं सर्वालंकारधरम्
वामदक्षिणहस्ताभ्यां नकुलीबीजपूरकधरं रत्नसंभव मुकुटं उत्पलमालाधरम्

The god is believed to possess extraordinary powers, bestowing wealth to his devotees. For the purpose of wealth, he was worshipped by the ascetics as well as the common mass.

29. B. Bhattacharyya, *op. cit.*, p. 60.
30. *Ibid.*, p. 73.
31. B. Bhattacharyya (ed.), *Sādhanamālā*, vol. II, no. 41, Baroda, 1968, pp. CLX-CLXI.

The images of the deity are met with in the monastic establishments of Orissa. Four images of Jambhala (all two-armed) from Ratnagiri, two from Lalitagiri, two from Udayagiri monasteries and one from Bārīpāḍā have been brought to light. All figures conform to the above-noted *dhyāna*, except one (now in the Ratnagiri Museum) which, made of chlorite stone, depict on the bejewelled crown the six miniature figures in two rows, five *dhyānī* Buddhas and one *bodhisattva* figure. The image holds a citron with the palm in *varada* pose and a mongoose on the left thigh vomiting jewel. He is pot-bellied, two-armed, adorned with anklets, *valaya*s, armlets, necklace, *upavīta*, ear-ornaments and a high conical *mukuṭa*. Seated in *lalitāsana*, he has seven *nidhi-kumbha*s arrayed around below. This is assigned to *c.* ninth century AD.[32]

The figures of Lalitagiri bear the same iconographic features, but do not have *dhyānī* Buddha on the crest. The other features are almost the same except that the number of jewel pots varies from three to five.

This god is akin to Kubera, the god of wealth in the Hindu pantheon. Now a question arises whether the concept of Jambhala is borrowed from the Hindu pantheon or viceversa. Since Jambhala appears first in the Gāndhāra art of early Christian era, he may have been borrowed from the Buddhist pantheon by the Hindus. Whatever the fact remains, from the artistic imagery it is an excellent piece of art, so also Kubera, both were worshipped for conferring wealth.

HERUKA

Heruka is one of the most important gods of the Buddhist pantheon. When he is depicted in *yab-yum* pose, he is associated with his *śakti*; when he is carved singly, he should have two arms. He is believed to confer Buddhahood on his worshipper. The images of the god are extremely rare. Translation of one *dhyāna* conforming to the available images is cited here:

> The worshipper should conceive himself as (Heruka) who stands on a corpse in the *ardhaparyaṅka* attitude, who is well-clad in human skin; whose body is besmeared with ashes; who wield the *vajra* in the right hand; in whose left is the *khaṭvāṅga* with a moving flag hanging from his shoulder like the sacred thread; who carries in his left hand the *kapāla* full of blood; whose necklace is beautified by a chain of half-a-hundred heads; whose face only tightly extorted with bare fangs and who revels in his blood-shot eyes; whose ear-ornament

32. Debala Mitra, *Ratnagiri (1958-61)*, vol. II, New Delhi, 1983, p. 371.

> is the *kuṇḍala* and who is decked in ornaments of bones; on whose head are the five skulls; who bestows Buddhahood and protects the world from the Māras.[33]

We have come across two such images of the two-armed Heruka, one from the Ratnagiri *mahāvihāra* and the other in bronze from Bānapur (now in the Orissa State Museum, Bhubaneśvar). The Ratnagiri image (5'2" × 2'6") is two-armed standing in *ardhaparyaṅka* pose on a corpse. He wears a long garland of human heads holding a *khaṭvāṅga* in the left arm and the right one in the pose of hurling a *vajra*. This piece is one of the most successful representations in art.

The bronze image of Heruka (height 12.2 cm) is greatly corroded and details of ornamentation are not distinct. The image is attributed to the eleventh century AD.[34] This is decked in beaded anklets, *valaya*s, two-beaded necklaces, ear ornaments, a short crown and a long garland of several human heads. The hair rises up like flames and is tied by a cord. He has a prominent body flexion dancing in *ardhaparyaṅka* posture with toe of his left foot placed on the chest of a corpse. The facial expression is fierce-looking with wide-open angry eyes, frowning eyebrows and open mouth showing fangs. His raised right hand is in the pose of hurling the *vajra* and the left holds a skull-cup full of blood. The *khaṭvāṅga* is in the left arm attached with three skulls. The long arched halo is edged by leaf-shaped tongues of flame. At its apex, there is an umbrella with two coiled banners.

The terrible looking god is iconographically equated to Bhairava, the *ghora* aspect of Śiva, who stands or dances on a corpse having garland of human heads, and the *khaṭvāṅga* tied with skull. The artistic representation in the two images is nicely executed.

HĀRĪTI

Hārīti is a very popular goddess of the Buddhist pantheon (*Pl.* 11.5). Originally a demoness of smallpox, was converted by the Buddha as the protectress of children. As the story goes, she, in the previous birth, was the wife of a cowherd at Rājagṛha, the old capital of Magadha. She was forced to dance in a festival when she was pregnant. The dance caused miscarriage. At this incident, she became terribly violent and took revenge by devouring children. She was supposed to be the guardian deity of Rājagṛha. Because of her spiteful act in the previous birth, she

33. B. Bhattacharyya, *The Indian Buddhist Iconography*, 1924, Calcutta, p. 62.
34. Debala Mitra, *Bronzes from Achutarajpur*, Orissa, Delhi, 1978, pp. 85-86.

developed the habit of stealing and eating children of the city of Rājagṛha. The terrified people of the city approached the Buddha, who was then staying there. To stop her cannibal habit, the Master miraculously enlarged His begging bowl and concealed her youngest child. Being unable to find out the child, the distressed Hārīti came to the Buddha, who told her, "Art thou so sorry for the lost child, thou beloved; how much more grieved are those who have lost their only one or two children on account of thy cruel vow." These words of the Tathāgata changed her heart and she left cannibal habit.[35] She was then admitted to the Buddhist order, and was entrusted with the protection of children. Hence, in art she is associated with children in different poses.

The earliest representation of Hārīti in sculptural art occurs in the Gāndhāra art. There are several sculptures of the goddess belonging to the Gāndhāra School preserved in the Indian Museum, Kolkata, in which her husband Pañcika is shown with her. One sculpture from Jamālgarh represents the couple under a tree. Hārīti stretches out her hand towards her husband. A naked child is standing in between the parents, and the other child is depicted in the upper background.[36] Like this several sculptures of the Gāndhāra School have been brought to light.

The Mathurā School of Art of the Kuṣāṇa period represent several sculptures of Hārīti with her husband Pañcika. The Mathura Museum preserves such sculptures.

In the medieval period, we come across sculptures of the goddess, now preserved in the Nālandā and Sārnāth Museums.

Two seated figures of Hārīti are met with in the art of Orissa — one in the Ratnagiri *mahāvihāra* and the other in the Lalitagiri Museum. Both of them are assigned to *c.* ninth-tenth century AD. The Ratnagiri figure (2.5' × 1.5') is placed in the right niche on the main passage into the monastery. Made of chlorite stone, the figure is seated in *lalitāsana*. She is two-armed — the right arm shows *varada-mudrā*, while the left one holds a child on her left lap. She is decked with all ornaments and a tiara on the head. In the monastery, she was represented as the protectress goddess. Lower part of the pedestal is flanked by a dancing peacock.

Similarly, the Lalitagiri image is two-armed — the right arm in *varada* pose and the left one holds a child on the lap. Her ornamentation is bold. The images

35. B. Sahai, *op. cit.*, p. 253.

36. N.G. Majumdar, *A Guide to the Sculptures in the Indian Museum*, Delhi, 1937, Part II, p. 110.

of the goddess in Orissa do not show the representation of Pañcika with her.

In sculptural art, she approximates the mother-goddess of the Hindu pantheon. Both are shown as mothers and the protectresses of children. The mother-goddesses have the respective *vāhanas*; but the Buddhist counterpart is devoid of *vāhana*. It is difficult to ascertain whether the concept of mother-goddess travelled from Buddhism to Hinduism or viceversa.

KURUKULLA

Kurukulla (*Pl.* 11.2), the Tāntric Buddhist goddesses emanated from the *dhyānī* Buddha Amitābha, is the most popular and important in the Buddhist pantheon. She is believed to bestow power to the *sādhaka* in the esoteric practice of *vaśīkaraṇa*, *sammohana* and *uccāṭana* to bewitch men, women, minister and kings. The method of achieving success in these Tāntric rites is prescribed in the *sādhanas*. There are as many as 14 *sādhanas* for the varieties of Kurukulla, such as Śukla Kurukulla, Tirodbhava Kurukulla, Oḍḍīyāna Kurukulla, Aṣṭabhuja Kurukulla are attributed. The *sādhana* of the Oḍḍīyāna Kurukulla is attributed to the Uḍḍīyāna Siddhācārya, Indrabhūti (1st part of the eighth century AD).

> This form of the goddess presents rather a fierce form in as much as she has the garland of heads, the five skulls on her head, protruding teeth and tongue, garments of tiger skin and brown hair rising above her head in the shape of a flame. Her eyes are three in number, which are red, round and moving. She is four-armed; the principal pair of hands is engaged in drawing to the full the flowery bow charged with an arrow of red lotus. The second pair holds the goad of flowers and the red lotus. She has red complexion and sits in the *ardhaparyaṅka* attitude on a corpse.[37]

How the extant images in Orissa correspond with the prescribed iconography is our concern. It is pertinent to mention that the important site of Bānapur-Achūtarājpur yielded 95 bronze figures, of which 75 are Buddhist, ten Jaina and five Brāhmaṇical, besides a series of *stūpa*-shaped bells. The bronze hoard was discovered in two big earthenware pots in 1963 at the time of laying foundation of the Godabarish Mahāvidyālaya. The recovered images are now preserved in the Orissa State Museum, Bhubaneśvar. The site has the earlier monuments and sculptures of Buddhist, Jaina and Brāhmaṇical pantheons. It appears from the antiquities of the site that all the three religious faiths flourished here side by side.

37. B. Bhattacharyya, *op. cit.*, p. 57.

The hoard contains an excellent image of Kurukulla (height 11.1 cm) conforming to the Oḍḍīyāna Kurukulla *sādhana*. She is four-armed holding an *aṅkuśa* (elephant goad) in the lower right hand; the upper right raised above her right ear is in the pose of shooting an arrow. She has a bow in the upper left arm and the lower left one holds an *utpala*. She has protruding teeth expressing extreme anger, three eyes dancing in the *ardhaparyaṅka* pose with the toes of her left foot on the chest of a corpse lying in the *kāyotsarga* posture on the pericarp of a *viśva-padma*. She is gorgeously decorated with beaded-anklet, bangles, necklace, beaded-girdle, ear-ornaments and a short crown with a lotus in the centre. Her hair-bun is tied in a string, shooting upward in the form of flames. She wears a short piece of cloth fitted lightly round the thighs, gives a vigorous stance. A garland of 15 human heads further enhances her ferocious attitude.[38] The icon in round with exquisite workmanship bears the Tāntric art tradition of the Bhaumakaras (ninth-tenth century AD).

Another image of the four-armed goddess was recovered from Udayagiri.[39] Seated in *lalitāsana*, she exhibits an *aṅkuśa* and *varada* in her two right hands and a bow and an *utpala* in the left ones. Her ornamentation is bold. In art and iconography, to a great extent, Kurukulla is akin to Cāmuṇḍā of the *mātṛkā* group in dancing form. Both have three eyes, protruding teeth, dancing or sitting on the corpse in *ardhaparyaṅka* pose, *muṇḍamālā*, tiger skin. Possibly the concept of Kurukulla is borrowed from Cāmuṇḍā.

APARĀJITĀ

This is an interesting goddess of the Buddhist pantheon, which illustrates the religious clashes in which a Buddhist deity superimposes the Hindu divinities. According to her *sādhana*, she is yellow in complexion, one-faced and two-armed, trampling under her feet Gaṇeśa *gaṇapatisamakrānta*, with her right hand in the pose of giving a slap, while the left carries the noose round the raised index finger against her chest. Her face is awful, terrible and ferocious. She is conceived as the destroyer of all wicked and the parasol over her is held by the wicked gods Brahmā and others.[40]

We have only one image of Aparājitā at Lalitagiri, standing in *ālīḍha* pose on two crouchant (*Pl.* 11.6) Gaṇeśa, one under each leg holds a flower in the uplifted

38. Debala Mitra, *op. cit.*, p. 116.
39. N.K. Sahu, *op. cit.*, p. 191.
40. B. Sahai, *op. cit.*, p. 215.

right hand and the left one shows the *tarjanī-mudrā*. An attendant goddess in the right side holds a parasol over her head. In the left side is seen another attendant figure. Her face is not awful and ferocious, but is lit with celestial smile. This is a unique figure remarkable with artistic grace and feminine delicacy. From religious point of view, it shows antagonism; but from the viewpoint of art, this is a wonderful piece.

TRAILOKYAVIJAYA

Trailokyavijaya image (*Pl.* 11.7), showing extreme antagonism against Śaiva-Śākta religion, is extremely rare in India. Since, he is not associated with any *dhyānī* Buddha, he is regarded as an independent Tāntric Buddhist god. According to the *sādhana*,

> The worshipper should realize himself as Trailokyavijaya Bhaṭṭāraka of blue complexion, four-faced and eight-armed; the first face displays the sentiment of wrathful passion, the right displays rage, the left disgust and the face behind the sentiment of heroism; who exhibits the *vajrahuṅkāra-mudrā* with the two hands bearing the *ghaṇṭā* and the *vajra* against the breast; and carries in his three right hands the *khaṭvāṅga*, the goad and the arrow, and in the three left, the bow, the noose and the *vajra*, who, standing in the *pratyālīḍha* attitude, tramples upon the head of Maheśvara with his left leg, while the right presses upon the bosom of Gaurī, who wears garments of variegated colours, and many ornaments and garlands pertaining to (the respective) Buddhas. . . .[41]

This image is extremely rare in India. Fortunately, we have two such images of the god in Orissa — one in bronze and the other in stone. The bronze image from the Achūtarājpur hoard (biggest of all measuring 47.3 cm (without umbrella which is missing)) marked for its excellent form of the heroic figure with its sturdy strong-built body having broad shoulders and chest, strong arms and wrathful facial expression.

> The modelling affords a perception of all the flesh having been hammered into a solid form. Further, the stout figure presents the impression of its power and vigour revealed in the treatment of the powerful leg with its vigorous stance.[42]

The icon may be datable to the middle of the tenth century AD. The Buddhists of the establishment made an attempt to curb down the rising power of the Śaiva-

41. B. Bhattacharyya, *op. cit.*, pp. 146-47.
42. Debala Mitra, *op. cit.*, p. 86.

Śākta religion by installing such an image in heroic form. The fierce image is shown trampling under his feet the Śaiva-Śākta divinities with an intention of drawing more followers from the Brāhmaṇical faith. The overcoming power of the image is emphasized by the depiction of scattered weapons of the multi-armed Śiva and Gaurī. The deity wears a short cloth in criss-cross manner in the waist befitting to the heroic posture.

> The ornaments consist of bangles (two around each wrist), beaded armlets with an ornate triangular central piece, a beaded *upavīta*, a broad elaborate necklace with a series of pendants, *puṣpa-kuṇḍala*s and an exceptionally high conical crown. The luxuriant coiled locks of hair fall on the shoulders in tiers.[43]

The face expresses terrible wrath with bulging angry eyes, frowned eyebrows, almost radiating flames symbolically depicted in the circular halo behind. With *vajraghaṇṭā* in the left fist and the thunderbolt in the right fist, the wrists are crossed against the chest in the *vajrahuṅkāra-mudrā*, which expresses diamond like strength and terrible anger.

The god stands in *pratyālīḍha* pose, one leg on the eight-armed Bhairava and the other on Gaurī. The *āyudha*s of the Brāhmaṇical deities are shown scattered on the circular part of the pedestal. These are a trident with a banner, a bell, a bow with the string broken, a couple of arrows, a noose, a kettle-drum, a sword and a hatchet. The attributes of Gaurī lying scattered are — a sword, a hatchet, a trident and a shield. Four *dhyānī* Buddhas are seen depicted on the crown. The circular halo is edged by a closely-knit flanks. The backside of the halo is engraved with the Buddhist *dhāriṇī*s.

The second image (42" × 26") of Trailokyavijaya at Amaraprasādgarh in the Prācī valley was recovered from the riverbed. This is seated in *ardhaparyaṅka* pose, is six-armed and three-faced, the two forearms carry a *vajra* and *ghaṇṭā* in criss-cross position at the chest displaying the *vajrahuṅkāra-mudrā*. The second and third right hands raise a sword over the heads and an arrow respectively, while the second and third left hands hold a bow and a long lotus stalk. Out of the three heads, the front and right ones are decorated with pyramidal crowns and the left one is provided with matted locks of hair. The right face exhibits *aṭṭahāsa* (loud laughter) and appears to be ferocious, the left one shows complete absorption in meditation, while the central one expresses *śānta* tranquil, bliss and

43. Debala Mitra, *op. cit.*, p. 87.

contentment. The image is remarkably chiselled of sandstone and his impressive muscular body is carved in round. This is assignable to the tenth-eleventh century AD.[44]

Trailokyavijaya cult is extremely rare in India. No other image of the Vajrayānic pantheon can be compared with Trailokyavijaya in so far as its iconographic features in expressing the intense wrath, anger and vengeance against Śaivism and Śaktism, and artistic imagery, are concerned. As a piece of art, the image is unparalleled maintaining physiognomy, strong built body, proportion, symmetry, wrathful expression, etc.

BUDDHA

The Buddha, originator of Buddhism came to be associated in the Hindu pantheon as the ninth incarnation of Viṣṇu. In regard to Buddha's origin and acceptance as an *avatāra* of Viṣṇu, the Purāṇas are divided in their views in the matter. The *Bhāgavata Purāṇa* mentions that Buddha as an *avatāra* was born as the son of Añjanā among the Kīkaṭas to delude the enemies of the gods. According to the *Agni Purāṇa,* the *suras* having been defeated by the *asuras* sought the protection of Viṣṇu, who was born as a deluder in the form of Buddha, the son of Jina. To save the gods, the Buddha deluded the *asuras* who accepted the religion of the Buddha and lost all powers as warriors. Many of them are recorded as heretics who have forsaken the Vedic religion. The stories of other Purāṇas describe Buddha as the deluding personage. Finally, the *Bṛhat-Saṁhitā*, the *Agni Purāṇa* and the *Dharmottara* give the following description of the image of Buddha:

> The figure of Buddha should have on its feet and the palms marks resembling the *padma* or lotus; the body should be full and fresh and of fair complexion; and the head should have short curly hair on it. The image as a whole should appear calm and full of grace, as though it represented Buddha as the father of all creatures and it must be seated on *padmāsana*. The lobes of the ears must be made pendant. The body should be covered with the *kaṣāya*, the yellow garb of the ascetics, and on the shoulder there should be a piece of *valkala* or clothing made out of the bark of certain trees. The hands should be in the *varada* and the *abhaya* poses.[45]

It is peculiar that the origin of the Buddha is distorted in the Purāṇas. The *Viṣṇu Purāṇa* speaks harshly against Buddhism and Buddhists. The protagonists of

44. N.K. Sahu, *op. cit.*, p. 217.

45. T.A. Gopinath Rao, *Elements of Hindu Iconography*, vol. I, part I, 2nd edn., Delhi, pp. 216-21.

Hinduism had developed animosity and wrath against the Buddhists, who on the other hand preached *ahiṁsā* (non-violence) and many more things, opposed to the path of the Vedas. But the description of the image of the Buddha is more or less the same in the Buddhist iconography.

In the sculptural representation of *daśāvatāra* images, when depicted in group, Buddha finds place as the ninth *avatāra* of Viṣṇu. The depiction of Buddha became more conspicuous from the time of Śrī Jayadeva who, in his famous *Gītagovinda*, gave a graphic picture of the *daśāvatāra* in the famous hymn *daśakṛtikṛte*. The *daśāvatāra* images with Buddha as the ninth *avatāra* in the temple of Jagannātha at Purī, in a *maṭha* of Purī, in the Mādhava Temple of Prācī valley, an in the two Kṛṣṇa-Viṣṇu images (one in the Orissa State Museum) (*Pl.* 11.8), has been nicely depicted. In one *daśāvatāra* panel, Jagannātha himself is placed as the ninth incarnation in place of Buddha. It is thus, no doubt a fact that Buddha's influence on Hinduism cannot be denied, though his origin is distorted by associating some Purāṇic myths under the garb of Hinduism.

Scholars have emphasized some Buddhistic traits in the cult of Jagannātha. The triad Jagannātha, Subhadrā and Balabhadra are identified with the *triratna* Buddha, *dharma* and *saṁgha*. The famous chariot festival of Śrī Jagannātha is stated to have been borrowed from the chariot festival connected with Gautama. The Buddha abhorred the caste system, and as such he accepted people irrespective of castes and creed in his *saṁgha*. Within the Jagannātha temple complex, there is no caste bar, particularly in taking the *mahāprasāda*.

TĀRĀ

Tārā, the primordial goddess of Buddhism, was multiplied with the enlargement of the Buddhist pantheon. Foucher has classified Tārās into seven in accordance with their colour. Only those images should be designated as Tārās, to whom the *mantra — oṁ tārā tuttare tūre svāhā* is assigned. The seven varieties of Tārās should carry each the *utpala* in the left hand and exhibiting the *varada-mudrā* in the right. Of these two, variations are stated to bear the *dhyānī* Buddha Amoghasiddhi on the crown and others do not have any *dhyānī* Buddha. It is thus difficult to identify the images of Tārā in stone on the basis of colour, when no colour is present.[46] Bhattacharyya has classified Tārās under two heads. The ordinary Tārās showing the *varada* in the right hand and carrying *utpala* or lotus in the left. The

46. B. Bhattacharyya, *op. cit.*, p. 135.

extraordinary forms of Tārā embrace all goddess designated as Tārās in the *Sādhanamālā*.[47]

There is no consensus among the scholars regarding the origin of the goddess Tārā. Some ascribe her origin to Hinduism and some to Buddhism. The *Śaktisaṅgama Tantra*[48] refers to seven forms of Tārā — Tārā, Ugrā, Mahogrā, Vajrā, Nīlā, Sarasvatī, Kāmeśvarī and Bhadra-Kālī. Chintaharan Chakravarty, referring to the Hindu Tantras, indicate eight forms of Tārā — Tārā, Nīlasarasvatī, Ugratārā, Ekajaṭā, Vidyārānī, Vāgīśvarī and Sarasvatī.[49] Hirananda Sastri has rightly pointed out the place of origin of Tārā and her incorporation in the Buddhist pantheon. To him Tārā worship was originated somewhere in Ladakh by the fifth century AD. From Ladakh she travelled to Tibet where she became the most popular deity. In about seventh century AD. Buddhism reached its culminating point spreading the form in different parts of India. In Buddhism Tārā is the highest female principle and is the Śakti of *bodhisattva* Avalokiteśvara.[50]

It is possible that the Buddhist Tārā might have travelled to Hinduism, where she is the second *mahāvidyā* of the cult of *daśamahāvidyās*. In this pantheon she appears as a fierce deity with different iconographic conception. Sastri, in support of her Buddhistic origin, says that the myth of Tārā arose about the fifth century AD and in about seventh century when the Tantra influence was at its zenith, she was Brāhmaṇized as the second *mahāvidyā*.

There are several *dhyānas* of Brāhmaṇic Tārā. The *dhyāna* of the *Nīla Tantra* corresponds to the extant iconic figure. According to this *dhyāna*, she is of dark blue complexion standing in *pratyālīḍha* pose on the bosom of Śiva, who is lying like a corpse; she is dreadful, short statured having a garland of several heads, a long belly, tiger skin in the waist. She is in the prime of her youth and adorned with *pañca-mudrās*. She is four-armed holding sword and dagger in her right hands and a skull and a blue lotus in the left ones. Her tongue is held out a bit and has one matted hair. She has three eyes dazzling like morning sun. She has protruding teeth, horrible face and smiling at the same time. She stands in the midst of burning funeral fire. She is laughing emotionally and is existing on the white lotus floating on the vast expanse of water.

47. B. Bhattacharyya, *op. cit.*, p. 135.

48. H.C. Das, *Iconography of Śākta Divinities*, vol. I, Delhi, 1997, p. 26.

49. *Ibid.*

50. Hirananda Sastri, *The Origin and Cult of Tārā*, 1977, A.S.I., No. 20, pp. 15-20.

We have an image of Tārā (2'5" × 1'2") in perfect state of preservation at Bhusandapur, about 50 km from Bhubaneśvar. The place where she is worshipped is the famous Tārā-pīṭha. Connecting to the local legends and her artistic imagery, this is assigned to the fourteenth century AD. Tārā images of Buddhist pantheon are numerous in Orissa like other Buddhist centres of India, which may be attributed to the period between the seventh and thirteenth centuries AD.

In addition to the above-noted cult images there are several others of the Vajrayāna period, which show interaction with the Hindu gods and goddesses. There are some images, which have been completely amalgamated in Buddhist pantheon. As for instance, Gaṇapati, who is a guardian goddess in the Buddhist iconography.

There are also cult images, which are accepted as the auspicious symbols of Hinduism, Buddhism and Jainism. They are, for example, Gaṅgā (*Pl.* 11.9), Yamunā (*Pl.* 11.10) and Gaja-Lakṣmī, who are depicted in the doorways. Such a depiction is common in almost all the monuments of Orissa.

It is indicated in the preceding pages how antagonism, sectarial rivalry and animosity of the Vajrayānists are expressed against the Hindus, who are called heretics. Their intense anger is expressed in the art depiction as shown above. It may not be out of place to indicate that, such rivalry is not a new phenomenon in Buddhism alone rather it was prevalent in almost all the sects, each attempting to superimpose its philosophy, cult, religion over the others. Whatever may be the fact behind, we cannot forget the contribution of Vajrayāna to the field of art, which grew in multi-dimensional proportions enlarging the horizon of art and architecture. Hence, from the point of view of religion, this attitude of antagonism does not seem to be congenial for the religious faiths but for art it is very important. It will also not be an exaggeration to say that without the Vajrayānic art reflected in the numerous Tāntric images, the Indian art could not have been so varied, so colourful and interesting. In essence, the Indian culture is reflected with greater exactitude through the visual art forms. The Buddhist art being the earliest art of India, it could naturally have greater influence on the art forms of other religions.

12

In Quest of Śiva-Buddha Cult

T.K. Biswas

THE collection of bronzes in the Asutosh Museum of Indian Art, University of Calcutta includes a unique and rare bronze image that hails from the district of Barisal in Bangladesh. To J.N. Banerjea, this image represents Śiva Lokeśvara. The image stands in *samapāda-sthānaka* pose on a double-petalled lotus, the latter being placed on a *tri-ratha* pedestal. The god is ithyphallic and is seen carrying a rosary *akṣa-sūtra* in his right hand and an indistinct object (a bunch of flowers?) in the left. On the top of his matted crest, there appears a tiny figure of *dhyānī* Buddha Amitābha. The standing figure of the god is flanked by attendants and seated donors. To the proper left of this image a long trident *triśūla* is found planted and near the left shoulder of the god appears a figure of Gaṇeśa.[1]

K.K. Dasgupta declined to accept the identification of Banerjea of the said image as Śiva Lokeśvara. Dasgupta could not find any *sādhana* in the Buddhist *Sādhanamālā* that described such an image. He, however, admitted that certain iconic features in this image called for its intimate Śaivite association such as the matted locks, rosary and trident. At the same time Dasgupta maintained that he could not trace in Indian Buddhist iconography, an icon of ithyphallic Lokeśvara. He could not find reflection of sectarian rivalry either. Dasgupta concluded that the image reflected an unknown form of Avalokiteśvara.[2] However, the image

1. J.N. Banerjea, *Development of Hindu Iconography*, Calcutta, 1956, p. 547.
2. Kalyan Kumar Dasgupta, "An Image of the so called Śiva Lokeśvara," in *Buddhism — Early and Late*, Calcutta 1985, pp. 103-05.

undoubtedly reflected an attitude of religious syncretism between Śaiva and Buddhist iconographical elements.

Interaction between Śaivism and esoteric Buddhism became quite conspicuous in the medieval Indian iconography and this tendency, subsequently, perhaps led to the evolution of a Śiva-Buddha cult. The mutual interaction of these two, largely found reflected in the crystallization of the iconographies of various aspects of *bodhisattva* Avalokiteśvara.

Buddhist text refers to Avalokiteśvara and said that he appeared on the Mount Potalaka as *Īśvara-deva* under the form of a *yogī* (a Pāśupati). In *Karaṇḍavyūha,* the nexus of Avalokiteśvara with Maheśvara has been established.[3] This is also established further when Avalokiteśvara takes the form of Maheśvara in his *amoghapāśa* aspect whose *mantra* contains the expression Mahā-Paśupati — an epithet of Śiva.[4] The *Guṇa Karaṇḍavyūha* deals in a very rare type of Avalokiteśvara called *Ekādaśa-Śira* or the Eleven-headed one. This *Ekādaśa-mukha* aspect refers to the conversion of the eleven violent gods of Vedic age, the *Ekādaśa-Rudra*. The *Ekādaśa-mukha* aspect with thousand arms and eyes had its prototype in the Vedic and Brāhmaṇical Viṣṇu, Indra and Śiva. When Avalokiteśvara appeared as *puruṣa* with thousand arms and eyes, Yama asked him in astonishment whether he was Maheśvara (Śiva) or Nārāyaṇa (Viṣṇu)? That Hari-hara, served as the prototype of this form of Avalokiteśvara becomes apparent from his epithet in his hymn.[5] At, one place, *Karaṇḍavyūha* also mentioned, that Śiva evolved from the forehead of Avalokiteśvara. In the *Yogāmbara Maṇḍala* of *Niṣpannayogāvalī* Śiva is found included in the family of Amitābha — *maheśvara amitābhena mudritaḥ*.[6]

Incidentally, a reference may also be made here of Ṣaḍākṣarī-Lokeśvara — a very popular aspect of Avalokiteśvara who personifies the six letters — *oṁ maṇi padme huṁ*. To Śaivites the word *maṇi* denotes *liṅga* while *padma* stands for *yoni*.[7]

---

3. Lokesh Chandra, *The Thousand Armed Avalokiteśvara*, New Delhi, 1988, p. 190.
4. T.K. Biswas, "Amoghapāśa : An Iconographic Analysis," *Kalā : The Journal of Indian Art History Congress*, 2003, vol. VIII, p. 57.
5. *Ṛgveda*, 2.135 (*indra sahasra cakṣus*), for thousand-eyed Rudra (*Atharvaveda*, 2.2), *Bṛhat-Saṁhitā*, 43.48 (*sahasrcakṣo*), *viṣṇu sahasradṛśa* (*Rāmāyaṇa*, 6.102.22), *Indra sahasrākṣa* (*Mahābhārata*, 3.670, 14.2444) and also see Lokesh Chandra, *op.cit.*, pp. 31-32.
6. M.T. Mallman, *Hindu Deities in Tantrik Buddhism*, tr. Simon Watson Taylor, *Zentralasiatische Studies*, 2, Bonn, pp. 41-54 and also see D.C. Bhattacharya, *Iconology of Composite Images*, Delhi, 1980, p. 62.
7. Vide Kalproth, *Journal Asiatique*, 7, pp. 185-206.

Certain other aspects of Avalokiteśvara such as Siṁhanāda-Lokeśvara, Lokanātha, Nīlakaṇṭha, Halāhala, Padmanartteśvara and Amoghapāśa bear direct adaptations from the iconic representations of Śiva. For instance, the *sādhanā* of Siṁhanāda-Lokeśvara may be cited here where the descriptions include such expressions as *śveta-varṇam, jaṭāmukuṭinām, trinetraṁ, nirbhūṣaṇam, vyāghracarma-prāvṛtaṁ, candrāsanaṁ, candraprabhaṁ, sitaphaṇiveṣṭitaṁ-triśūlam* and these refer to direct borrowings of iconic features of Śiva's iconography.[8] If the tiny image of *dhyānī* Buddha Amitābha is withdrawn from the headgear of this aspect of the *Bodhisattva,* he could be easily identified as Śiva. Curiously enough, like Lord Śiva, Siṁhanāda-Lokeśvara is also considered as the healer of diseases.[9] Likewise Amoghapāśa, another aspect of Avalokiteśvara appears like Śiva as a *tapasvī*; he is found draped in tiger skin, bears on shoulder a gazelle skin sash and holds *tridaṇḍa* and *kamaṇḍalu* and all these remind his closeness with Śiva.[10]

Lokesh Chandra while discussing the structure of *garbhadhātu, maṇḍala* mentions the quarter of *susiddhi* that has eight deities and these are related to eight *siddhis* of *Haṭha-Yoga* of Patañjali. The *siddhis* are considered as the direct and indirect results of a quest for enlightenment of knowledge — *parā-siddhi* (Transcendent power). Interestingly, these eight *siddhis*, are taken to denote eight *vibhūtis* of Śiva. The fact that Avalokiteśvara represents the excellence of *susiddhi* once again preserves the reminiscences of his closeness to Śiva.[11]

A reference needs to be made here of a Śaivite adaptation from the Buddhist iconography. Lakulīśa, the twenty-eighth incarnation of Śiva in eastern India (especially in Orissa) is found represented with certain features of a Buddha image. Like Buddha, Lakulīśa is seen seated on a double-petalled lotus being raised up by two *nāga* kings and his hands are engaged in *dharma-cakra-mudrā* and sometimes, the two deer and the wheel *dharma-cakra* are found carved in the pedestal.[12]

---

8. Benoytosh Bhattacharya, *Sādhanamālā*, vol. I, Gaekwad Oriental Series, No. 26, Baroda, 2nd edn., p. 63.
9. J.N. Banerjea, *op. cit.*, 4th edn., 1985, p. 24.
10. Pratapaditya Pal, "The Iconography of amoghapāśa Lokeśvara," *Oriental Art*, vol. VII, no. 4, Winter, 1966, and also see P.H. Pott, *Introduction of Tibetan Collections of National Museum of Ethnology*, Leiden, 1951.
11. Lokesh Chandra, "The Structure of Garbhadhātu Maṇḍala," *Buddhist Iconography*, Sambhota Series 11, Tibet House, Delhi, 1989, pp. 189-90.
12. J.N. Banerjea, *op. cit.*, 4th edn., 1985, Calcutta, p. 6.

The association of deer (*mṛga*) with Śiva has been traced from the so-called Paśupati seal of Mohenjo-Dāro and subsequently, the *kṛṣṇa-mṛga* became an established attribute of Śiva but what could be the justification of the combined wheel and deer, a typically Buddhist device, with the image of Lakulīśa? K.K. Thaplyal thinks, quite justifiably, that the common factor between Buddha and Lakulīśa was that both were great philosophers and were most prominent of their sect and hence this incorporation.[13]

The closeness between Śiva and Buddha could be established further with the help of certain rare images. The famous Śiva image of Badrīnātha temple resembles a Buddha figure, seated in *bhūmisparśa-mudrā* and it is curious to note that the Buddha is worshipped here as Śiva following the traditional belief of the people that Śiva and the Buddha are one and the same deity.[14] Śiva and Avalokiteśvara are identified in the same person as the Lord of the three worlds in a shrine at Trilokanātha in the Chenub gorge and finally, in the collection of Svayambhūnātha Museum in Nepal there is a dated sculpture entitled *lokeśvara śiva parivāra sahita*. In this panel, to the right of Śiva-Pārvatī, there appears a male figure (Avalokiteśvara) with one hand in *varada* pose and the other carries a lotus flower. Two royal ladies occupy the other side in the panel. According to the epigraphic record, this image was executed in Nepali *Saṁvat* 797, i.e., AD 1677 on the advice of the crown prince Nripendra Malla of Kantipur.[15]

Not only in Nepal, the Śiva-Buddha cult could be traced in Sumatra, Java and Bali. A large stone Bhairava, which significantly contains a small *bodhisattva* on its head, has been found at Sungai Langsat in Central Sumatra. This refers to the extension of the said cult in Sumatra. There is a reference to this cult in a thirteenth-century eastern Javanese temple, called Tjandi Djawi. A fourteenth-century poetical work known as *Nagara Kertāgama* written by poet Rakawi Prapañca, recorded that the temple of Djawi was a two storied building. The

13. Kiran Kumar Thaplyal, "Transformation of Symbols: A case study of Wheel and Deer Device," vide, *Buddhist Iconography*, pp. 49-50.

14. K.P. Nautiyal, *The Archaeology of Kumayun*, Varanasi, 1969, p. 153 and for detail see Rahul Sankrityayan, *Himalaya Parichay*, Part I, p. 475.

15. Pratapaditya Pal, "A note on the ancient shrine of Paśupatinātha, Nepal," *Proceedings of the Indian History Congress*, 24th session, Delhi, 1961, Calcutta, 1963 pp. 33ff and also see Amita Ray, "The Paśupatinātha Temple," *Man in India*, 39, no. 1, January-March, 1969, pp. 50ff and also see D.C. Bhattacharya, *op. cit.*, p. 42 and Ram Niwas Pandey, "Iconography of Lokeśvara Image," *Buddhist Iconography*, *op. cit.*, p. 173.

sanctum below enshrined a splendid and immeasurable likeness of Śiva while the upper story of the temple installed an equally majestic image of *dhyānī* Buddha Akṣobhya.[16]

It appears that the religious life of east Java in the thirteenth-fourteenth centuries was marked by a growing tendency of syncretism. Śaivite and Buddhist cults overlapped and fused, and were strongly tinged by Tāntric conceptions. King Kr̥tanagara, the last king of Singasari in eastern Java was deified as Śiva Buddha at Tjandi Djawi. Likewise, King Viṣṇuvardhana was deified as Śiva in Tjandi Mleri and as *bodhisattva* Amoghapāśa at Tjandi Djago. In the present Balinese religion there are two kinds of high priests *pedanda*, the *pedanda* Buddha and the *pedanda* Śiva. They both officiate at the same temple and sometimes simultaneously.[17] The iconographic and architectural examples discussed above persuade us to believe that there had been a Śiva-Buddha cult in medieval period, the nucleus of which was formed in eastern India and then it migrated to Nepal and Indonesia subsequently.

---

16. Rakawi Prapañca, *Nagara Kertagama*, tr. Dr. Pigeaud, *vide* Java in the Fourteenth Century, The Hague, 1960, see Canto 56, stanza 2.
17. Clare Holt, *Art in Indonesia, Continuity and Change*, New York, 1967, p. 68.

13

Vāsudeva-Viṣṇu-Padmapāṇi and Avalokiteśvara-Śiva

Gouriswar Bhattacharya

IF anybody nowadays asks a Hindu painter or sculptor to paint or make a sculpture of the god Viṣṇu for him, without any doubt or thinking he will represent the deity with four arms and holding the essential four attributes ascribed to him, viz., *śaṅkha, cakra, gadā* and *padma* (*Pl.* 13.1). In the vast Purāṇic literature, the dark-complexioned deity is described holding the above four attributes, i.e., *caturbhujaṁ pañkaja-rathāṅga-śaṅkha-gadā-dharma*.[1] And in the Pāñcarātra doctrine, the *caturviṁśati* or 24 forms of Viṣṇu were contemplated with various arrangements of these four attributes and the deity was named differently; the most common form being Trivikrama in which Viṣṇu holds *padma, gadā, cakra* and *śaṅkha* clock-wise in the four hands. But in the earlier images, the deity is devoid of a lotus. The early text *Bṛhat-Saṁhitā* (*c.* sixth century), chapter 57, verse 31-35, describes three forms of Viṣṇu but in none of the forms the god holds lotus in any hand; for example,

> Eight, four or two should be the number of Viṣṇu's hands; his chest should be adorned with the *śrīvatsa* mark and the *kaustubha* jewel; his colour should be of that of the *atasī* flower (yellowish green), he should wear yellow garments, ear-rings, jewelled crown; when eight-armed, his right hands should show a sword, a mace, an arrow and *abhaya-mudrā*; while his left ones should hold a bow, a shield, a wheel and a conch-shell; if he is four-armed, his right hands should show an assurance pose (*abhaya-mudrā*) and a mace, the left

1. *Bhāgavata Purāṇa*, Nirnaya Sagar Press, Bombay, 1950, p. 2.2.8b.

> hands holding a conch-shell and a wheel; in a two-armed Viṣṇu, the right hand should be in the *abhaya* pose, the left one holding a conch-shell.[2]

The deity has already been called Viṣṇu.

> *kāryo'ṣṭa bhujo bhagavāṁś caturbhujo dvibhuja eva vā viṣṇuḥ* |
> *śrīvatsāṅkita-vakṣaḥ kaustubha-maṇi-bhūṣitoraskaḥ* || 31 ||
> *atasī-kusuma-śyāmaḥ pītāmbara-nivasanaḥ prasanna-mukhaḥ* |
> *kuṇḍala-kirīṭa-dhārī pīna-galoraḥsthalāṁsabhujaḥ* || 32 ||
> *khaḍga-gadā-śara-pāṇir dakṣiṇataḥ śāntidaś caturtha-karaḥ* |
> *vāma-kareṣu ca kārmuka-kheṭaka-cakrāṇi śaṅkhaś ca* || 33 ||
> *atha ca caturbhujam icchati śāntida eko gadā-dhāraś cānyaḥ* |
> *dakṣiṇa-pārśve tv evaṁ vāme śaṅkhaś ca cakraṁ ca* || 34 ||
> *dvibhujasya tu śānti-karo dakṣiṇa-hasto'paraś ca śaṅkha-dharaḥ* |
> *evaṁ viṣṇoḥ partimā kartavyā bhūtim icchadbhiḥ* || 35 ||
>
> — *Bṛhat-Saṁhitā*,[3] 57.31-35

It is quite interesting to know that the *Bṛhat-Saṁhitā* does not prescribe the *varada-mudrā*, which is a quite common for Viṣṇu (compare *Pl.* 13.2 of the red sandstone image of Vāsudeva-Kṛṣṇa from Mathurā, *c.* AD 300, now in the Museum of Indian Art, Berlin, MIK I 5878). The four-armed deity shows *varada-mudrā* with the front right hand, holds *gadā* in the back right hand, *cakra* in the back left hand and *śaṅkha* in the front left hand. This is an image of the Vṛṣṇi-hero Vāsudeva. The *Mahābhārata*[4] describes Vāsudeva-Kṛṣṇa with the attributes, *śaṅkha*, *cakra* and *gadā*. In the later descriptions, a lotus *padma* is given instead of the *varada* hand of the deity, and he is called Trivikrama. For Vāsudeva showing *śāntida-mudrā* (according to *Bṛhat-Saṁhitā*), see *Pl.* 13.3 from Mathurā, now at the Mathura Museum, belonging to the Kuṣāṇa period and illustrated by Härtel.[5] The standing deity shows *abhaya-mudrā* with the front right hand and holds a long *gadā* in the back right hand, *cakra* in the back left hand and *śaṅkha* in the front left hand. No lotus has been shown as attribute.

---

2. Jitendra Nath Banerjea, *The Development of Hindu Iconography*, Calcutta University, rpt. 1985, New Delhi, 1956: 396, fn.3.
3. The *Bṛhat-Saṁhitā* of Varāhamihira, ed. H. Kern, rpt. 1982, Osnabrück Biblio Verlag.
4. *Mahābhārata*, vs 2015, Gita Press, Gorakhpur.
5. R.C. Sharma, *The Splendour of Mathurā Art and Museum*, D.K. Printworld (P) Ltd., New Delhi, 1994, *fig.* 74.

This tradition of showing the deity with *śāntida-mudrā*, same as *abhaya-mudrā* and not *varada-mudrā* and without any lotus, is carried out even in the buffstone image of Viṣṇu (Vāsudeva?) from Rataul, Meerut, now at the Mathura Museum (No. 88.10), of the medieval period (eighth-ninth century) (*Pl.* 13.4).[6]

It is in the *Viṣṇudharmottara,* the most important Hindu iconographic text, where Viṣṇu is described with a lotus attribute. The text was composed most probably in the Kashmir region and should be dated in the seventh century, although Priyabala Shah dates it in "between *circa* 450 and 650 AD" (p. xxvi). In the 85th chapter of the text, the four-armed Vāsudeva is described as dark-complexioned *salilādhmāta-meghābhaḥ,* wearing a long *vanamālā* and a *yajñopavīta,* and holding in the front right hand a full-blown lotus *utphulla-kamala,* and *śaṅkha* in the front left hand. In his back right hand, he holds the anthropomorphized form of *gadā gadā-devī,* and in the back left hand, the anthropomorphized form of *cakra cakra-puruṣa.* The earth *kṣoṇī* is shown between his feet in a female form watching the god with astonishment. No mention of Garuḍa is made. This type of image originated in the Kashmir region (*Pl.* 13.5).

In the Bodhisattvayāna, or popularly Mahāyāna Buddhism, Avalokiteśvara is the most important *bodhisattva;* and in the Gāndhāra art of Buddhism, he is so prominent as next to the future Buddha Maitreya. Avalokiteśvara's main attribute is a full-blown lotus; hence he is called Padmapāṇi. Earlier he is two-armed and is illustrated standing or seated as an independent deity or accompanying the Śākyamuni-Buddha (*Pl.* 13.6). The later Buddhist iconographic text *Sādhanamālā*[7] (*c.* eleventh century) contains thirty-eight *sādhana*s of Avalokiteśvara, in which the deity holds a lotus invariably (*Pl.* 13.7). This important fact perhaps suggests that the lotus, as an attribute, was ascribed to Vāsudeva-Viṣṇu after the concept of Padmapāṇi. We are not very sure when and where the first Viṣṇu image was created with a lotus in hand. But it is evident that the Kashmir region most probably was the origin of Viṣṇu with a lotus attribute (*Pl.* 13.8). The three-headed and four-armed bronze image of Viṣṇu from the Swāt Valley, belonging to the beginning of the seventh century, is now in the Museum of Indian Art, Berlin (MIK I 24), 48.5 cm high. This is one of the earliest Vāsudeva-Viṣṇu images holding a lotus. For the Kashmir images of Vāsudeva holding a lotus (see *Pls.* 13.9 & 13.10).

6. H. Härtel, Zur Typologie einer Kaschmir-Skulptur, Einblicke-Einsichten-Aussichten, Berlin, S. 95-115 (Jahrbuch Preussischer Kulturbesitz, Sonderband 1), 1983, fig. 32.
7. Benoytosh Bhattacharya, *Sādhanamālā*, ed. GOS, 26, 41, Oriental Institute, Baroda, 1968.

Avalokiteśvara-Śiva

The two-armed deity holding only a lotus *padma* Padmapāṇi develops certain iconographic features, which are quite common to the Hindu god Śiva or Īśvara. To call a Buddhist deity Avalokiteśvara with Īśvara as a designation is rather unusual in the early phase of Buddhist iconography. For the Hindu god Śiva it is a technical and unique appellation, and it is known to all that when a *śiva-liṅgam* was installed by a devotee, the object was called Īśvara of the donor. In the hundreds of Śaivaite inscriptions we have references of this fact. Already in the early-Gupta period, two *śiva-liṅga*s were known after the disciples, Upamiteśvara and Kapileśvara.[8] Śiva is known for his *jaṭā*. His attributes are — *akṣamālā, kapāla* and *triśūla*. The last one is a weapon for killing or subduing an enemy.[9] Avalokiteśvara in the post-Kuṣāṇa period is invariably shown with a *jaṭā-mukuṭa*. In the caves of Maharashtra, during the seventh-century Avalokiteśvara is exhibited with an elaborate *jaṭā-mukuṭa*.[10] The *sādhana* describes, *śrīmal-lokanāthaṁ jaṭā-mukuṭa-dharaṁśāntaṁ . . . vāmena padmadharaṁ dakṣiṇe varadaṁ*, here of course the deity shows *abhaya* (compare also *sādhana*s 18 and 19). We are not sure if this early image should be called Lokanātha following the description of a late iconographic text. Compare also, for example, the Kashmir pensive Padmapāṇi/ Avalokiteśvara of the eighth century, where the seated deity wears a nice *jaṭā-mukuṭa* in which the transcendent Buddha Amitābha is shown.[11] From about the tenth century onwards, Avalokiteśvara carries an *akṣamālā* also, which is an attribute of Śiva or Brahmā.[12] The six-armed deity wears a beautiful *jaṭā-mukuṭa* and carries an *akṣamālā* in the upper right hand (*Pl.* 13.11).

In the Pāla period (eighth-thirteenth centuries), the Buddhist deities were much influenced by the manifestation of the Hindu divinities. The reason is obvious. Generally, it is mistaken that all the Pāla rulers were Buddhists, but we

8. D.C. Sircar, *Select Inscriptions*, vol. I, 2nd edn., University of Calcutta, 1965: 278.
9. Jitendra Nath Banerjea, *The Development of Hindu Iconography*, Calcutta University, rpt. 1985, New Delhi, 1956 pl. XXXII, no. 1, Standing Śiva Candraśekhara of the tenth century, from Khiciṅg, Orissa, is quite interesting for a Buddhist deity.
10. S.K. Saraswati, *Tantrayāna Art: An Album*, The Asiatic Society, Calcutta, 1977, No. 41, Auraṅgābād, Cave VII, *c.* seventh century; No. 46, Ellorā, Cave VIII, *c.* seventh century; and No. 57, Ellorā, Cave IV, *c.* seventh century, this time the deity is seated. Sarasvatī calls the deity Lokanātha following the eighth *sādhana* of the *Sādhanamālā*.
11. Pratapaditya Pal, *Bronzes of Kashmir, Graz* Austria, 1975, nos. 46a-b.
12. Pratapaditya Pal, *Bronzes of Kashmir, Graz* Austria, 1975, nos. 46a-b, nos. 51a-b, Six-armed seated Avalokiteśvara from Kashmir, AD 980-1003.

know that at least one ruler, viz., Nayapāla, became a Śaiva, the Bāngarh *praśasti* is an eloquent testimony to it.[13] We know further, from the Bhagalpur *praśasti* of Nārāyaṇapāla that the ruler got constructed a huge Śiva temple for the adherents of the Pāśupata Śaivism.[14] And the famous Pāla ruler, Mahīpāla I, father of Nayapāla, installed a Śaiva *maṭha* for the Pāśupata *ācārya* Indraśiva.[15] The ministers of the Pāla rulers were brāhmaṇas, and the wives of the kings were Hindus. Therefore, it is no wonder that during the Pāla period, hundreds of stone and bronze sculptures of the Hindu divinities were produced in the ateliers of Bihar-Bengal. The Buddhist iconographic text *Sādhanamālā* of this period bears testimony to the fact how the iconography of a Buddhist deity got mixed up with the Hindu iconography and viceversa. Generally, a four-armed form of Avalokiteśvara of this period wears a *jaṭā-mukuṭa* and holds an *akṣamālā.*[16] In Ratnagiri, Orissa, the four-armed Avalokiteśvara is also shown with a *jaṭā-mukuṭa* and *akṣamālā* (*Pl.* 13.12). Śiva is known as Nīlakaṇṭha because he swallowed the poison *halāhala* during the churning of the milk-ocean. A parallel image with the same nomenclature of the *bodhisattva* Avalokiteśvara is to be found at the Nalanda Museum, No. 79, *c.* eighth century.[17] Bhattacharya, 1956, p. 140 translates *sādhana* 39,

> The worshipper should think himself as the god Nīlakaṇṭha, who is yellow in colour and whose *jaṭāmukuṭa* is adorned with the crescent and the effigy of Amitābha. He sits in the *vajraparyaṅka* attitude on a red lotus, on which is spread the skin of black antelope. He exhibits the *samādhi-mudrā* with his two hands carrying the *kapāla* (bowl) filled with a variety of gems. His sacred thread is made of the deer-skin *aiṇeya-carma.* He wears the tiger-skin, and bears no ornaments (on his person). His throat shows the blue pill (of poison). The two sides of the god are occupied by two cobras with jewels on their hoods and tails entwined with each other. They look towards the god.

Another deity with the nomenclature *halāhala* was created for Avalokiteśvara with the description,

---

13. D.C. Sircar, "Bāṇgaḍh Stone Inscription of the time of Nayapāla," *JAIH*, vol. VII, part I-II, 1973-74, pp. 135-158, 264, Calcutta., 1975, pp. 135ff.
14. F. Hultzsch, "The Bhagalpur Plate of Nārāyaṇapāla," *The Indian Antiquary*, vol. 15, pp. 304ff., Calcutta, pp. 304ff.
15. Sircar, *ibid.*
16. S.K. Saraswati, *Tantrayāna Art*: *An Album,* The Asiatic Society, Calcutta, 1977, No. 67.
17. *Ibid.*, 1977, No. 67.

> The worshipper should think himself as Halāhala, the Great Compassionate, originating from the sacred syllable Hrīḥ, with three eyes, three faces and matted hair rising upwards in the shape of a crown. . . . He bears on his head the crescent and the *kapāla*. . . . He has six arms, a smiling face and is fond of garments of tiger-skin.[18]

For a painting of the figure in the Machhandar Vahal, Kāṭhmāṇḍu, (see Bhattacharya, p. 401, Fig. 3(A)). And for a painting of Nīlakaṇṭha Lokeśvara, (see p. 405, *fig*. 17(A)).

Śiva is well-known as a dancer, popularly called Naṭarāja, but in Bengal he is known as Nartteśvara from a pedestal inscription. Strangely enough, several forms of Avalokiteśvara are described as Padmanaratteśvara in the *Sādhanamālā*. Compare, for example, *sādhana*s 30, 31, 32 of *Sādhanamālā*. In *sādhana* 31, eight-armed Padmanartteśvara is described as:

> *. . . rakta-varṇam eka-mukhaṁ jaṭā-mukuṭinaṁ trinetraṁ aṣṭa-bhujaṁ . . . sarppa-yajñopavītaṁ arddhaparyyaṅkena tāṇḍavaṁ . . . evambhūtaṁ padmanartteśvara-lokanāthaṁ bhāvayet,*

> The worshipper should think himself as Padmanaratteśvara . . . red in colour with one face, the *jaṭā-mukuṭa*, three eyes and eight arms . . . wears a sacred thread of a snake, and dances in the *ardhaparyaṅka* attitude.[19]

For a bronze image of Padmanartteśvara from Nepal, see Bhattacharya, p. 260, *Fig*. 110. And finally for a very interesting form of Avalokiteśvara seated on a lion and associated with a *triśūla* entwined by a snake, verily an attribute of Śiva, compare *sādhana* 25,

> *. . . ātmānaṁ siṁhanādaṁ lokeśvara-rūpaṁ bhāvayet śvetavarṇaṁ trinetraṁ jaṭāmukuṭinaṁ nirbhūṣaṇaṁ vyāghracarmma prāvṛtaṁ siṁhāsanasthaṁ mahārājalīlāṁ candrāsanaṁ candraprabhaṁ bhāvayet । dakṣiṇe sita-phaṇi-veṣṭitaṁ triśūlaṁ śvetaṁ vāme nānā-sugandhi-kusuma-paripūrita-padma-bhājanaṁ vāma-hastāduttha padmopari jvalat-khaḍgaṁ . . .*

> The worshipper should think himself as Siṁhanāda Lokeśvara of white complexion, with three eyes, and the *jaṭā-mukuṭa* (crown of matted hairs). He is without ornaments, is clad in tiger-skin, and sits on a lion in the attitude of princely ease. He is seated on the orb of the moon and is radiant like her. In his right, there is a white trident entwined by a white snake, and in his left there is a lotus-bowl, full of fragrant flowers. From his left hand rises a lotus,

18. *Sādhanamālā*, ed. Benoytosh Bhattacharya, GOS, 26, 41, Oriental Institute, Baroda, 1968.
19. Benoytosh Bhattacharya, *The Indian Buddhist Iconography*, Calcutta, rpt. 1968, 1958, p. 135.

> on which there is a sword burning like fire.[20]

For an excellent stone sculpture of Siṁhanāda Lokeśvara, see MIK I 576 from the region between Nālandā and Lakkhī Sarāi, eleventh-twelfth century[21] (*Pl.* 13.13) Taran Kumar Biswas rightly comments,

> In the *Sādhanamālā* there are as many as 38 *sādhana*s on Avalokiteśvara, from which . . . Siṁhanāda Lokeśvara, Nīlakaṇṭha, Halāhala and Padmanartteśvara disclose definite Śaivaite association.[22]

Bibliography

Banerjea, Jitendra Nath, 1956, *The Development of Hindu Iconography*, Calcutta University, reprinted 1985, New Delhi.

Banerji, R.D., 1933. *Eastern Indian School of Medieval Sculpture*, Delhi, 1933.

Bautze-Picron, Claudine, 1985, "Limage de l'Adimurti Vasudeva au Bihar et au Bengale," du 5e au 12e siecle, *Annali*, vol. 45, pp. 437-81, Napoli.

Bautze-Picron, Claudine, 1998, *The Art of Eastern India in the Collection of the Museum für Indische Kunst, Berlin: Stone & Terracotta Sculptures*, Dietrich Reimer Verlag, Berlin.

Bhāgavata Purāṇa, Nirnaya Sagar Press, Bombay, 1950.

Bhattacharya, Benoytosh, 1958, *The Indian Buddhist Iconography*, Calcutta, rpt. 1968.

Biswas, T.K., 1996-97, "Metamorphosis of Avalokiteśvara," *Kala*: *The Journal of Indian Art History Congress*, vol. III, pp. 26-29, Varanasi.

The *Bṛhat-Saṁhitā* of *Varāhamihira*, ed. H. Kern, reprinted 1982, Osnabrück Biblio Verlag.

Härtel, H., 1983, Zur Typologie einer Kaschmir-Skulptur, Einblicke-Einsichten-Aussichten, Berlin, S. 95-115 (Jahrbuch Preussischer Kulturbesitz, Sonderband 1).

Hultzsch, F., 1886, "The Bhagalpur Plate of Nārāyaṇapāla," *The Indian Antiquary*, vol. 15, pp. 304ff., Calcutta.

Mahābhārata, vs 2015, Gita Press, Gorakhpur.

Pal, Pratapaditya, 1975, *Bronzes of Kashmir*, Graz, Austria.

Sādhanamālā, 1968, ed. Benoytosh Bhattacharya, GOS, 26, 41, Oriental Institute, Baroda.

Saraswati, S.K., 1977, *Tantrayāna Art*: *An Album*, The Asiatic Society, Calcutta.

Sharma, R.C., 1994, *The Splendour of Mathurā: Art and Museum*, D.K. Printworld (P) Ltd., New Delhi.

Sircar, D.C., 1965, *Select Inscriptions*, vol. I, 2nd edn., University of Calcutta.

Sircar, D.C., 1975, "Bāṇgaḍh Stone Inscription of the time of Nayapāla," *JAIH*, vol. VII, part I-II, 1973-74, pp. 135-58, 264, Calcutta.

Viṣṇudharmottara Purāṇa, Third Khaṇḍa (vol. I), 1958, edn. Priyabala Shah, Oriental Institute, Baroda.

Zwalf, Wladimir, 1996, *A Catalogue of the Gandhāra Sculptures in the British Museum*, London.

---

20. Benoytosh Bhattacharya, *The Indian Buddhist Iconography*, Calcutta, rpt. 1968, 1958, p. 127.
21. Claudine Picron Bautze, *The Art of Eastern India in the Collection of the Museum für Indische Kunst, Berlin: Stone & Terracotta Sculptures*, Dietrich Reimer Verlag, Berlin. 1998, Cat. No 51.
22. T.K. Biswas, "Metamorphosis of Avalokiteśvara," *Kalā*: *The Journal of Indian Art History Congress*, Vol. III, pp. 26-29, Varanasi, 1996-97: 26.

14

Concept and Iconography of Buddhist Goddess Parṇaśabarī

Kamal Giri and M.N.P. Tiwari

THE two most important iconographic Buddhist texts, namely, *Sādhanamālā* (*c.* CE 1165) and *Niṣpannayogāvalī* (Abhayakargupta — latter half of twelfth century CE) conceived a number of goddesses under the Tāntric impact of Vajrayāna. These goddesses were mainly the emanatory forms of supreme Buddhist goddess Tārā. According to the *Mañjuśrīmūlakalpa*, Tārā was the personification of compassion (*karuṇā*) and she is visualized as the remover of obstacles and fear (*vighna* and *bhayanāśinī*) and also boon conferring (*varadāyinī*) goddess.[1] The entire process of evolution of the Buddhist as well as the Jaina pantheon is based on the socio-religious needs and concepts having multi-dimensional interactions with the Vedic-Purāṇic traditions of greater antiquity. This has to be accepted as historical truth and the study of Buddhist and so also Jaina and other religions and their art forms must be undertaken in this backdrop. It is with this historical perspective that we have endeavoured to take-up the study of Buddhist goddess Parṇaśabarī, who is said to have been an emanatory form of Tārā (Pītatārā). Like Tārā she is also conceived in the *dhyāna*s enunciated in the *Sādhanamālā* as the healer of all the epidemics and diseases (*sarvamārīpraśamanī*). She is also very close to the tribal people and thereby to the Nature to derive the immense power of pacifying and curing various epidemics and diseases through the medicinal property of Nature itself. It is due to this fact that she not only tramples under her

1. M. Ghosh, *Development of Buddhist Iconography in Eastern India (A Study of Tārā, Prajñā of five Tathāgata and Bhṛkuṭi)*, New Delhi, 1980, pp. 11-12.

feet, various *vighnas* (shown in visual examples as the personified diseases lying prostrate) but also carries cluster of leaves (*parṇamañjarī*). She wears tiger-skin and cloth of leaves (*parṇavasanā*) along with garland of leaves.[2]

According to Grunwedel, Parṇaśabarī was worshipped by the aboriginal tribes of India, especially the Śabaras and Kirātas. Her name, the leaf garment, and the characteristic epithet *paiśācī* distinctly indicate her association with the leaf-clad Śabara tribe. Thus as the remover or pacifier of diseases she assumes the form of a Mother Goddess on the one hand and through her name, dress and leave like symbol, penetrates into the tribal people on the other.[3] D.C. Bhattacharyya and Parnasabari Bhattacharyya have lucidly shown that the Mahāyāna Buddhists adopted Parṇaśabarī in their pantheon from the non-Āryan Śabaras for their multifarious ritualistic practices as is proved from her name and attributes. At first she was the goddess of Śabaras, later when she was inducted in the higher religion, she came to be known as *sarva-śabarāṇāṁbhagavatī*, i.e., Goddess Bhagavatī of all the Śabaras.

On the basis of *Agni Purāṇa* (*c.* ninth century CE), *Skanda Purāṇa* (*c.* twelfth century CE) and *Tantrasāra*, N.P. Joshi[4] and D.C. Bhattacharyya[5] have discussed some forms of Pārvatī or Durgā as Tvaritā, Kairātī and Śabarī who were provided with leave cloth or peacock feathers, dress and ornaments. D.C. Bhattacharyya has further mentioned that it is significant that the Buddhists did not take the *Parṇakairātī* for a form of Tārā, rather they preferred the name Parṇaśabarī — evidently to give more importance to the Śabaras than to the Kirātas. Incidentally it may also be interesting to note that in about tenth-eleventh centuries CE the Śvetāmbara Jain tradition (*nirvāṇakālikā*) also visualized Mānavī (12th Vidyādevī) as four-armed and showing *viṭapa* (tree leaves) along-with *varada-mudrā*, noose and rosary.

Different scholars have so far published about eight images (including four bronzes from Kurkihar, Bihar) of Parṇaśabarī found mainly from Bihar and east Bengal (now Bangladesh).[6] These images are now preserved in Patna Museum

2. *Sādhanamālā*, pp. 306-08, *dhyāna*, 148-50.
3. D.C. Bhattacharyya, *Studies in Buddhist Iconography*, New Delhi, 1978, pp. 14-18.
4. N.P. Joshi, "Goddess Tvaritā Śabarī, Manasā and Tulajā and Allied Problems," *Kalā*, no. VIII, p. 11.
5. D.C. Bhattacharyya, *op. cit.*
6. N.K. Bhaṭṭaśāli, *Iconography of Buddhist and Brāhmaṇical Sculptures in the Dacca Museum*, Dacca, 1929; Bhagawant Sahai, *Iconography of Minor Hindu and Buddhist Deities*, New Delhi, 1975; →

(four examples), Indian Museum, Calcutta (one example), Sahitya Parishad, Dhaka (one mutilated image showing three-faced elephant-heads, two-armed Vināyaka on the pedestal); and Dhaka Museum (two examples with identical details from Vikrampur and Vajrayoginī — three-faced, three-eyed, six-armed goddess in *pratyālīḍha* with five *dhyānī* Buddhas overhead — Amoghasiddhi (in *abhaya*) being in the centre. She holds hatchet, arrow and thunderbolt in right hands and bow, *tarjanī* (in place of *tarjanī-pāśa*) and cluster of leaves in left hands. Of all the images, only the last two examples of Dhaka Museum with identical details conform almost fully with the *dhyāna-mantras* of *Sādhanamālā*. These images also contain some very interesting features and figures which speak of the positive interaction with the Brāhmaṇical cult and art which will be discussed in the following pages. All other images however, need reconsideration as to their identification with Parṇaśabarī because their details (as we would see in case of bronze figures of *c.* eleventh century CE in Patna Museum) do not conform to the injunctions as envisaged by the *Sādhanamālā*.

The available images of Parṇaśabarī and the *dhyāna*s of *Sādhanamālā* suggest that the crystallization of iconographic form and its visual representation took place in about eleventh-twelfth centuries CE. It is interesting to note that the Brāhmaṇical goddess Śītalā was also worshipped as the controlling goddess of diseases, specially small-pox. According to the *Skanda Purāṇa* she is propitiated for good health of children.[7] She is referred to as a presiding goddess of diseases and she is supposed to remove all sorts of fear and diseases (*sarvarogabhayāpahā*).[8] The goddess also reveals the *mātṛkā* aspect. The margosa (*nīma*) leaves and twigs are offered in oblation to the goddess which according to the pharmaceutical system of *Āyurveda* are employed in medication and natural relief to person specially suffering from small-pox. Like Parṇaśabarī, the form and iconography of Śītalā were also crystallized sometimes in the eleventh-twelfth centuries CE, as

→ Parnasabari Bhattacharyya, "Parṇaśabarī: A Tāntric Buddhist Goddess," *Tantric Buddhism (centennial Tribute to Dr. Benoytosh Bhattacharyya)*, ed. N.N. Bhattacharyya, New Delhi, 1999, pp. 215-21, *Eastern Indian Bronzes*, Pt. II (Karl Khandelavala and Sadashiv Gorakashkar), Lalit Kala Akademi, New Delhi, 1986, p. 146, figs. 197-99.

7. *Skanda Purāṇa* 7.134.2, 7.135.1-7.

8. See for detail Jeanine Auboyer and Marie-Thérése De Mallmann, "Śītalā-La-Froide, Déesse Indienne de la petite vérole" (Śītalā-the-Cold, Indian Goddess of Small-pox), *Artibus Asiae*, vol. 13, 1950, pp. 207-27; Maruti Nandan Tiwari, "Concept and Manifestation of Goddess Śītalā," *Kalā*, vol. VII, 2000-01, pp. 73-78.

evidenced by the literary references of *Nārada, Skanda* and *Bhaviṣya* Purāṇas and also by the sculptures of the goddess from the Sūrya-kuṇḍa-*devakulikā*, Sun temple, Moḍherā (Mahesana, Gujarat, eleventh century CE), Saccikāmātā temple, Osiāñ (Jodhpur, Rajasthan, 1177 CE) and a number of other places in Gujarat and Rajasthan.[9] In conformity with the descriptions of the texts Śītalā rides a donkey and holds a winnowing basket (*śūrpa* — in two upper hands) and sweeping broom (*mārjanī*). She is also shown nude. Thus the goddess Śītalā in Brāhmaṇical and Parṇaśabarī in the Buddhist traditions have close semblance in respect of being the goddess worshipped for removing all sorts of fear and diseases. Śītalā is nude while Parṇaśabarī wears a apron of leaves.

It is further interesting to find the presence of Śītalā in diminutive form on the left flank of the two images of Parṇaśabarī from Vikrampur and Vajrayoginī (now in Bangladesh). Both the images preserved in Dhaka Museum, are datable to *c.* eleventh century CE. These images depict Śitalā as two-armed goddess riding on a donkey and holding a sweeping broom and winnowing basket. This indeed was the positive interaction.

The prostrate figure of elephant-headed deity with sword and shield, usually identified as Gaṇeśa, and as running away from the wrath of Parṇaśabarī may be taken instead as the form of Vināyaka (the proto-type of Śiva-*putra* Gaṇeśa). The texts like *Mānava Gṛhyasūtra, Yājñavalkya-Smṛti* and *Mahābhārata* describe the Vināyakas who were prone to possess men and women and make them failures in life. The Vināyaka is said to put obstacles in the performance of good deeds.[10] The elephant-headed figure with sword and shield and lying prostrate on the pedestal in such a way as if fleeing out of the fear of Parṇaśabarī has relevance as the deity of obstacles (*vighnarāja*). The elephant-headed figure however, does not have any distinctive features of Gaṇeśa such as *modaka* or *modaka-pātra, paraśu* and *mūṣaka vāhana*.

In Parṇaśabarī images of Dhaka Museum, the goddess tramples upon two prostrate human figures symbolizing diseases and pestilences. The figure under the right leg of goddess, as remarked by Bhattacharyya, is apparently that of the man attacked with small-pox as it shows certain circular marks over the body, while the figure under the left foot is probably attacked with some fatal disease. On the right side of goddess in both the examples a horse-faced and two-armed figure,

9. Maruti Nandan Tiwari, *op. cit.*, pp. 75-78.
10. J.N. Banerjea, *Development of Hindu Iconography*, Calcutta, 1957, p. 358.

either facing the goddess or moving in the opposite direction with folded hands or with one hand being raised in adoration, is carved who has been identified as Hayagrīva, the Hindu god of fever which is not acceptable. *Jvara* (fever) is visualized in the *Viṣṇudharmottara* as a form of Śiva. According to this text *jvara* should be made three-faced (each with three eyes), three-armed and three-legged.[11] Further the Brāhmaṇical god Hayagrīva related to Viṣṇu is perhaps no where associated with fever. On the other hand, the *Sādhanamālā* and *Niṣpannayogāvalī* refer to Hayagrīva with several forms of Avalokiteśvara but nowhere he is conceived as horse faced, instead he is to be shown with three faces, three eyes and multi-armed. Under the circumstance we propose to identify the horse-faced figure as Aśvīnikumāra, the son of Sūrya, shown with folded hands in the images of Sūrya.

Further in both the *dhyāna-mantras* of *Sādhanamālā* referring to Parṇaśabarī, there is no mention of Śītalā, Hayagrīva, Aśvinīkumāra and Gaṇeśa. However, the *dhyāna-mantras* refer only to *vighnas* being trampled by Parṇaśabarī which is represented through the two lying human figures under the feet of goddess suggesting diseases. The rendering of prostrate figure of elephant-headed Vināyaka (personifying obstacles) with sword and shield, making fast escape out of the fear of goddess, apparently has contextual relevance. The presence of Śītalā and Aśvinīkumāra is virtually the outcome of some local Śāstric tradition of East Bengal, now lost to us. In any case it was an intelligent assimilation suggesting the positive interaction which indeed was a localized tradition because no other figure of Parṇaśabarī from anywhere else does show these Brāhmaṇical deities who are assisting Parṇaśabarī in her work of eradicating different diseases.

Thus the concept and iconography of Parṇaśabarī is a little bit different in terms of interaction with Brāhmaṇical deities. Contrary to the forms like Aparājitā, Ucchuṣma-Jambhala, Samvara, Trailokyavijaya, Hevajra, Vajrahuṅkāra, Bhūtaḍāmara, Vighanāntaka and Kālacakra showing Brāhmaṇical deities like Brahmā, Viṣṇu, Śiva, Śakti, Gaṇeśa, Dhanada in subdued and humiliated positions, sometimes even trampled by the Buddhist deities, Parṇaśabarī is a unique example of positive interaction.

---

11. P. Shah, ed., *Viṣṇudharmottara Purāṇa*, Khaṇḍa III, chap. 73, Śloka 40. Baroda, 1958.

15

Exchange of Formal Concepts between Buddhist and Brāhmaṇical Pañcāyatana Complexes

Falk Reitz

THE remains of a pedestal (*Pls.* 15.1-15.4) in the archaeological park of Sārnāth appealed me since 1994, when I started with the fieldwork for my Ph.D. thesis "Pañcāyatana Complexes in North India — Formation, Development and Regional Variations of an Indian Architectural Design," which had been submitted and defended at the Free University, Berlin in 1998.[1]

This basement[2] has extensions at all the four corners (*fig.* 15.2), which according to my opinion, had been the platforms for the four sub-structures. Following the style of the terracotta decorations at the basement (*Pls.* 15.5, 15.6, 15.9, 15.10 &15.11) I would like to suggest a date for this structure at the end of the fourth century or in the first decades of the fifth century AD.[3] If one accepts the hypotheseis

1. I am very thankful to the German Acedemic Exchange Service (DAAD) and the Indian Council for Cultural Relations (ICCR) which sponsored my fieldwork and the research in the library and archives of the American Institute of Indian Studies (AIIS), Center for Art and Archaeology (then at Vārāṇasī, Rāmnagar) with an one-year-scholarship. I will never forget the help and support of Prof. M.A. Dhaky and all his colleagues of the AIIS during my research in India.

2. It must have been excavated after 1915 since it is not shown in the excavation report on Sārnāth in the *Annual Report* 1914-15: pl. LX. Other excavation reports on Sārnāth are in *Annual Report* 1907-08 (see pl. XI) and *Annual Report* 1904-05 (see pl. XVI). It is also not included in Sahni's guide book of 1917.

3. Cf. Plaeschike 1982 : 134 ff. The terracotta decorations from the *stūpa* at Devnimorī (Mehta 1966: pl. LVI A) had been taken as parallel. This *stūpa* is dated by Mehta (1966: 29) to the third quarter of the fourth century AD. Important is the form of the leaves in the terracotta decorations which are structured in the following decades less realistically and more stylized. According to the stylistic development suggested by Plaeschike, the basement of Sārnāth should be close to the Devnimorī decorations.

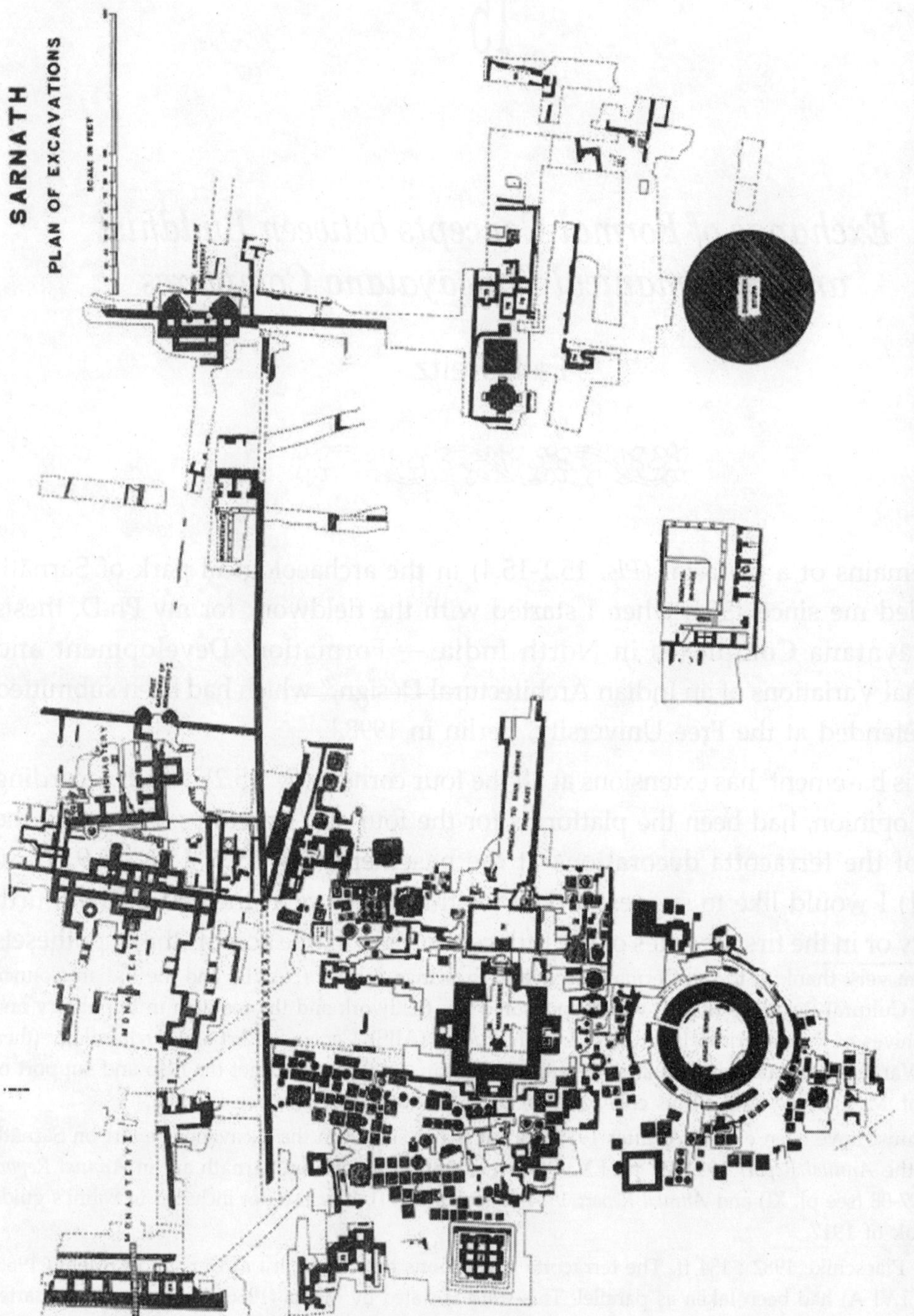

*fig.*15.1. Sārnāth, plan of the excavated area from the Annual report of the Archaeological Survey of India 1907-08: pl. XI.

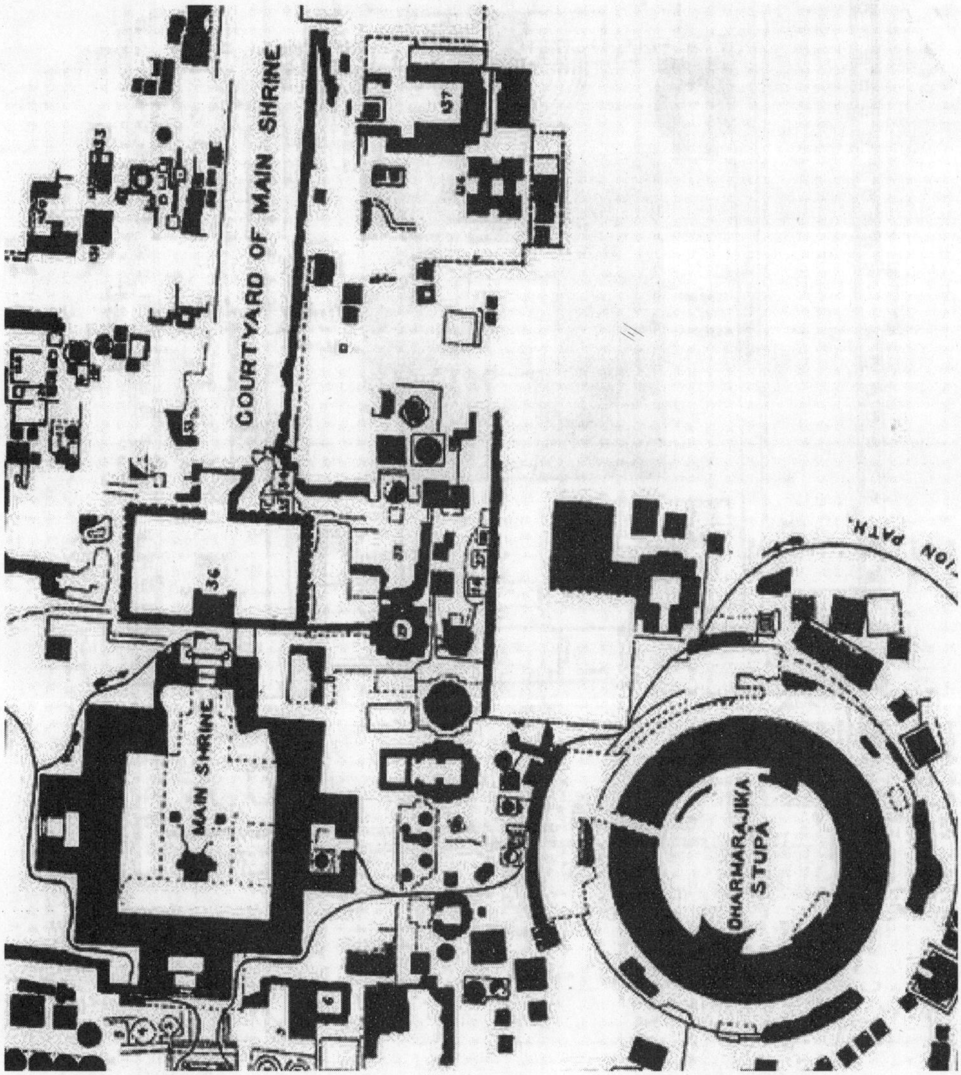

fig. 15.2. Sārnāth, plan of the excavated area in the year 1926 with the pedestal no. 136 south of the courtyard of the main shrine (after: D.R. Sahni 1926: plan of excavations, after p. 45).

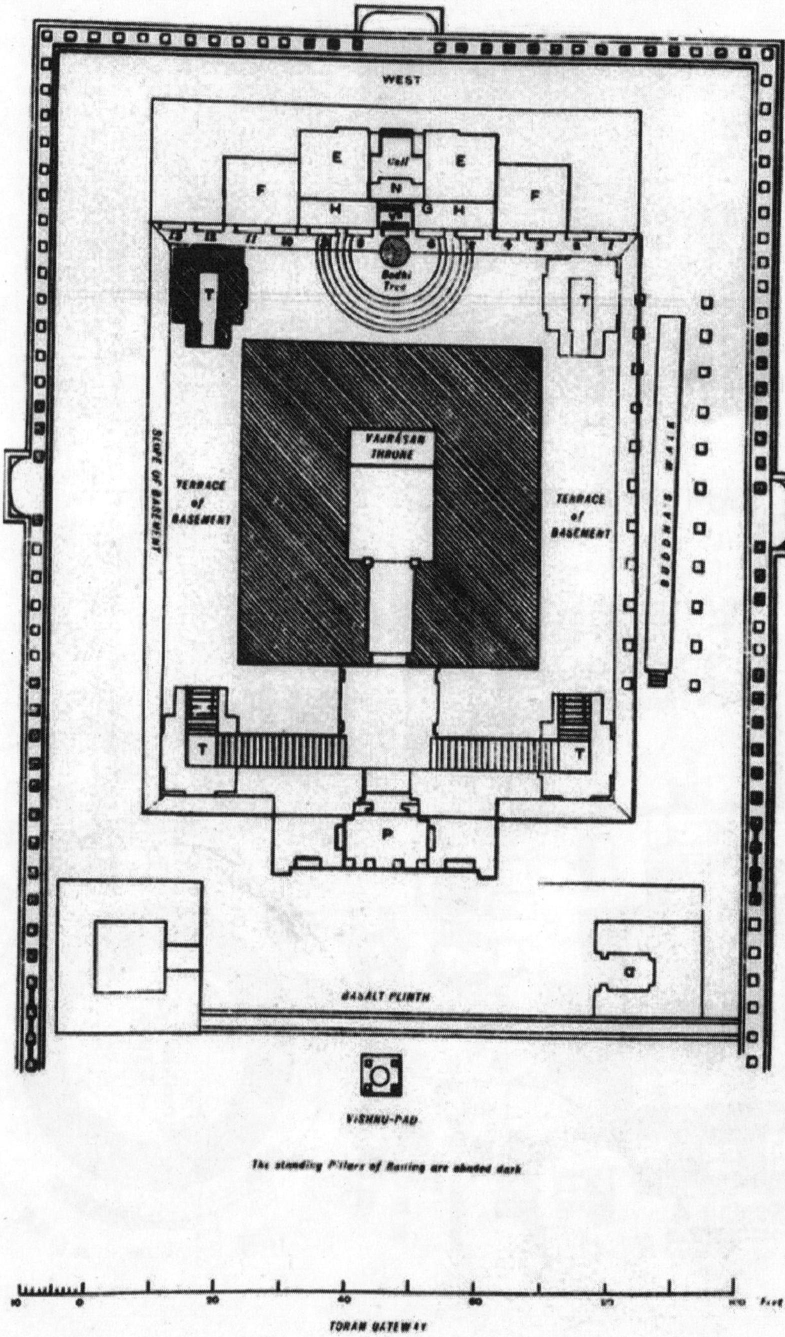

*fig.*15.3. Bodha-Gayā, Mahābodhi temple groundplan (after Cunningham 1892: pl XI).

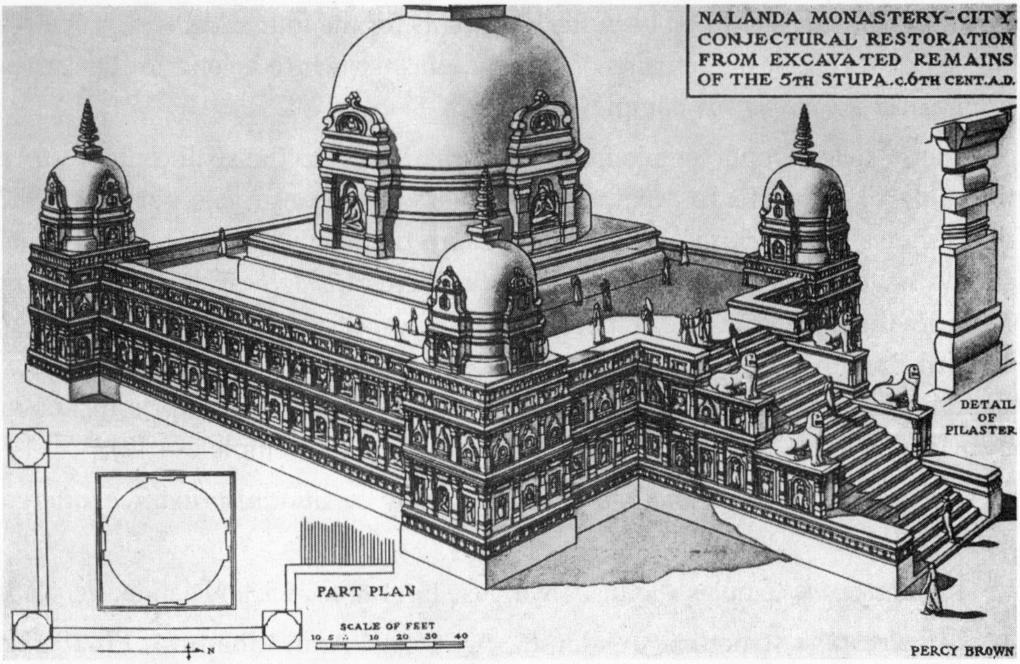

fig.15.4.Nālandā, site no. 3, fifth-period *stūpa* with four sub-*stūpa*s (recons-truction of P. brown 1965: p. C xxxii).

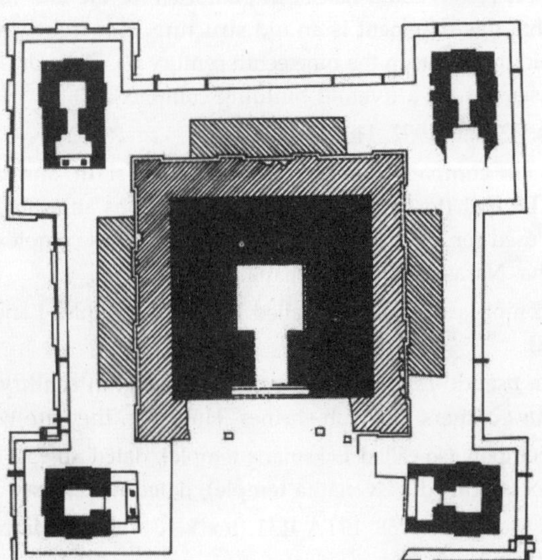

fig.15.5. Nālandā, temple no. 12, groundplan (after EITA II/ 12, text: p. 399).

that the four extensions had been the basements for the four small sub-structures, we can deduce that the remains of this Buddhist structure belong to the earliest example of a *pañcāyatana* complex in India.[4]

The so-called Gupta temple from Deogarh, datable to the sixth century AD,[5] is the earliest known Hindu *pañcāyatana* complex. The reconstruction of Vats (1952: pl. V) shows how a central Viṣṇu temple is surrounded by four sub-temples which should have had idols of Viṣṇu *avatāras* in their *garbhagṛhas*.[6] In the following centuries the *pañcāyatana* model became popular especially in the different capitals of north Indian Hindu kingdoms, as at Osian,[7] Bhubaneśvar,[8] and Khajurāho.[9] Buddhist five-fold temple complexes comparable to the Hindu examples are known from Bodha-Gayā (Mahābodhi temple)[10] and Nālandā (temple no. 12).[11]

The scheme of *pañcāyatana* had been adopted by the Buddhists in three different concepts:

1. *pañcāyatana* temples (Bodha-Gayā, *Pls*. 15.14 & *fig*. 15.3; Nālandā, *fig*. 15.5).
2. *pañcastūpa* structures (Nālandā, *fig*. 15.4,[12] Anurādhāpura, *Pl*. 15.12,[13]

4. We discussed the different possibilities during the site visit on the 17.02.2003 : Prof. R.C. Sharma suggested that the extensions could had been platforms for the four figures. Prof. Kamal Giri did not believe at all that this basement is an old structure. She argued that it could have been put together from the old fragments in the nineteenth century (?). Only Dr. Amar Singh fully supported my view-point (basement for a fivefold building complex).
5. See EITA II/1(text): 52 Vats 1952: 11.
6. The Viṣṇu *pañcāyatana* complex at Rājim (datable to the sixth, and the additions to the eighth centtury AD, see EITA II/1 (text): 230, 232) might be used as an example to the how even today this complexes are used for worship. In the sub-shrines of this complex are seated different Viṣṇu *avatāras*, like Varāha, Narasiṁha and Vāmana.
7. Viṣṇu *pañcāyatana* complexes I and II (so-called Hari-Hara temples I and II), eighth century AD, see EITA II/2: 167, 182).
8. The Vetāl Deul is a pseudo-*pañcāyatana* temple of the eighth century AD, see EITA II/2: 416. It shows at the *maṇḍapa* corners four sub-shrines. However, they are without *garbhagṛhas*.
9. Viṣṇu *pañcāyatana* complex (so-called Lakṣmaṇa temple), dated AD 954, see EITA II/3: 68, and Śiva *pañcāyatana* complex (so-called Viśvanātha temple), dated AD 999, see EITA II/3: 75.
10. Cunningham 1892, Malandra 1988, EITA II/1 (text): 104-08, 108: dated to early seventh century AD, with later additions.
11. See EITA II/2: 399: founded early in the seventh century AD, with later additions. A comparative study of the 46 Hindu *pañcāyatana* complexes in north India is included in my Ph.D. dissertation (Reitz 1999).
12. See EITA II/1(text): 108-10, datable in the last quarter of the sixth century AD.
13. Ratnamāli Mahāstūpa, second century BC and later additions, see Seneviratna 1994: 99-106.

Polonnaruva, *Pl.* 15.13[14]).

3. *pañcāyatana vihāra*s (Anuradhāpura[15]).

The *pañcāyatana* structure of the Mahābodhi temple at Bodha-Gayā had been particularly popular, and was copied quite often as miniature replicas. Few of these copies had been used as souvenirs.[16] The Mahābodhi temple had been so famous in the neighbouring Buddhist countries that the local rulers there intended to have at least one similar temple complex itself. So it is not surprising to find adaptations of the Mahābodhi temple in accordance with the local architectural design patterns in Burma and Thailand.[17]

It is difficult to decide from the remains of the pedestal no. 136 at Sārnāth whether it had been used as the basement for the central temple and four sub-shrines, similar to the example of the Mahābodhi temple at Bodha-Gayā or for one central and four smaller *stūpa*s as in the case of the Ratnamāli *mahāstūpa* at Anurādhapura. But one point, according to my understanding, is quite clear. The pedestal no. 136 at Sārnāth had obviously been the lower part of a Buddhist *pañcāyatana* structure since all the surrounding structures are also Buddhist. This type of architectural design, however, later became very popular in Vārāṇasī and was adopted within the Hindu cultural context. The connecting feature between the three different Buddhist types and the Hindu type of *pañcāyatana* is the basement. Either five *stūpa*s, or five temples, or five *vihāra*-buildings are located on one common platform that connect the main and the sub-structures as well as elevate them above the common ground.

Besides the formal aspect for the reconstruction of the pedestal no. 136 in Sārnāth, it would be interesting to know the intended functional purpose of the complex. During our discussion at the site in Sārnāth it had been proposed by Dr. Amar Singh that the main building at the centre of the base could have been the *āyatana* for Vairocana, and the four sub-structures the *āyatana*s for Akṣobhya, Ratna-sambhava, Amitābha and Amoghasiddhi. It should not be a surprise to have a building complex for the five Tathāgatas at Sārnāth at the end of the fifth century AD[18] however, the

14. Potgul Vehera, twelfth century AD, see Seneviratna 1998: 99-102.

15. See Bandaranayake 1974: 86-101.

16. See Malandra 1988: 12, fig. 2.

17. Mahābodhi temple, Pagan, thirteenth century AD (Brown 1988: 62, fig. 1), wat Chet Yot, Chiengmai, fifteenth century AD (Brown 1988: 65, fig. 4).

18. The culminating period of the Mahāyāna Buddhist system, in which the doctrine of the five *tathāgata*s had been in use, continued during the fifth century AD.

position of the four sub-structures in the north-eastern, south-eastern, south-western and north-western corners of the platform is rather disappointing. One usually expects the architectural reminiscence of the *tathāgatas* in the cardinal directions north, east, south, and west,[19] nevertheless, the sub-structures could have had openings in these directions in the case of sub-temples, or niches in the case of sub-*stūpas*.

The intention of publishing this paper is not to give a conclusive explanation about the form and function of the structure no. 136 at Sārnāth, but to provoke more opinions,[20] which could help to establish in future a better understanding of this small monument as the starting point of an architectural development.

Bibliography

Annual Report 1904-05, ed.: Archaeological Survey of India, Calcutta 1908.

Annual Report 1907-08, ed.: Archaeological Survey of India, Calcutta 1911.

Annual Report 1914-15, ed.: Archaeological Survey of India, Calcutta 1920.

Bandaranayake, S., 1974, *Sinhalese Monastic Architecture — The Vihāras of Anurādhapura*, Leiden 1974.

Brown, R.L., 1988, "Bodhgayā and South-east Asia," *Mārg* XXXX/1: 61-84.

Brown, P., 1965, *Indian Architecture, Buddhist and Hindu Periods*, Bombay.

Cunningham, A., 1892, *Mahābodhi: or the Great Buddhist Temple Under the Bodhi Tree at Buddha-Gayā*, London.

Encyclopaedia of Indian Temple Architecture, EITA, eds. M.A. Dhaky, K. Deva, M.W. Meister, New Delhi 1988 (vol. II, part 1), 1991 (vol. II, part 2), 1998 (vol. II, part 3).

Kölver, B., 2003, Das Weltbild der Hindus, ed. A.J. Gail, Berlin.

Mehta, R.N., 1966, *Excavation at Devnimori (A Report of the Excavation conducted from 1960 to 1963)*, Baroda.

Malandra, G.H., 1988, "The Mahābodhī Temple," *Mārg* XXXX/1: 9-28.

Plaeschike, H.I., 1982, *Indische Felsentempel und Höhlenklöster*, Leipzig.

Reitz, F., 1999, *Pañcāyatana-Komplexe in Nordindien — Entstehung, Entwicklung und regionale Besonderheiten einer indischen Architekturform*, Berlin 1999 (2 vols.).

Sahni, D.R., 1917, *Guide to the Buddhist Ruins of Sārnāth*, Calcutta.

Sahni, D.R., 1926, *Guide to the Buddhist Ruins of Sārnāth with a Plan of Excavations*, Calcutta.

Seneviratna, A., 1994, *Ancient Anuradhāpura — The Monastic City*, Colombo.

Seneviratna, A., 1988, *Polonnaruva — Medieval Capital of Sri Lanka*, Colombo.

Vats, M.S., 1952, *The Gupta Temple at Deogarh*, Delhi (Memoirs of the Archaeological Survey of India no. 70).

---

19. Cf. the Svayambhū *stūpa*, Kāṭhmāṇḍu, drawing in : Kölver 2003: 267.
20. Please send your opinions to Dr. Falk Reitz, Lecturer, Institut für Indische Philologie und Kunstgeschichte, Freie Universität Berlin, Koenigin-Luise-Str. 34a, 14195 Berlin, Germany, or to rishab@zedat.fu-berlin.de.

16

Interaction between Buddhist and Brāhmaṇical Art

Evidence from Bengal

Enamul Haque

THE gradual stages in the progress of Aryanization of Bengal are yet to be established.[1] It is generally believed that since the days of the Epics the pre-Āryan primitive tribes of Bengal were having a slow fusion with the immigrant Āryans from the Madhyadeśa and that it was not until a comparatively late period, towards the closing of the first millennium BC, the people of Bengal first began to adopt the social and religious customs of the Āryans. By the early centuries of the Christian era, gradually increasing number of high class Āryans were pouring into Bengal, following thee military or peaceful pursuits. So came the followers of the Brāhmaṇical, Buddhist and Jaina religious sects. By the time the Guptas emerged, the essential features of the Āryan dominated society were well established. The archaeological evidences of the Early Historic period discovered during the last six decades also confirm this assumption. Hundreds of terracotta figures and plaques, recovered from the explorations and excavations at Mahāsthāngarh, Bāngarh, Candraketugarh, Tāmralipta and such other places, do not convincingly prove that the Buddhism, Jainism and the Hinduism flourished in the deltaic Bengal till about the establishment of the Gupta rule in the fourth century AD.

In fact, although in the identification of certain categories of art objects we have used the dynastic appellations of Mauryan, Śuṅga or Kuṣāṇa, based on the

1. R.C. Majumdar (ed.), *History of Bengal*, vol. 1, Dacca University, Dacca, 1943: 426.

known stylistic traits, yet the rule of these dynasties in Bengal is no more than a mere conjecture. Recently, in an extensive study of terracottas from Candraketugarh,[2] only a handful of figurines have been found which have been tentatively proposed to be the prototypes of later Hindu/Buddhist divinities. They are the pot-bellied squatting males, provisionally called Kubera, used mostly as rattles for the children; the beautiful young heavily bejewelled standing female on a jar (*ratna-bhaṇḍāras*) and holding two lotuses in her two hands called Lakṣmī/Śrī; and, human figures riding on one or more rams/horses/elephant, etc., calling Brahmā, Sūrya or Indra, respectively.

From Gupta period onwards, we have extensively reliable literary evidences, supported by archaeological evidences too, about the continued co-existence of the three religions, namely, the Hinduism, Buddhism and Jainism with substantial interaction among them. For the present paper, Jainism has been excluded, as it never became a dominant religion in this region, nor it received any royal patronage of any dynasty from any where in Bengal. From the seventh century AD till the coming of the Muslims in Bengal, the Khaḍgas, the early Devas, the Candras, the Pālas and the Kāmbojas and the individual rulers like Dhanadatta and his son Kāntideva, and Raṇavaṅkamalla, were Buddhists. Vainyagupta, Śaśāṅka, Lokanātha, Dommanapāla, and the early Sena rulers were Śaivas. The Varmans, the later Sena kings and the later Devas were Vaiṣṇavas.[3] However, it is to be noted that by far the large majority of images and inscriptions which may be assigned to the period between AD 750 and 1200 are Brāhmaṇical, and not Buddhist. This evidence leaves no doubt that the Buddhists and the Jainas were far outnumbered by the followers of the Brāhmaṇical sects from the seventh century onwards.

Perhaps there can be no further argument against the general supposition that, as in the Indian sub-continent, the art was basically a hand-maid of religion, or all the hieratic arts emanated from the contemporary religions. Therefore, the interaction between the Buddhist and Brāhmaṇical arts, in fact, would reveal the actual interaction between the two religions. At this stage, we may take note of the role of the political powers in dealing with the two major religions.

At the beginning of the fourth century AD Mahārāja Śrī-Gupta is said to have established a "Chinese temple" near the *stūpa* Mṛgasthāpana (or Mi-li-kia-si-kia-

2. Enamul Haque, *Chandraketugarh: A Treasure-House of Bengal Terracottas*, Dhaka, 2001.
3. R.C. Majumdar (ed.), *History of Bengal*, vol. 1, Dacca University, Dacca, 1943 : 426.

po-no) in Varendra or north Bengal, for the use of the visiting Chinese Buddhist *bhikṣus*. He donated 24 villages for its upkeep.[4] King Vainyagupta of East Bengal, who was a *Śaiva-mahādevapādānudhyāta* at the beginning of the sixth century AD, according to the Gunaighar copper-plate from Comilla district, donated land for the maintenance of a Buddhist monastery built for a Mahāyānic *bhikṣu* Śāntideva and dedicated in the name of Ārya-Avalokiteśvara — and also for the worship of a Buddha image established by the Mahāyānic *bhikṣu saṁgha*.[5] In *c.* sixth-seventh century, during Paramavaiṣṇava Mahārāja Śrī-Dharanarata of East Bengal, his Buddhist *mahā-sandhivigrahādhikārī* Jayanātha donated land for the Buddhist as well as the Brāhmaṇical establishments.[6] According to the Ashrafpur copper-plate from Dhaka district of Buddhist king Devakhaḍga, his Queen Prabhāvatīdevī dedicated (*c.* seventh-eighth centuries AD) an inscribed eight-armed Sarvāṇī image (*Pl.* 16.1), a representation of Śakti of Śiva.[7] Paramasaugata Mahārāja Kāntideva's mother was Śivapriyā and an exponent of *Rāmāyaṇa-Mahābhārata*-Purāṇas.[8]

Most of the Pāla kings were professedly Buddhists. *Paramasaugata* king Nārāyaṇapāla who was *vāsudeva-padābja-pūjā-nirata-mānasaḥ* claimed to have established one thousand temples, and his brother king Nayapāla (AD 1027-42) is known for adopting Śiva as his *ārādhya devatā* and established many images and temples.[9] King Mahīpāla donated land to Hindu brāhmaṇas after taking his ritual bath on the *Viṣuva-Saṅkrānti*.[10] King Rāmpāla in his capital city Rāmāvatī erected several temples dedicated to Śiva, Sūrya, Skanda and Gaṇapati.[11] King Madanapāla's Queen Citramatikā had her husband donate land to a brāhmaṇa for recitation of the *Mahābhārata*. King Madanapāla was said (in Sandhyākaranandī's *Rāmacaritam*) as *caṇḍīcaraṇa-saroja-prasāda-sampanna vigrahaśrī*.[12] Candra king Paramasaugata Śrī-Candra donated land to the brāhmaṇas.[13] King Rāmapāla plunged into the river Ganges on hearing the death of his uncle

4. Niharranjan Ray, *Bangalir Itihas: Adiparva* (in Bengali), rpt., Calcutta, 1993: 502.
5. Niharranjan Ray, *Bangalir Itihas: Adiparva* (in Bengali), rpt., Calcutta, 1993.
6. *Ibid.*, 503.
7. *Ibid.*, 522.
8. *Ibid.*
9. *Ibid.*
10. *Ibid.*
11. *Ibid.*
12. *Ibid.*
13. *Ibid.*

Mathana.[14] Paramasaugata king Lāḍhacandradeva established a Viṣṇu image and named it after himself as Lāḍhamādhava-Bhaṭṭāraka.[15] What one unmistakably notice from the above references is that there had been a cordial relationship between the Hindu and Buddhist religions and a cosmopolitan perception worked at the root of religious activities.

The religious life was marked by a "spirit of catholicity and mutual respect and understanding." This realization has been so perfectly depicted in the Śrī-Dharmapāladeva *mahāvihāra* at Pahārpur (*Pl.* 16.2) established by king Dharmapāladeva, the second ruler of the Pāla dynasty, in the beginning of ninth century AD.[16] In the cruciform temple complex at the centre of the courtyard of the monastery, on the walls of the lowermost *pradakṣiṇāpatha*, are fixed 63 stone sculptures, all except one representing the Brāhmaṇical themes (*Pls.* 16.3 & 16.4). These sculptures predates the monastery by about more than a century at least. They possibly belonged to an earlier Hindu temple which might have been in ruined condition. King Dharmapāladeva, liberal as he was, must have personally permitted the preservation of these images within the Pahārpur Buddhist monastery as an essential scheme of architecture. In the same monastery, on the walls of the *pradakṣiṇāpatha*s at two upper levels of the temple, hundreds of terracotta plaques depict, apart from ordinary secular themes, a large number of Hindu thematic representations. In fact, the artists were given full freedom to choose Hindu divinities and related figures for decorations on the walls of this pride Buddhist monument.

From the availability of innumerable Buddhist and Brāhmaṇical sculptures from *c.* ninth century onwards, quite a few sculptural production centres can be identified all over Bengal. It is also natural to contemplate that these ateliers were simultaneously producing the both, Buddhist and Brāhmaṇical images, to cater to the respective votaries. Consequently, there were not only stylistic similarities between the two, rather in a good number of pieces there were actual transplantation of motifs between them, which were otherwise typical for a particular religious sculpture. The rather notable stone image of Viṣṇu at Lakṣmaṇakāṭi (*Pl.* 16.5), Barisal district, Bangladesh,[17] shows the deity in Buddha-

14. Niharranjan Ray, *Bangalir Itihas: Adiparva* (in Bengali), rpt., Calcutta, 1993, 522.
15. R. Mukherji, and S.K. Maity, *Corpus of Bengal Inscriptions Bearing on History and Civilization of Bengal*, Calcutta, 1967: 27.
16. K.N. Dikshit, *Paharpur, Memoirs of the Archaeological Survey of India*, no. 55, New Delhi. 1938.
17. Enamul Haque, *Bengal Sculptures: Hindu Iconography till c. 1250 AD*, Dhaka, 1992: 88, plate 60.

like *lalitāsana*, Śrī and Puṣṭi seated on the palms of the upper two hands, and a four-armed seated *dhyānī* figure on the crown, reminding us of such Mahāyānic Buddhist practices. The seated bronze Viṣṇu from Sāgardighi, Murśidābād district, West Bengal, depicts the *śaṅkha*, *cakra* and *gadā*, all placed on the lotuses in the Buddhist fashion of Mañjuśrī or Prajñāpāramitā.

There are a number of images from different parts of Bengal showing syncretic development between the Brāhmaṇical and Buddhist sculptures taking elements from one another. A stone image (*Pl.* 16.6) from Ghyāsābād, Murśidābād district, shows a 12 armed standing male in *samapādasthānaka*,[18] under snakehoods, holding each emblem placed on a lotus, with a *vanamālā* falling up to the knees. Two of its arms are placed on two figures on the sides, like the *āyudhapuruṣa*s in Viṣṇu. On the pedestal of a similar sculpture from Rājshāhī district is depicted Preta Sūcīmukha, a recognized follower of Avalokiteśvara.[19] On one similar image (*Pl.* 16.7) from Sonargang, Dhaka district, above the head is depicted the seated *bodhisattva* Amitābha.[20] A stone figure of Viṣṇu from Surohor, Dīnājpur district and now in the Varendra Museum, shows the deity standing under a canopy of seven serpent hoods, the *gadā* and *cakra* in the back hands placed on full-flown lotus flowers, and the *cakra-puruṣa* and *śaṅkha-puruṣa* on two sides where the attributes are shown on *nīlotpala*s held by the respective figures.[21] An Amitābha-like figure (*Pl.* 16.8) is placed just above the central snakehoods and a six-armed dancing figure of Śiva is carved in the middle of the pedestal below. These images are probably an amalgam of Bhāgavata Viṣṇu and Mahāyānī Lokeśvara, which flourished during the eleventh-twelfth centuries.

There are quite a few Brāhmaṇical images (*Pl.* 16.9) from Bengal which depict above their heads the miniature figures of Kārttikeya, Brahmā, Viṣṇu, Śiva and Gaṇeśa, reminding us of the depictions of *pañcadhyānī* Buddhas (*Pl.* 16.10) of the Mahāyānic pantheon.[22]

A large number of images illustrating the ten incarnations of Viṣṇu have been discovered from different parts of Bengal. The list generally followed in Bengal, with slight modifications here and there, included Matsya, Kūrma, Varāha,

18. R.C. Majumdar (ed.), *History of Bengal*, vol. 1, Dacca University, Dacca, 1943: 468, plate xxi 55.
19. Niharranjan Ray, *Bangalir Itihas: Adiparva* (in Bengali), rpt., Calcutta, 1993: 535.
20. Enamul Haque, *Bengal Sculptures: Hindu Iconography till c. 1250* AD, Dhaka, 1992: 96.
21. *Ibid.*, 75-75, plate 31.
22. *Ibid.*, 96 : Plates 26, 178, 199, 203, etc.

Narasiṁha, Vāmana, Paraśurāma, Rāma, Balarāma, Buddha and Kalki. Jayadeva, in his *Gītagovinda* (*c.* AD 1170), endorses this list. Apart from finding individual sculpture of each of the *avatāra*s, the ten incarnations in miniature are depicted on the upper part of the *prabhāvalī*s of a variety of Viṣṇu images. The author could locate 33 such images[23] from Bengal showing the main deity surrounded by the ten incarnations. The order of attributes in the hands of Viṣṇu was of the *trivikrama* variety of the 24 forms of Viṣṇu.[24] Since Kṛṣṇa is not depicted among these incarnations, the main deity was identified as the Vāsudeva Kṛṣṇa.

The inclusion of Buddha as an incarnation of Viṣṇu (*Pl.* 16.11) shows a remarkable example of the capacity for assimilation, a characteristic of the Brāhmaṇical revival during the period of the Gupta supremacy.[25] It is also to be noted that although the list of ten incarnations in Bengal and their chronological placements vary occasionally, the inclusion of Buddha and his penultimate placing at the ninth position are without any exception. This is further corroborated by the representation of the ten incarnations on the reverse sides of the square stone or metal slabs which are frequently found in different parts of Bengal. On the analogy of the well-known *āyāgapaṭṭa*s of the Jainas, Bhaṭṭaśāli denominated them as *viṣṇupaṭṭa*s. The author noticed 23 *viṣṇupaṭṭa*s (*Pls.* 16.12a & 16.12b) from Bengal.[26] The general characteristics of the slabs are that the obverse is divided into several square and rectangular compartments, nine or 25 in number, demarcated by narrow raised bands, and in the centre of them the four-armed Viṣṇu is invariably shown seated either in *lalitāsana*, *padmāsana* or *mahārājalīlāsana*. The reverse of these slabs depict a circle of raised band enclosing a *padma* in low relief. Each of the ten petals form the background of an incarnation and the Buddha is always there. As far as we have seen, these *viṣṇupaṭṭa*s are the products of the tenth-twelfth centuries AD when in spite of the dominance of the Buddhist Pālas and the Candras for quite some time, the general population were overwhelmingly the followers of the Brāhmaṇical faiths. Still their perpetual acceptance of Buddha as an incarnation of Viṣṇu is perhaps the single major

23. Enamul Haque, *Bengal Sculptures: Hindu Iconography till c. 1250 AD*, Dhaka, 67; Plates 23, 24, 25 and 26.

24. Enamul Haque, *Bengal Sculptures: Hindu Iconography till c. 1250 AD*, Dhaka, 1992: 96.

25. N.K. Bhaṭṭaśālī, *Iconography of the Buddhist and Brāhmaṇical Sculptures in Dacca Museum*, Dacca, (Bhaṭṭaśālī 1929:103; Enamul Haque, *Bengal Sculptures: Hindu Iconography till c.* 1250 AD, Dhaka, Plates 23, 24, 25 and 26, 1992 : 99-120.

26. Enamul Haque, *Bengal Sculptures: Hindu Iconography till c.* 1250 AD, Dhaka, 1992: 125, plates 97A, 97B, 98A, 98B, 99A and 99B).

example of interaction between the Buddhist and Brāhmaṇical faiths and, therefore, arts.

But in spite of this assimilative gesture, some questions remain which need to be answered. Bengal has yielded a large number of independent Buddha images. Is there any evidence that some or any one of them were the creations of the Hindus to be worshipped as an *avatāra* of Viṣṇu? What was the reaction from the Buddhist side of incorporating their Master as one of the many gods of the Hindu pantheon, and that also in a subordinate manner? Was there any denunciation? Are there any other respectful representation of Buddha in any Hindu sculptural art beyond the depiction among the *daśāvatāra*s?

The interaction between the Buddhist and Brāhmaṇical arts had also other manifestations in Bengal. The Mahāyānist answer to the Brāhmaṇical Sūrya (*Pl.* 16.13) was the goddess Mārīci.[27] She travels on a chariot drawn by seven pigs (*Pl.* 16.14) matching the seven horses of the Sūrya. Jambhala (*Pl.* 16.15) was created[28] against the Hindu god Kubera, almost with the identical characteristics. Ṣaṣṭhī has her parallel in Hārīti, Manasā in Jāṅgulī. But these positive developments, side by side there were a few attempts to ridicule some Hindu god like Gaṇeśa. Bhaṭṭaśāli located an image of a Bhṛkuṭi Tārā (*Pl.* 16.16) from Bhavānīpur, Munśīgañj district.[29] where the eight-armed goddess is seated in *vajrāsana* with the representation of Gaṇeśa, crawling on floor, right below the seat. Similarly, there are two images of three-headed six-armed Parṇaśabarī (*Pl.* 16.17), one from Nayananda and the other from Vajrayoginī, both in Munśīgañj district and both are now in Bangladesh National Museum. In each case, Gaṇeśa is represented at the bottom prostrate with a sword and a shield in hands, "evidently vanquished after a fight with the goddess."[30]

The examples of the Buddhist attempt to portray a Hindu deity in an undignified manner were very few in number and were almost of no significance at least in the arena of art activities. The thirteenth century began with the establishment of Turko-Afghan Muslim supremacy in Bengal. The subsequent eight centuries did not see any restoration of Hindu or Buddhist royal power. In

27. N.K. Bhaṭṭaśālī, *Iconography of the Buddhist and Brāhmaṇical Sculptures in Dacca Museum*, Dacca, 1929: 43 ff.
28. *Ibid.*, 34 ff.
29. *Ibid.*, 55 ff.
30. *Ibid.*, 58 ff.

the meantime the Buddhist community had almost totally withered away from Bengal, except a very small enclave in the south-east corner. The Hindu community flourished with all their religious practices and deities, but with lots of compromises and adjustments within itself compelled by the inner and external forces. The religious Hindu art continued responding to the realities of the time but without discarding the few elements of Buddhist art which were incorporated in its heydays till the twelfth century AD.

Bibliography

Bhaṭṭaśālī, N.K., *Iconography of the Buddhist and Brahmanical Sculptures in Dacca Museum*, Dacca, 1929.s

Dikshit, K.N., *Paharpur, Memoirs of the Archaeological Survey of India*, N0. 55, New Delhi, 1938.

Haque, Enamul, *Bengal Sculptures: Hindu Iconography till c. 1250 AD*, Dhaka, 1992.

———, *Chandraketugarh: A Treasure-House of Bengal Terracottas*, Dhaka, 2001.

Majumdar, R.C. (ed.), *History of Bengal*, vol. 1, Dacca University, Dacca, 1943.

Mukherji, R. and Maity, S.K., *Corpus of Bengal Inscriptions Bearing on History and Civilization of Bengal*, Calcutta, 1967.

Ray, Niharranjan, (reprint), *Bangalir Itihas: Adiparva* (in Bengali), Calcutta, 1993.

17

Sūrya-Candramaṇḍalas in the Art of Nepal

Gerd J.R. Mevissen

DURING the fourteenth century, the art of the Kāṭhmāṇḍu valley witnessed the rise of *maṇḍala*s depicting the sun god Sūrya or the moon god Candra as the principal figure. Although the worship of the sun god in Nepal dates back to the first millennium, as indicated by the existence of a few ancient Sūrya images,[1] it is only in the fourteenth century that *maṇḍala*s[2] were created in which the central figure, either Sūrya or Candra, is encircled by figures of the other eight planetary deities or *grahas*,[3] viz., Maṅgala (Mars), Budha (Mercury), Bṛhaspati (Jupiter), Śukra (Venus), Śani (Saturn), Rāhu (moon node, demon of eclipses) and Ketu (comet),[4] and in some cases by a number of additional astral deities such as *nakṣatra*s (lunar constellations), *āditya*s (solar gods), *kalā*s (personification of the moon's digits), *rāśi*s (zodiac signs), or *dikpāla*s (directional deities). This outburst of astral-inspired iconography relating to time and space took place not only in

1. For discussions on early Sūrya images from Nepal, cf. Pal/Bhattacharyya 1969: 9-20, esp. 9-10, Bangdel 1982: 46-51, Bangdel 1987: 151-52; Gail 2001: 59-63.
2. In the present context, the term *maṇḍala* is used for any representation in which a large central figure is surrounded by conceptually related smaller figures, no matter whether the layout of the representation is circular (as in the paintings or metal images), or half-circular, or even linear (as in many stone sculptures).
3. For another type of Nepalese Sūrya images in which the Sun god is accompanied by a multitude of deities other than *grahas*, see Pal/Bhattacharyya 1969: 14-15, 18-19, 29-30, figs. 5-6; Tchekhoff 1980: 97, *fig.* [3]; Śimkhada 1984a; Śimkhada 1984b: *fig.* 6; Bangdel 1987: 169, Abb. 121; Bangdel 1989: pls. 40, 105; Bangdel 1995: 98 sec. 5.5, 101 sec. 6.7, 129 sec. 22.7, 246 sec. 13.6, 255 sec. 19.1, 395 sec. 6.1.
4. For comprehensive studies on the imagery of the Indian planetary deities in general, and on the development of Rāhu and Ketu in particular, see Markel 1990, 1991, 1995.

the Hindu context, but also in the Buddhist sphere, where it eventually lead to the creation of a special and so far unexplained form of Buddhist *maṇḍala*s.

In the following I will present a survey of such circular representations. The 42 images (see Appendix) have been organized in three broad categories with regard to the central figure (Sūrya, Candra, Budha). They have further been subdivided into twelve groups according to (i) the religious context in which they appear, as indicated by the depiction of certain sectarian details in the images, (ii) the medium in which they are worked (stone, metal, painting), and (iii) the subsidiary deities that are represented (*graha*s and/or other astral deities). Special attention has been paid to the sequential order in which the remaining *graha*s are arranged around the central figure. The different iconographic concepts of the *graha* figures require a separate study and will be touched upon only cursorily.

Sūryamaṇḍalas (S) with Eight Graha Figures

Of the nineteen *sūryamaṇḍala*s listed in this category, five images (S10, S12, S13, S16, S17) bear dated inscriptions. The reading of the earliest one (S16) is uncertain (AD 1370? or 1379?) while the other dates range from AD 1462 (S10) to AD 1537 (S17).

STONE SŪRYAMAṆḌALAS WITHOUT INDICATION OF RELIGIOUS CONTEXT

Nine such sculptures[5] — four from Kāṭhmāṇḍu (S1-S4), three from Bhaktapur (S5-S7), one from Panauti (S8) and one from Pharping (S9) will be described below. With regard to their location within the layout of the urban space it is interesting to note that most of them are found in the south or south-east quarters of the cities (S2-S7) or of the valley (S8, S9), thus corresponding to the directional placement of the *sūryapīṭha*s (*navagraha-maṇḍala*s with Sūrya in the centre) in south Indian Śiva temples after the fourteenth century.

The first image (S1) is now in the National Museum, Kāṭhmāṇḍu (*Pl.* 17.1), probably dating from the fourteenth or fifteenth century. Sūrya is shown standing on a double-petalled lotus pedestal wearing boots. There is no indication of a chariot or horses. The remaining eight *graha*s, all seated and two-armed, flank the central figure on either side. Their order is clockwise, starting with Candra (without lotuses) at the bottom on the right side and continuing upwards with

5. In the descriptions, the terms "right" and "left" have always been used as viewed from the image and not from the observer, i.e., in the sense of "proper right" and "proper left."

Maṅgala (spear), Budha (bow and arrow), and Bṛhaspati (water jar), Śani (staff with globular top), Rāhu (large bust) and Ketu (snakehood and snake-tail; sword). Two flying *vidyādhara*s are depicted above the head of Sūrya, and two male attendants, Piṅgala and Daṇḍin, stand at the bottom on either side of the pedestal.

An image (S2) of roughly the same date is located in a courtyard at Purana Bhansar, Ombahaltol, south Kāṭhmāṇḍu (*Pl.* 17.2). It is part of a *pañcāyatana* arrangement of four freestanding subsidiary sculptures (Gaṇeśa, Devī, Sūrya, Skanda) around a *śiva-liṅga* in the centre. Sūrya is shown standing on a lotus wearing boots (?), accompanied by two female attendants holding *cāmara*s. At the bottom of the image the chariot is indicated by seven-winged horses driven by the seated charioteer Aruṇa, and beneath are the remnants of small seated figures of Piṅgala (right) and Daṇḍin (left) in a rocky landscape.[6] The surrounding *graha* figures, all two-armed and seated on lotus pedestals, are arranged in clockwise order, but in contrast to the previous image the sequence starts with Candra (crescent behind head) in the second position from below on the right side and continues upwards with Maṅgala (spear) and Budha (bow); on the left it runs from top to bottom with Bṛhaspati, Śukra, Śani and Rāhu (damaged); it ends with Ketu (snake-tailed and snakehooded) beneath Candra. Although the image itself does not show any detail pointing to the religious context, its location within a Śiva temple complex would suggest a Śaiva context.

Another image (S3) is located not far away in south Kāṭhmāṇḍu, in the large courtyard of Tebahal (*Pl.* 17.3). Sūrya is shown standing on his chariot, flanked by two female figures shooting arrows; his feet are concealed behind Aruṇa who directs the seven winged horses. Above Sūrya is an umbrella. The other *graha*s are arranged in the usual clockwise order (see S1). They are all seated, Maṅgala, Budha, Śani and Ketu, in aggressive poses. At the bottom, in the centre beneath the horses and above an inscription of six or seven lines, is an eight-petalled lotus bud, perhaps symbolizing the one wheel of Sūrya's chariot, flanked by two-armed demonic figures who shrink away from it.

A second, considerably damaged, image in Tebahal (S4) seems to be of a later date (*Pl.* 17.4). Sūrya is flanked by two arrow-shooting female figures; he is exceptionally shown seated in *padmāsana* on his chariot drawn by seven winged

6. Seated representations of Piṅgala and Daṇḍin are very rare. The two figures are now very mutilated but were almost completely intact when the photograph published by Bangdel (1987: 168, Abb. 120) was taken.

horses[7] directed by Aruṇa, and there is an umbrella above his head. Four of the remaining *graha* figures are preserved but only partially visible. Assuming the usual clockwise order they may be identified as Budha and Bṛhaspati on the right and Śukra and Śani on the left, respectively. The *graha*s are seated and seem to be two-armed, although Śani may also be four-armed.

The three images at Bhaktapur belong to the same type as the one in the National Museum (S1), the one from Parphing (S8) and the one from Panauti (S9), they all do not show Sūrya's chariot.

The image in the compound of the Tilamādhava Nārāyaṇa temple at Taumadhitol (S5) shows the sun god standing on a double-petalled lotus (*Pl.* 17.5), his feet are wearing boots. There is a large umbrella above his head. The eight remaining *graha*s, all two-armed and seated, are arranged in a peculiar combination of vertical and horizontal order: the sequence starts with Candra (two lotuses) at the upper right side and runs down to Maṅgala (spear) and Budha (bow and arrow), then continues on the left from the top downwards with Bṛhaspati, Śukra and Śani (staff with globular top); Rāhu appears at the bottom of the right side beneath Budha, and Ketu (snake-tailed, sword and shield) at bottom on the left beneath Śani. The image is only a short distance from the only known Nepalese stone frieze depicting the *navagraha*s in a row (the usual mode followed throughout the northern and eastern India), located in a *dhārā* (well) probably constructed in AD 1328 as part of the Viṣṇu temple.[8] The Sūrya image may date from the same period. Although no iconographic detail in the image itself does point to its religious context, the location would suggest a Vaiṣṇava context.

Not far away, in Bhelukhel in south Bhaktapur, is another *sūryamaṇḍala* (S6) of the fourteenth-fifteenth centuries (*Pl.* 17.6). Sūrya is shown standing, as are the surrounding *graha*s. All figures are two-armed. Sūrya's feet are mutilated, perhaps he is wearing boots. In contrast to the previous image there is no umbrella above his head. Some *graha* figures are damaged and only closer scrutinization can determine whether their order duplicates the combined vertical and horizontal arrangement of the previous image or is register-wise from top to bottom; in any case the sequence starts on the upper right side with Candra holding two lotuses

7. The heads of the animals seem to have ears implying that they are horses. However, it could also be possible that they are seven geese. In this case the image would represent Candra.
8. Tchekhoff 1980: 97, *fig.* [2]; Slusser 1982: 168, *fig.* 233; Bangdel 1995: 340-42, sec. 31.5-13.

and ends with Ketu, who is shown as a complete figure holding a sword in his right hand, on the lower left side.

The third image in Bhaktapur (S7) is now housed in a private shrine near a cinema compound (*Pl.* 17.7). Sūrya is shown standing barefooted beneath an umbrella, the remaining *graha*s are seated on double-petalled lotuses. Their order is register-wise reverse, starting with Candra on the upper left side and ending with Ketu on the lower right. Ketu is again shown as a complete human figure holding a sword in his left hand.

The well-known *sūryamaṇḍala* (S8) from the Śikhara (or Sekha or Śeṣa) Nārāyaṇa temple tank near Pharping in the south of the Kāṭhmāṇḍu valley, dating from the fourteenth century, was stolen in the early 1980s and again in October 1996 (*Pl.* 17.8). The standing figure of Sūrya, who is wearing boots, is flanked by the eight remaining *graha*s. They are shown seated and arranged in the usual clockwise order (see S1), starting with Candra (without lotuses) at the bottom on the right and ending with Ketu (snakehooded and snake-tailed) at the bottom left. A shallow lotus bud is incised above Sūrya's head, flanked by two (female?) *vidyādhara*s holding garlands.

The image from the Triveṇīghāṭ (S9) at Panauti was also stolen in the early 1980s (*Pl.* 17.9). It resembles the one from Bhelukhel, Bhaktapur (S6), in showing the *graha*s standing on lotus pedestals. Sūrya does not wear boots, his bare feet are visible. The sequential arrangement of the *graha*s follows the usual clockwise order (see S1). Bṛhaspati's figure is missing, and Ketu is shown as a full male human figure holding a sword (as in S6 and S7).

STONE SŪRYAMAṆḌALAS INDICATING ŚAIVA CONTEXT

Two images clearly point to a Śaiva context of origin. The first one (S10) is dated AD 1462; it is now in the National Art Gallery at Bhaktapur (*Pl.* 17.10). Sūrya is exceptionally shown seated (as in S4) behind Aruṇa and flanked by two female arrow-shooters. The seated *graha*s are arranged in the usual clockwise order (see S1). Interestingly, the snake-tailed figure of Ketu on the left side is symmetrically counter-balanced by a *nāga* figure on the opposite side holding the axle of Sūrya's chariot, drawn by seven winged horses. Two demons shrink away from a half lotus at the bottom. The apex is occupied by a *śiva-liṅga*, inserted between the figures of Bṛhaspati and Śukra.

The other image (S11) is located at Panauti, in a newly-built *parivāra* chapel to the west of the Indreśvara temple, probably dating to the fifteenth century (*Pl.* 17.11). Sūrya is shown seated in a chariot drawn by seven winged horses. He is flanked by two arrow-shooting female figures, and the lower part of his body is concealed by Aruṇa. The eight remaining *graha*s, all two-armed, are shown standing, with the two malevolent *graha*s, Maṅgala and Śani, in an aggressive posture. The sequential arrangement follows the usual clockwise order (see S1). A small *śiva-liṅga* surmounted by an umbrella is depicted above Sūrya's head, between Bṛhaspati and Śukra. Two frightened demonic figures are shown in the bottom corners.

METAL SŪRYAMAṆḌALAS INDICATING ŚAIVA CONTEXT

Proceeding to the metal images of *sūryamaṇḍala*s we know of four examples, all pointing to a Śaiva context of origin. The first is a gilt copper image (S12), dated AD 1480, now in an American private collection (*Pl.* 17.12). Sūrya is shown standing in a chariot drawn by seven winged horses directed by Aruṇa. On either side of the horses are two demonic figures. Sūrya is flanked by two standing attendants and two arrow-shooting figures, all female. Sūrya, Candra and Ketu are two-armed, the other *graha*s four-armed. Their sequential order resembles the one of S7 in being register-wise reverse: Listed by location on the face of a clock, we find Candra in the 1 o'clock position, Maṅgala at 11 o'clock, Budha at 2 o'clock, Bṛhaspati at 10 o'clock, Śukra at 3 o'clock, Śani at 9 o'clock, Rāhu at 4 o'clock and Ketu at 8 o'clock. All *graha*s are seated on their respective mounts: Candra on a goose, Maṅgala on a ram, the *vāhana*s of Budha, Bṛhaspati, Śukra and Śani are unclear, but the latter can be identified by his crippled right leg.[9] Rāhu is exceptionally depicted as a full figure including legs; Ketu rests with his snake-tail on a bird. The apex is embellished with a small *liṅga*, and just below that, in the 12 o'clock position, is an additional so far unidentified four-armed figure, seated on a lion-like animal.

The provenance and present location of the following two metal images is unknown. One of them (S13) is dated AD 1485, i.e., five years after the previous image, which it resembles in many respects, including the arrangement of the attendant figures (*Pl.* 17.13). However, the iconography of the *graha*s follows the usual Nepali pattern, regarding the number of hands (all are two-armed) and the *vāhana*s. The sequential order of the *graha*s is also the usual one (see S1),

9. On this special feature of Śani, see Mevissen 1997 and 2000.

running clockwise from Candra at 7.30 to Ketu at 4.30. As in the previous image (S12), an additional four-armed figure is seated on a lion (?) at 12 o'clock; the attribute in his upper left hand is clearly a *triśūla*. Apparently there is no *liṅga* at the apex.

The other *sūryamaṇḍala* (S14) is undated (*Pl.* 17.14). The iconography and sequential order of the *grahas* is identical with the previous one (S13), but there is a *liṅga* at the apex, while the unidentified four-armed figure is not represented.

The last image in this group (S15) is an interesting example in the National Museum, Kāṭhmāṇḍu (*Pl.* 17.15), perhaps dating from the eighteenth or nineteenth century. The *sūryamaṇḍala* is depicted on one face of a standard *dhvaja* having a wooden core mounted on a wooden shaft. The central Sūrya is flanked by two standing females holding *cāmaras*; he is seated behind Aruṇa on a chariot drawn by seven horses. The remaining eight *graha* figures are four-armed, except Candra who has only two arms like Sūrya. Ketu sits on his snake-tail. The sequential order is clockwise but differs from the one of S1 in starting with Candra in the 12 o'clock position. The *maṇḍala* on the reverse (or obverse) side of the *dhvaja* centres upon a six-faced and 12-armed figure of the war god Skanda-Kārttikeya riding his peacock *vāhana*. This feature would suggest that the *dhvaja* was once used in warfare, in which the constellation of the stars and eventual propitiation of the *navagrahas* plays an important role.[10] It also points to a Hindu (Śaiva) context of origin.

PAINTED SŪRYAMAṆḌALAS INDICATING ŚAIVA CONTEXT

Turning our attention to the few painted *sūryamaṇḍalas* that have surfaced so far,[11] we note that three are Śaiva and only one is Bauddha. The earliest belongs to the Zimmerman collection, New York (S16). It bears a dated inscription referring either to AD 1370 (?) or 1379 (?). The elaborate composition includes, in the periphery, figures of all the major and minor Hindu gods (like Śiva and Pārvatī, Brahmā, Gaṇeśa, Skanda, Durgā, *aṣṭadikpālas*, etc.), but apparently no figure of Viṣṇu. The central core of the *maṇḍala* depicts Sūrya seated on his chariot, flanked

10. I am thankful to Marianna Kropf, who has been working extensively on the *navagraha* rituals in Nepal, for this suggestion.

11. Slusser's statement (1982: 265), "Curiously, in Nepal there are no stone sculptures of Candra, but numerous *maṇḍala* paintings; Sūrya who has so many stone sculptures, has no *maurya* who has so many stone sculptures, has no *maṇḍalas*", is misleading, even if the term *maṇḍala* is applied only to the painted *maṇḍalas*.

by two *cāmara*-bearing and two arrow-shooting females. He is surrounded by the eight remaining *graha*s in the first (inner) circle, all seated on *vāhana*s and, except Sūrya, Rāhu and Ketu, all four-armed. Their order is quite unusual and may be termed "modified clockwise": starting with Candra on a goose at 1.30, the sequence continues with Maṅgala on a ram at 3 o'clock, then moves to the opposite with Budha on a lion at 9 o'clock, continues clockwise with Bṛhaspati on an elephant at 10.30 and Śukra on a horse at 12 o'clock, then runs down vertically to Śani on a tortoise at 6 o'clock, continues anti-clockwise with Rāhu on a lion-like animal at 4.30, and ends with Ketu on a *mṛga* at 7.30. The second circle contains the 28 goddesses of the constellations *nakṣatra*, and in the corner spaces occur the 12 zodiacal signs *rāśi*, several auspicious signs, a number of other deities (e.g., Agastya), and again Candra and Sūrya. In the row above the central core are the twelve solar *āditya*s, each seated on a green horse and resembling the central Sūrya figure.

Another painting (S17), dated AD 1537, is now in a Dutch private collection. It differs from the previous one in the sequential order of the *graha*s, which runs clockwise starting with Candra at the bottom. The second circle accommodates the 12 *āditya*s, while the third circle includes the twenty-eight *nakṣatras*. The four corner spaces are again filled with the 12 *rāśi*s, starting with Aries at the bottom on the right side. The *aṣṭadikpāla* appear in a row beneath the central core. Another difference is the presence of Viṣṇu on Garuḍa in the upper left corner space, though the other gods in the painting are basically Śaiva.

The latest painting in this group (S18) is in the Museum of Indian Art, Berlin (*Pl.* 17.16). It may date from the seventeenth century. The top row shows Śiva and Pārvatī in the centre, flanked on their right by Brahmā and Sarasvatī, on their left by Viṣṇu and Lakṣmī, and at the extreme ends are dancing Gaṇeśa and Skanda. Sūrya is seated in the centre, encircled in the first ring by the 12 *āditya*s. Another unique feature is that the second circle contains the complete group of *navagraha*s instead of only the remaining eight *graha*s, all apparently without *vāhana*s. With the exception of Sūrya, who is inserted in the 8.30 position, the other *graha*s are arranged in exactly the same unusual "modified clockwise" sequential order, which has already been noticed in the Zimmerman painting (S16). The third circle contains 27 *nakṣatra*s instead of 12 *rāśi*s in clockwise order, starting with Aries at the top centre. The surrounding square band shows the *aṣṭadikpāla*s in the cardinal and intermediate directions, starting with Indra at the top centre.

PAINTED SŪRYAMAṆḌALAS INDICATING BUDDHIST CONTEXT

The small, sixteenth-century *maṇḍala* (S19) in the Ford Collection, USA, is the only *sūryamaṇḍala* that can be assigned to a Buddhist context,[12] as indicated by the figures of the five transcendental Buddhas *pañca-tathāgata* in the upper row, with Vairocana in the central position. Sūrya, who is shown standing on a chariot exceptionally drawn by only five-winged horses,[13] is encircled by the remaining eight *graha*s, arranged in clockwise order starting with Candra at the bottom (as in S17). Except Budha, Śukra and Rāhu, the *graha*s are shown seated on their respective *vāhanas*. The second circle accommodates the 12 *ādityas*, each seated on a horse. The corner spaces are filled with the eight auspicious symbols of the Buddhists *aṣṭamaṅgala*.

Summing up the survey of the *sūryamaṇḍala*s, it has to be pointed out that the majority of the 19 images shows signs of Hindu, especially Śaiva affiliation (nine items), whereas only one image is certainly of Buddhist origin. Two different types of representing the central Sūrya image can be discerned, with the chariot (S2-S4, S10-S19) or with it (S1, S5-S9).

Different modes of arranging the sequence of the *graha*s have been found, of which the clockwise order is the most commonly used, though in four different variations with regard to the starting point of the sequence. With the exception of the Berlin *maṇḍala* (S18), the number of the surrounding *graha*s is usually eight, and that of the *nakṣatra*s 28.

It should also be noted that the figures of the solar *āditya*s appear only in the painted *sūryamaṇḍala*s, and are never exclusive rather they are together with other groups of astral deities. In contrast to a considerable number of stone sculptures from Bengal that show a central Sūrya figure encircled by the 11 remaining *āditya*s, but not by other astral deities,[14] i.e., only by iconographically identical figures of purely solar character, not a single image of this type, neither

12. A painted Buddhist *maṇḍala* with Sūrya surrounded by eight *graha*s from Kharakhoto, China, now in the Hermitage's collection, St. Petersburg (Samosyuk 1997/98b), indicates that such *maṇḍala*s were already in use in the Tangut empire before the fourteenth century.

13. Such a deviation from the general rule is in rare cases also found with Candra images; see, e.g., Bangdel (1995: 299, sec. 4.4) for a Candra on a chariot drawn by only five geese, at Bhaktapur, *c.* seventeenth century.

14. See, e.g., Bhaṭṭaśāli, 1929: pls. LVII. b, LX, LXI. a, LXI. b.

in sculpture nor in painting, has been reported so far from Nepal.[15]

Candramaṇḍalas (C)

Generally, the *candramaṇḍalas* strongly resemble the *sūryamaṇḍalas* in almost every respect including the attendant figures. Sculptural representations differ only in the nature of the animals that draw the chariot, seven geese in the case of Candra instead of seven horses in the case of Sūrya. Since Sūrya's horses are almost invariably depicted with wings, it is sometimes difficult to distinguish them from Candra's *haṁsas* (e.g., S4). In paintings, however, the deities are easily distinguishable by their colour, Sūrya being red and Candra white.[16]

The 18 Candra images encircled by the astral deities follow two different concepts: they are (A) either accompanied by the eight remaining *graha* figures (14 items), or (B) by anthropomorphic representations of the *kalās*, the digits of the moon cycle (four items). The latter concept, i.e., encircling a central Candra figure only by iconographically identical figures of purely lunar character and not by the other astral deities, is exclusively found in *candramaṇḍalas* from Nepal and has no parallel in the Nepalese *sūryamaṇḍalas* (*supra*).

Seven images bear dated inscriptions (C3, C4, C6, C9, C10, C12, C15), ranging from AD 1426 (C3) to AD 1669 (C12). The reading of the date of one image (C6) is uncertain (AD 1416 or 1426 or 1456).

Candramaṇḍalas with Eight Graha Figures

STONE CANDRAMAṆḌALAS WITHOUT INDICATION OF RELIGIOUS CONTEXT

Two images belong to this group. One is located in the courtyard of Tebahal, Kāṭhmāṇḍu (C1). It may be contemporary with one of the *sūryamaṇḍalas* in the same location (S3), which it resembles strongly in showing an eight-petalled lotus bud and two demonic figures at the bottom (*Pl.* 17.17). Candra stands in a chariot drawn by seven geese directed by a charioteer and flanked by two arrow-shooting females. Above his head is an umbrella with garlands. The remaining eight *grahas* are all two-armed and seated without *vāhanas*. Their sequential arrangement

15. A possible exception may be a *c.* nineteenth-century stone sculpture of Sūrya from Lele, in the south of the Kāṭhmāṇḍu valley (illustrated in Bangdel 1995: 430, see. 1.7), which shows 11 (mostly twelve-petalled) lotus buds on the inner rim of the back-slab, perhaps symbolizing the 11 remaining *ādityas*. For the symbolic representation of astral deities, see Mevissen 2003.

16. Cf. Slusser 1982: 265. See also note 11.

follows the usual clockwise order of the *sūryamaṇḍala*s (see S1), here starting with Sūrya at the bottom on the right side and ending with Ketu on the left.

The second image (C2) hails from the Kumbheśvara temple tank at Patan (*Pl.* 17.18). It strongly resembles the previous image in every respect, including the attendant figures, the rendering of the bottom register and the sequential arrangement of the *graha*s. Its location might suggest a Śaiva context of origin.

STONE CANDRAMAṆḌALAS INDICATING ŚAIVA CONTEXT

Two sculptures show a *liṅga* at the apex, thus pointing clearly to a Śaiva context. The one in the Patan Museum (C3) is dated AD 1426 (*Pl.* 17.19). Candra is shown seated in *padmāsana* behind the charioteer on his chariot drawn by seven geese; he is flanked by two *cāmara*-bearing and two arrow-shooting females. The sequential order of the surrounding two-armed *graha* figures is clockwise (as S15), starting with Sūrya on a horse in the top position (beneath the *liṅga*) and continuing with Maṅgala on a ram, Budha (no *vāhana*), Bṛhaspati on an elephant, Śukra on a horse (? damaged), Śani (damaged), Rāhu on a fire pit, and Ketu on a *makara*. At the bottom of the image is an inscription with a ram reclining in a rocky landscape carved in the centre.

The provenance and present location of the other image in this group (C4) is unknown (*Pl.* 17.20). It is dated AD 1429, three years after the previous one. Candra appears to be seated behind the charioteer, flanked by two arrow-shooting females. The chariot is drawn by seven geese. The sequential order of the two-armed *graha* figures is similar to the previous image (C3). They are, however, shown without *vāhana*s. There seems to be a very small *liṅga* at the apex above the figure of Sūrya.

METAL CANDRAMAṆḌALAS INDICATING ŚAIVA CONTEXT

Only one metal image (C5) is known that clearly shows Śaiva affiliation (*Pl.* 17.21). Its provenance and present location is unknown. Candra is shown standing behind the charioteer, flanked by two *cāmara*-bearing and two arrow-shooting females. The chariot is drawn by seven geese, flanked by two demonic figures. Above Candra is a prominent *liṅga*. The sequential arrangement of the *graha*s follows the usual clockwise order (C1). The *graha*s are two-armed and seated on *vāhana*s (except Budha, Śukra and Rāhu). Sūrya's and Ketu's (?) figures are missing, Maṅgala sits on a ram, Bṛhaspati on an elephant, and Śani on a tortoise.

PAINTED CANDRAMAṆḌALAS INDICATING BUDDHIST CONTEXT

At least nine such paintings are presently known, thus forming the most numerous group of *candramaṇḍalas*. Each example depicts the *pañca-tathāgatas* in the top register.

The earliest one (C6), now in the Zimmerman Collection, New York, bears a dated inscription either referring to AD 1416, 1426 or 1456. Candra is shown seated on his chariot accompanied by the charioteer and two arrow-shooting females. Exceptionally, he is of dark grey/green complexion. The inner circle accommodates the remaining eight *grahas* in clockwise order, starting with Sūrya at the bottom (similar to S17); all are two-armed and seated on *vāhanas*. The second circle shows 16 *kalā* figures, the third circle 40 deities, eight of which can be identified as the *aṣṭadikpālas* placed in the cardinal and intermediate directions. In the corner spaces are four of the five Buddhist protective goddesses *pañca-rakṣā* and the 12 *rāśis*.

Another painting (C7), considerably damaged along the top, is undated though roughly contemporaneous with the first one. It is now in the Los Angeles County Museum of Art. Candra, of white complexion, is seated on his chariot accompanied by the charioteer, two attending and two arrow-shooting females. The order and iconography of the *grahas* in the first circle is similar to the previous one (C6), but there is only one further circle filled with figures of the 28 *nakṣatras*. In the corner spaces are four Buddhist deities, each flanked by two of the *aṣṭadikpālas*.

A painting in the Jucker collection, Basel, is even more reduced, having only a single circle, which is occupied by the *grahas* (C8). Their iconography and sequential arrangement is the same as above (C6). The painting has been assigned to the end of the fifteenth century.

The next two paintings resemble each other strongly regarding the internal structure of the *maṇḍala*. Their inscribed dates differ by only three years. The one in the Prince of Wales Museum, Mumbai, is dated AD 1522 (C9). The four circles are occupied (from the inner to the outer one, respectively) by the eight remaining *grahas*, 16 *kalās*, 28 *nakṣatras*, and 40 deities and symbols including the *aṣṭadikpālas* and perhaps the *rāśis*. The painting in the Museum of Asiatic Art, Amsterdam, is dated AD 1525 (C10). The contents of the two inner circles are the same as in the previous one. However, the third circle has 36 figures, viz., eight *dikpālas* and 28 *nakṣatras*, and the fourth circle depicts 24 symbols including the 12 *rāśis* and the eight auspicious symbols *aṣṭamaṅgala*.

Another *candramaṇḍala* (C11) in the Zimmerman collection, New York, is undated; it has been assigned to the third quarter of the sixteenth century. As in the previous examples, the first circle contains the eight *graha*s in the usual clockwise order (see C6). The second circle accommodates 40 deities including the *aṣṭadikpālas*.

The present location of a painting dated AD 1669 (C12) is unknown (*Pl.* 17.22). Candra is shown seated on his chariot, accompanied by the charioteer, two attending *cāmara*-bearing and two arrow-shooting figures, all apparently male. Another quite unusual feature is the *makara-toraṇa* under which Candra is seated.[17] The *graha*s occupy the first circle, all seated but apparently without *vāhanas*, arranged in the usual clockwise order (C6). The second circle contains 16 seated figures of different colours, some of them female, all showing *abhaya-mudrā* with their right hand and holding a flower in their left, which is placed on the left knee.[18] They may or may not represent the 16 *kalā*s. The third circle is filled with figures of the 28 *nakṣatra*s.

Two more paintings of *candramaṇḍala*s (C13, C14) have been reported, but since they have not been published as to my knowledge, nothing can be said about their iconography and arrangement.

Candramaṇḍalas with Kalā Figures

STONE CANDRAMAṆḌALAS WITHOUT INDICATION OF RELIGIOUS CONTEXT

Only one stone sculpture depicts Candra encircled by 16 *kalā* figures, the personified digits of the moon cycle (C15). The image is dated AD 1468 and kept in the National Art Gallery at Bhaktapur (*Pl.* 17.23). The 16 surrounding figures resemble the central Candra in being two-armed and holding a lotus in each hand. Candra is shown standing on a chariot accompanied by his charioteer and two arrow-shooting females. The chariot is drawn by seven geese. Below the chariot, above the socle bearing a six line inscription, is a large centrally placed lotus bud flanked by two-armed demons.

PAINTED CANDRAMAṆḌALAS INDICATING BUDDHIST CONTEXT

Three paintings belong to this group. The earliest is in the Jucker Collection, Basel, dating from the fifteenth century (C16). Candra is of white complexion and shown

17. Similar *makara-toraṇa* appear also above the central Buddha figure in B1, B2 and B3.

18. They strongly resemble the 16 seated figures in the second circle of B1, B2 and B3.

seated on a chariot drawn by seven geese, accompanied by two attendants and the charioteer. Candra is encircled by only 15 white-complexioned *kalā* figures, each seated on a goose. Seven appear on white ground composed of two superimposed white squares, presumably symbolizing the *śukla-pakṣa* (bright half of the lunar month), and eight on the surrounding blue ground, presumably symbolizing the *kṛṣṇa-pakṣa* (dark half of the lunar month).

Though the depiction of only 15 *kalās* could be regarded as the correct mode of representing the *kalās*, since Candra himself is considered as the 16th digit; this number of *kalās* is found only in this painting. The place of the 16th *kalā* is occupied by a white *caitya*, just above Candra. The second circle accommodates the 28 *nakṣatras*, the outer circle 40 deities including the *aṣṭadikpālas* and the *aṣṭanāgas*. The *grahas* are not represented. In the top row of the painting are the *pañca-tathāgatas* with Vairocana in the centre, corresponding to the bottom row showing the *pañca-rakṣā* goddesses with Mahāpratisarā in the centre.

Another painting in the Jucker Collection may be assigned to the late seventeenth or even the eighteenth century (C17). Its internal structure is much simpler than the previous one. Candra is surrounded by only one circle containing the 16 *kalā* figures without *vāhanas*. In the corner spaces are two flying winged figures (above) and two fleeing armed demons (below). The top row is occupied by the *pañca-tathāgatas* seated on their respective *vāhanas* with Vairocana on a lion in the centre.

A *candramaṇḍala* painting (C18) of unknown location (*Pl.* 17.24) resembles the previous one (C17) so strongly, regarding the internal structure, style, iconography, and size, that one is tempted to suggest it having been painted in the same atelier, or even by the same hand. The only, though insignificant, difference is the absence of *vāhanas* below the figures of the *pañca-tathāgatas* in the top register.

From our survey of the *candramaṇḍalas* it is obvious that, in contrast to the *sūryamaṇḍalas*, most of them (12 items) belong to the Buddhist context, while only three items clearly show the Śaiva affiliation, and another three items do not indicate their religious context.

Buddhamaṇḍalas (B)

After having examined all the regular *candramaṇḍalas*, we now come to our last category comprising four rather enigmatic *maṇḍalas*. Although in at least two of these paintings the central figure is shown riding in a chariot drawn by seven geese *haṁsaratha*, i.e., the usual chariot of Candra, it is not the moon god who is represented but a Buddha displaying the *dharma-cakra-mudrā*.

The identity of this Buddha figure is not clear: the *dharma-cakra-mudrā* would point to Vairocana, the transcendental Buddha of Light, though the light red complexion in at least one painting[19] does not coincide with his usual white body colour.[20] Another possible identification would be the Buddha Tejaprabha who in Central Asian paintings is often surrounded by the planetary deities.[21] However, the cult of the Buddha Tejaprabha appears to be confined exclusively to Central Asia, and no images (nor any *sādhanas*) of this Buddha seem to have been found so far from India or Nepal. Furthermore, in the images he does not display the *dharma-cakra-mudrā* but has his hands either joined in *samādhi-mudrā* holding a sun wheel, or the right hand displays the *vyākhyāna-mudrā* while the left is in the lap holding a sun wheel;[22] and also his complexion is red rather than white. Further research is necessary to identify the central Buddha figure properly and to explain the significance of these paintings.

PAINTED BUDDHAMAṆḌALAS WITH NAVAGRAHAS

The earliest painting in this group (B1) is in the Musée Guimet, Paris, dating from the early fifteenth century. The Buddha in the centre, of light red complexion, is seated on a chariot drawn by seven geese and surmounted by a *makara-toraṇa* flanked by two lotus buds.[23] He is accompanied by two attending *bodhisattvas* but not by the two arrow-shooting figures that are usually found on either side of the central deity in most *sūrya* and *candramaṇḍalas*. The eight lotus petals constituting the inner circle accommodate the nine *graha* figures: Sūrya and Candra are placed side by side in the bottom position, but in reverse order; the other *grahas* follow in the usual clockwise order (C6, etc.). All the *grahas* are

19. Unfortunately only B1 has been published in colour. The complexion of the central Buddha figures in B2, B3 and B4 is unknown.
20. Some forms of Vairocana can also be of golden or yellow complexion; cf. Mallmann 1975: 393.
21. For *maṇḍalas* of the Buddha Tejaprabha surrounded by planetary and astral deities, indicating the importance of the planet cult in the Buddhist art of the Tangut empire (China) in the eleventh and twelfth centuries, see Piotrovsky 1993: 228-31, no. 57, col. Pl.; Samosyuk 1997/98a: 356-58, figs. 1-4a; Menzies 2001: 80, no. 54, col. Pl., detail p. 5; Sen 1999: figs. 17, 20, 21, 22, 23.
22. Cf. Samosyuk 1997/98a: 360.
23. A similar *makara-toraṇa* is also found above the central Candra figure in C12. In the same painting, the *cāmara*-bearing attendants are apparently male figures, somehow resembling *bodhisattvas*.

seated on their respective *vāhana*s. The second circle contains 16 figures of different complexion, some of which may be female. As far as can be judged from the worn-out details, they all hold their right hand in front of the breast while the left hand is placed on the lap.[24] They apparently do not represent the *kalā*s, but perhaps a group of 16 *bodhisattva*s. The outer circle is sub-divided into eight sections, each section containing one of the *aṣṭadikpāla*s flanked by two (female?) deities. The small rosettes in the corner spaces, now almost completely rubbed off, may once have contained the symbols of the twelve *rāśi*s.

The present location of the second painting (B2) is unknown (*Pl.* 17.25). It may date from the sixteenth century and is more elaborate than the previous one. The central Buddha figure, of light complexion, is again shown seated below a *makara-toraṇa*, but the two attending *bodhisattva*s are not depicted, and the quality of the photograph does not permit us to state with certainty if there is a *haṁsaratha* beneath the double-petalled lotus seat of the Buddha or not. The first circle contains the *navagraha*s in the same clockwise order as above. The following square band shows 16 figures of different colour, probably the same deities as in the previous painting as can be judged from their hand gestures. The whole central part of the painting is again enclosed by two circles, the inner one of which accommodates 28 seated figures, probably the *nakṣatra*s. Each of the eight sections of the outer circle shows one of the *aṣṭadikpāla*s flanked by four other deities.

The third *maṇḍala* (B3) is also of unknown location (*Pl.* 17.26). Its structure and iconographic programme strongly resemble the Paris painting (B1), though there are some differences. The first circle contains the *navagraha*s in the usual clockwise order, but Sūrya and Candra are not reversed. The second circle shows the same 16 figures, while the third circle is filled with 36 deities, viz., eight *dikpāla*s and 28 *nakṣatra*s. The *pañca-tathāgata*s with Vairocana in the centre in the top register are counter-balanced by the *pañca-rakṣa*s with Mahāpratisarā in the centre in the bottom register.

The last painting (B4), again of unknown location, differs considerably from the three previous ones (*Pl.* 17.27). It may date from the late nineteenth or even the twentieth century. It shows the central Buddha not seated on a chariot, but on a white cushion resembling a moon cycle. There is neither a *makara-toraṇa* above him nor is he flanked by two *bodhisattva*s. The first circle depicts eight seated figures, probably *bodhisattva*s. The second circle is sub-divided into ten

24. They thus resemble the appearance of the 16 figures in the second circle of C12.

sections containing the *navagrahas* in the usual clockwise order plus an additional, hitherto unidentified white figure at the end of the sequence. This enigmatic figure is Janma, a pseudo-planetary deity who seems to represent the astrological components which are defined by the birth time of a person, and who often appears in Newār ritual texts as the final member of the group of *navagrahas*. He may also symbolize the astrological essence of the nine conventional *grahas*.[25] Interestingly, from the eighteenth century onwards such a white figure is invariably found at the end of *navagraha* groups in Nepalese paintings commemorating the *bhīmaratha*, a rite celebrated when a person reaches the age of 77 years, seven months and seven days.[26] The chariot procession depicted at the bottom of our painting does relate to this ritual, for which paintings are regularly commissioned even today.

Conclusion

Summing up our survey, it has to be pointed out that the high time of *sūrya* and *candramaṇḍalas* extends from the fourteenth through the sixteenth centuries (34 out of 42 items), though the tradition continues up to modern times. Most of the *sūryamaṇḍalas* originated in Hindu, especially Śaiva contexts, whereas the *candramaṇḍalas* are predominantly Buddhist. A strong connection between the Buddhism and the Candra is also indicated by the enigmatic *buddhamaṇḍalas* presented in the last group, which came into vogue from the fifteenth century onwards. Certain iconographic details, e.g., the strong resemblance of the 16 figures in the second circle of the *candramaṇḍala* C12 and the *buddhamaṇḍalas* B1, B2 and B3 or the presence of the five Buddhist protective goddesses *pañca-rakṣā* in the *candramaṇḍalas* C6 and C16 and the *buddhamaṇḍala* B3, establish further links between the *candra* and the *buddhamaṇḍalas*. Future research might explain the connection between the preaching Buddha and the *grahas*, and especially between the Buddha and the moon god, whose goose-drawn chariot is assumed by him.

Most *maṇḍalas* depict the *grahas* as subsidiary deities. In addition, certain groups of other astral divinities occur : in the painted *sūryamaṇḍalas* we often find the 12 solar *ādityas* (S16, S17, S18, S19), while many *candramaṇḍalas* include

25. I am thankful to Marianna Kropf for this information, which is based on her recent research on Nepalese ritual texts dealing with *graha* worship.

26. See Mevissen forthcoming : chapter 4. The tenth figure is also depicted at the end of the *navagraha* panel above the door lintel of the Nepalese temple in Vārāṇasī, which was built in the middle of the nineteenth century.

the 16 lunar *kalās*, both in paintings (C6, C9, C10, C16, C17, C18) and in stone sculpture (C15). The constellations *nakṣatra*, usually numbering 28 (with one exception: S18), the 12 zodiacal signs *rāśis*, and the eight guardians of the directions *aṣṭadikpāla* occur in a number of images of all the three types *nakṣatras*: S16, S17, S18, C7, C9, C10, C12, C16, B2, B3; *rāśis*: S16, S17, S18, C6, C9?, C10, B1?; *aṣṭadikpālas*: S16, S17, S18, C6, C7, C9, C10, C11, C16, B1, B2, B3.

An additional, so far unidentified deity is found within the group of *grahas* in two metal *sūryamaṇḍalas* of the fifteenth century (S12, S13) and in one late *buddha-maṇḍala* (B4). According to some recently surfaced ritual texts the additional figure in B4 most probably represents Janma, a deity based on astrological concepts, who occurs regularly in paintings, and rarely in wood carving, from the eighteenth century onwards. Further research is required to verify whether this deity has already been depicted in the early *sūryamaṇḍalas* (S12, S13).

As regards the arrangement of the *graha* figures, most often we notice a clockwise order in all the three categories. The sequence usually follows the temporal order of the planets based on the Western seven-day week calendrical system, which was introduced in India from the third century onwards.[27] Two painted *sūryamaṇḍalas* (S16 and S18) differ considerably from the usual scheme. In both of them, the sequence is interrupted by unexpected "jumps" to the opposite side, which cannot be explained satisfactorily on the basis of the temporal order. It somehow reminds one of astrological birth charts in which the planets can also be placed in certain angles from each other, including oppositions. The internal structure of these two paintings, however, suggests that they can certainly not be understood as duplicating astrological birth charts.[28] On the other hand, at the present state of our knowledge it would be unwise to rule out completely that the two *maṇḍalas* might have been influenced to some extent by astrological concepts.

Acknowledgement

I would like to thank Dr. Bharat Rawat, Kāṭhmāṇḍu, for his help in studying the images S1 and S15 in the National Museum of Nepal and for the permission to publish them.

---

27. Cf. Markel 1995: 69-84.

28. Since in astrology Rāhu and Ketu symbolize the ascending and descending moon nodes, they are always placed in opposition to each other in the birth charts. This is not the case in S16 and S18.

Appendix

List of Sūrya- and Candramaṇḍalas from Nepal

I. *Sūryamaṇḍalas* (S) with eight *graha* figures (19 items).

1. Stone images without indication of religious context (9 items).

(S1) Kāṭhmāṇḍu, National Museum, 75 × 56 × 28 cm, fourteenth/fifteenth century; unpublished? (*Pl.* 17.1).

(S2) Kāṭhmāṇḍu, Purana Bhansar, Ombaaltol, 71 × 56 cm, fourteenth/fifteenth century; Publ. : Slusser 1982: pl. 438; Bangdel 1987: 168, Abb. 120; (*Pl.* 17.2)

(S3) Kāṭhmāṇḍu, Tebahal, 84 × 46 cm, *c.* fifteenth century; Publ. : Bangdel 1995: 111, sec. 12.6 (*Pl.* 17.3).

(S4) Kāṭhmāṇḍu, Tebahal, fifteenth/sixteenth century; unpublished? (*Pl.* 17.4).

(S5) Bhaktapur, Taumadhitol, Tilamādhava Nārāyaṇa temple complex, 81 × 69 cm, fourteenth/fifteenth century; Publ. : Slusser 1982: fig. 436-37; Bangdel 1995: 339, sec. 31.1 (*Pl.* 17.5).

(S6) Bhaktapur, Bhelukhel, 58 × 48 cm, fourteenth/fifteenth century; Publ.: Bangdel 1995: 298, sec. 3.1-2 (*Pl.* 17.6).

(S7) Bhaktapur, private shrine near cinema compound, fourteenth-fifteenth century; Publ.: Deva 1984: pl. 70. B; Nagar 1995: pl. 59; Srivastava 2000: 94-95, fig. (left) (*Pl.* 17.7).

(S8) Formerly Pharping, Śikhara (or Sekha or Śeṣa) Nārāyaṇa temple tank, stolen in the early 1980s and again in October 1996, *c.* fourteenth century; Publ.: Pal/Bhattacharyya 1969: 18-19, 29-30, figs. 10-11; Pruscha 1975: 190-191, photo 7; Detmold/Rubel 1979: fig. opp. p. 101; Schick 1989: 30, Abb. 106; Bangdel 1989: pls. 200-01; Höfer 1991: 128, col.pl.; Schick 1998: 55, 101, pl. 68 (*Pl.* 17.8).

(S9) Formerly Panauti, Triveṇīghāṭ, stolen in the early 1980s, height. 66 cm, *c.* fourteenth century; Publ.: Bangdel 1989: pl. 133 (*Pl.* 17.9).

2. Stone images indicating Śaiva context (2 items)

(S10) Bhaktapur, National Art Gallery, 66 × 41 cm, AD 1462; Publ.: Bangdel 1995: 327, sec. 24.4 (*Pl.* 17.10).

(S11) Panauti, Indreśvara temple compound, 78 × 70 cm, *c.* fifteenth century; Publ.: Macdonald/Stahl 1979: 55, fig. 42; Gail 1980a: fig. 18; Gail 1980b: fig. 19; Toffin 1984: 257, fig. 77; Bangdel 1995: 443, sec. 4.4 (*Pl.* 17.11).

3. Metal images indicating Śaiva context (4 items)

(S12) Michael Douglas Collection, USA, formerly on loan to the Los Angeles County Museum of Art (TR. 6847.1), 34.1 × 22.5 × 13 cm, AD 1480, reportedly dedicated by the grandsons-in-law of Yakṣa Malla; Publ.: Alsop 1986: fig. 8 (*Pl.* 17.12).

(S13) Prese Kāṭhmāṇḍu nt location unknown, height. 37.8 cm, NS 605 — AD 1485; Publ.: South NY 25.3.1999: lot 42 (*Pl.* 17.13).

(S14) Present location unknown, height. 27.3 cm, *c.* seventeenth century; Publ.: Chri NY 3.10.1990: lot 166; South NY 30.11.1994: lot 97; Mevissen 1997: 129, pl. 10.8 (*Pl.* 17.14).

(S15) Kāṭhmāṇḍu, National Museum, *dhvaja* with wooden core and shaft, total length 220 cm, diameter 50 cm, eighteenth-nineteenth century?: unpublished? (*Pl.* 17.15).

4. Paintings indicating Śaiva context (3 items)

(S16) Zimmerman Family Collection, New York, 92.1 × 53.3 cm, 1370 (?) or 1379 (?) AD; Publ.:

Pal 1978: 75-76, fig. 82 (ca. 1400); Pal 1991: 70-71, 192, col. Pl. 33 (1379?); Pal 1992: fig. 4 (1370-9); Leidy/Thurman 1997: 75, 146, no. 14 (about 1379), (*col. Pls.*).

(S17) Private collection, Netherlands, NS 657 — AD 1537; Publ.: Van der Wee (1995): 138-141, (*fig.* 65).

(S18) Museum of Indian Art, Berlin (inv. No. MIK I 10013), 102 × 77.5 cm; *c.* seventeenth century; Publ.: Thomsen (1977): col. Pl. 25; MIKB 1986: 80-81, no. 277 (not ill.); MIKB 2000: 130-131, no. 198 (b/w. ill.) (*Pl.* 17.16).

5. **Painting indicating Buddhist context** (1 item)

(S19) Ford Collection, USA, 48.3 × 41.3 cm, *c.* sixteenth century; Publ.: Ray 1986: 202, 204, col. Pl. 16; Pal 2001: 220-221, no. 128, col. Pl.

II. *Candramaṇḍalas* (C) (18 items)

II. A. *Candramaṇḍalas* with eight *graha* figures (14 items)

6. **Stone images without indication of religious context** (2 items)

(C1) Kāṭhmāṇḍu, Tebahal, fourteenth/fifteenth century; unpublished? (*Pl.* 17.17)

(C2) Patan, reportedly at Kumbheśvara temple tank, sixteenth/seventeenth century; Publ.: Banerji 1972: pl. I; Deva 1984: pl. 68B (*Pl.* 17.18).

7. **Stone images indicating Śaiva context** (2 items)

(C3) Patan, Patan Museum (inv. No. SS 335), ht. 55 cm, AD 1426; Publ.: Slusser 2002: 115, col. Pl (*Pl.* 17.19).

(C4) Present location unknown, ht. 57 cm, NS 549 — AD 1429; Publ.: Soth Lon 15.6.1987: lot 140 (*Pl.* 17.20).

8. **Metal image indicating Śaiva context** (1 item)

(C5) Present location unknown, ht. 25.4 cm, *c.* sixteenth century; Publ.: Soth Lon 12.12.1977: lot 157; Mevissen 1997: 130, pl. 10.9 (*Pl.* 17.21).

9. **Paintings indicating Buddhist context** (9 items)

(C6) Zimmerman Family Collection, New York, 53.3 × 43 cm; NS 536 or 546 or 576 = 1416 or 1426 or 1456 AD; Publ.: Pal 1978: *fig.* 81 (1426); Rawson 1978: 148, *fig.* 123 (sixteenth century); Bangdel 1987: 324, Abb. 252 (1416); Mevissen 1989: cat. M. IV.A.4, Abb. 123; Pal 1991: 72-73, col. pl. 35 (ca. 1450; Alsop in App. I, p. 192: 1456?); Pal 1992: 39, *fig.* 5 (*ca.* 1450).

(C7) Los Angeles County Museum of Art (inv. No. M.83.113), 68 × 59.7 cm, first half of fifteenth century; Publ.: Pal 1985: 63 col. pl. P12 (detail), 208 b/w illustrations (complete).

(C8) Jucker Collection, Basel, 55 × 35 cm, the second half of fifteenth century; Publ.: Kreijger 1999: 40-41, col. pl. 7 [a,b].

(C9) Prince of Wales Museum, Mumbai, 80 × 63.5 cm, NS 642 — AD 1522; Publ.: Pal 1967b: 9-10, *fig.* 10; Pal/Bhattacharyya 1969: 30-31 (*fig.* 14).

(C10) Museum van Aziatische Kunst/Rijksmuseum, Amsterdam (inv. no. MAK 1246), NS 645 — AD 1525; Publ.: Pal 1967a: 5-9, 32-34, *fig.* 1; Pal 1967b: 9-10, fig. 11; Pal/Bhattacharyya 1969: 30-31, fig. 15; Kooij 1978: 33, pl. XLVIII.

(C11) Zimmerman Family Collection, New York, 61 × 48.3 cm, *c.* third quarter of sixteenth century; Publ.: Pal 1978: *fig.* 104; Reynolds 1986: *fig.* 10; Pal 1991: 76-78, col. pl. 39.

(C12) Present location unknown, 96 × 67 cm, NS 789 = 1669 AD; Publ.: Lauf 1972: no. 6608, *fig.* 36. (*Pl.* 17.22)

(C13) Haridas K. Swali Collection, Bombay; mentioned in Pal 1967b: 9, fn. 7 (not ill.).

(C14) National Museum, New Delhi; mentioned in Pal 1967b: 9, fn. 7 (not ill.).

II. B. *Candramaṇḍala*s with kalā figures (4 items)

10. Stone image without indication of religious context (1 item)

(C15) Bhaktapur, National Art Gallery, 107 × 58 cm, NS 589 — AD 1468; Publ.: Bangdel 1987: 166, Abb. 118; Bangdel 1995: 327, sec. 24.3. (*Pl.* 17.23)

11. Paintings indicating Buddhist context (3 items)

(C16) Jucker Collection, Basel (inv. no. 425); 62 × 53 cm, *c.* fifteenth century; Publ.: Jünemann 1989: col. pl. May; Mevissen 1989: cat. M.IV.A.11, col. pl. 32; Kreijger 1999: 34-35, col. pl. 4; apparently the same painting is described in Lokesh Chandra 1996: 46-47 (not illustrated).

(C17) Jucker Collection, Basel, 93 × 65 cm, late seventeenth or eighteenth century; Publ.: Kreijger 1999: no. 15.

(C18) Present location unknown, 94.6 × 65.1 cm, late seventeenth/eighteenth century; Publ.: SothNY 24.9. 1997: lot 31 (*Pl.* 17.24).

III. *Buddhamaṇḍala*s (B)

12. Paintings of buddhamaṇḍalas with navagrahas and other astral deities (4 items).

(B1) Musée Guimet, Paris (MA 5169), 51 × 46 cm, early fifteenth century; Publ.: Béguin 1990: 40, 42, 44, col. pl. 14; Béguin 1993: no. 10.

(B2) Present location unknown; 107 × 83 cm, *c.* sixteenth century; Publ.: SothLon 9.7.1979: lot 147 (*Pl.* 17.25).

(B3) Present location unknown, 64 × 51 cm, *c.* sixteenth century; Publ.: Tibetica 24/1973: no. 8071, b/w *fig.*; Uhlig 1976: 82 (*fig.*), 84; Mevissen 1989: cat. M. IV.A.15, Abb. 125 (*Pl.* 17.26).

(B4) Present location unknown, 58.5 × 74.7 cm, late nineteenth or twentieth century; Publ.: SothLon 23.6.1980: lot 157 (*Pl.* 17.27).

Bibliography

Alsop, Ian (1986), "Repoussé in Nepal," *Orientations* 17/7: 14-27.

Banerji, N.R. (1972), "The Moon in Legends, Literature and Records of the Hindus and Buddhists," *Insian Museum Bulletin* 7/2: 7-13.

Bangdel, Lain S. (1982), *The Early Sculptures of Nepal*, New Delhi.

Bangdel, Lain S. (1987), *Zweitausendfünfhundert Jahre nepalesischer Kunst*, Nepal.

Leipzig (1989), *Stolen Images of Nepal*, Kāṭhmāṇḍu.

Leipzig (1995), *Inventory of Stone Sculptures of the Kathmandu Valley*, Kāṭhmāṇḍu.

Béguin, Gilles (1990) "Art ésotérique de l'Himālaya," *Catalogue de la donation Lionel Fournier*, Paris.

Béguin, Gilles (1993), "Maṇḍala," *Diagrammes ésotériques du Népal et du Tibet*, Paris.

Bhattasali, Nalini Kanta (1929), *Iconography of Buddhist and Brahmanical Sculptures in the Dacca Museum*, Dacca.

Chri NY — Christie's New York, Auction Catalogues [Citing date of auction].

Detmold, Geoffrey and Mary Rubel (1979), *The Gods and Goddesses of Nepal*, Kāṭhmāṇḍu.

Deva, Krishan (1984), *Images of Nepal*, New Delhi (Memoirs of the Archaeological Survey of India 81).

Gail, Adalbert J. (1980), *Planets and Pseudoplanets in Indian Literature and Art with Special Reference to Nepal*, [a] Proceedings of the First Symposium of Nepali and German Sanskritists 1978, Kathmandu 1980: 121-136. [b] East and West 30/1-4: 133-46.

Gail, Adalbert J. (2001), *Sonnenkult in Indien. Tempel und Skulpturen von den Anfängen bis zur Gegenwart*, Berlin.

Höfer, Hans *et al.* (1991), *Kathmandu Insight City Guides*, Singapore.

Jünemann, Wolfgang (1989) (ed.), *Thangka Kalender 1990*, Durach.

Kooij, Karel Rijk van (1978), *Religion in Nepal*, Leiden (Iconography of Religions XIII/15).

Kreijger, Hugo E. (1999), *Kathmandu Valley Painting: The Jucker Collection*, London.

Lauf, D.I. (1972), *The Buddhist sculpture in India and her influence on the art of Tibet*, Stuttgart (Tibetica 20/1972).

Leidy, D.P. and R.A.F. Thurman (1997), "Mandala," *The Architecture of Enlightenment*, New York.

Lokesh Chandra (1996), *Transcendents Art of Tibet*, New Delhi (Śata-Piṭaka Series 385).

Macdonald, A.W. and A. Vergati Stahl (1979), *Newar Art, Nepalese Art during the Malla Period*, Warminster.

Mallmann, Marie-Thérèse de (1975), *Introduction a l'iconographie du tāntrisme Bouddhique*, Paris.

Markel, Stephen (1990), "The Imagery and Iconographic Development of the Indian Planetary Deities Rāhu and Ketu," *South Asian Studies*, 6: 9-26.

Markel, Stephen (1991), "The Genesis of the Indian Planetary Deities," *East and West*, 41/1-4: 173-188.

Markel, Stephen (1995), *Origins of the Indian Planetary Deities*, Lewiston-Queenston-Lampeter.

Menzies, Jackie (2001) (ed.), "Buddha Radiant Awakening," *Catalogue*, Art Gallery of New South Wales. Sydney.

Mevissen, Gerd J.R. (1989), "Ikonographie der Pañcarakṣās." M.A. Thesis, Freie Universität Berlin (unpublished).

Mevissen, Gerd J.R. (1997), "The Mahisantosh Sūrya Image: Some Iconographic Considerations," *Journal of Bengal Art* 2: 121-40.

Mevissen, Gerd J.R. (2000), "Īṣat-paṅgu Śanaiścara, the Lame Planetary God Saturn and His *Vāhanas*," *South Asian Archaeology*, 1997, eds. M. Taddei and G. De Marco, vol. 3: 1267-97. Rome.

Mevissen, Gerd J.R. (2003), "Corpus of Hindu and Jaina devī Images Bearing Figures or Symbols of Astral Deities," *Berliner Indologische Studien* 15/16.

Mevissen, Gerd J.R. (forthcoming), Images of Buddhist Goddesses Accompanied by Astral Deities, "To be published in Festschrift Enamul Haque," eds. G. Bhattacharya, G.J.R. Mevissen, M. Mitra, S. Sinha.

MIKB (1986) = H. Härtel, M. Yaldiz, V. Moeller, W. Lobo, G. Bhattacharya. Museum für Indische Kunst Berlin. Katalog 1986. Ausgestellte Werke, Berlin.

MIKB (2000) — M. Yaldiz, R.D. Gadebusch, R. Hickmann, F. Weis, R. Ghose. Magische Götterwelten. Werke aus dem Museum fūr Indische Kunst, Berlin. Potsdam.

Nagar, Shanti Lal (1995), *Sūrya and Sun Cult* (*In Indian Art, Culture, Literature And Thought*), New Delhi.

Pal, Pratapaditya (1967a), *Two Buddhist Paintings from Nepal, Amsterdam* (Nos. 15/16, 1967, Third series of the Bulletin, Vereeniging van Vrienden der Aziatische Kunst).

Pal, Pratapaditya (1967b), "Paintings from Nepal in the Prince of Wales Museum," *Prince of Wales Museum Bulletin* 10: 1-26.

Pal, Pratapaditya (1978), *The Arts of Nepal*, Part II: Painting. Leiden, Kḷln.

Pal, Pratapaditya (1985), *Art of Nepal, A Catalogue of the Los Angeles County Museum of Art Collection*, Berkeley, Los Angeles, London.

Pal, Pratapaditya (1986) (ed.), "American Collectors of Asian Art," Marg Publications, Bombay.

Pal, Pratapaditya (1991), "Art of the Himalayas," *Treasures from Nepal and Tibet* [in the Zimmerman Collection], New York.

Pal, Pratapaditya (1992), *Himālayan Mandalas in the Zimmerman Collection,* Orientations 23/2: 36-45.

Pal, Pratapaditya (2001), "Desire and Devotion," *Art from India, Nepal, and Tibet in the John and Berthe Ford Collection,* London.

Pal, Pratapaditya and Dipak Chandra Bhattacharyya, (1969), *The Astral Divinities of Nepal,* Varanasi.

Piotrovsky, Mikhail (1993) (ed.), "Lost Empire of the Silk Road," *Buddhist Art from Khara Khoto X-XIIIth century,* Milano.

Pruscha, Carl (1975), *Kathmandu Valley: The Preservation of Physical Environment and Cultural Heritage, A Protective Inventory,* vol. 1. Vienna.

Rawson, Philip (1978), *The Art of Tantra,* rev. edn., London.

Ray, Eva (1986), John Gilmore Ford (1934 -), In: Pal 1986: 185-204.

Reynolds Valrae (1986), The Zimmerman Family Collection. In: Pal 1986: 165-84.

Samosyuk Kira (1997/98a), *The Planet Cult in the Tangut State of Xi Xia — The Khara Khoto Collection,* State Hermitage Museum, St. Petersburg, Silk Road Art and Archaeology 5: 353-68.

Samosyuk, Kira (1997/98b), "A Twelfth Century 'Stellar Magic Circle from Khara Khoto," *Silk Road Art and Archaeology 5,* 369-76.

Schick, Jürgen (1989), *Die Götter verlassen das Land. Kunstraub in Nepal,* Graz.

Schick, Jürgen (1998), *The Gods are Leaving the Country, Art Theft from Nepal,* Revised English Edition. Bangkok.

Sen, Tansen (1999), "Astronomical Tomb Paintings from Xuanhua: Maṇḍalas?," *Ars Orientalis 29: 29-54.*

Shimkhada Deepak (1984a), "The Masquerading Sun: A Unique Syncretic Image in Nepal," *Artibus Asiae* 45/2-3: 223-229.

Shimkhada, Deepak (1984b), "Museum Without Walls A Wayside Sculpture in the Kathmandu Valley," *Arts of Asia* 14/4: 96-100.

Slusser, Mary Shepherd (1982), *Nepal Maṇḍala, A Cultural Study of the Kathmandu Valley,* 2 vols., Princeton.

Slusser, Mary Shepherd, et al. (2002), *Patan Museum Guide,* Nepal.

SothLon — Sotheby's London. Auction Catalogues [Cited according to date of auction].

SothNY — Sotheby's New York. Auction Catalogues [Cited according to date of auction].

Srivastava, K.M. (2000), "The Art of Nepal," *Arts of Asia* 30/1: 82-100.

Tchekhoff, Geneviève (1980), "Surya: Icons of the Sun-God," *Arts of Asia* 10/4: 95-101.

Thomsen, Margrit (1977), Geheimnisvolles Nepal. Tempelschätze aus zwei Jahrtausenden. Ausstellungskatalog, Hannover, n.d.

Tibetica, Sale Catalogues, Schoettle Ostasiatica, Stuttgart [Cited according to catalogue no. and year].

Toffin, Gérard (1984), *Société et religion chez les Néwar du Népal,* Paris.

Uhlig, Helmut (1976) (ed.), Buddistische Kunst aus dem Himalaya: Kaschmir — Ladakh — Tibet — Nepal — Bhutan, Ausstellungskatalog, Berlin.

Van der Wee, Pia and Louis (1995), *A Tale of Thangkas, Living with a Collection* [Antwerp], n.d.

18

The Bhāgavata Purāṇa and the Later Descriptions of Buddhist Hell

Ineke Van Put

ACCORDING to the *Bhāgavata Purāṇa*[1] (Skandha V, Chapter 26) there are 28 hells, providing 28 tortures for 28 different crimes (cf. Table 1). These came into existence as the result of "the (commission of) the thousands of prohibited sinful acts committed by those who indulge in desires (of various kinds) due to the influence of *avidyā* (ignorance) dominating them from time immemorial (verse 3)." Further their location is said to be "within the three worlds. They lie in the Southern direction below the earth and above the waters (verse 5)."

In Buddhism, as is the case in Brāhmaṇism, there are many different descriptions of hell. Nevertheless it is possible to make abstraction of these descriptions and give a general picture. The kernel of this image is the *Devadūtasūtra*'s[2] description of *mahāniraya*, the Great Hell, which is surrounded by several adjacent hells. From this primitive image, a more elaborate system of eight Great Hells, surrounded by 16 *utsādas* developed.[3] The idea of cold hells is

1. The text I have used is "Chapter 26: Description of Hells" in Dr. G.V. Tagare: 2002, 764-72.
2. In particular, the versions found in the Pāli *Majjhima Nikāya* (M. 130) and the Chinese *Madhyamāgama* (*Tianshijing*; T. 1 no. 26.64). Other *Devadūtasūtras* are the *Tīni Devadūtani* of the *Aṅguttara Nikāya* (A. III, 35), the second half of the *Devadūtasūtra* of the Chinese *Ekottarāgama* (T. 2 no. 125.32.4) and the *Yanluowangwutianshizhejing* (J. *Enraṛgotenshishakyṛ*; T. 1 no. 43). Besides these texts, Akanuma Chizen (2000, 96) also considers the *Wukuzhangjujing* (J. *Gokushṛkukyṛ*; T.1 7 no. 741) as belonging to the same. In this article the plural *Devadūtasūtras* refers to the first two only.
3. On the development of the single hell structure into a structure with eight great hells, see my article "Some Remarks on the Eight Great Hells in the Northern Buddhist Tradition" in *The Indian International Journal of Buddhist Studies*, no. 1 (1999-2000): 75-82.

Table 1: Offences and Punishments in the *BP*

Hell name	*Translation*	*Offence*	*type*	*Punishment*	*type*
1. *Tāmisra*	Darkness	taking away someone's wealth, children or wife	stealing	beaten with cudgels; hunger and thirst	beaten; hunger and thirst
2. *Andhatāmisra*	Obscure Darkness	enjoying someone's wife (property, etc.) by decei-ving him	stealing	loss of sight and consciousness	[blindness]
3. *Raurava*	Screaming	wrongly indentifying one's Soul, regarding one's wealth as one's own and comforting and nourishing his family by maliciously treating others	wrong view	killes by *rurus*	[death]
4. *Mahāraurava*	Extreme Screaming	to be solely occupied with the nourishment of one's body by any unscrupulous means	desire	killes by *kravyādas*	[death]
5. *Kumbhīpāka*	Cooking Cauldron	cooking living beasts or birds	killing	fried in oil	boiled
6. *Kālasūtra*	Black Rope	bearing malice towards one's parents, the Brāh-maṇas and the Vedas	defilement/ disrespect of social rules or religion	burnt on a plan of a copper sheet; hunger and thirst	burnt
7. Asipatravana	Forest of the Leaves	embracing a heretic sect ("when there was no calamity")	wrong view	whipped; cut in pieces by the iron leaves	whipped; cut

8. *Śūkaramukha*	Hog's Mouth	(Kings or their servants) inflicting punishments on innocent people or inflicting corporal punishments on brāhmaṇas	abuse of power	crushed	crushed
9. *Andhakūpa*	Dark Pit	(Persons capable of understanding agony caused to others) causing creatures who feed on human bodies pain	abuse of power	harassed by animals and insects leading to loss of sleep and mental peace	[mental torture]
10. *Kṛmibhojana*	Worm's Food	eating whatever is available without sharing or performing the five daily great sacrifices	desire	born as a worm in of worms, the evil-prayed upon by and feeds himself worms	fed with filthy/hot substances*
11. *Sandaṁśa*	Pair of Tongs	stealing or robbing (without justification)	stealing	cut by red hot iron balls or tongs	cut*
12. *Taptasūrmi*	Hot Image	sexual intercourse with an inappropriate/unwothy partner	lewdness	burnt by a red hot iron image	burnt
13. *Vajrakaṇṭaka śālmalī*	Cotton Trees with Adamantine Thorns	indiscriminate sexual intercourse with all (humans and aminals)	lewdness	cut by adaman tine thorns	cut
14. *Vaitaraṇī*	*Vaitaraṇī*	(Kṣatriyas or noble officers of Kings) having joined a heretic sect	wrong view	eatern by aquatic animals in this river which carries a flood of excretion, urine, pus, blood, hair, nails, bones, fat, flesh and marrow.	devoured; filth

15. *Pūyoda*	Sea of Pus	(those of higher caste) keeping lower caste women, neglecting purity, righteous conduct and self-discipline and leading a beastlike life	defilement/ disrespect of social rules or religion	thrown in a sea of pus, excretion, urine, phlegm and dirt and made to eat these things	fed with filthy/hot substances
16. *Prāṇa(ni)-rodha*	Life's Extinction	(Brāhmaṇas and others) hunting and killing animals with donkeys and hounds on other occasions than those prescribed by the Śāstras	killing	pierced by arrows	pierced
17. *Viśasana* (*Vaiśasa*)	Dissection	killing beasts in sham sacrifices	killing	cut	cut
18. *Lālābhakṣa*	Eating Semen	(*dvija*) making his wife of his own caste drink his semen	lewdness	thrown in a stream of semen and being forced to drink it	fed with flithy/hot substances
19. *Sārameyā-dana*	Offer to the Dogs	dacoits, perpetrators of arson and poisoning plundering villages or caravans of merchants	killing and stealing, arson	devoured by hounds with adamantine teeth	devoured
20. *Avīci(mat)*	Without Ripples	lying at the time of disposing evidence, money transactions or donating gifts	lying	hurled down from a steep mountain to a place with rocky surface appearing as water, His body is shattered to pieces but he does not die.	crushed
21. *Ayaḥpāna*	Drinking Iron	unallowed consumption of *soma*	intoxicants	being poured molten iron into the mouth	fed with filthy/hot substances

22. *Kṣārakar-dama*	Causticmud Pool	(those of the lowest strata) not paying duly respect to those who are superior	defilement/ disrespect of social rules of religion	hurled down with downwards and subjected to endless tortures	crushed
23. *Rakṣogaṇa-bhojana*	Food for the *rākṣasas*	offering human sacrifice and eating it	defilement/ disrespect of social rules or religion merrily	cut in slices by *rakṣasas* like butchers, who drink their blood, dance and sing	cut
24. *Śūlaprota*	Impalement	allure people in order to torture them by means of transfixing them on an iron pike or by binding them with ropes.	abuse of power	transfixed on iron pikes; attacked and pecked on by hell hellish birds such as *kaṅka* and *vaṭaka;* distressed with hunger and thirst	pierced
25. *Daṇḍaśūka*	Snake bites (?)	tormenting other people	abuse of power	devoured by snakes	devoured
26. *Avaṭani-rodhana*	Confinement in a Hole	confining living beings in dark holes	abuse of power	shut up in dark places full of poisonous fire and smoke.	
27. *Paryāvartana*	Having [one's eyes] turned away	getting angry with guests arriving at one's door	anger	pecked one's eyes out by birds of adamantine beaks like vultures, crows, *kaṅka, vaṭaka*	
28. *Sūcīmukha*	Needle Snouts	being proud of one's wealth and full of egotism only thinking of the preservation and supplementation of his wealth while looking suspicious to others	desire	stitched on all sides by Yama's servants	stretched

an addition, which is important but not essential for the general image of Buddhist Hell. Essential features are the eight Great Hells including *avīcī* as the successor of the *mahāniraya*, the presence of the 16 *utsāda*s and the tortures executed therein. These are the structural characteristics of Buddhist hell. The names of the eight great hells are the same in every text, as are the names of certain *utsāda*s, especially those borrowed from the *Devadūtasūtra*s. Certain tortures, such as pouring molten iron into the offender's mouth, appear in any text. The hell descriptions offered in the *Lokaprajñaptisūtra* of the Chinese *Dīrghāgama* (T. 1.30) and related texts, the *Abhidharmakośabhāṣya*, the *Mahāprajñāpāramitopadeśa*, the *Saddharmasmṛtyupasthānasūtra*, etc., correspond to this general image of Buddhist hell. They will be discussed in detail hereafter.

Hell Structure and Hell Names

When comparing the *Bhāgavata Purāṇa* with the general Buddhist hell image, some interesting differences and similarities become clear. The *BP* counts 21 + 7 hells; there are no *utsāda*s. Of the 28 hells, four names can be recognized as the names of Great Hells of Buddhism and three as popular *utsāda*s:

BP	*Buddhist Hells*
	Great Hells
3. *Raurava* (Screaming)	*Raurava* (Screaming)
4. *Mahāraurava* (Extreme Screaming)	*Mahāraurava* (Extreme Screaming)
6. *Kālasūtra* (Black Rope)	*Kālasūtra* (Black Rope)
20. *Avīcimat* (Without Ripples)	*Avīci* (Without Interruption)
	Utsādas
7. *Asipatravana* (Forest of the Iron Leaves)	*Asipatravana* (Forest of the Iron Leaves)
13. *Vajrakaṇṭakaśālī* (Trees with Adamantine Thorns)	*Ayaḥśālmalīvana* (Forest of the Iron Cotton Trees)
14. *Vaitaraṇī*	*Vaitaraṇī*

The *BP*'s etymology for *raurava* (as well as *mahāraurava*) and *avīcimat* differs from the Buddhist versions:

Ruru is the name of a creature much more cruel than a serpent. Hence, this hell is called *Raurava.* Chapter 26, verse 11 —

> [In *Avīcimat,*] he is hurled down headlong from a (steep) mountain top one

> hundred *yojana*s in height to a place with a rocky surface appearing as water. Hence it is called *avīcimat* (a place with a hard surface but appearing like water with ripples). — Chapter 26, verse 28; tr. in Tagare: 2002, 766 and 770.

The *Kośa* says of *Avīci*:

> Because, unlike the other *naraka*s, one receives in there suffering without interval and because the suffering is extreme, it is called Without Interval. . . . There is another master who explains: 'In *Avīci* there is suffering without happy intervals'. Therefore it is called Without Interval. In the other hells happy intervals occur Although [these] are no maturation *vipāka* they are of an equal consequence *niṣyanda* (T. 29 no. 1558: 58b6, 58b9-58b11). *Raurava* is usually said to mean "Screaming."

The other names do not resemble any Buddhist hell or *utsāda*, but the description of many reminds one of popular tortures. Quite common examples are: the Cooking Cauldron (cf. 5. *kumbhīpāka*) and Hot Liquid Iron (cf. 21. *ayaṣpāna*, Drinking Iron). *Tāmisra* and *andhatāmisra* are related to the names of the *SUS' utsāda*s Darkness, Complete Darkness, Total Darkness, etc. Darkness is, however, not always the main torture in these secondary hells. Also the names of the *SUS' utsāda*s Dark Smoke and Forest of Burning Smoke remind one of the tortures in *avaṭanirodhana* ("Confinement in a Hole"). In the Bone Eating Insect Hell and the Burning Hell of String like Worms, one is eaten by worms, which is characteristic of *kṛmibhojana* ("Worms' Food"), but also of the *utsāda kuṇapa*.

Types of Torture

The tortures described in the Buddhist hell texts can be categorized according to the 14 types. In combination with the various implements used by the *narakapāla*, however, they are countless. The 14 main types are:

1. being beaten (with cudgels, whips, etc.).
2. being boiled (in a cauldron, oil, etc).
3. being burned (by fire, a hot floor, etc.).
4. being crushed (by a mountain, mortar, grinding stone, etc.).
5. being cut (by iron tools such as knife, axe, sword, iron leaves; by a sharp wind).
6. being devoured (by wild animals, insects, snakes).

7. (brains/eyes) being pecked at (by birds).
8. being pierced (by iron tools such as arrows, awls, spikes, nails, thorns).
9. (skin/tongue) being stretched (by nails).
10. being torn apart (by a charriot).
11. being peckled (in caustic brine or excretions such as excrements, pus, blood, etc.).
12. being fed with filthy or hot substances such as pus, blood, iron balls, liquid iron, etc.
13. being winnowed (by a hot iron winnow).
14. infliction of various kinds of suffering (e.g., cold, disease, hunger and thirst).

Most of the tortures described in the *BP* correspond to one of these 14 types. But there are exceptions. A striking example, for instance is "harassment leading to loss of sleep and mental peace" and "loss of sight and consciousness." Especially mental tortures are seldomly seen in the Buddhist scriptures. One of the rare examples is the *SUS' utsāda* "Watching Evil." In this *utsāda* child molesters are forced to watch how their children are being molested by the demons of hell.

Purāṇic creatures, which do not inhabit the hells of the Buddhist texts mentioned above, are the *rurus*,[4] *kravyādas*,[5] *kaṅkas*[6] and *vaṇakas*. Also snakes and carnivorous aquatic animals are rare. On the other hand, (sharp beaked) worms and birds, as well as sharp-toothed dogs are common.

Finally, there are some tortures, which the *BP* shares with only one or two Buddhist texts. *Taptasūrmi* (Hot Image), for instance is described only in the *SUS*, but in no other Buddhist text that I have so far studied. An interesting detail is that the *SUS* reserves this punishment for homosexuals, whereas in the *BP* it applies to heterosexuals, more precisely only "to a man who indulges in a sexual intercourse with a woman whom he should not have approached or to a woman who does so with a man unworthy of such an approach." The *SUS* and the *Mppo*, both share the following tortures with the *BP*: no. 16: being pierced by

4. *Ruru:* a kind of deer (Wogihara 1132b).

5. *Kravyāda* means "meat-eating." In Chinese it is usually translated as "meat" or "lion" (Wogihara 386b).

6. *Kaṅka* means "blue heron." It is usually translated with the Chinese character for "eagle," or the uniquely Japanese character for *mamema washi*, which is a kind of eagle (Wogihara 307, b).

arrows,[7] no. 25: being devoured by snakes[8] and no. 26: being shut up in dark places full of poisonous fire and smoke.[9] Further, the description of hell no. 23, namely "being cut in slices by *rākṣasas* like butchers," reminds one the *Mppo*'s comparison between the *rākṣasas*' treatment of the evil doers and cooks preparing meat.

To regard these descriptions as mere exceptions from the Buddhist point of view, however, would be wrong. Although it is true that they do not occur in the "classical" descriptions, they did become part of the perception of Buddhist Hell as seen in East Asia. The medieval Japanese paintings of hell are hereof proof (see *Pls.* 18.1, 18.2, 18.3 & 18.4).

Offences Leading to Hell

As mentioned above, the *BP* names 28 hells, providing 28 tortures for 28 different crimes. According to the offence committed, one falls into a different hell. In many cases, the tortures received seem to be retributions in the literal sense: the person who cooked living animals will be boiled, the hunter will be pierced by arrows, unallowed drinking of *soma* will be punished by being poured molten iron through one's throat, etc.

In Buddhist literature, it seems that only from the occurrence of the Eight Great Hells onwards the tendency to link certain hells with specific offences starts to develop. In classical Buddhist texts such as the *Devadūta* and *Bālapaṇḍitasūtras*, crime specific punishments are a-typical and so are detailed descriptions of offences.

Buddhist morality prescribes various kinds of precepts and meritorious acts. The precepts for lay Buddhists, the five *śīla*, include abstention from: 1. murder, 2. theft, 3. lewd behaviour, 4. lying, and 5. drinking alcohol. Abstention from murder, theft, lewd behaviour, and lying are also part of the ten good acts, which developed into the ten good precepts of Mahāyāna Buddhism. The ten (good/bad) acts[10] are usually classified according to the three kinds of actions (*karma*), namely, physical, verbal and mental actions:

7. Cf. the *utsādas* are Fearful Vulture of Kālasūtra and Field of Steel Trees of Raurava in the *SUS*, and Raurava in the *Mppo*.
8. Cf. *Mppo*'s *Ayaḥśālmalīvana* and *SUS' utsādas* Field of Steel Trees of Raurava, Black Bile of *avīci*, etc.
9. Cf. the *SUS' utsādas* Large Sword Forest and Plantain Smoke Forest of Raurava, as well as *Mppo*'s *raurava* and *mahāraurava*.
10. Opposite to the ten good acts and the ten good precepts, are the ten bad acts and the ten grave prohibitions (violation of them constitute a *pārājika* offence) with some minor differences.

- Abstention from the three physical actions of: 1. murder, 2. theft, and 3. lewd behaviour
- Abstention from the four vocal actions of: 4. lying, 5. harsh words, 6. slanderous speech, and 7. idle talk
- Abstention from the three mental actions of: 8. desire, 9. anger, and 10. holding wrong views

The *Lokaprajñapti* of the Chinese *Dīrghāgama,* one of the first hell texts to pair each of the hells with an offence, frequently mentions the three kinds of actions:

1. *Sañjīva*: physically acting wrongly without verbally or mentally doing good;
2. *Kālasūtra*: offending father, mother, a *tathāgata* or a *pratyekabuddha;*
3. *Saṅghāta*: doing the three kinds of wrongful deeds without doing the three kinds of good deeds;
4. *Raurava*: killing with evil intend;
5. *Mahāraurava*: indulging in sexual activity only;
6. *Tapana*: burning living beings;
7. *Pratapana*: discarding all meritorious deeds and doing nothing but wrong;
8. *Avīci*: committing any of the worst of criminal actions.

With "the worst of criminal actions" probably the five actions of immediate retribution, or *ānantarya* are meant. These are 1. matricide (*mātṛghāta*); 2. patricide (*pitṛghāta*); 3. shedding the blood of a *tathāgata*; (*tathāgatasyantike-duṣṭacittarudhirotpādana*); 4. causing a schism (*saṅghabheda*); 5. killing a *arhat* (*arhadghāta / arhadvadha*).[11] In fact, the text mentions only three concrete offences, 1. killing, 2. lewd behaviour, and 3. offensive behaviour towards father, mother, a *tathāgata* or a *pratyekabuddha.* The association of *ānantarya*, "immediate retribution," with *avīci*, "without interruption," — in Chinese both *wujian* (J. *mugen*) — is clear.

With the exception of the *kośa,* later texts usually give more detailed descriptions of the various offences leading to hell. Quite elaborate are *Mppo* and the *SUS*. The *SUS* links the eight hot hells with the following eight offences:

11. The order of the offences may differ according to the text and tradition. For example, in China and Japan, patricide precedes matricide.

1. *Sañjīva*: killing.
2. *Kālasūtra*: stealing (and killing).
3. *Saṅghāta*: sexual indulgence (and killing, stealing).
4. *Raurava*: intoxication (and killing, stealing, sexual indulgence).
5. *Mahāraurava*: lying (and killing, stealing, sexual indulgence, intoxicants).
6. *Tapana*: heresy (and killing, stealing, sexual indulgence, intoxicants, lying).
7. *Pratapana*: sexual abuse of virtuous people; sexual activity by monks (and killing, stealing, sexual indulgence, intoxicants, lying, heresy).
8. *Avīci*: five actions of immediate retribution *ānantarya*.

The first five correspond to the five offences stipulated by the lay precepts discussed above. The sixth, Heresy, is related to Wrong Views of the ten acts and the seventh is once more related to Lewdness. The five actions of immediate retribution lead again to *avīci*.

In the surrounding *utsāda*s, not only the offences, which is related to the main crime of the hell they belong to is punished, but also the offences committed in one of the foregoing main hells.[12] The *utsāda*s of *raurava,* for example, punish crimes related to intoxication combined with the main crimes of the first three hells, namely killing, stealing and sexual indulgence. Exception to this rule, are the *utsāda*s of *avīci.* They punish crimes which damage the *saṅgha,* its members and its possessions, but which do not fall under the five *ānantarya*. The fifth *utsāda*, for example, punishes evil-doers who set fire to the possessions or buildings of the *saṅgha*.

The second text, the *Mppo* does not organize the different hells as systematically as the *SUS*. The offences, which are punished in the various hells, are manifold. They also do not necessarily include the offences of the former hells. Major offences include killing, stealing, abuse of power, arson, causing death by lying, cheating, false views and the five actions of immediate retribution *ānantarya*. However, the *Mppo*'s definition of the five *ānantarya*, deviates from the common one, which is given above. In the *Mppo* they are: 1. Destroying wholesome roots; 2. Calling right "wrong"; 3. Calling wrong "right"; 4. Denying cause and effect and 5. Detesting good people.

12. One exception is the first *utsāda* of *Kālasūtra*, which is destined for "those who deny belief in true morality and preach lies." According to Matsunaga (1972, 109) this *utsāda* might be an addition by a later editor, which might explain the inconsequency.

In its description of the *utsādas*, the *Mppo* again specifies which offences lead to which *utsāda*. But it does so only for nine of its sixteen *utsādas*. The punishment prescribed in all cases is closely related to the offence committed:

1. *Kukūla*, or "Embers," punishes (those who are guilty of violation of precepts; inducing lay people to disparage the Buddhist Law);
2. *Kuṇapa*, or "Excrements," punishes those who lead a beastly life or who defiled somebody else's body or food;
3. *Ādīptavana*, or "Burning Forest," punishes hunters who putting fire on the forest caused a bloodbed and damaged insects;
4. *Asipattravana*, or "Forest of Iron Leaves," punishes those who killed (or wounded) others with a sword or crushed them under a tree by cutting it. It also punishes those who leak a secret that had been confined to them;
5. *Kṣuramārga*, or "Road of Blades," punishes those who pierce their enemies with sharp knives or spears; who destroy roads or ponds and who destroy the road of the Good Law;
6. *Ayaḥśālmalīvana*, or "Iron Cotton Tree Forest," punishes those who give way to luxury; take other men's wives; who covet and experience "agreeable contacts" *sukhasparśana*. In this case the association between offence and punishment is not clear. On the other hand, it may be that *ayaḥśālmalīvana* was commonly associated with (sexual) desire. Also the *BP* links *ayaḥśālmalīvana* with lewdness;
7. *Vaitaraṇī/Khārodakānadī*, punishes those who pushed living beings in the water or threw them into boiling or ice cold water, or those who killed (or wounded) aquatic animals;
8. *Tāmrastambha*, or "Copper Pole," punishes those who steal without emergent reason; monks pretending to be sick in order to get molten butter or honey; hurting people by offending them; acceptance of many presents deprived of morality, concentration and wisdom. There is no immediate connection between a "copper pole" and giving way to desire. However, the text further explains that in this hell the offenders are forced to drink liquid copper and eat iron balls. The latter two tortures clearly punish gluttony and avarice;
9. *Arbuda*, the first "cold" *utsāda*, punishes those who rob people during the winter months or those who rob people from fire and combustibles when

they suffer from cold; those who cause a rain of hail and ice to damage people during one's life as a *nāgā*; those who offend the Buddha, his disciples and people of the Way; those who ignore the four vocal prohibitions.

On the whole it seems that the *Mppo* is inspired by the ten acts, rather than by the *śīla*: no reference is made to offences related to intoxication and very little attention has been paid to sexual desire and lewdness. Also the uncommon definition of the five actions of immediate retribution *ānantarya* points to the scholastic character of the text.

Thus, in the *Lokaprajñapti* of the Chinese *Dīrghāgama*, the *SUS* and the *Mppo* those who fall into hell are mostly violators of the five *śīla* or the ten good actions, or those guilty of commiting one of the five *ānantarya*. The graveness of the five *ānantarya*, which in a sense overlap again with the *śīla* and the ten actions, is related to the fact that they refer to offences, which aim at the destruction of the Three Treasures and of basic human relations. Apart from the *ānantarya*, there are other instances in the *Mppo* as well as in the *SUS* where (sometimes literal) defilement of social relations and religious law are punished in hell. In all, with the addition of the *Mppo* offences of arson and abuse of power, the three texts discussed above speak of 14 different offences:

Offences leading to hell	***Karmapatha***	
Physical actions	*3 Physical actions*	*5 Śīla*
1. killing	1. killing	1. killing
2. stealing	2. stealing	2. stealing
3. lewdness	3. lewdness	3. lewdness
4. offences related to alcohol		4. drinking spirits
5. arson		5. lying
6. abuse of power		
Verbal actions	*4 Verbal actions*	
7. lying	4. lying	
8. harsh words	5. harsh words	
9. slanderous language	6. slanderous language	
10. idle talk	7. idle talk	

Mental actions	*3 Mental actions*
11. desire	8. desire
12. anger	9. anger
13. wrong view	10. wrong view
Actions, which can be physical, vocal and/or mental	
14. Defilement/disrespect of social rules and the Three Treasures	

An analysis of the offences found in the *BP* according to the above categories, leads to the following list (in order of importance):

5-4 times	*3 times*	*once*
- killing	- lewdness	- drinking alcohol
- stealing	- desire	- arson
- abuse of power	- wrong view	- lying
	- defilement/disrespect of social rules and religion	- anger

Since the three wrongful actions are not unfamiliar to Brāhmaṇism,[13] it is not surprising to find all the four physical offences, one verbal action — lying, and all the three mental actions among the offences of the *BP*. The three offences of the *Mppo*, which do not belong to the *karmapatha* or *śīla*, 1. abuse of power, 2. arson and 3. defilement/disrespect of social rules and religion also occur in the *BP*.

The *BP*'s description of lewdness is rather detailed as it disapproves of oral sexual practice and bestiality. This kind of explicity can only be seen in the *SUS*, which adds anal sexual practice, paedophilia, rape, incest and homosexuality. The *BP*'s punishment for one who made his wife of his own caste drink his semen as being thrown in a stream of semen and being forced to drink it, however, has no equal in the Buddhist literature.

13. For example, *Law of Manu*, Chapter 12:

"5. Coveting the property of others, thinking in one's heart of what is undesirable, and adherence to false (doctrines), are the three kinds of (sinful) mental action.

6. Abusing (others, speaking) untruth, detracting from the merits of all men, and talking idly, shall be the four kinds of (evil) verbal action.

7. Taking what has not been given, injuring (creatures) without the sanction of the law, and holding criminal intercourse with another man's wife, are declared to be the three kinds of (wicked) bodily action."

The *BP*'s emphasis on gluttony and avarice is another conspicuous characteristic. And so are the descriptions of animal abuse, including culinary preparations: hunting and killing animals with donkeys and hounds on other occasions than those prescribed by the Śāstras; cooking living beasts or birds; killing beasts in sham sacrifices, confining living beings in dark holes. The latter is a characteristic, which the *BP* shares with the *SUS* as well as the *Mppo.* Both the Buddhist texts frequently mention abuse and killing of animals.

Final Remarks

At this point I have discussed the differences and similarities between the *BP's* description of Hell and Buddhist Hell. Perhaps the main difference is the number of different hells and the independent hell structure. Of the 28 hell names only one-fourth is also common in a Buddhist context. Most tortures are the same or at least very similar. The occurrence of mental tortures and the depravement of sight stands out, although it is not exclusively Brāhmaṇic.

In Buddhist scriptures, only later ones such as the *Mppo* and *SUS* relate different offences to specific punishments in hell. When were these texts written? Most authors agree that the *SUS Sadharmasmṛtyupasthānasūtra* T. 721 was written after the *Mppo* and the *Abhidharmamahāvibhāṣā Śāstra* (T. 1545), probably towards the end of the fifth or the beginning of the sixth century CE (Ishida: 1995, 110; Matsunaga: 1972, 75-76, etc.). According to the Taishā's colophon, the Chinese translation was made by Gautama Prajñārūci, who lived at the end of the fifth and the first half of the sixth centuries. Yamabe Shóshaku, the translator of the text into Japanese, thinks that Prajñārūci in fact composed the text himself.[14] There is also a Tibetan translation. The original Sanskrit is lost. The doctrinal affiliation is another point of discussion. A. Matsunaga and D. Matsunaga (1977, 75) classify it as a Mādhyamika/Vijñānavāda work and M. Ishida (1995, 110) as *sarvāstivāda*. More convincing, however, is the opinion of Lū Cheng (1979, 64). According to Lū, it belongs to the *pudgalavāda* tradition, probably the Bhadrāyanīya sub-school of the Vātsīputrīyas and not the Sammitīya sub-school as a Tang tradition says. Typical for the *pudgalavāda*s is their belief in the existence of the ego as well as their acceptance of six, sometimes seven *gati*. The seventh *gati* is intermediary existence, *antarābhava* (Lū: 1979, 63 and 68).

14. See Yamabe's introduction to the text in *Kokuyaku Issaikyṛ*, vol. 8, pp. 1-7 (Tokyo 1933) in Matsunaga & Matsunaga (1972, 75).

The *Mppo* by Kumārajīva (350-409, 413?), is traditionally attributed to Nāgārjuna (*ca.* 200 CE). New insights in the developments of *sarvāstivāda* Buddhism, as proposed by Charles Willemen, lead to the conclusion that its author might have been Kumārajīva himself. Lamotte's suggestion that the *Mppo* was written about one century after Nāgārjuna supports this view. Kumārajīva, who was educated in Kashmir, probably wrote the work as a *Mādyamika Abhidharma* after the example of the *Kashmir Abhidharma* he had studied.

Thus, the *SUS* as well as the *Mppo*, which are both important texts for the image of hell in East Asia and in particular in Japan, both are relatively late texts. Their shared interests therefore could be a sign of the time as both are also directly or indirectly the products of north-western Indian Buddhism. Their age is an age of Gupta rule characterized by the Sanskritization of Buddhism and increasing Brāhmaṇic influence. Especially the *pudgalavāda*s must have felt akin to certain Hindu philosophies as also these acknowledge the existence of the ego.

There are other peculiarities. In its discussion of killing and torturing, five hells are destined for those who kill or torture animals, six against the case of human beings. Interestingly, we see the same kind of concern for animals in both *Mppo* and *SUS*. In about half of the cases animals are mentioned along with humans. Sometimes, there is even a hell specifically for the maltreatment of animals.

Class-consciousness is another striking feature. More than one hell is meant especially for people in power and of high rank ("Kings and their servants," "Kṣatriyas or noble officers of Kings," "those of higher caste," *dvija*s) when transgressing certain rules. Other groups of people who risk punishment in specific hells are "Persons capable of understanding agony" and "those of the lowest strata." The group with the highest risk for rebirth in hell are the powerful. They are well represented in the *Mppo*, which uses the term "magistrates." The *BP* considers abuse of power as a serious crime as well.

Bibliography

1. Akanuma, Chizen, 2000, "Tetsujṛnairikyō," in *Bussho kaisetsu daijiten*, ed. Ono Genmyō, p. 96. Shukusatsuban. Tait shuppansha.
2. Ishida, Mizumaro, 1995, "Jigoku to wa nani ka," in *Jigoku no sekai*, ed. Sakamoto Kaname, 97-129. Keisuisha.
3. Lū, Cheng, 1979, *Yindu Faxue Yuanliu Luejiang* (Lectures about the Origin and Development of Indian Buddhism), Shanghai Renmin Chubanshe.

4. Matsunaga, Alicia and Daigan Matsunaga, 1972, *The Buddhist Concept of Hell*, New York: Philosophical Library.
5. Tagare, G.V. (tr.) 2002, *The Bhāgavata Purāṇa*, Part II, *Ancient Indian Tradition and Mythology*, vol. 8. Delhi: Motilal Banarsidass Publishers.
6. Wogihara Unrai. 2001. *Kan'yaku taishō. Bon-wa daijiten*. Kṛdansha.

Abbreviations

1. *Kośa* — *Abhidharmakośabhāṣya*
2. *Mppo* — *Mahāprajñāpāramitopadeśa*
3. *SUS* — *Saddharmasmṛtyupasthānasūtra*
4. *BP* — *Bhāgavata Purāṇa*

19

Xie He's "Liu Fa (Six Rules of Art)" and Buddhist Painting

Charles Willemen

It is a widespread view that Xie He's six rules of painting, written down in his *Guhuapinlu*, Old Record of the Classifications of Painters, shortly after 532 CE, were inspired by the *ṣaḍaṅga* of Indian art. The word used by Xie He for a rule is *fa*, i.e., law or canon. This word, of course, has its original Chinese meanings, i.e., law, rule, method, etc., but after the introduction of Buddhism in China, ever since the oldest translations by the Parthian An Shigao in the second half of the second century, this *fa* was used to translate *dharma*. This fact greatly contributed to the search for an Indian origin of the six rules. Yaśodharā's commentary (thirteenth century) to Vātsyāyana's *Kāmasūtra* (*ca.* 400 CE) mentions six links or members: 1. *rūpabhedāni* (variety of manifestations); 2. *pramāṇāni* (measurements); 3. *bhāva*(*-yojanam*) (nature, emotion); 4. *lāvaṇyayojanam* (embodiment of charm, "savour"), 5. *sādṛśyam* (likeness); 6. *varṇikābhaṅga* (preparation or analysis of pigments). These six members are six norms. The discussion about which *aṅga* agrees with which Chinese rule, has brought hours of intellectual enjoyment for many scholars. My predecessor, W. Acker, has studied this problem extensively in his study about Zhang Yanyuan's *Lidaiminghuaji*, a critical history of Chinese painting up to 847, the year of its publication (Tang dynasty 618-907).[1]

He said that the six Chinese rules, which all consist of four characters, are inspired by the six members. The Chinese also mentions six canons, each time explained by the second half of the rule. W. Acker translates (p. 4):

1. *Some T'ang and Pre-T'ang Texts on Chinese Painting*, Sinica Leidensia VIII, Leiden 1954, ed. E.J. Brill. See esp. pp. xxviii-xiv.

> First, Spirit Resonance which means vitality; second, Bone Method, which is (a way of) using the brush; third, correspondence to the Object, which means the depicting of forms; fourth, Suitability of Type which has to do with the laying on of colours; fifth, Division and Planning, i.e. placing and arrangement; and sixth, Transmission by Copying, that is to say the copying of models.

Not everybody agreed with W. Acker's interpretation. Western, i.e., European (including North America) translations are extremely numerous.[2] Japan certainly did not lag behind. This has led me to an investigation of the earliest composition of the Chinese rules.[3] When were these rules conceived? My conclusion was and is that they were most probably conceived during the Wei-Jin (220-420) period, a remarkably creative and formative period in Chinese philosophy, literature, painting and calligraphy. The original composition of the rules should probably be dated in the third century, may be even the early third century, i.e., at the end of the Han (220 CE).

The six rules can be divided in four plus two. Rules one to four describe the painting process in figure painting. Landscape painting became synonymous with Chinese painting as late as the eleventh century, the Northern Song with the famous Guo Xi and Fan Kuan.[4] Jing Hao, tenth century, may be considered to represent the transition between the figure and the landscape painting. Rules one to four are: (1) As the consonance of the vital spirit produces movement, (2) Use the brush for the skeletal structure! (3) Give a resemblance of the form responding to things, and (4) Set forth the colours according to type!

One may see these four rules as four verses of one stanza describing the painting process. Each verse has a caesura after the second syllable. The third syllable is a verb. No rhyme is required in this technical poetry. The first two verses, *qi yū sheng dong* and *gu fa yong bi*, just state that when nature's vital spirit (*qi*) accords with the vital energy of the artist, i.e., when the artist is talented, he may start painting. This means he may first draw a general outline, contours, in black. The caricature of the figure may be "written down," as if it were a Chinese

2. See, e.g., Mai-mai Sze, *The Tao of Painting*, 2 vols., Bollingen Series XLIX, New York 1956, vol. I, pp. 33-55, *The First Canon of Painting*, vol. II, p. 19, esp. Note 6.
3. Charles Willemen, "The Stanza of the Six Rules of Painting," in: *Studi in Onore di Lionello Lanciotti*, Istituto Universitario Orientale, Dipartimento di Studi Asiatici, Series Minor LI, Napoli 1996, pp. 1413-29.
4. Michael Sullivan, *An Introduction to Chinese Art*, Faber and Faber, London 1961, pp. 142-47.

character. Verse three informs us that the next step is to draw the texture, the surface, i.e., *cunfa*, offering an outward appearance. Verse four tells us to apply the right colours, the washes, after which the painting is completed.

Chinese poetry has stanzas of four verses during the Han and later. Four tetrasyllabic verses form a stanza. In this case the stanza is didactic, technical, not real literature. The confucianist or daoist elite did not bother to elaborate on this stanza, which was nothing more than a mnemotechnic means for a figure painter. There is no reason to see any Indian influence in this stanza. A cultured Chinese probably came up with these four verses in the third century. Rules five and also six seem to have been added under Indian influence. They say: (5) Locate while arranging the layout, and (6) copy according to the tradition! The Chinese reads: *Jingying weizhi*, and *Chuanyi muxie*. Here we have a different grammatical construction, namely predicative compounds, verbs. Rule five tells us to place a figure on a surface, having made an architectural plan, layout, i.e., *jingying*. *Jing* gives the vertical lines (Sanskrit *sūtra*), and *ying* arranges the circles, the arcs. This rule immediately reminds one of Indian *śilpa-vidyā*. Indian *tālamāna*, iconometry, is mentioned in rule five. A direct Indian influence can be seen in this rule for which the Buddhism seems to be responsible. Rule six tells us that we should follow the tradition. This tradition may be of India, or it may be a Chinese tradition from master to disciple. Rules five and six place the painting in space and in time. All rules make a stanza of six verses *pada*, which is common in Buddhist literature. Rules five and six were added to the first five rules at a later time, but probably still in the third century.

The six rules had nothing to do with the six members in India. They were four verses (not nouns), plus two. The unmistakable Indian influence does not come from the *ṣaḍaṅga*, but from Indian painting technique, from iconometrical design. Chinese have hardly ever paid attention to this technical literature. When in the third-century confucianist officials were graded and classified for public service, the six rules, even though not conceived to grade artists, could still be used as criteria to grade painters (and calligraphers). So they were written down by such people as Xie He, and later by Zhang Yanyuan and others. The Chinese intellectual was not interested in technical "literature." The rules were orally transmitted, until they became useful to classify artists. Even the Chinese Buddhist intellectuals did not elaborate on the artisanal rules. Traditional Chinese culture does not really value artisanal skills. The oldest *tālamāna* text in Chinese dates from 1742.

Before that, it was written that making images was meritorious, but the "grammar" of image-making was not written down. The eighteenth-century Chinese text is a translation of a Tibetan text, which is the translation of the Sanskrit *Pratimālakṣaṇa.* The Chinese text was not even written by a Han Chinese, but by the Mongol mGon-po skyabs, Gongbuchabu in Chinese, who explained and commented on the text, using Tibetan texts, especially, the Tibetan *Saṁvarodayatantra* and the *Kālacakratantra*, of which there are no Chinese versions. The earliest of the added prefaces is dated Qianlong 6, 12th month, 8th day, which is 14.01.1742. The translator may also have used the Tibetan *Pratimālakṣaṇa*, the *Pratimālakṣaṇavivaraṇa*, and the *Citralakṣaṇa*. All these texts have a Tibetan, but no Chinese version. The Chinese title is: *Foshuo Zaoxiangliangdujing Jie* (Taishå 1419), The Scriptural Text: Measurements in Image-making, expounded by Buddha, and its Explanation. Buddha expounded the text to Śāriputra in Śrāvastī, before he ascended to the *trayastriṁśa* Heaven in order to expound the doctrine to his mother. Both Haridas Mitra and J.N. Banerjee[5] have edited a manuscript of the Sanskrit text, found in the Darbar Library in Nepal. J.N. Banerjea also gave an English translation. Sakaki[6] Ryåzaburå had edited the text in 1918, based on a manuscript in the library of Kyoto University. He also gave a Japanese translation. The Tibetan version is the work of Dharmadhara, who recited the work, and of the Tibetan translator Grags-pa rgyal-mtshan from Yarlong. It was composed in southern Tibet, in Gungthang in Man-yul, north of Kyirong. The Tibetan translator is known as a "respected uncle" of the Sas-kya-pa rulers of Tibet, probably from 1306 to 1331, during the Yuan in China. He was a layman, who lived in Shalu for a while.

There is a Japanese literary translation of the complete Chinese text, given by Henmi Baiei.[7] Cai Jingfeng gave an English translation, but this is absolutely not the final rendering.[8] Recently the text has been studied in China, by example Hongxue, Li Dingxia and Bai Huawen. The studies appearing in China are mainly based on Tibetan literature, not on the Sanskrit versions.[9]

5. Haridas Mitra, *Buddhapratimālakṣaṇam*, Banaras 1933, *Princess of Wales Sarasvatz Bhavana Texts* 48. J.N. Banerjea, *Pratimālakṣaṇam*, Calcutta 1932. Texts from Nepal 2, Calcutta University Press.
6. R. Sakaki, "Bussetsu Zåzåryådokyå no Bonpon Kenky.," in *Geibun* 9, 1918, pp. 251-67.
7. "Bussetsu Zåzåryådokyå," in *Kokka* 40, 1930.
8. *The Buddhist Canon of Iconometry*, Ulm 2000, Fabri Verlag.
9. Our edition of the Sanskrit text, transcribed and translated, and also the English translation of the Chinese, with Chinese-Sanskrit glossary, will appear in 2004.

20

Interaction between Buddhist and Brāhmaṇical Art

In the Far Eastern Perspective

Preety A. Trivedi

IF the meaning of interaction, i.e., "a mutual or reciprocal action or influence" is taken in the true sense, the Buddhist and Brāhmaṇical art of India could be taken as its supreme example. The art of both the sects sprang from a single source, of the Hindu ethics, and flowered side by side from the earliest times. In other words, they could be termed as offsprings of a basic Indian concept of *pratyakṣadevatā* for offering *ekātmikabhakti*.[1] The emergence of the Buddha image is said to be the outcome of the same religious impulse that characterized the followers of the Brāhmaṇical religion.[2] Hence, the mutual influence and interaction was inevitable.

Prior to 600 BC, i.e., the historical period of ancient Indian history, Indian art probably formed a part of the art of Jambūdvīpa, comprising the whole of Asia. Some of its art forms were inherited from the common heritage of the area consisting of Bhadrāśva or China up to Ketumāla[3] or Iran and Mesopotamia. These art forms were the winged lion, two-headed eagle, winged bison, etc. Thus, Indian art in the proto-historic period, was a part of Asiatic art.[4]

1. A.S. Altekar (ed.), *Age of Imperial Unity*, p. 365.
2. V.S. Agrawal, *Origin of the Buddha Image*, p. 29.
3. According to Dr. N.P. Joshi, these terms may be found in the *Viṣṇu Purāṇa* or any of the *Bhuvana Kośas*, where they imagined a land of seven islands and Bhadraśva and Ketumāla were two of them.
4. V.S. Agrawal, *Indian Art*, p. 71.

The period from the late fourth century BC, shows two parallel streams of art existed in India in the form of the Mauryan "court art" and "folk art." The court art depended upon the artisans brought to India from Iran, whereas the "folk art" depended upon the pre-existent traditions of *yakṣa* and *nāga* worship.[5] The "court art" was developed solely by Aśoka, for the purpose of propagating his *dhamma* all over his empire and adjacent areas also. Since, his sphere of influence covered countries with varied cultures, languages and beliefs, it was suitable to use an art style, which could be identified with India as well as other parts of the world. However, from the point of view of art history, this was an isolated effort evidently having no influence on the parallel folk art traditions in India.

The art of the Śuṅga-Sātavāhana age, which followed after the Mauryas, was clearly a continuation of the "folk art" traditions. It was on the basis of this that the earliest images of Buddhist and Brāhmaṇical deities were made.

From this period onwards, followed the most creative and luxuriant period of Indian art, which promulgated its religious concepts of Buddhism and also Brāhmaṇism not only within the country, but also in Asia.

The Golden Age,[6] extending from the fourth to the eighth century AD and coinciding with the rule of the Gupta dynasty, gave a great stimulus to the colonial and cultural expansion of India in the Asiatic World. This age is considered to be grand for its literary compositions and artistic renderings. Here, the nature of Indian art, combining the supreme metaphysical concept with its imaginative form or image *mūrti* played a key role in disseminating religious abstractions, along with art, to other parts of the Asian continent. Many different races and cultures in Asia emulated the Indian Art and reproduced the images of Indian deities, Buddhist or Brāhmaṇical, according to their cultural ethos. Images of Buddha, *bodhisattva*s, Śiva, Viṣṇu and Devī were made in far-off places like West Asia, Central Asia, Far East and South-East Asia.[7] This diffusion of culture and art followed for many centuries. The metamorphoses that Indian art and religious ideologies passed through were transmitted to these regions in successive waves. Thus, when there was interchange and interaction in the various schools of Indian art, there was change in the art of these countries too.[8] The factors, which

5. Niharranjan Ray, *Maurya and Sunga Art*, pp. 22 & 63.
6. R.C. Majumdar, *The Age of Imperial Unity*, p. 510.
7. Radhakamal Mukherjee, *The Culture and Art of India*, p. 20.
8. *Ibid.*, p. 27.

made this dissemination possible were trade, trade-routes,[9] missionary activities of monks, pilgrims, vaiśya merchants, kṣatriya nobles, brāhmaṇa priests, Buddhist monks, etc.

In order to get a better understanding of the nature and means of the spread of Indian Culture to the countries of Asia, we may divide the entire continent into three broad zones, viz., the Western, South-Eastern and Eastern zones.

In the Western zone, we have countries to the east of Euphrates and Tigris (including Middle East and Central Asia), up to Turkistan. The architecture, sculpture and paintings of this region show that while Buddhism was predominant in these areas, Brāhmaṇism was not altogether absent.

The south-eastern zone includes countries like Burma, Indonesia, Java, Cambodia, Thailand, Vietnam (as the kingdom of Champa), etc. These countries were "colonized" by Indians in the true sense of the term. The missionary zeal of the brāhmaṇas and Buddhists and the spirit of adventure of the kṣatriya princes and nobles helped the "Hinduization" of the society. Sometimes, the Hindu kingdoms were also established by seizing political power. Hence, the influence of Indian culture and religion in these parts was more prominent and lasting than in the other zones; so much so, that many islands and land masses lying between India and China were included in Bhāratavarṣa and termed as *dvīpāntara*, meaning the collection of *dvīpa*s or islands between *antara* India and China.[10]

The Eastern zone, comprising the main area of our study, includes countries coming within the modern connotation of Far East, i.e., China, Korea, Mongolia, Japan, etc.[11] These far-off lands also came within the Indian sphere of religious influence; however, they adapted the Buddhist and Hindu elements coming from India according to their understanding and preference. Hence, the art we get to see in these countries shows a unique blend of Indian artistic themes with the local styles. Sometimes, these infiltrating perceptions of art were difficult for the people of these far-off lands to understand; hence, they came up with such iconographic forms, which were unknown to Indian art itself. For example, the images of Indra (known as Taishakuten) were quite popular in Japan, where the god was shown with his *vāhana* Airāvata. The size of the elephant in these images

9. R.C. Majumdar (ed.), *op.cit.*, p. 637.
10. Radhakamal Mukherjee, *op.cit.*, p. 22.
11. Scholars like R.C. Majumdar have included Java, Champa, Burma, Cambodia and the neighbouring countries within their study of the Far East. *Hindu Colonies in the Far East*, 1944.

was reduced to that of a horse, probably because the ancient Japanese may not have been able to imagine what an actual elephant looked like.[12] Or we may take the example of the *Rāmāyaṇa* in China where Rāma, Lakṣmaṇa and Sītā are stated to be brothers and sister.

However, from the point of view of studying the level of interaction between the Buddhist and Brāhmaṇical art in the Far East, it would be appropriate here to understand when and how these countries opened to religious and artistic influence from India.

It is generally held that Indian religious concepts travelled to the Far East via northern India and Gāndhāra to pass first into Central Asia and then across the interior of the Asiatic continent to enter China. From there it reached Korea in the fourth-fifth centuries AD and finally disseminated in Japan.[13]

The name of China was familiar to the Indians from a very early period. With the gaining of popularity of Mahāyāna Buddhism, also called Northern Buddhism, a great deal of cultural interaction took place between India and China. As Buddhism underwent many changes in India, they were reflected in the religious practices of China and other countries also. Hence, the interactive nature of the Mahāyāna sect, which was not averse to accepting idol-worship, was felt in the Far Eastern countries also. The official account of the introduction of Buddhism into China is dated to AD 65 in the reign of the Han emperor Ming-Ti.[14] With the growing trend in Mahāyāna Buddhism of accepting ritualism and a variety of iconographic forms in imagery, the Buddhist ideals in China may also have accepted these diversities in the religion. An interesting example of the co-mingling of Buddhist and Brāhmaṇical ideologies in China may be cited here. The *Rāmāyaṇa* or the *Rāma-kathā* was incorporated in the Buddhist *jātaka*s in China. It was called the *Daśaratha Jātaka* and was translated from Pāli or Sanskrit to Chinese.[15]

Thus, the interactive Buddhist and Brāhmaṇical art of India was transmitted to China, and from thence to Korea and Japan. In the early medieval period, the growing influence of the esoteric Vajrayāna sect also contributed greatly to the iconography of the Far Eastern countries. This is the period in which we see either the depiction of Brāhmaṇical deities or as associate deities to the Buddhist

12. Tokamichi Okabe, *Nepalese Deities of Japan*, Embassy of Japan.
13. Robert Paine & Alexander Soper, *The Art and Architecture of Japan*, p. 10.
14. P.C. Bagchi, *India and China*, pp. 7 & 32.
15. H.K. Chaturvedi, "Rāmāyaṇa in Asia," *India's Contribution to World Thought and Culture*, p. 182.

pantheon all over the Far Eastern countries. The cave paintings of Tun-huang are an excellent example of the interaction between the Buddhist and Brāhmaṇical art in the Far East. (Although Tun-huang comes within the area of Central Asia, we may consider this site in this context due to its proximity to the Far East and also because it posed as an important way-station on the trade route between Central Asia and China.) Buddhist Cave No. 285 here shows an assemblage of deities painted in the non-Chinese style, depicting Gaṇeśa, Kumāra and Śiva on the top.[16] The emulative examples of the Śiva Trinity have been found in far-off places, like the Yun-Kang Cave in China and as Daiitoku in Japan, displaying the Hindu concept of the synthesis of the male and female principles.

Korea was also greatly influenced by the Tāntric form of Buddhism. This could be because of the fact that it was open to influence from China on the one hand and was a transmitter of culture to Japan on the other. Buddhism in Korea is recorded as being introduced in AD 372; but the interactive aspect of the Buddhist and Hindu sects may mainly be seen here in the incorporation of Hindu gods in the Buddhist pantheon.

As long as Japan was open to influence through Korea up to the seventh century AD, it showed a great amount of stylistic similarity to its immediate neighbour. However, by ninth century AD, during the Heian period, there was a marked change in the iconography of Japan. We see the marked popularity of Hindu deities in the Buddhist iconography. Kichijoten, originally the Hindu goddess Śrī Devī, was incorporated into the Buddhist pantheon. She was considered to be a goddess of beauty and virtue and represented as an elegant lady in Japanese art.[17] Gaṇeśa was among the Hindu deities depicted in China and Japan as separate from Buddhist art or iconography. Two aspects of Gaṇeśa were generally known in China and Japan, viz., Vināyaka was the single form and Kangi-ten was the double form. Vināyaka was the generally accepted form, whereas Kangi-ten was secretly worshipped and was related to esoteric practices.[18]

The depiction of the 12 *āditya*s in the Japanese iconography is also noteworthy here. These were the 12 Guardian-*deva*s in Esoteric Buddhism. Symbolizing the

16. Priyatosh Banerjee, *A Śiva Icon from Piandjikent*, www.ibiblio.org.
17. Hugo Munsterberg, *The Art of Japan*, p. 82.
18. M.K. Dhavalikar, "Gaṇeśa beyond the frontiers," *India's Contribution to World Thought and Culture*, p. 13.

12 directions, including the four cardinal directions and four semi-directions, up and down, sun and moon, their origin may be traced to Hindu iconography. Chief among these were Bonten (Brahmā), Taishakuten (Indra), Katen (Agni), Enmaten (Yama), Rasatsu (Rākṣasa), Suiten (Varuṇa), Nitten (Sūrya) and Gatten (Candra).[19] It would be worth noting here that Vaiśravaṇa was also included as one of the *ādityas* in the Far East. In India, he is taken to be the precursor of *yakṣa* and the father of Nalakubera.[20]

Some stray examples of Hindu Buddhist deities in Mongolia may also be cited here, like the depiction of Mahākāla in one of the Mongolian paintings.[21]

Thus, the Reformations and Renaissance that captured the whole of India, and witnessed in the interactive elements of the Buddhist and Hindu sects, mainly due to Tāntric beliefs, also contributed essential elements to the Asian art. This led to a kind of "cultural mimesis" which characterized the Buddhist and Brāhmaṇical art in Asia in general.

Bibliography

Agrawala, V.S., "Origin of the Buddha Image," *Shatabda Kaumudi*, 1964.

Bagchi, P.C., *India and China*, Calcutta, 1944.

Banerjee, Priyatosh, *A Śiva Icon from Piandjikent*, www.ibiblio.org.

Chakravarty, N.P., *India and Central Asia*, Calcutta, 1927.

Chatruvedi, H.K., "Rāmāyaṇa in Asia," *India's Contribution to World Thought and Culture.*

Dhavalikar, M.K., "Gaṇeṣa Beyond the Frontiers," *India's Contribution to World Thought and Culture.*

Majumdar, R.C., *The Age of Imperial Unity*, Bombay, 1990.

Majumdar, R.C., *The Classical Age*, Bombay, 1990.

Majumdar, R.C., *The Age of Imperial Kanauj*, Bombay, 1990.

Majumdar, R.C., *Hindu Colonies in the Far East*, Calcutta, 1944.

Mukherjee Radhakamal, *The Culture and Art of India*, London, 1959.

Munsterberg, Hugo, *The Art of Japan, An Illustrated History*, London, 1957.

Paine Robert and Alexander Soper, *The Art and Architecture of Japan*, Middlesex, 1955.

Pandey, Mishra, Rao, *India's Cultural Relations with South-East Asia*, Delhi, 1995.

Rubissow Helen, *Art of Asia*, New York, 1954.

---

19. Mark Schumacher, *Japanese Buddhist Corner*, www.onmarkproduction.com.
20. This information has been taken from the *Paurāṇika Kathā-Kośa*, Dahyabhai Derasari, p. 540, I am grateful to Dr. B.S. Mehta, an eminent scholar, Varanasi, for providing this bit of information.
21. Radhakamal Mukherjee, *op.cit.*, plate 28.

Visuals

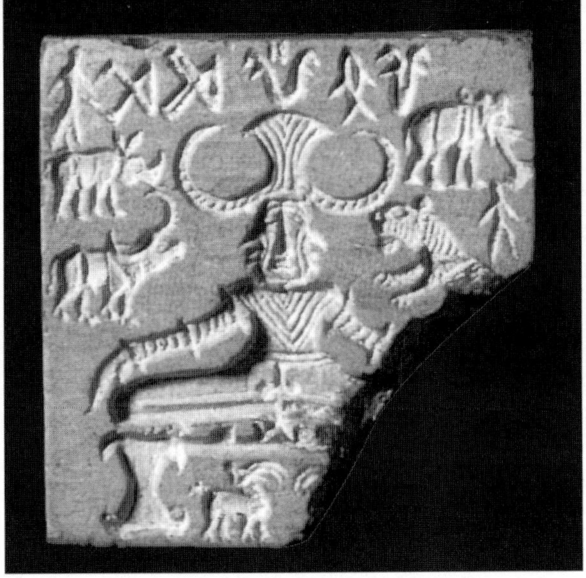

Pl. 4.1.Paśupati on Indus seal.

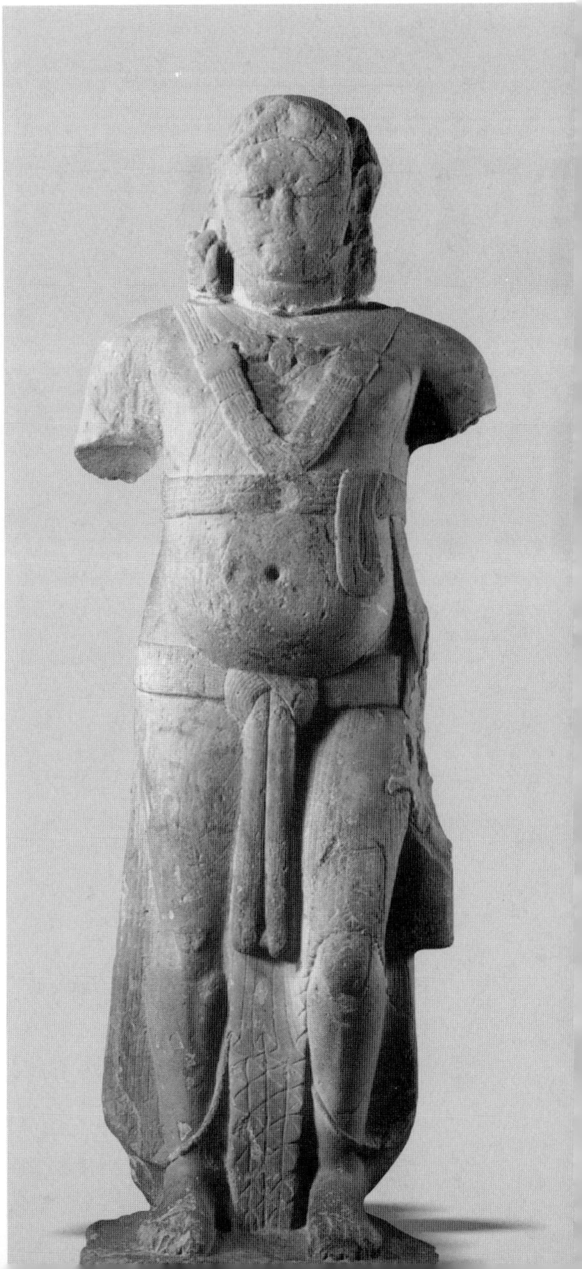

*Pl.*4.2.Yakṣa from Parkham,
Mauryan Śuṅga, Mathura Museum.

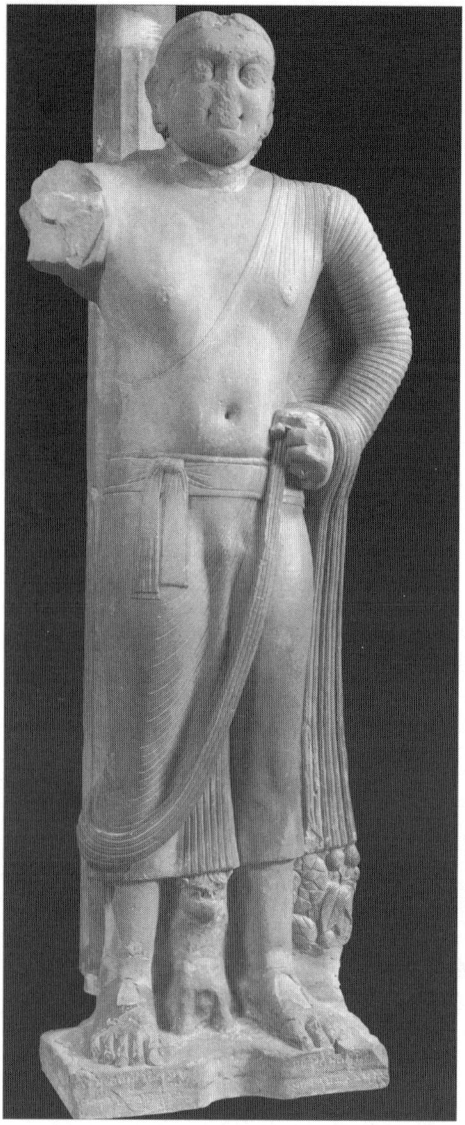

Pl. 4.3.Bodhisattva from Mathurā of Kaniṣka year 3, Sarnath Museum.

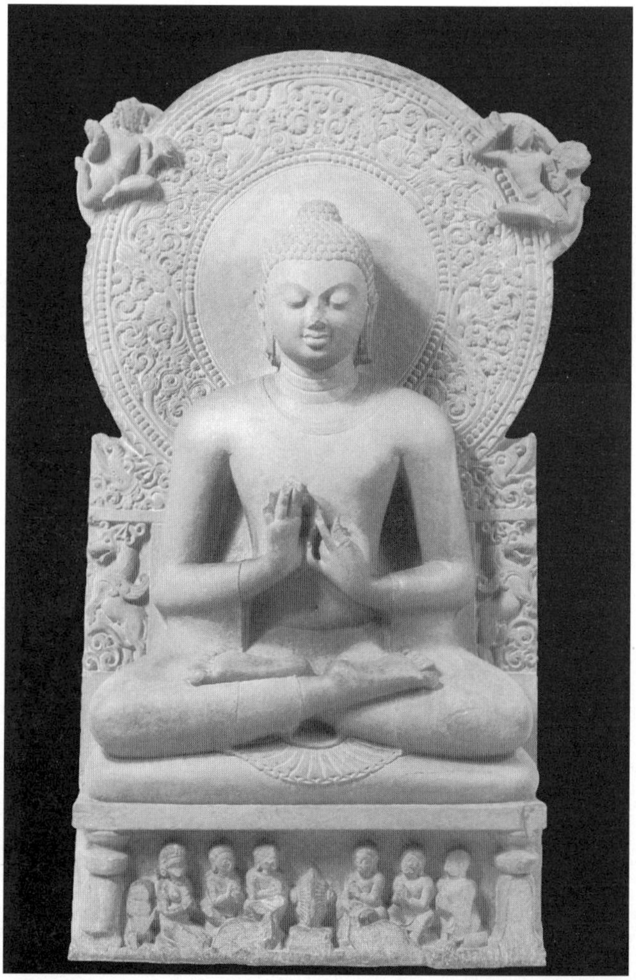

Pl. 4.4.Preaching Buddha, Gupta period, Sarnath Museum.

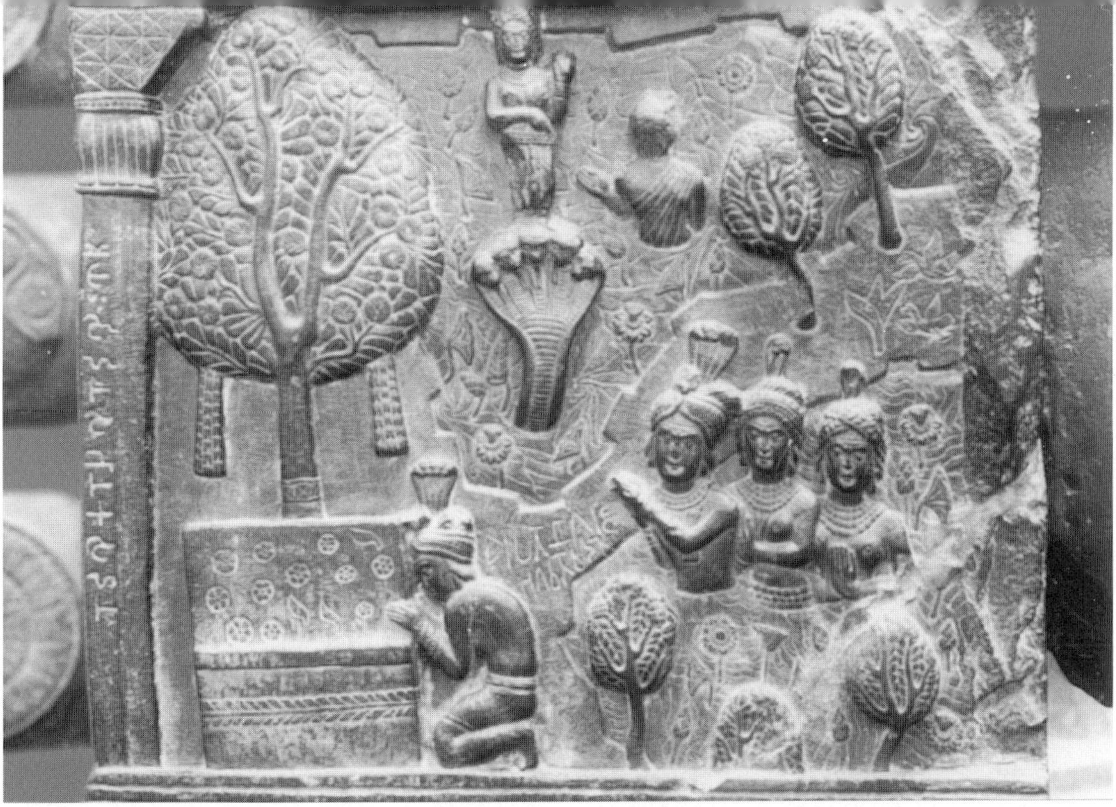

Pl. 5.1. Nāga king Erāpatra worshipping *bodhi* tree (Buddha), Bharhut, second century BC.

Pl. 5.2. Nāgarāja Mucalinda, Sañcī.

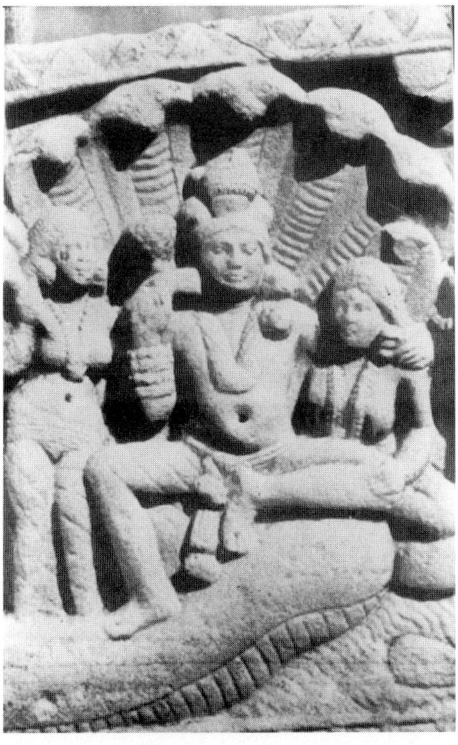

Pl. 5.3. Nāga Mucalinda, Sañcī, first century BC.

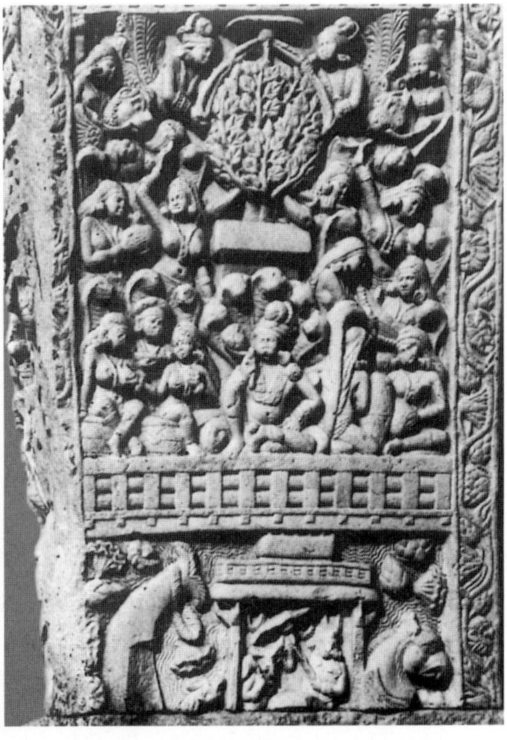

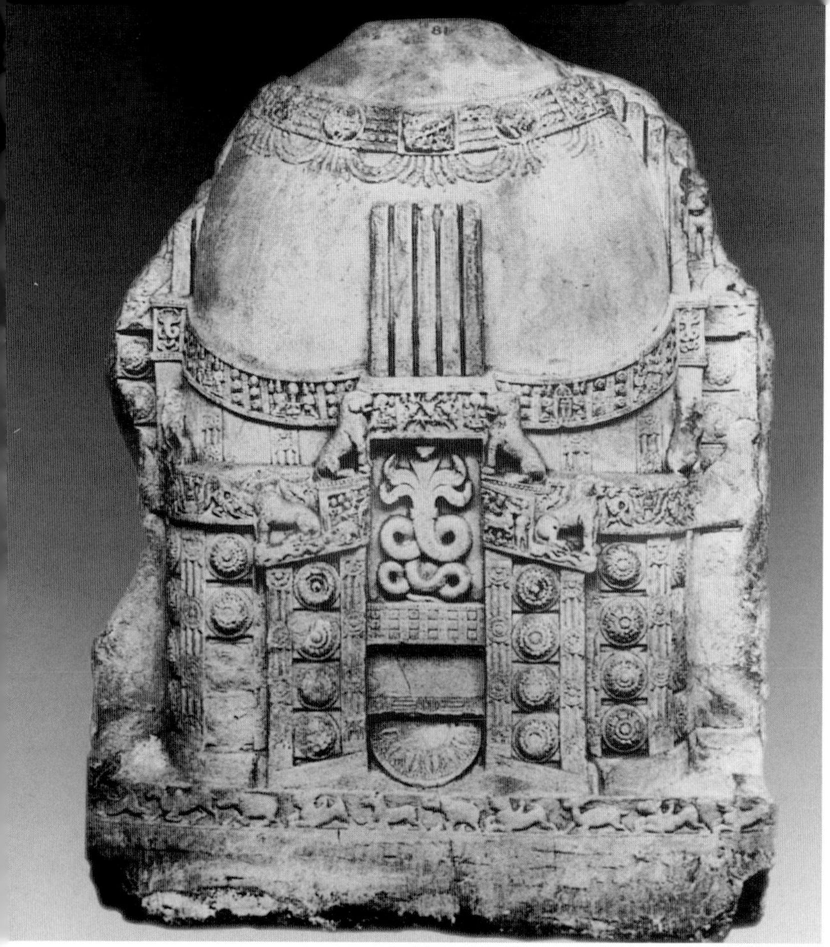

Pl. 5.4. Nāga depicted on a stone slab, Amarāvatī.

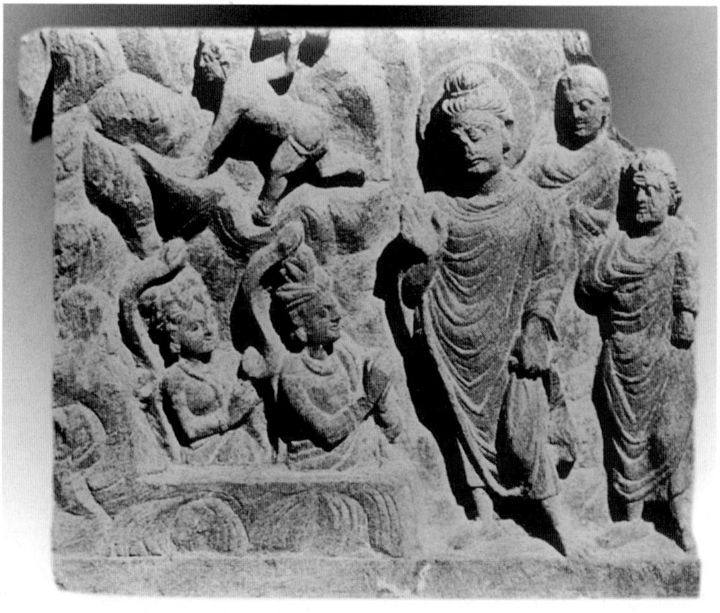

Pl. 5.5. Nāga in human form, worshipping Buddha, Gandhāra.

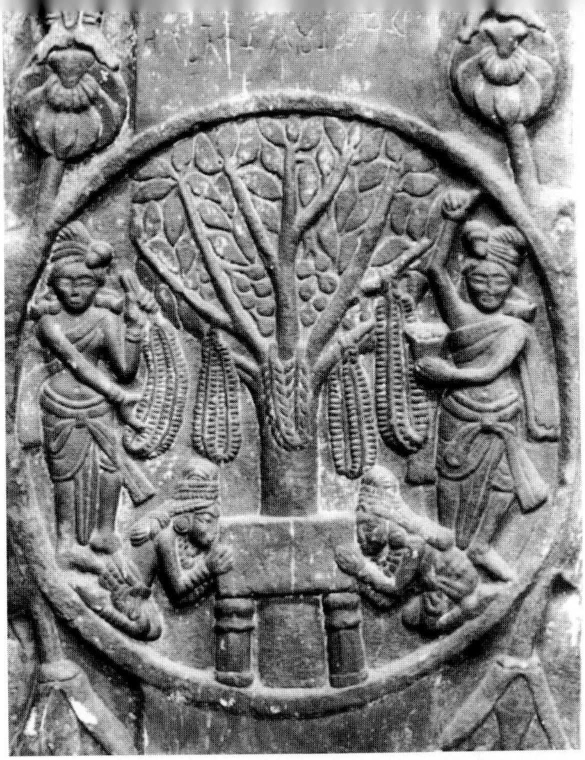

Pl. 6.1. *Bodhi*-tree of Kanaka Muni, Bharhut, Great Railing Pillar, first century BC.

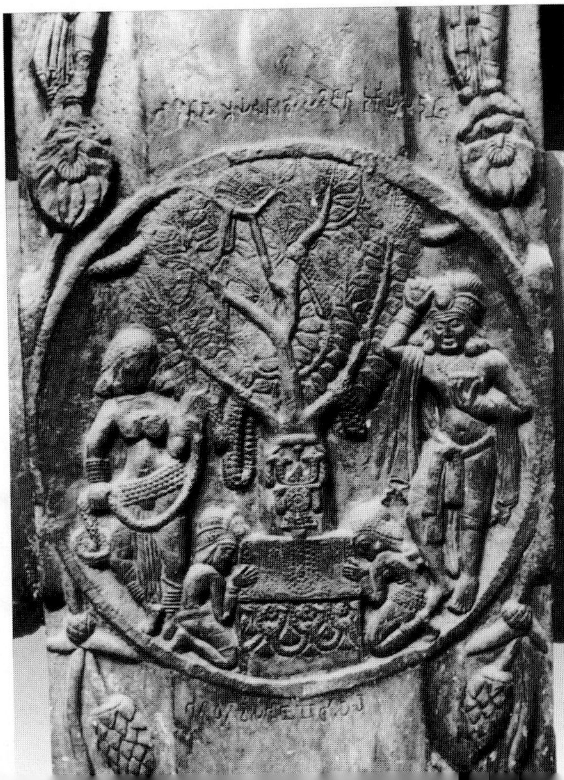

Pl. 6.2. *Bodhi*-tree of Viśvabhū, Bharhut, Great Railing Pillar, first century BC.

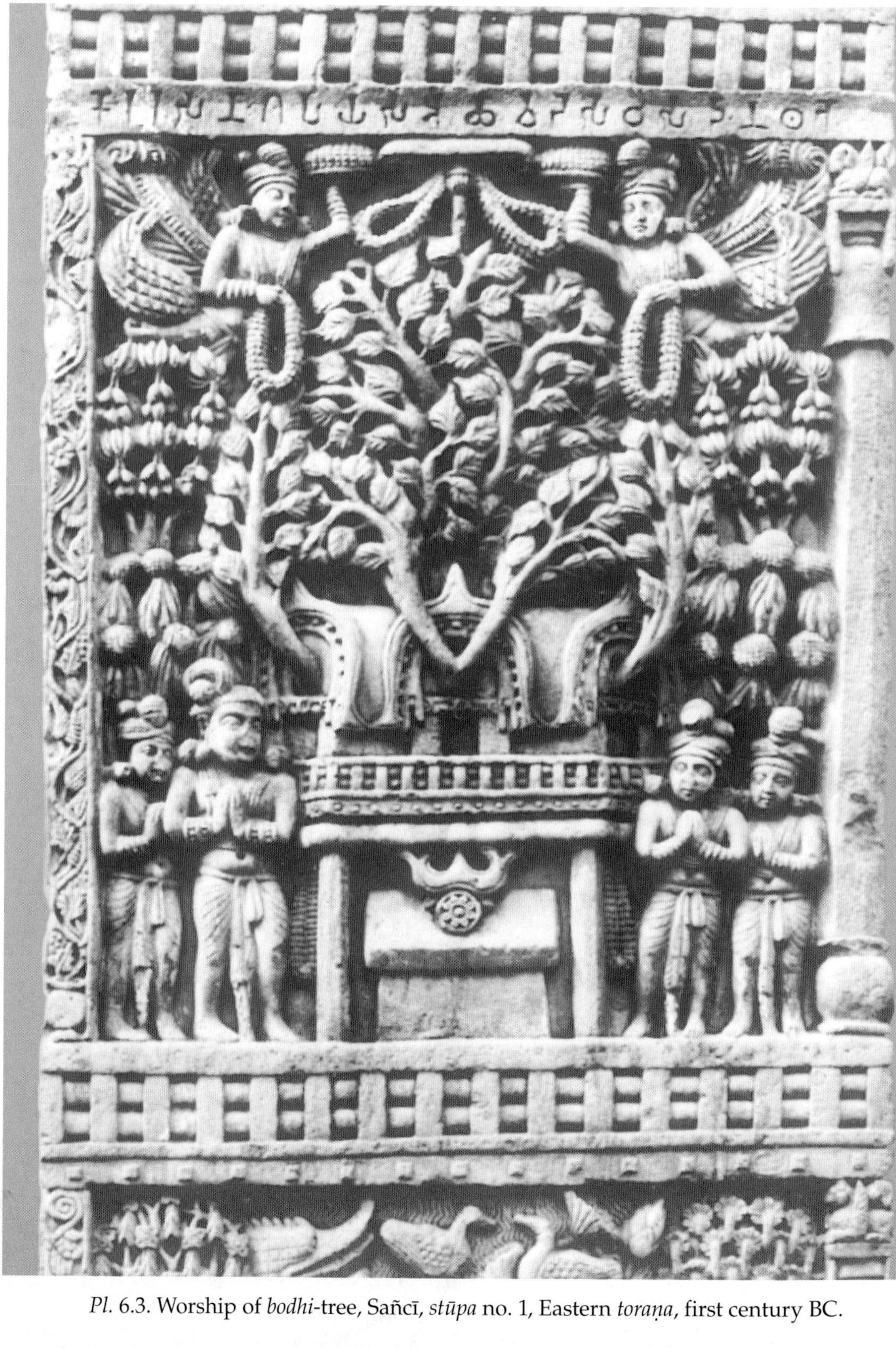

Pl. 6.3. Worship of *bodhi*-tree, Sañcī, *stūpa* no. 1, Eastern *toraṇa*, first century BC.

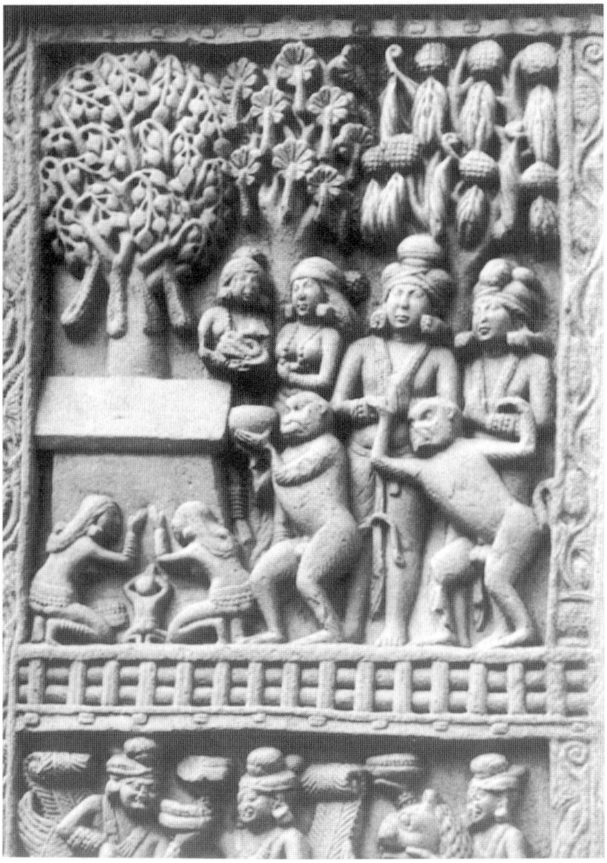

Pl. 6.4. Monkey offering Honey, Sañcī, *stūpa* no. 1, Northen *toraṇa*, first century BC.

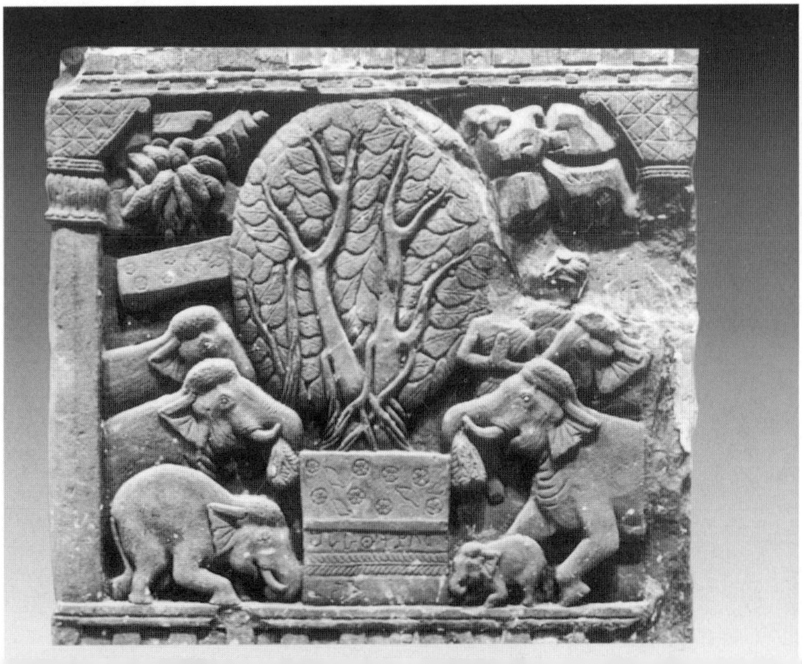

Pl. 6.5. Elephants worshipping *bodhi*-tree, Bharhut, Great Railing, Southern gate, Corner Pillar, first century BC.

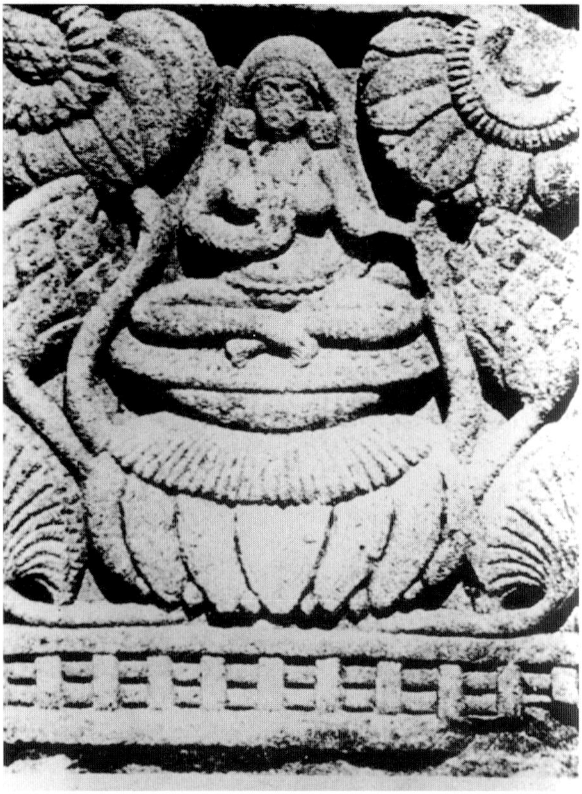

Pl. 6.6. Śrī-Lakṣmī, Sañcī, first century BC.

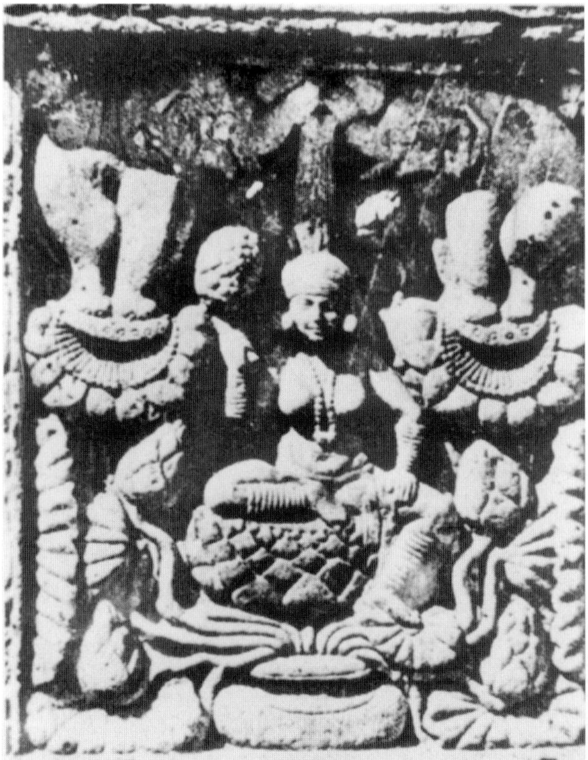

Pl. 6.7. Gaja-Lakṣmī, Sañcī, first century BC.

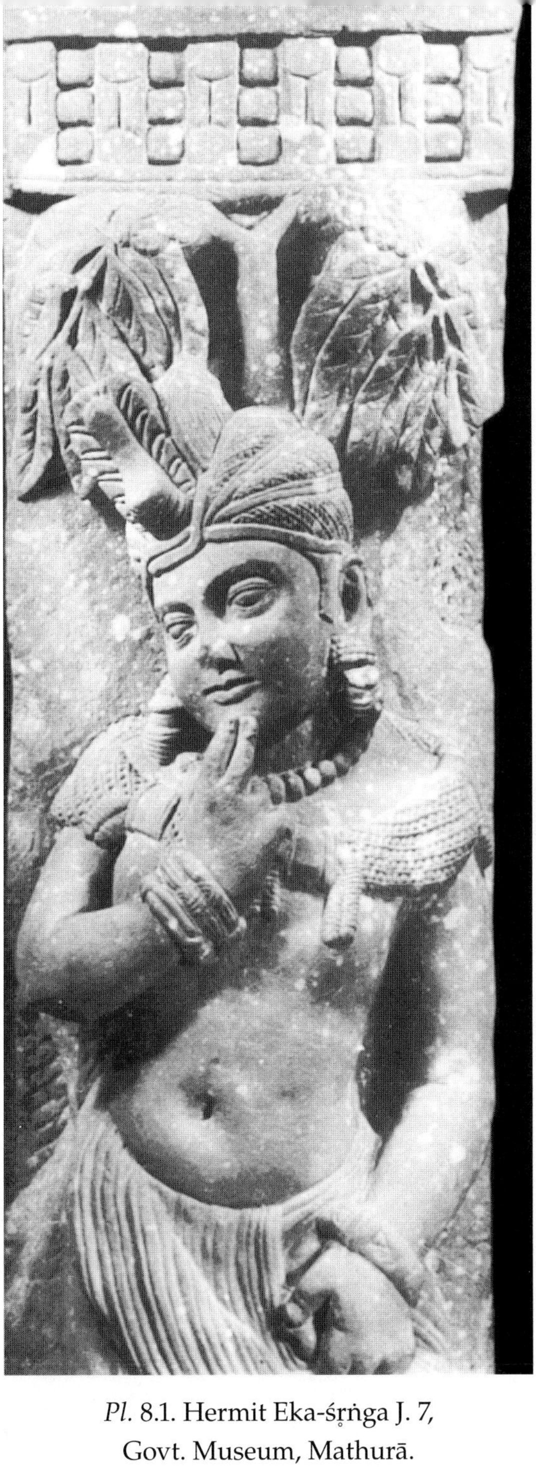

Pl. 8.1. Hermit Eka-śṛṅga J. 7,
Govt. Museum, Mathurā.

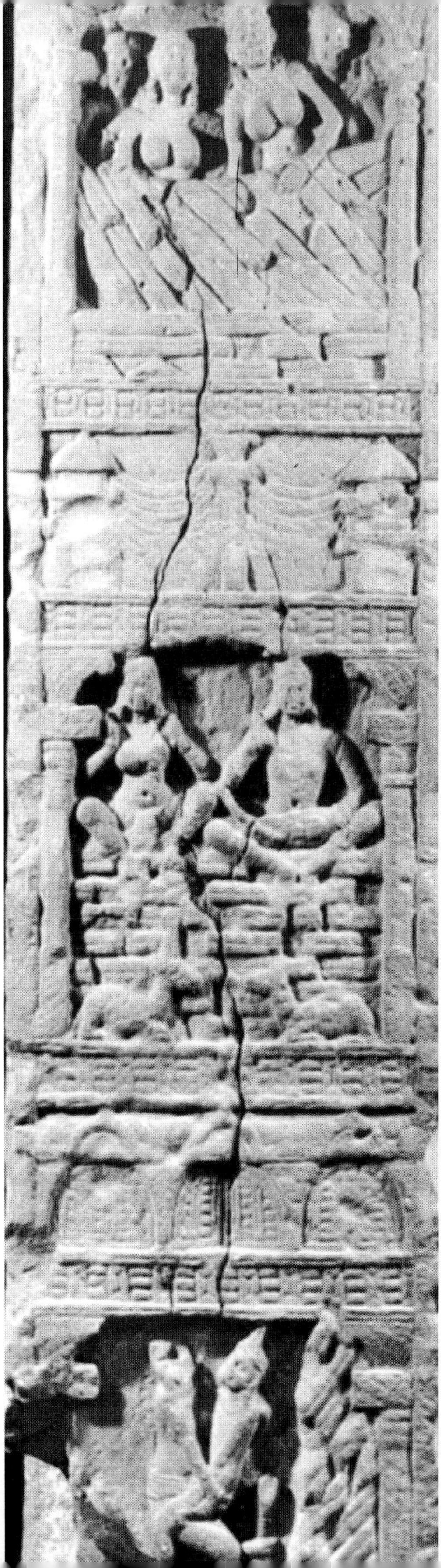

Pl. 8.2. The Episode of
Eka-śṛṅga 11.151,
Govt. Museum, Mathurā.

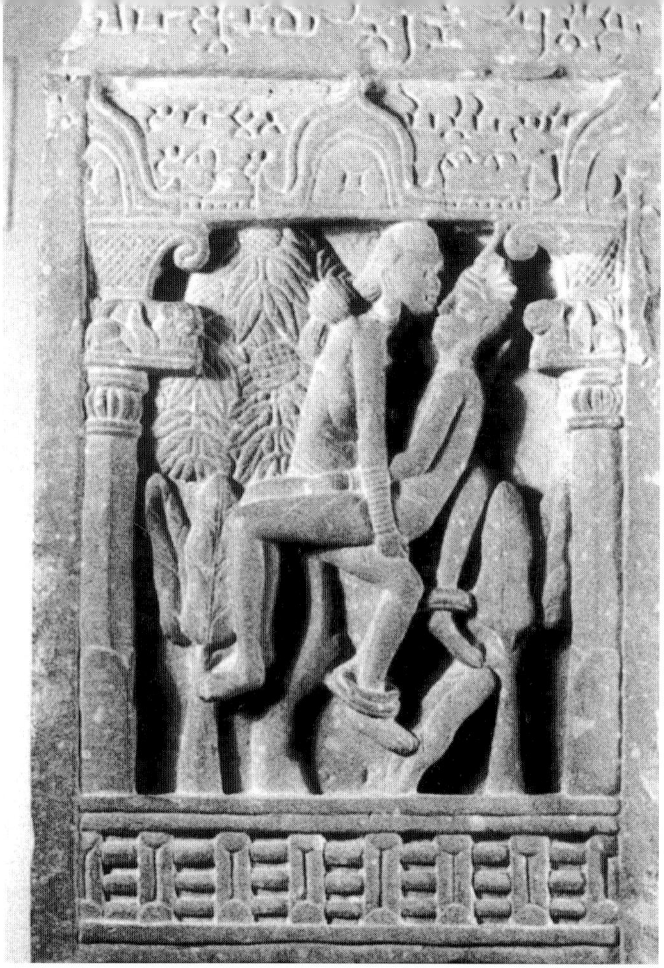

Pl. 8.3. A Horned Youth sitting in the lap of a lady J.7, Govt. Museum, Mathurā.

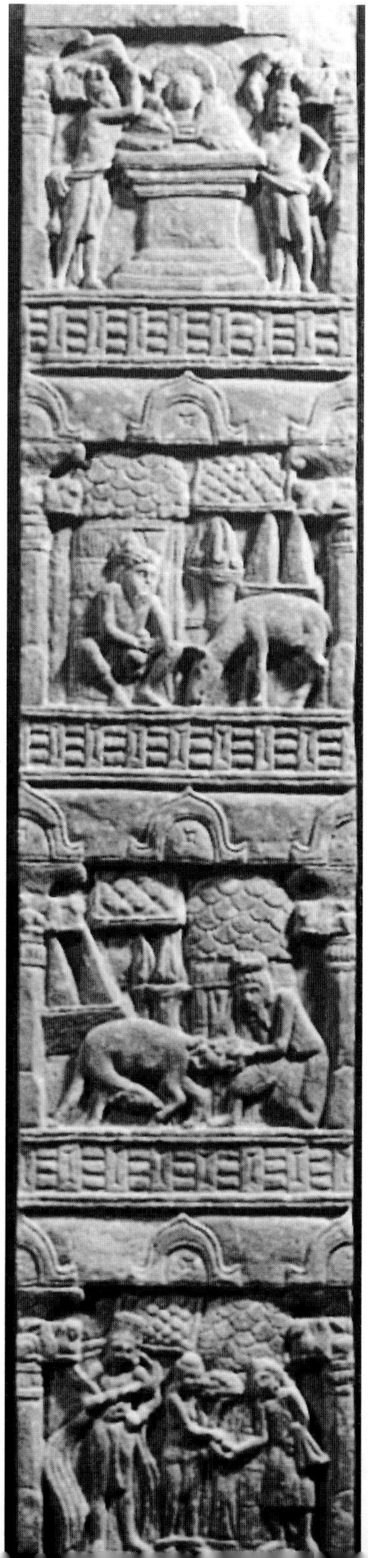

Pl. 8.4. Birth of Ṛṣyaśṛṅga 76. 40, Govt. Museum, Mathurā.

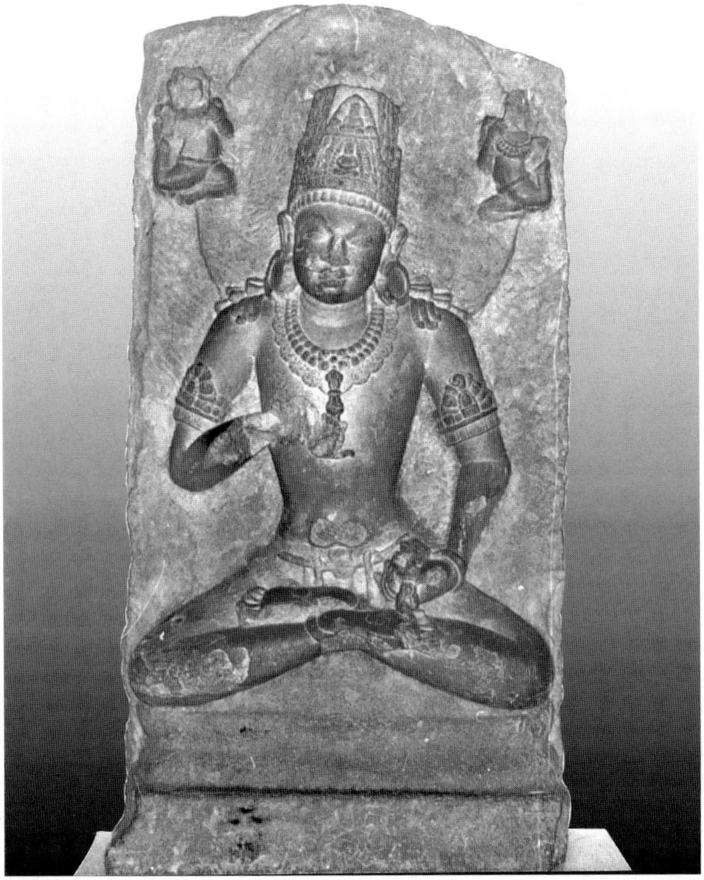

Pl. 9.1. Vajrapāṇi.

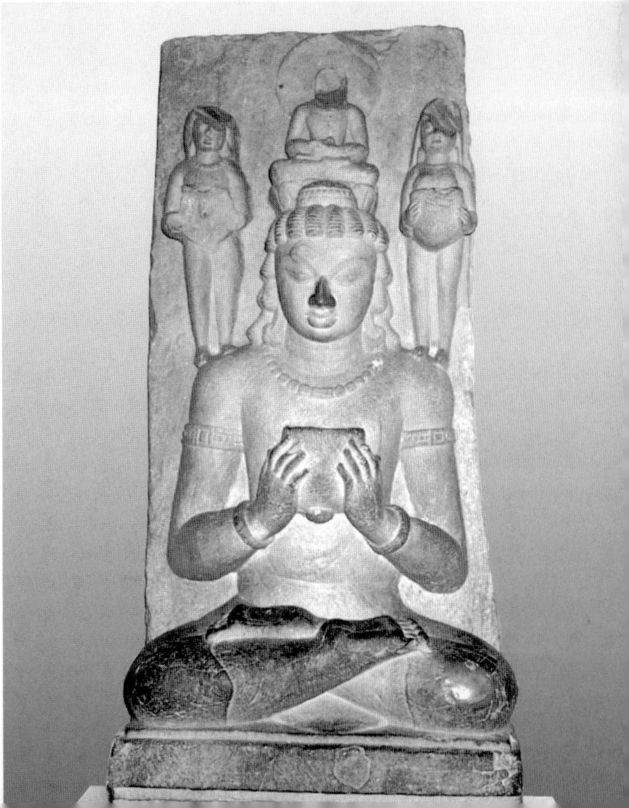

Pl. 9.2. Amitābha with Meditating Buddha on head.

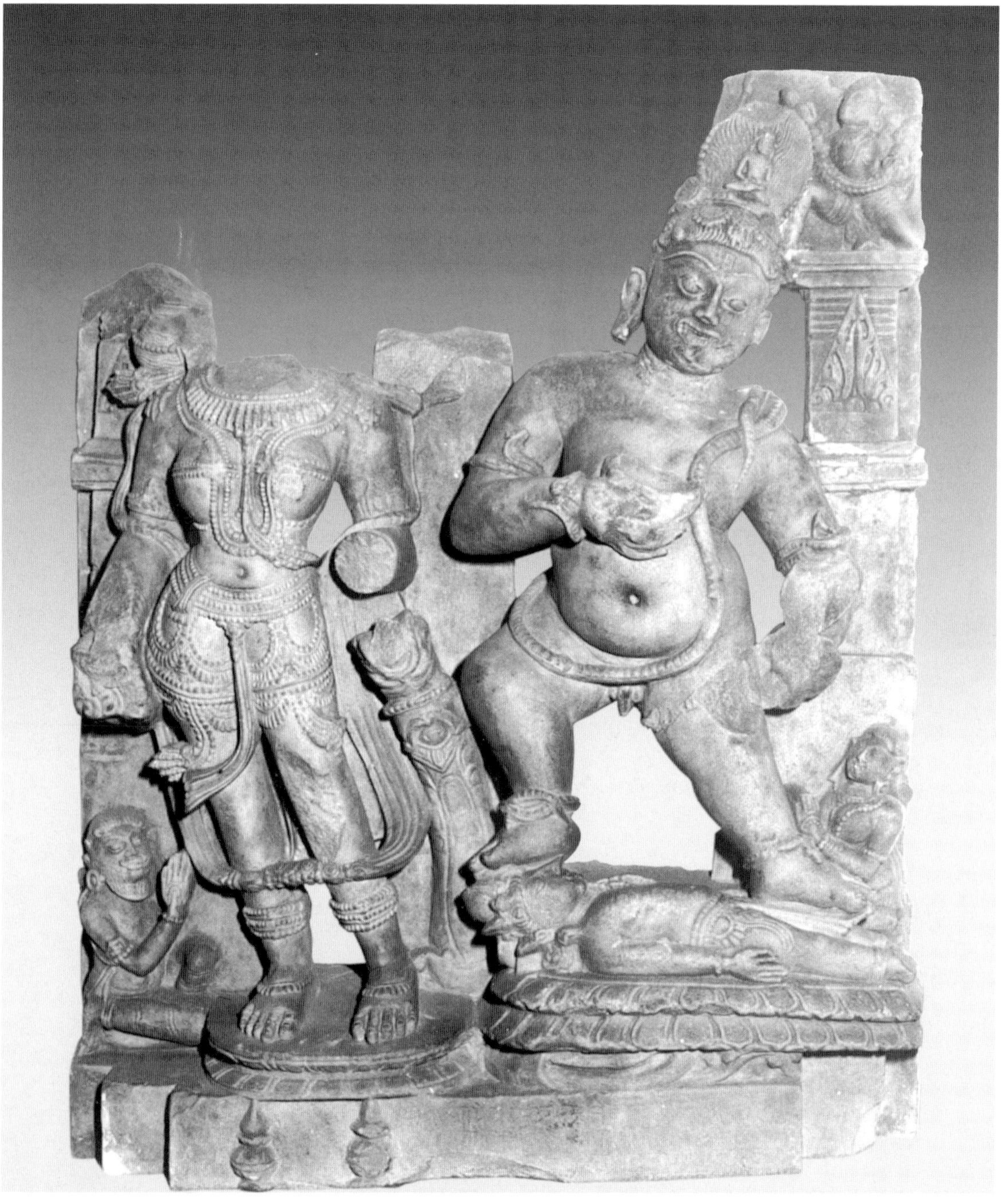

Pl. 9.3. Jambhala and Vasudhārā.

Pl. 11.1. Bhāskareśvara *śivaliṅga* (an Aśokan pillar converted to *śivaliṅga*).

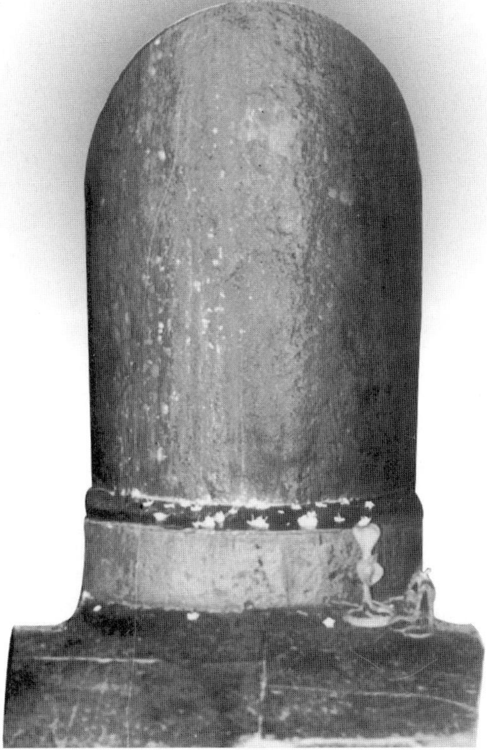

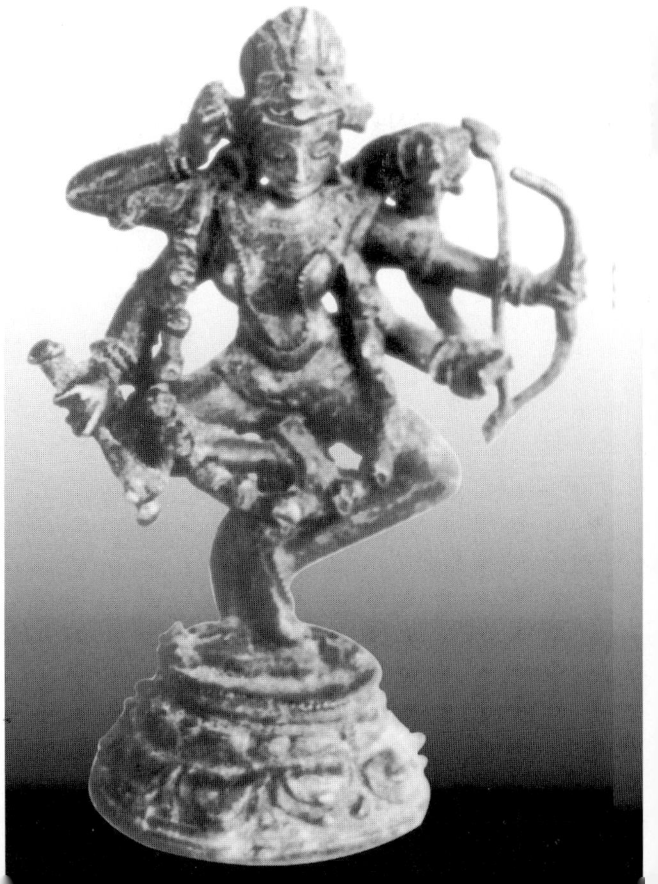

Pl. 11.2. Kurukulla (bronze) Bānpur ninth century AD.

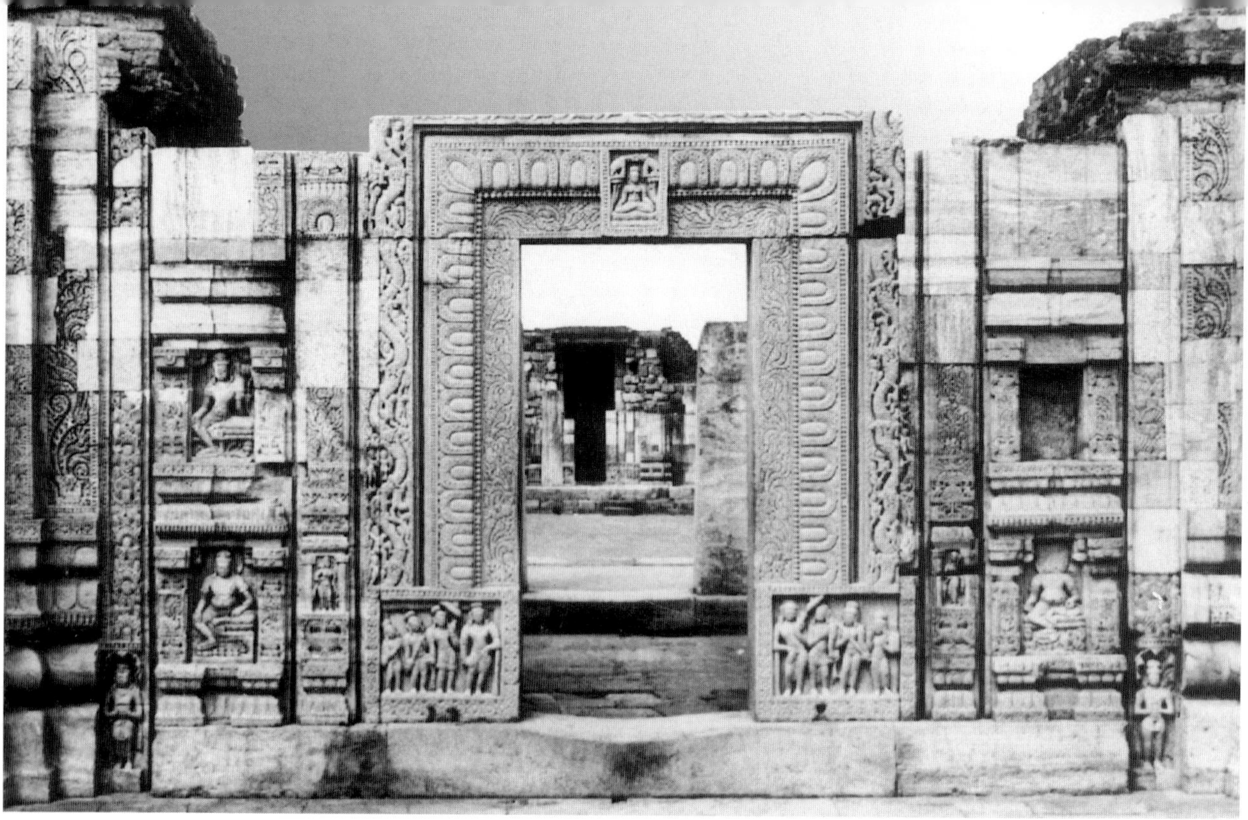

Pl. 11.3. Main gateway to Ratnagiri monastery.

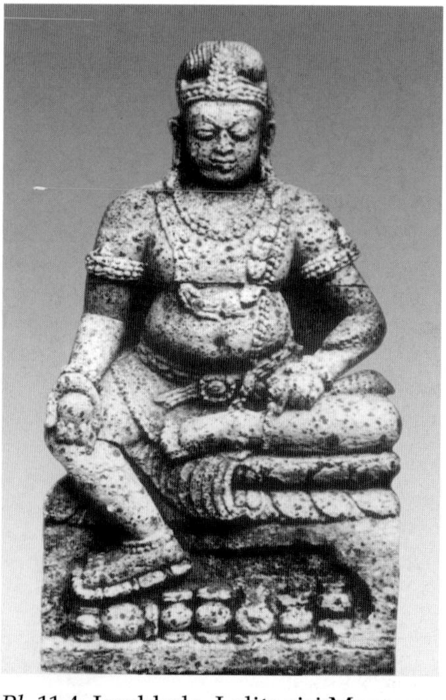

Pl. 11.4. Jambhala, Lalitagiri Museum, *c.* ninth century AD.

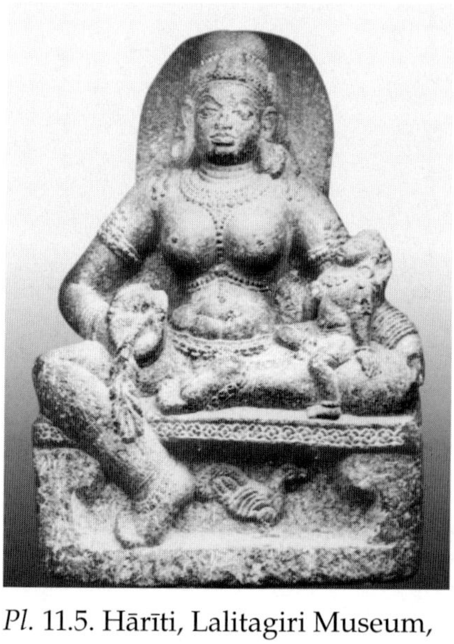

Pl. 11.5. Hārīti, Lalitagiri Museum, *c.* ninth century AD.

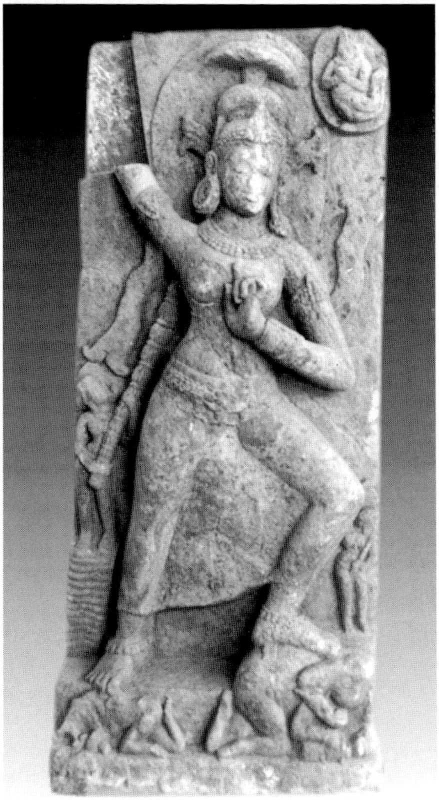

Pl. 11.6. Aparājitā, Lalitagiri Museum, *c.* ninth century AD.

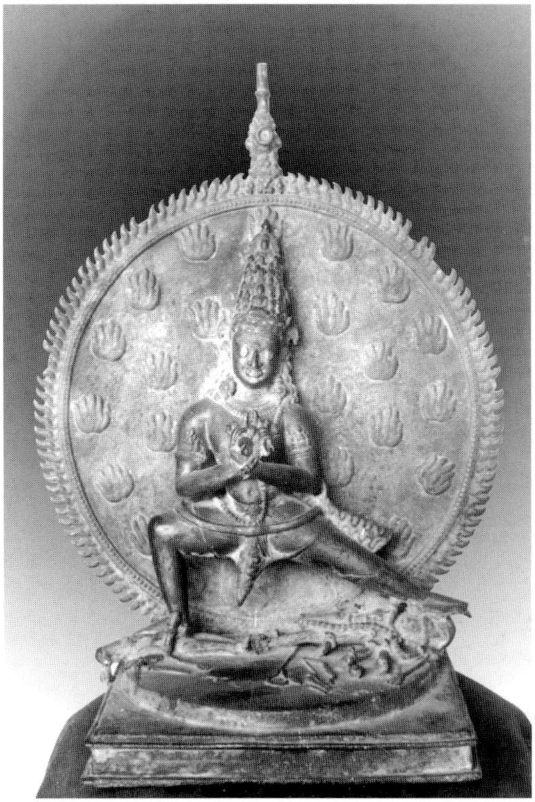

Pl. 11.7. Trailokyavijaya (bronze), Bānpur, tenth century AD.

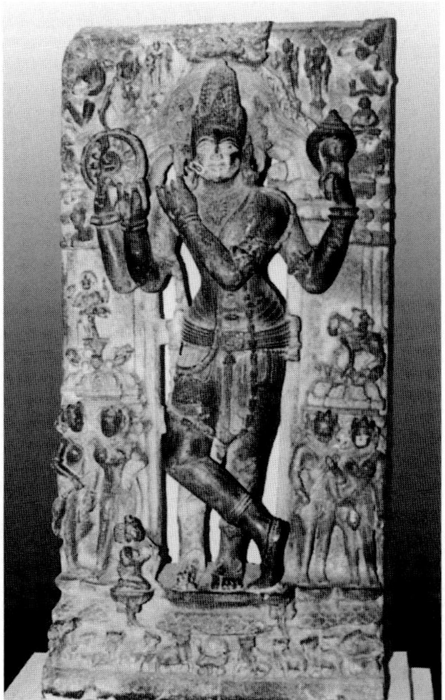

Pl. 11.8. Kṛṣṇa-Viṣṇu, Orissa State Museum, twelfth century AD.

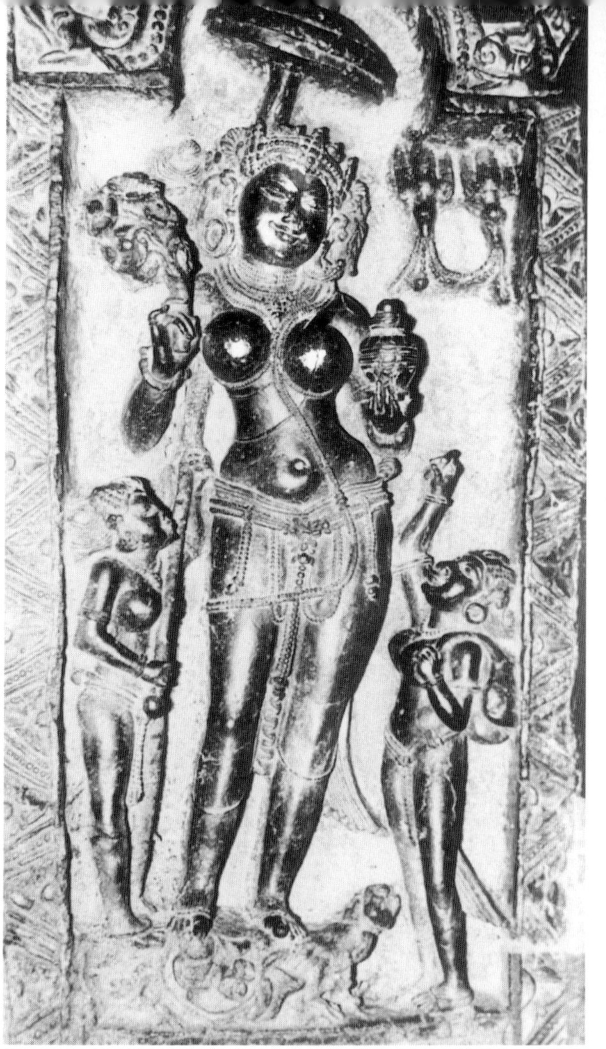

Pl. 11.9. Gaṅgā, Khiciṅg, *c.* tenth century AD.

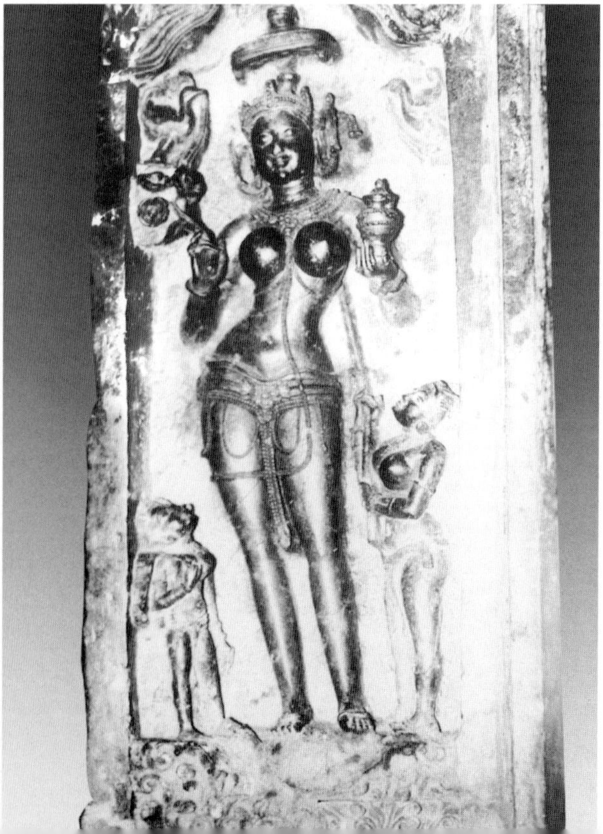

Pl. 11.10. Yamunā, Khiciṅg, *c.* tenth century AD.

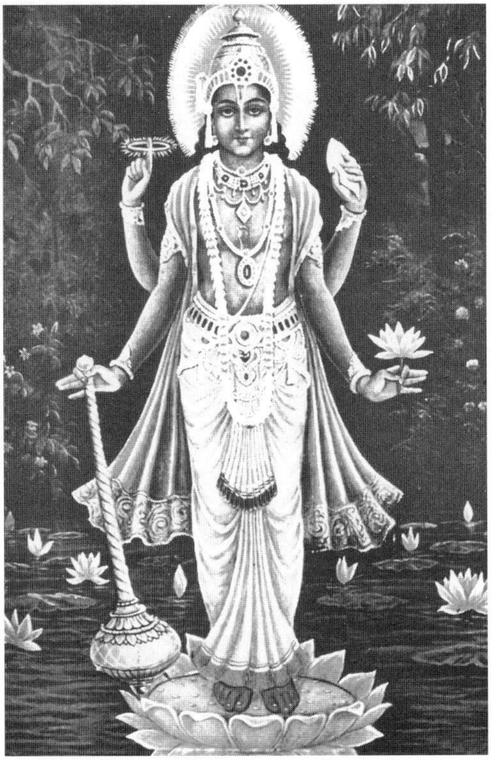

Pl. 13.1. Viṣṇu, modern painting, reproduced from the *Viṣṇupurāṇam*, Gita Press, Gorakhpur.

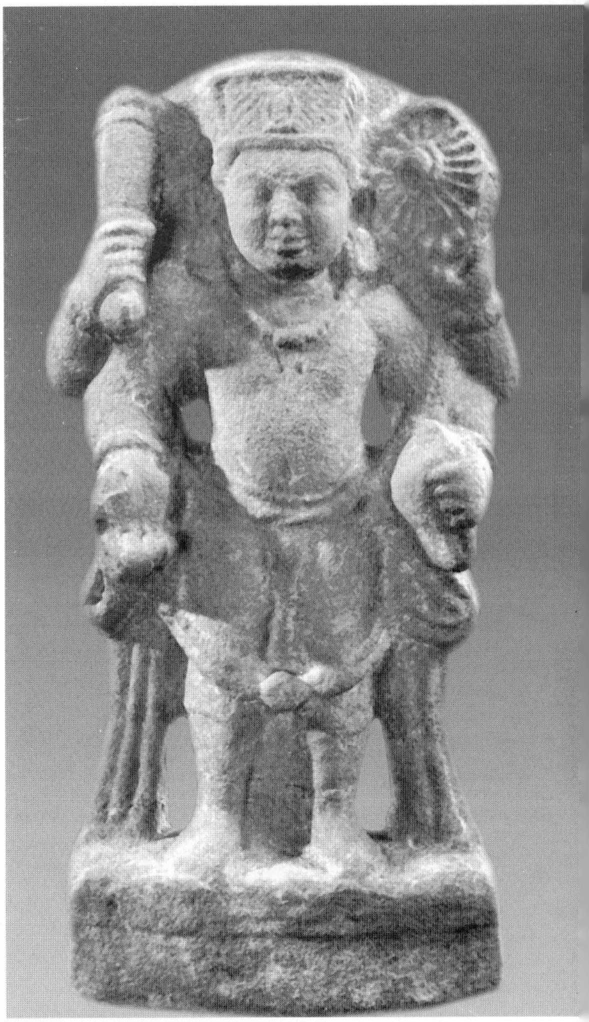

Pl. 13.2. Vāsudeva, Mathurā, spotted red sandstone, *c.* AD 300, now Museum of Indian Art Berlin, MIK I 5878, after: H. Härtel and W. Lobo, Schätze indischer Kunst, Berlin 1984, no. 21.

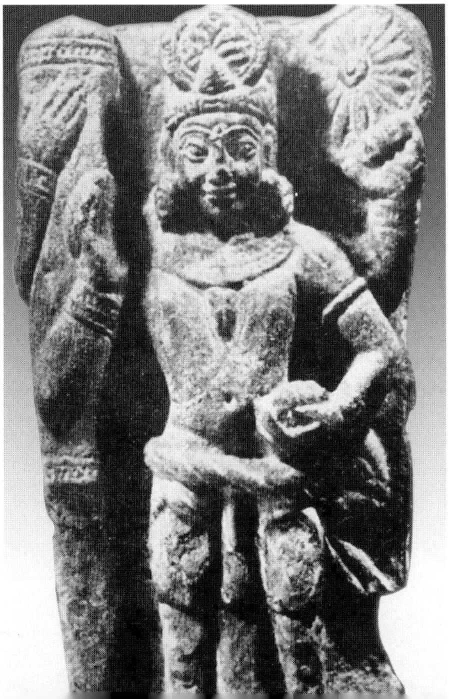

Pl. 13.3. Vāsudeva, Mathurā, spotted red sandstone, Kuṣāṇa period, now Govt. Museum Mathurā, after: Härtel 1983, fig. 32.

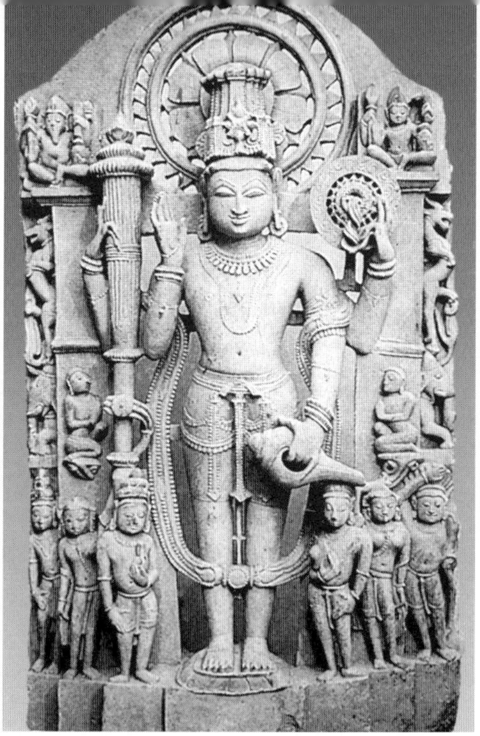

Pl. 13.4. Viṣṇu (Vāsudeva?), from Rataul, Meerut, now Govt. Museum, Mathurā (no. 88.10), medieval, after: Sharma 1994, fig. 74.

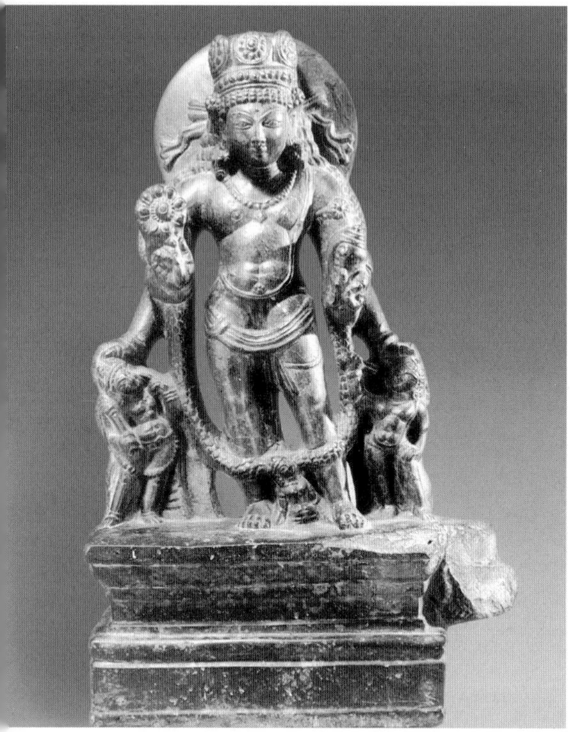

Pl. 13.5. Viṣṇu (Vāsudeva), Kashmir, grey sandstone, ninth-tenth centuries, after: Sotheby's New York, Sept. 19, 1996, lot 125.

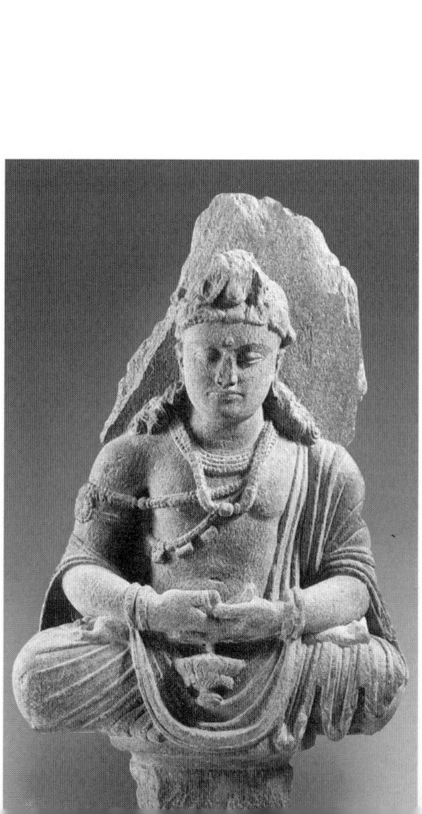

Pl. 13.6. Bodhisattva Padmapāṇi, grey schist, Gandhāra, now British Museum, London (no. OA 1913.1-8.14), after: Zwalf 1996, no. 77.

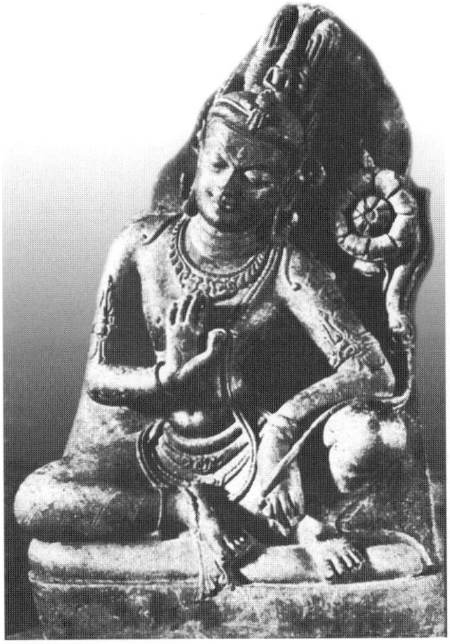

Pl. 13.7. Avalokiteśvara Padmapāṇi, black schist, Pāla, from Bishenpur, Tandawa, now Patna Museum, *c.* eleventh century, after: Banerji 1933, pl. XXXIIa.

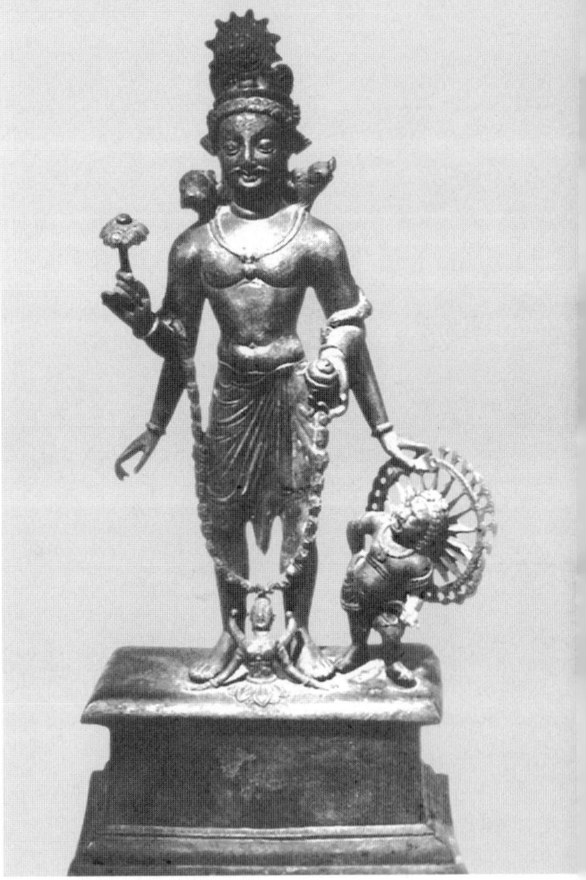

Pl. 13.8. Three-headed bronze Viṣṇu from Swat Valley, now Museum of Indian Art, Berlin (No. I 24), seventh century, after: Härtel 1983.

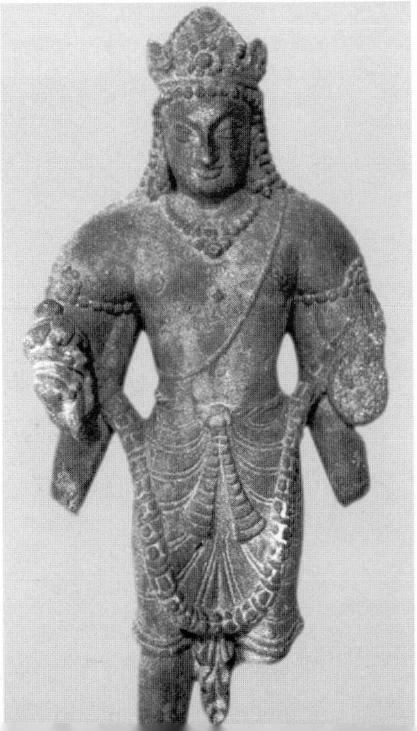

Pl. 13.9. Vāsudeva, grey schist from Kashmir, three arms damaged, holding lotus in the front right hand, eighth-ninth centuries, after: Sotheby's London, 4th July 1983, lot 69.

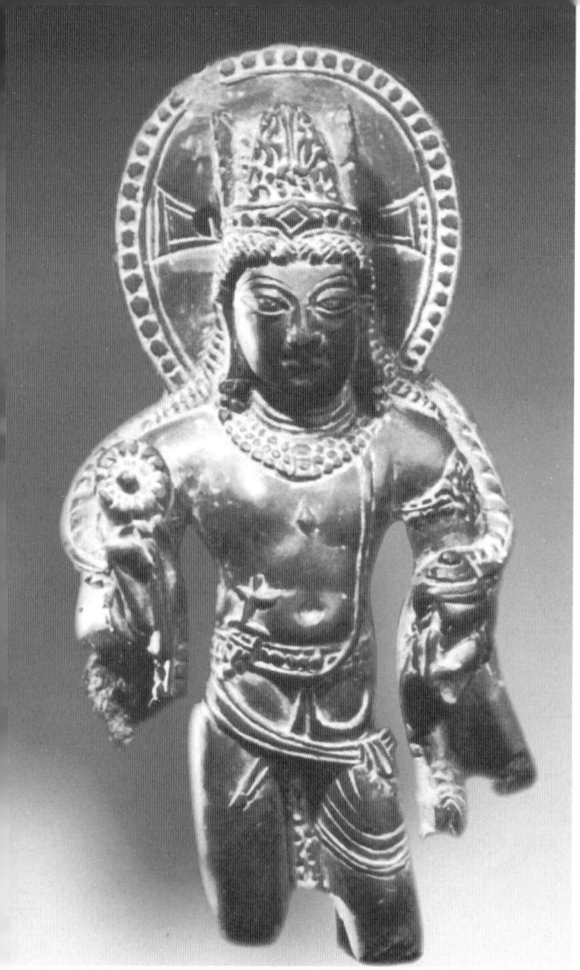

Pl. 13.10. Vāsudeva, grey schist from Kashmir, two arms damaged, holding lotus in the front right hand and conch in the front left hand, *c.* ninth century, after: Spink & Son London, n.d., illustration 23.

Pl. 13.11. Inscribed bronze Sugatisandaśana Lokeśvara from Kashmir, now Sri Pratap Singh Museum, Srinagar, 980-1003 AD, after: Pal 1975, No. 51a.

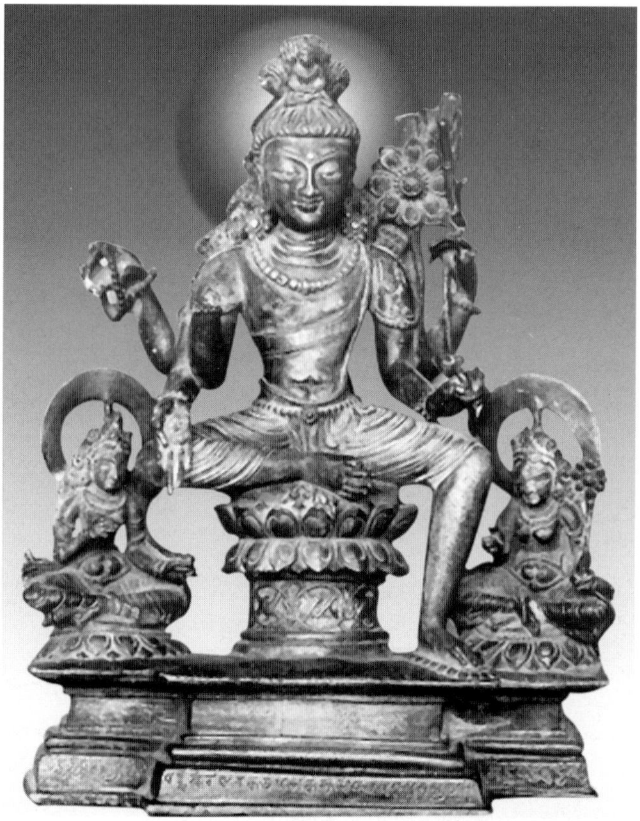

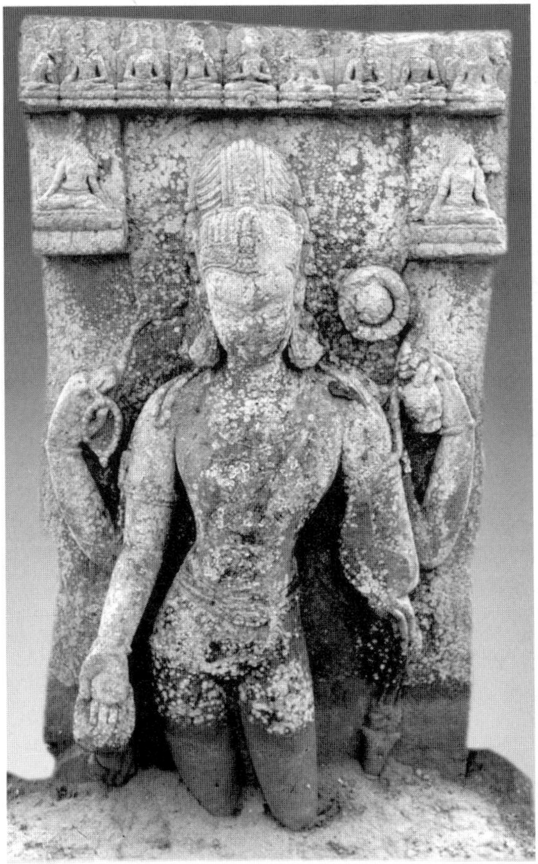

Pl. 13.12. Avalokiteśvara from Ratnagiri, Orissa, *c*. ninth century, Photo: G. Bhattacharya.

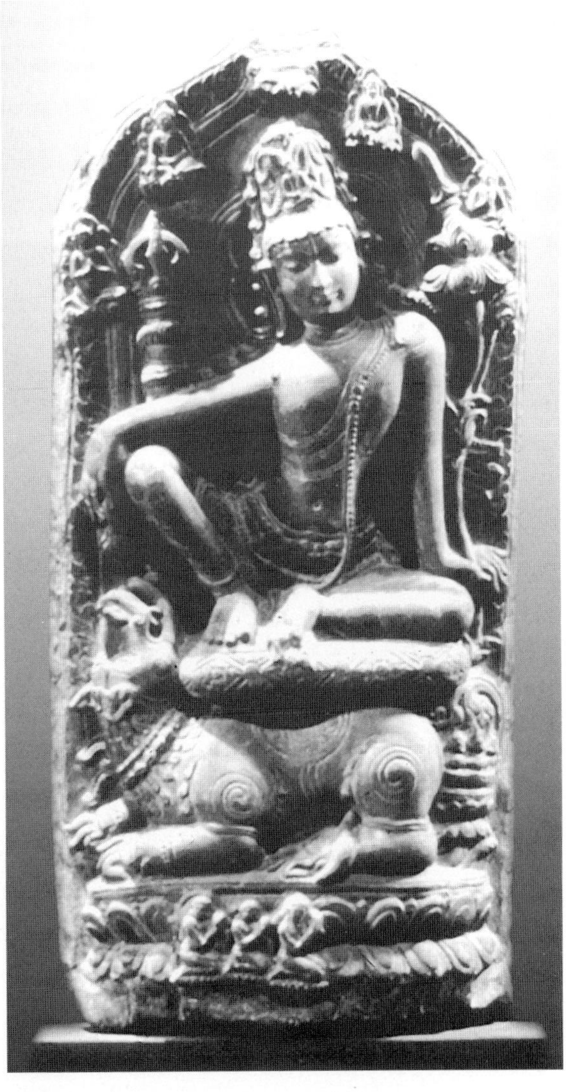

Pl. 13.13. Siṁhanāda-Lokeśvara, grey phyllite, from between Nalanda and Lakhi Sarai, eleventh-twelfth centuries, now Museum of Indian Art, Berlin (no. I 576), after: Bautze-Picron 1998, no. 51.

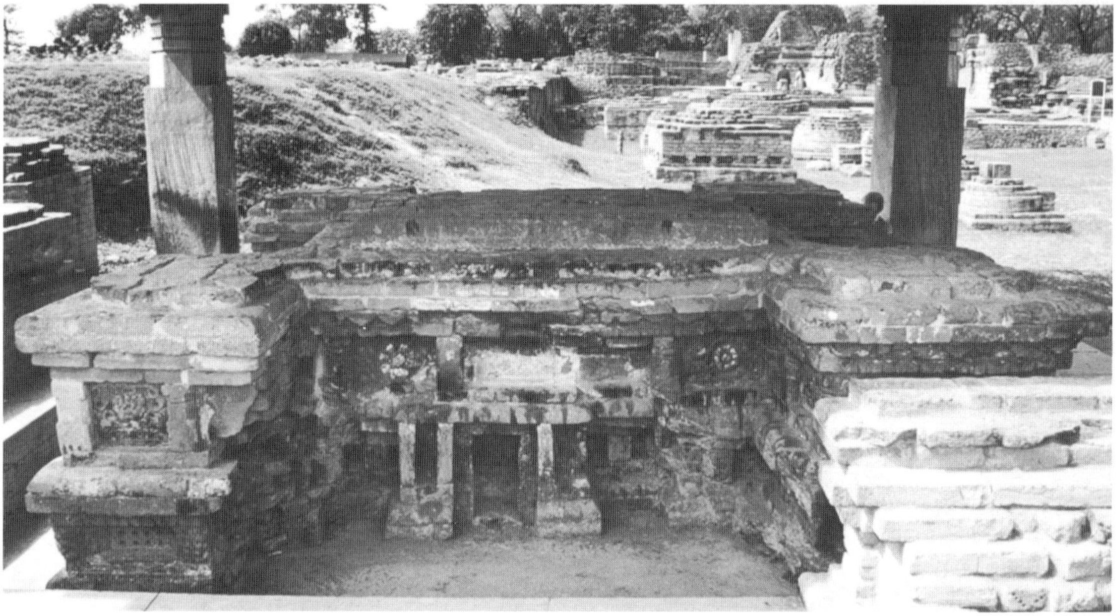

Pl. 15.1. Sārnāth, pedestal with *pañcāyatana* structure (no. 136 in Sahni's plan of 1926), view from E.

Pl. 15.2. Sārnāth, pedestal no. 136, view from S.

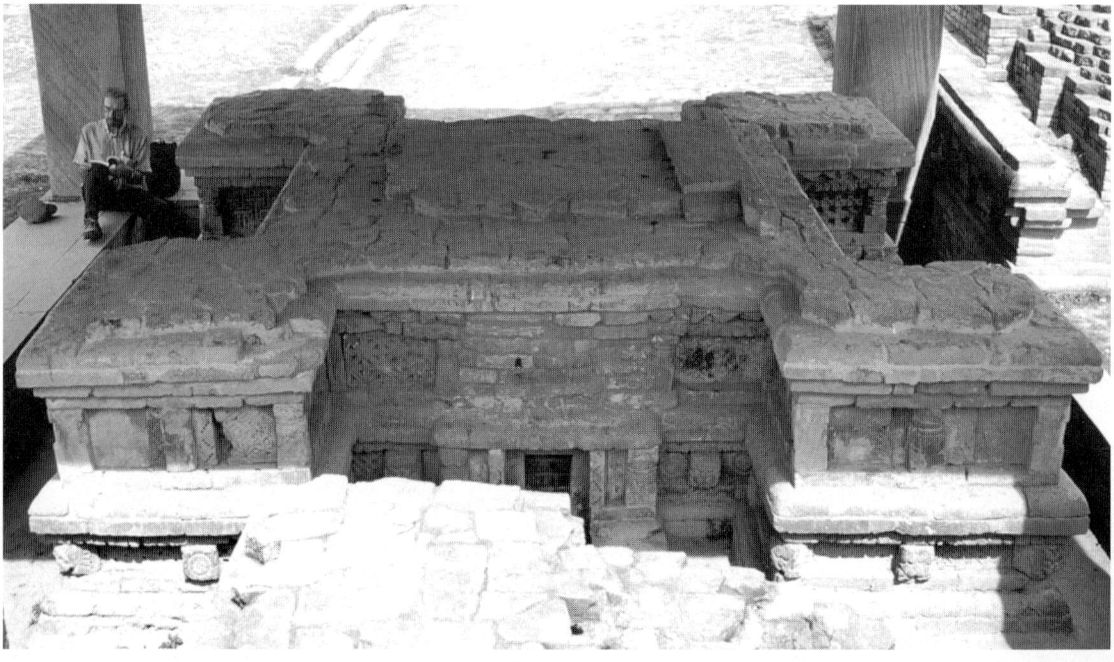

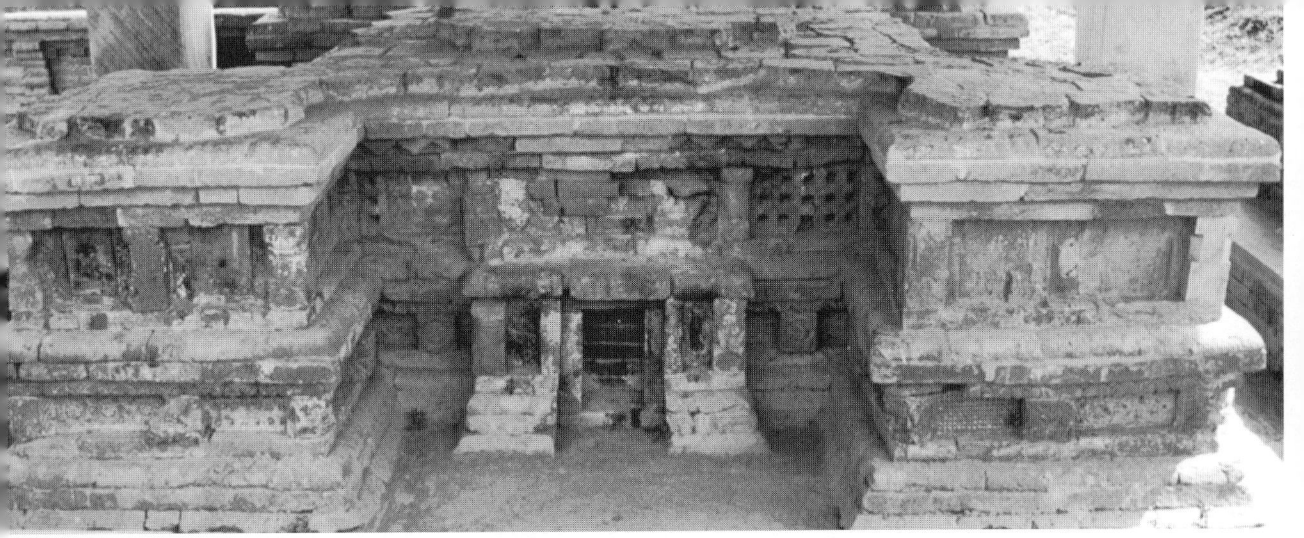

Pl. 15.3. Sārnāth, pedestal no. 136, view from W.

Pl. 15.4. Sārnāth, pedestal no. 136, view from N.

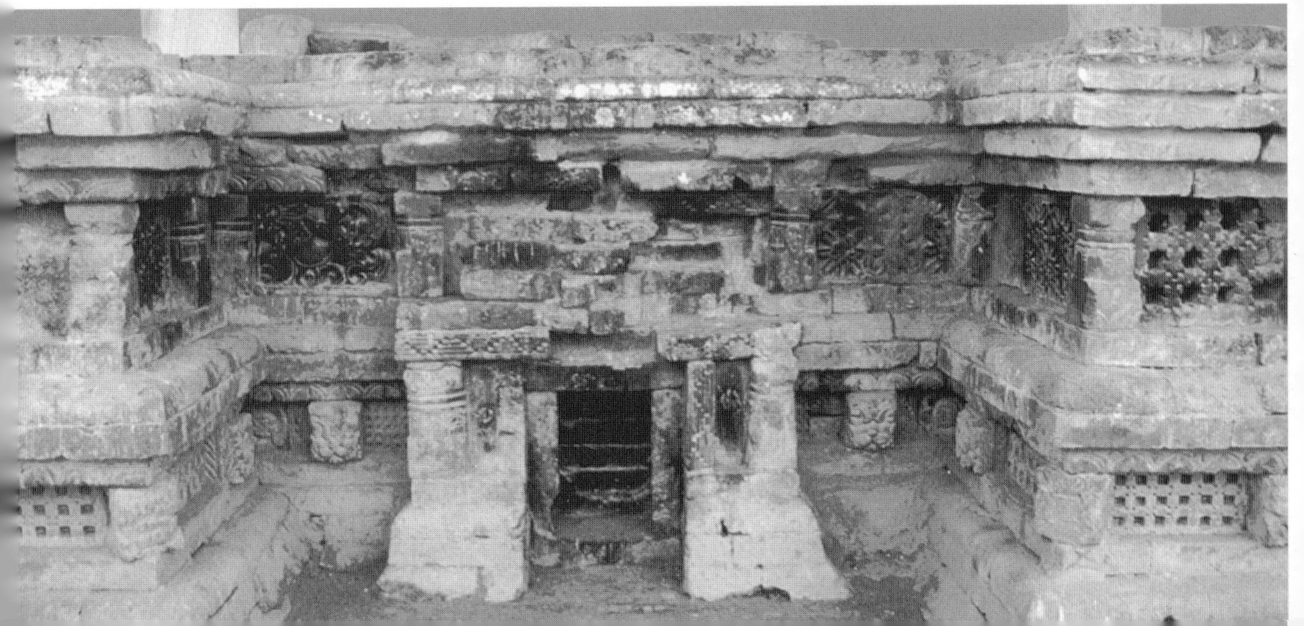

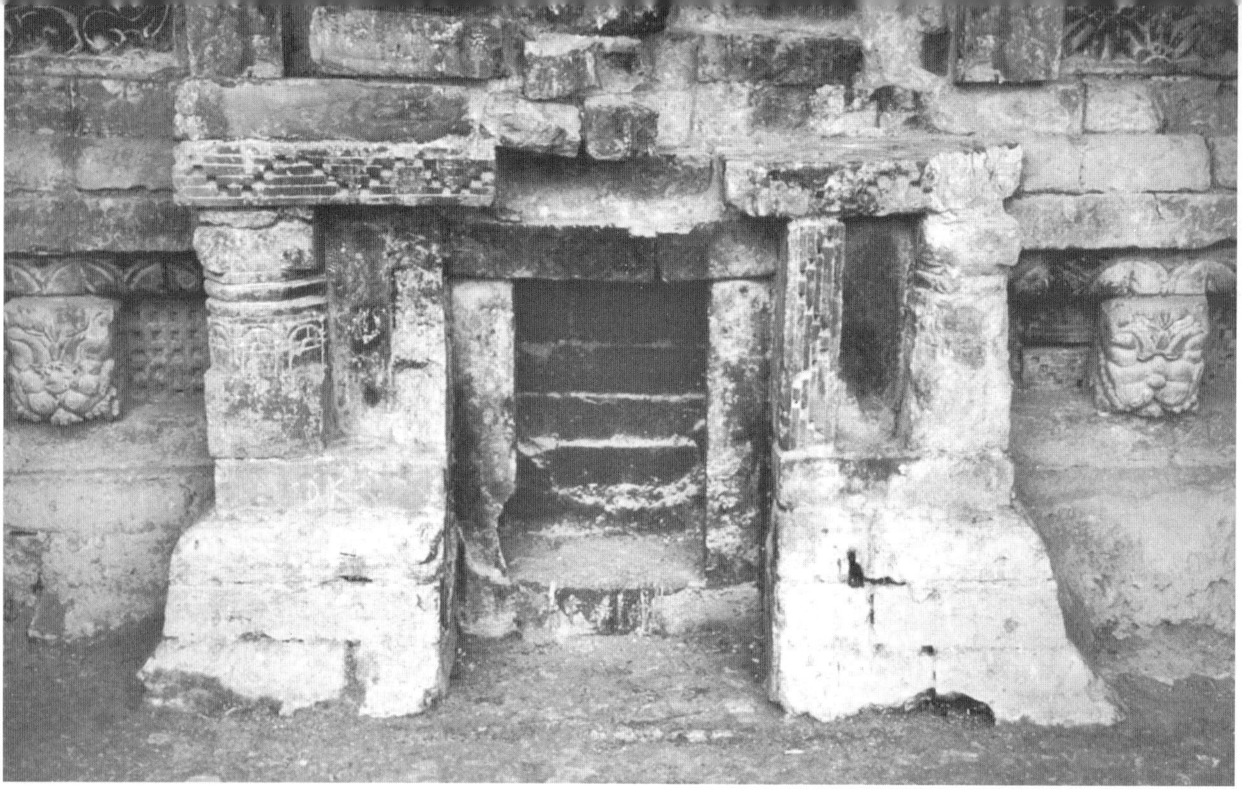

Pl. 15.5. Sārnāth, pedestal no. 136, details of N-façade.

Pl. 15.6. Sārnāth, pedestal no. 136, NE-corner from SE.

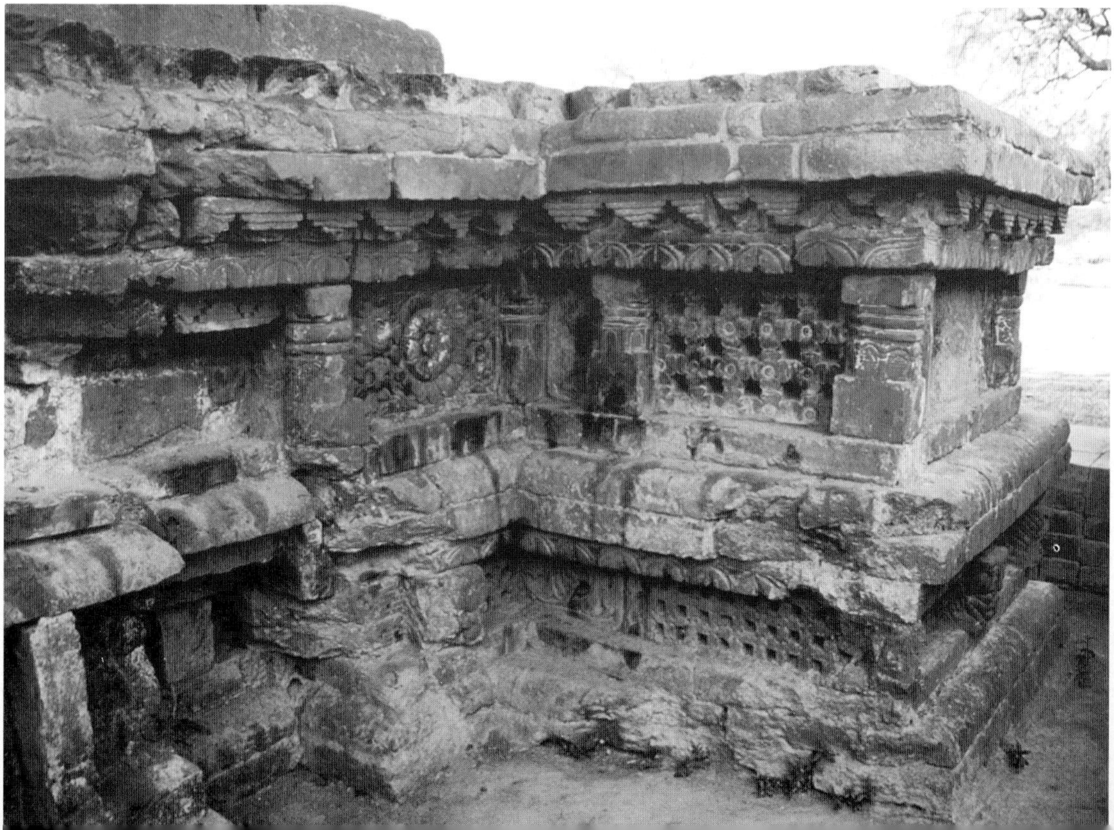

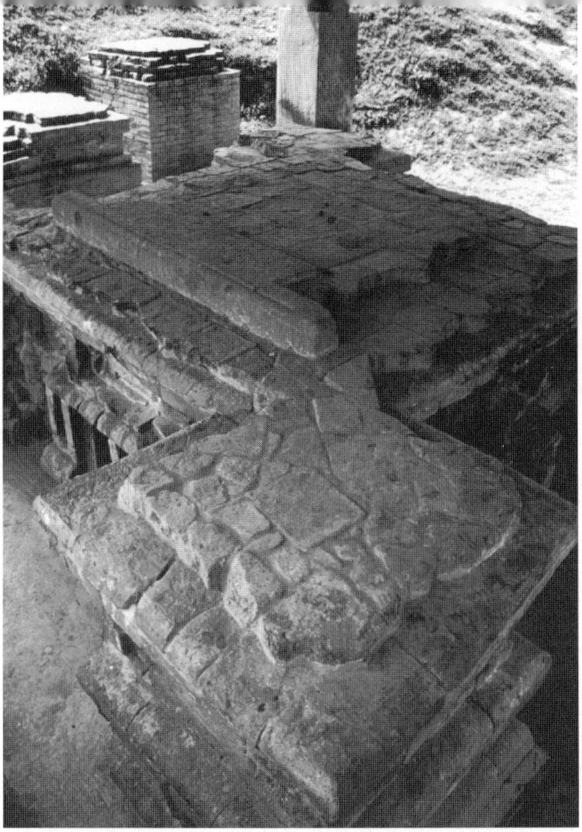

Pl. 15.7. Sārnāth, pedestal no. 136, NE-corner from NE.

Pl. 15.8. Sārnāth, one of the *Kīrttimukha*s at the lower part of pedestal no. 136.

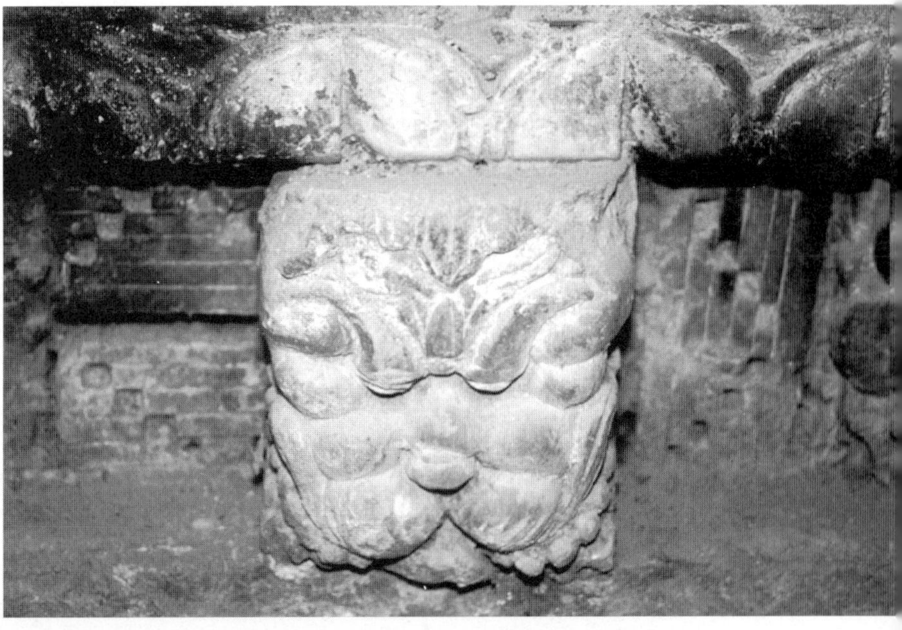

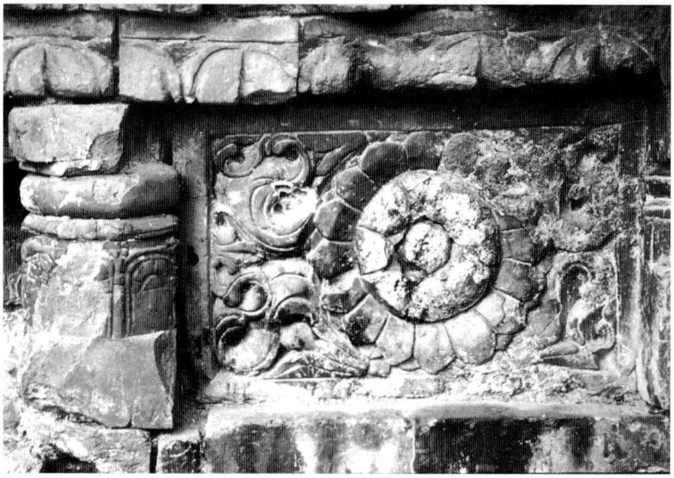

Pl. 15.9. Sārnāth, pedestal no. 136, E-façade.

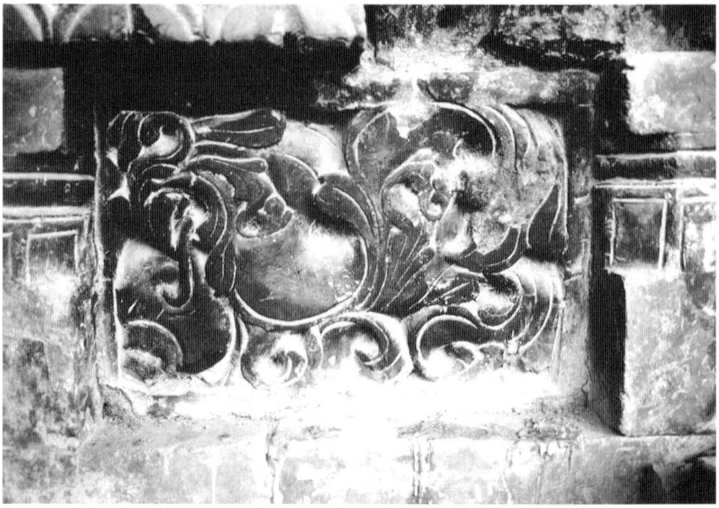

Pl. 15.10. Sārnāth, pedestal no. 136, detail of N-façade.

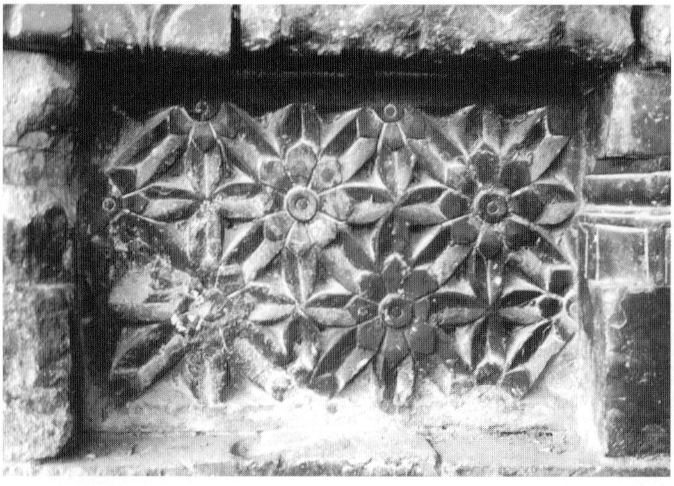

Pl. 15.11. Sārnāth, pedestal no. 136, details of N-façade.

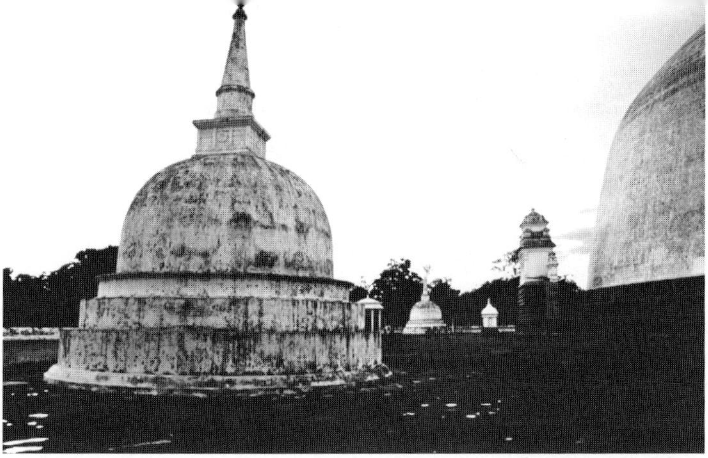

Pl. 15.12. Anurādhapura, Ratnamāli-Mahāstūpa, two of the four sub-*stūpa*s.

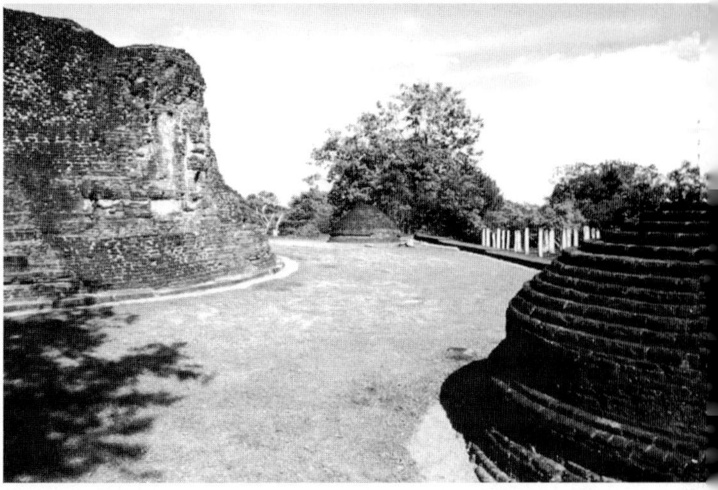

Pl. 15.13. Polonnaruva, Potgul-Vehera, two of the four sub-*stūpa*s and the central structure with circular ground-plan.

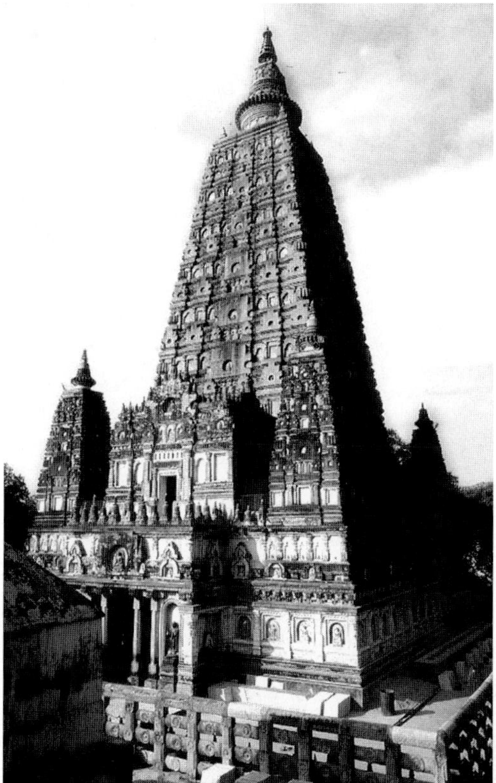

Pl. 15.14. Bodha-Gayā, Mahābodhi temple (after Malandra 1988: p. 11).

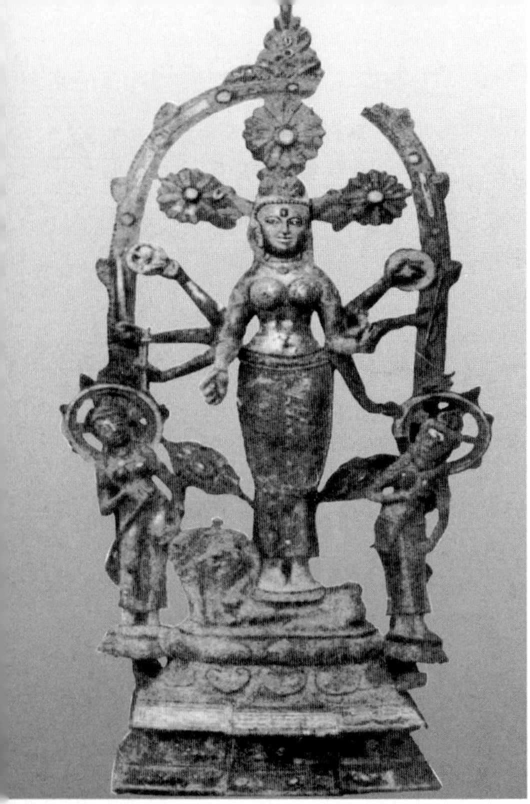

Pl. 16.1. Bronze image of Sarvāṇī from Deulbari, Comilla district.

Pl. 16.2. View of the Pahārpur Monastery, Nāogāon district.

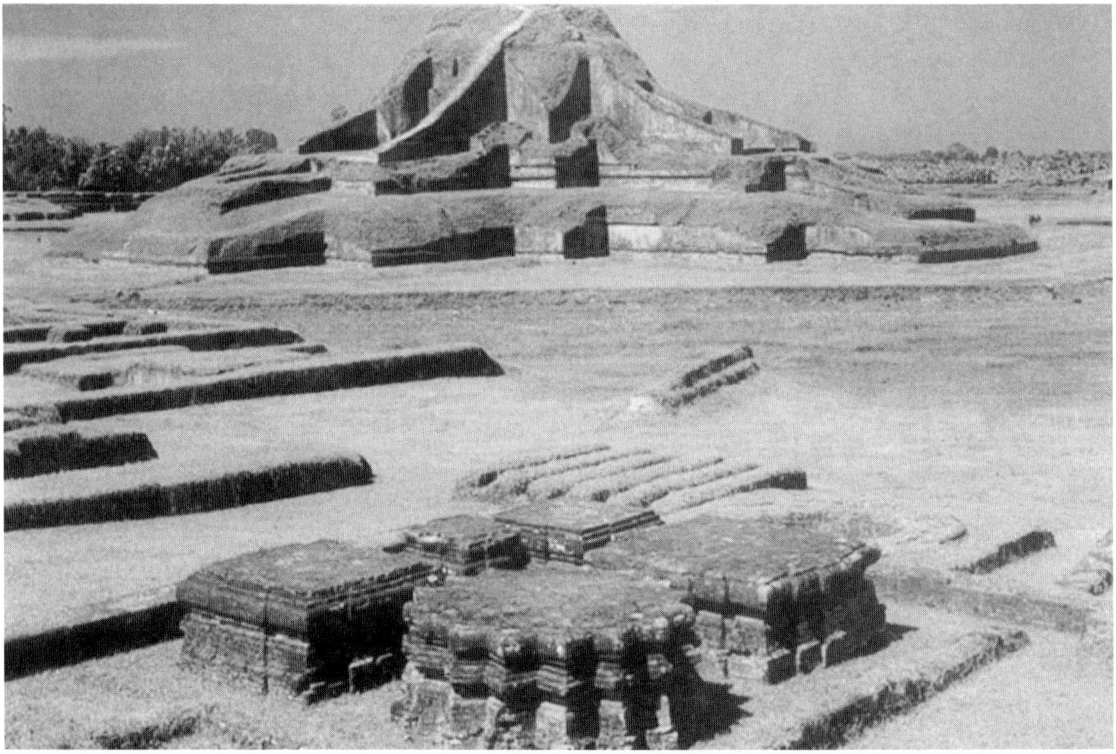

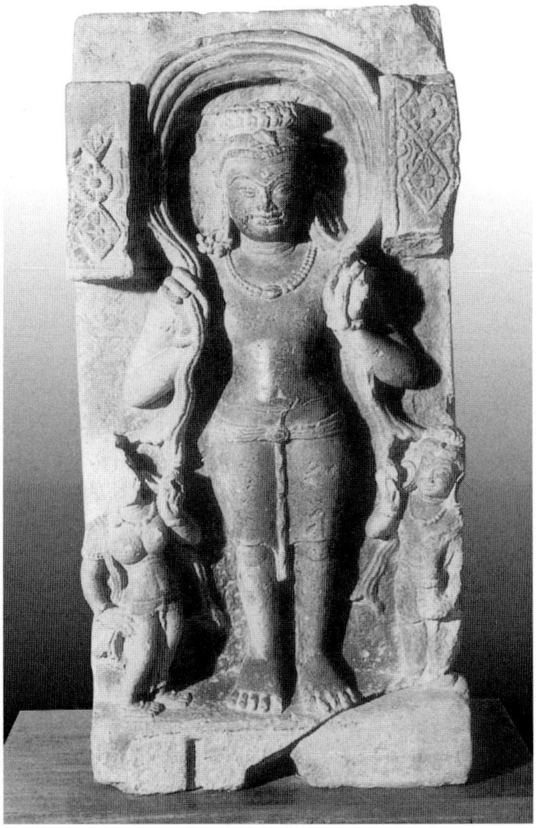

Pl. 16.3. Image of Vāyu, stone,
from Pahārpur Monastery.

Pl. 16.4. Amorous couple, stone,
from Pahārpur Monastery.

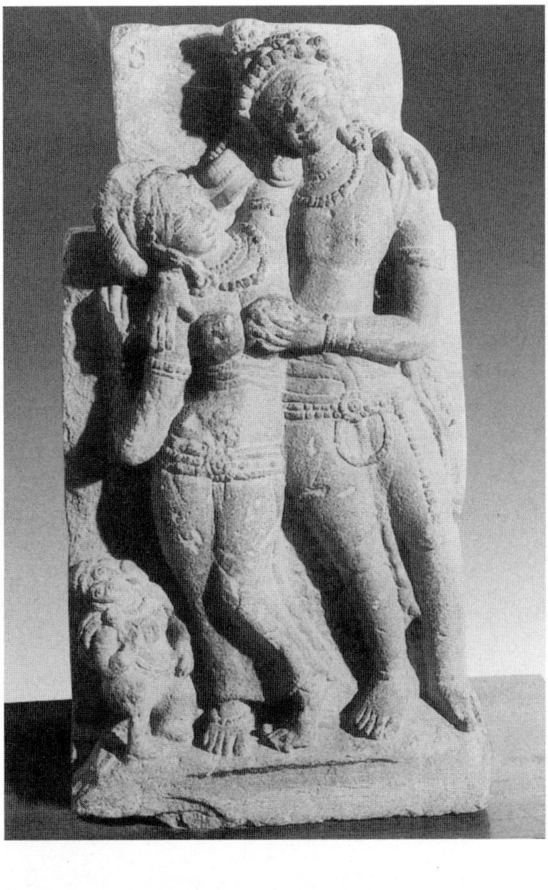

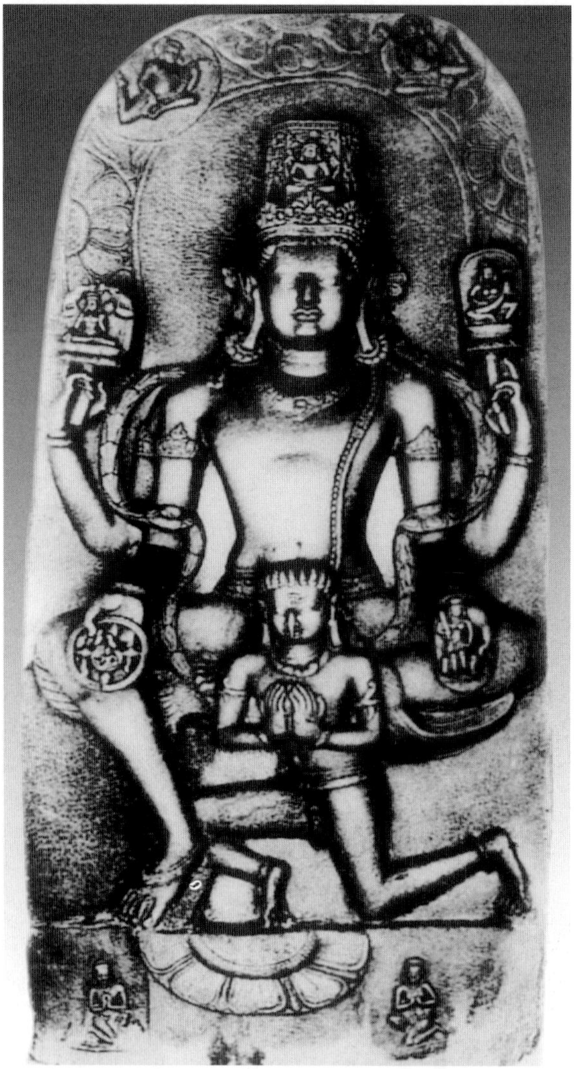

Pl. 16.5. Viṣṇu, stone, at Lakṣmaṇkati, Barisal district.

Pl. 16.6. Viṣṇu-Lokeśvara, stone, from Ghyāsābād, Murśidābād district.

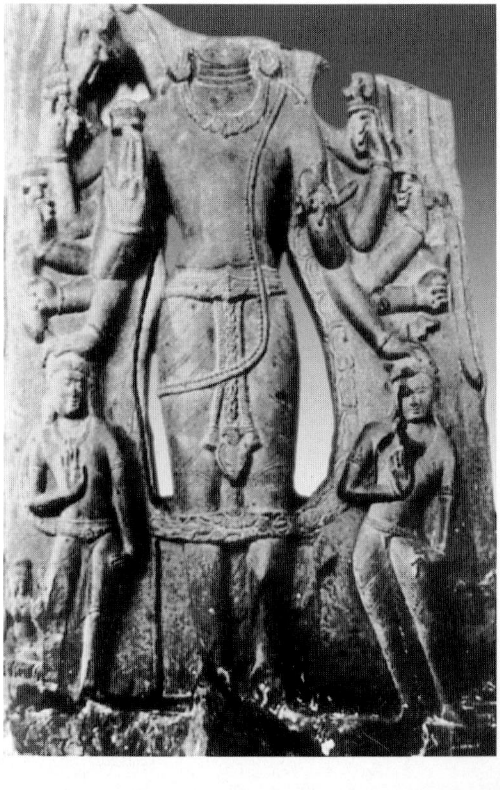

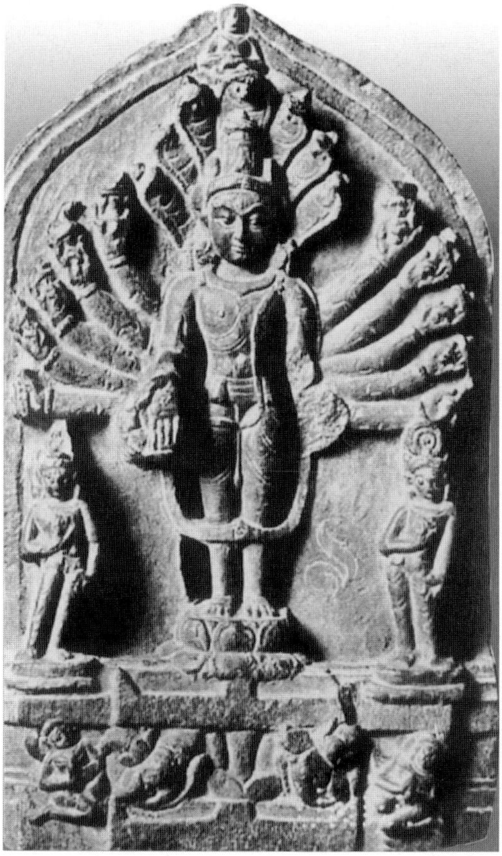

Pl. 16.7. Viṣṇu-Lokeśvara, stone, from Sonarang, Munśigañj district.

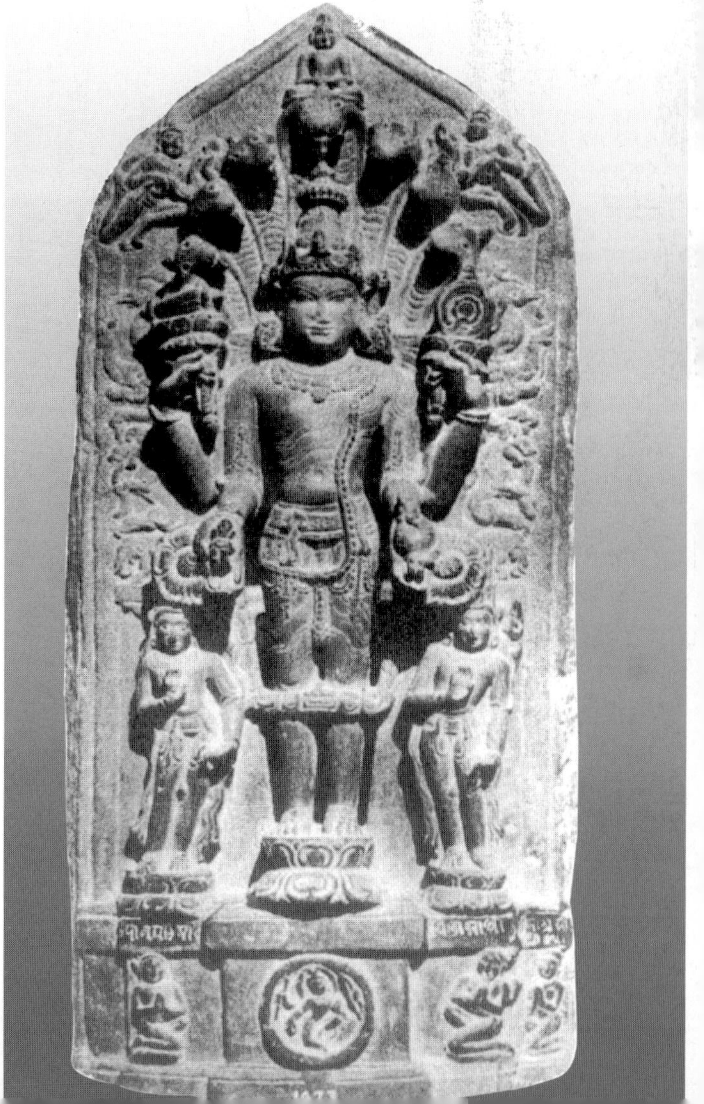

Pl. 16.8. Viṣṇu, stone, from Surohar, Dīnājpur district.

Pl. 16.9. Devī, stone, from Muhammadpur, Comilla district.

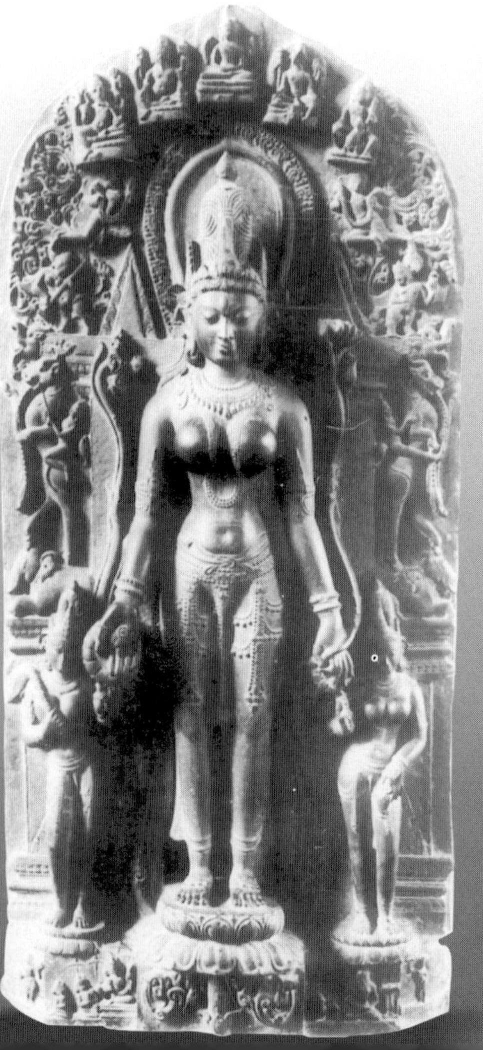

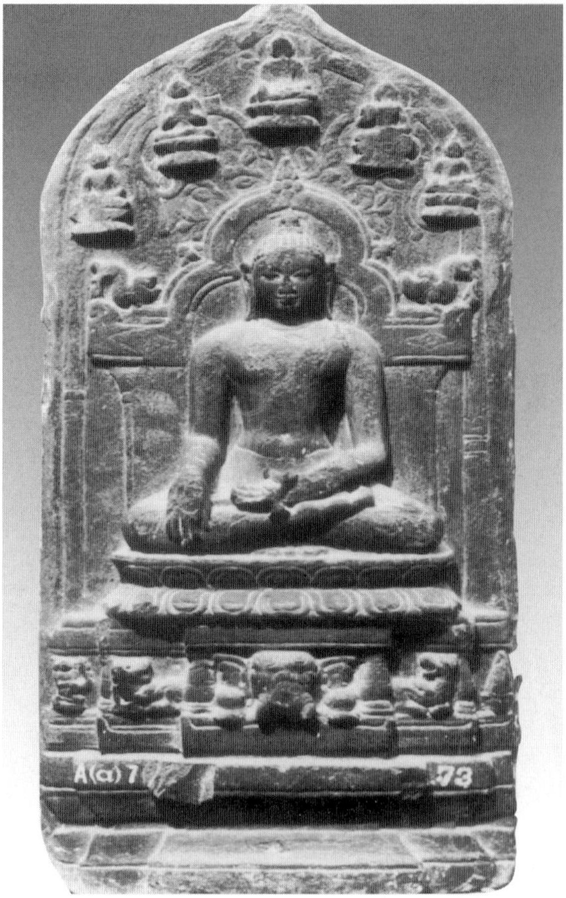

Pl. 16.10. Dhyānī Buddha Akṣobhya, stone, in Varendra Museum, Rajshāhī.

Pl. 16.11. Viṣṇu with 10 incarnations, stone, in Bangladesh National Museum.

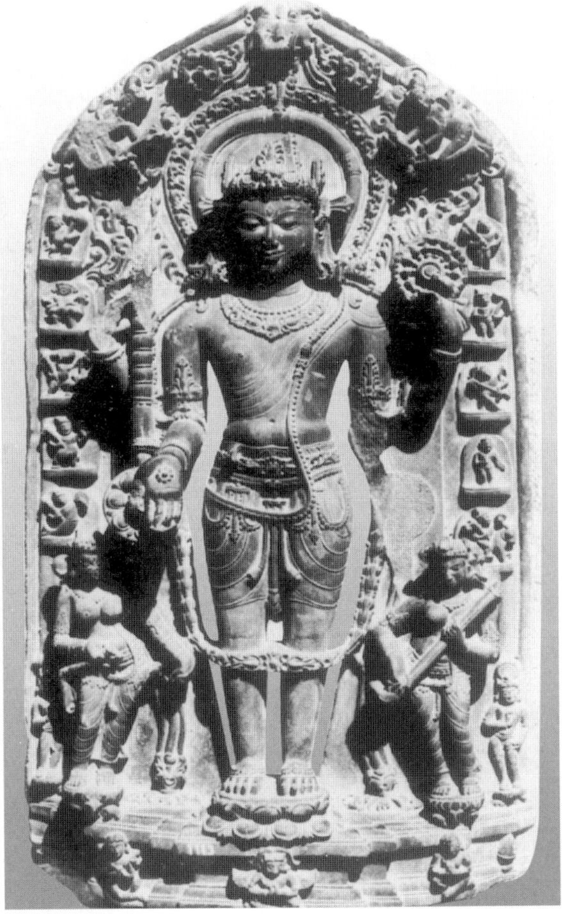

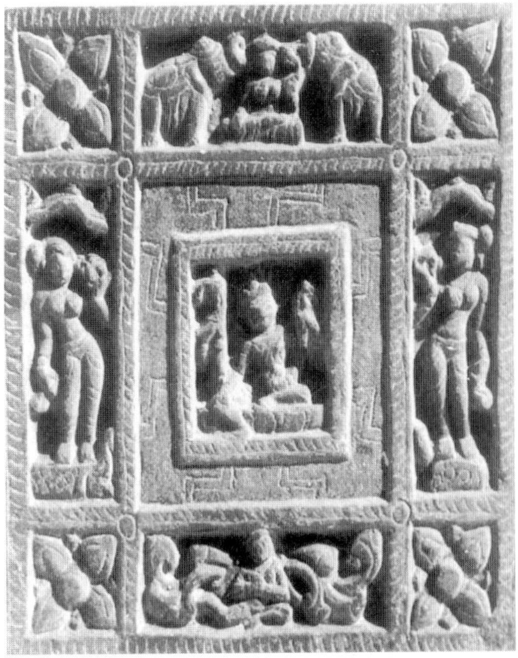

Pl. 16.12a. Viṣṇu, stone, in Bangladesh National Museum.

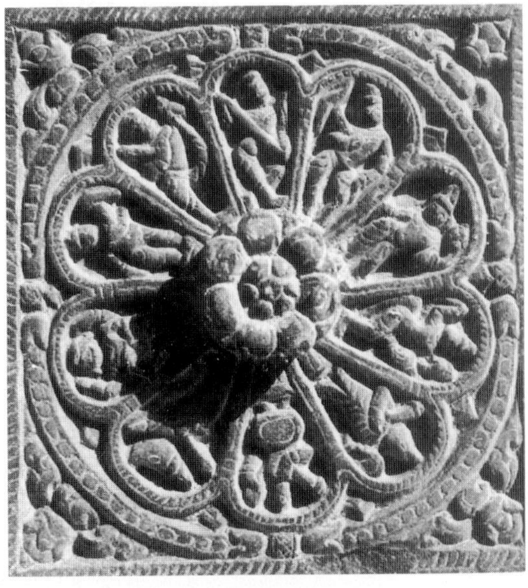

Pl. 16.12b. *Viṣṇupaṭṭas*, stone, in Bangladesh National Museum.

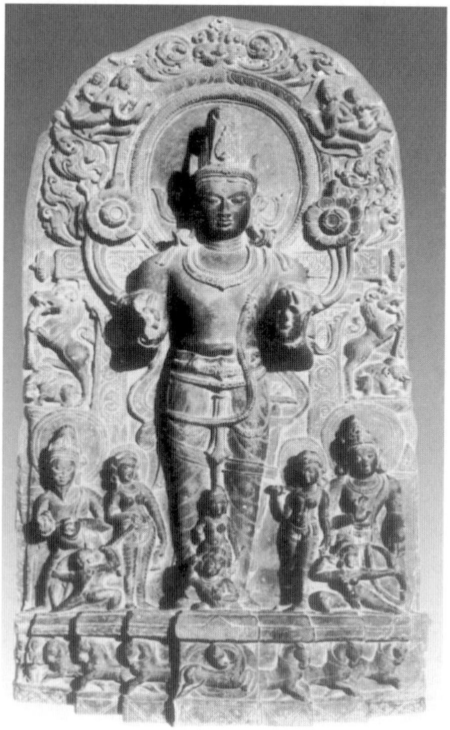

Pl. 16.13. Sūrya, stone, in Bangladesh National Museum.

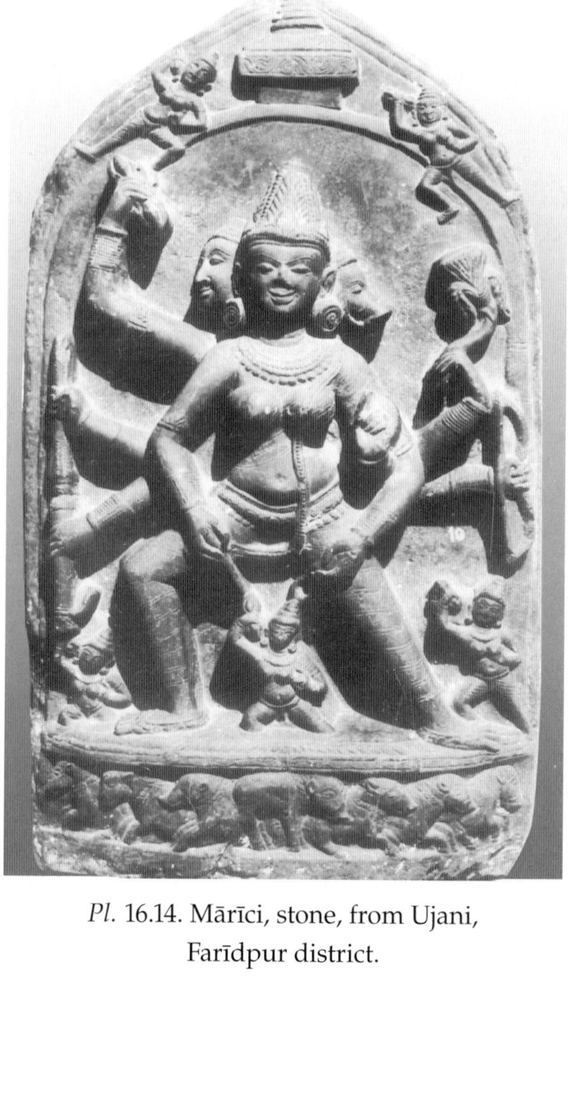

Pl. 16.14. Mārīci, stone, from Ujani, Farīdpur district.

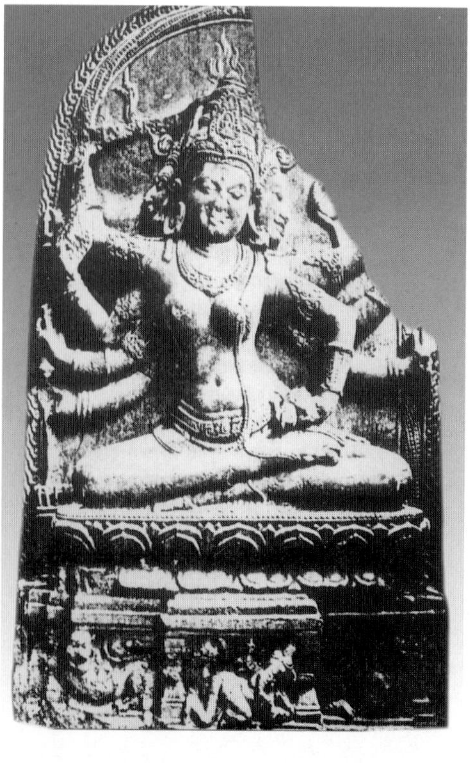

Pl. 16.15. Jambhala, stone, in Varendra Museum, Rajshāhī.

Pl. 16.16. Bhṛkuṭī Tārā, stone, from Bhavānīpur, Munśigañj district.

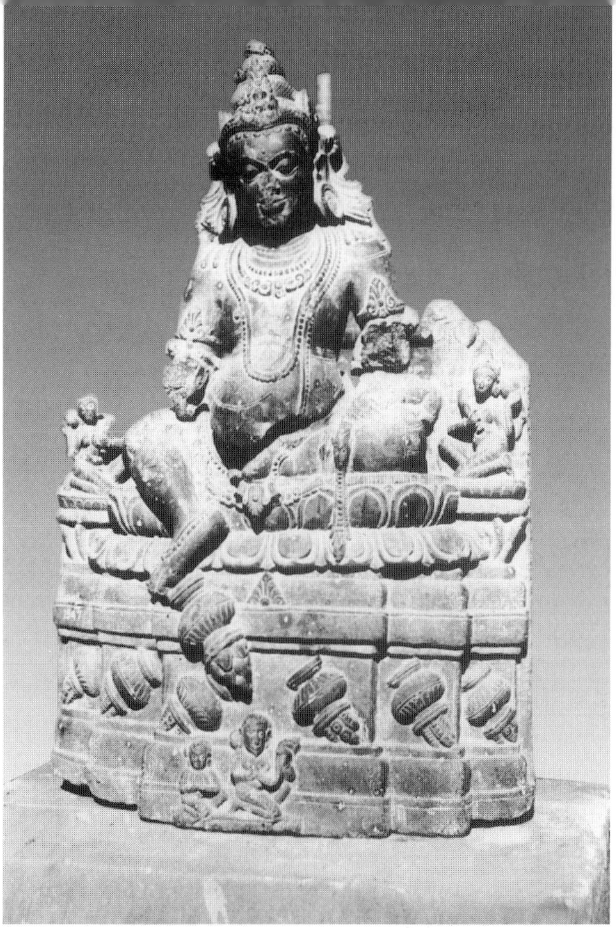

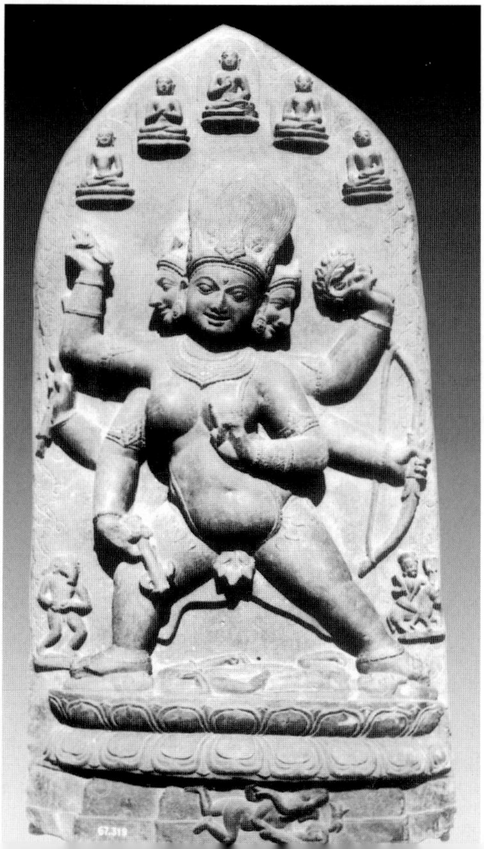

Pl. 16.17. Parṇaśabari, stone, from Nayananda, Munśigañj district.

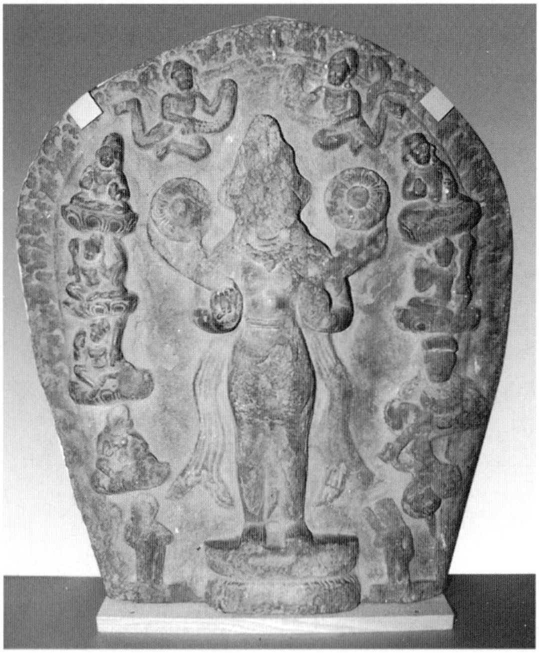

Pl. 17.1. *Sūryamaṇḍala* (S1), Kāṭhmāṇḍu, National Museum, Photo: Mevissen 2003.

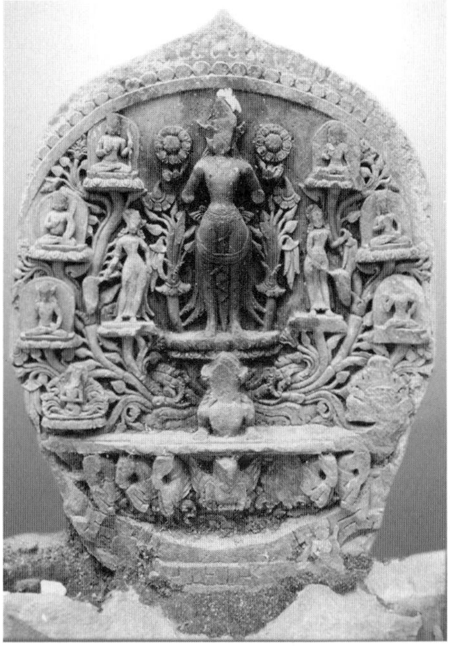

Pl. 17.2. *Sūryamaṇḍala* (S2), Kāṭhmāṇḍu, Ombahaltol, Photo: Mevissen 2003.

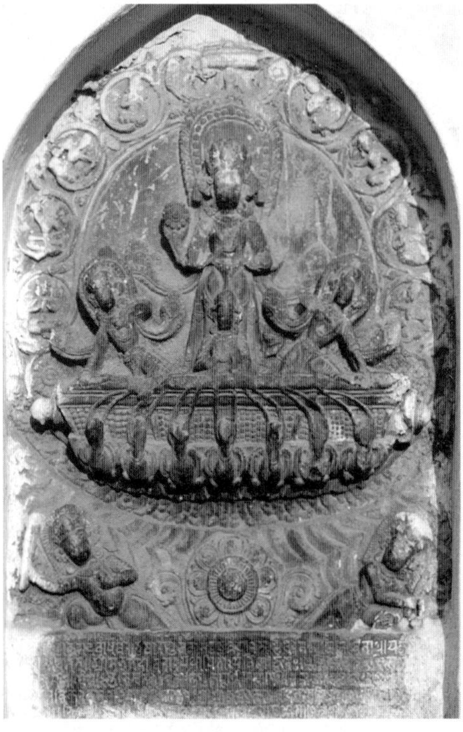

Pl. 17.3. *Sūryamaṇḍala* (S3), Kāṭhmāṇḍu, Tebahal, Photo: Mevissen 2003.

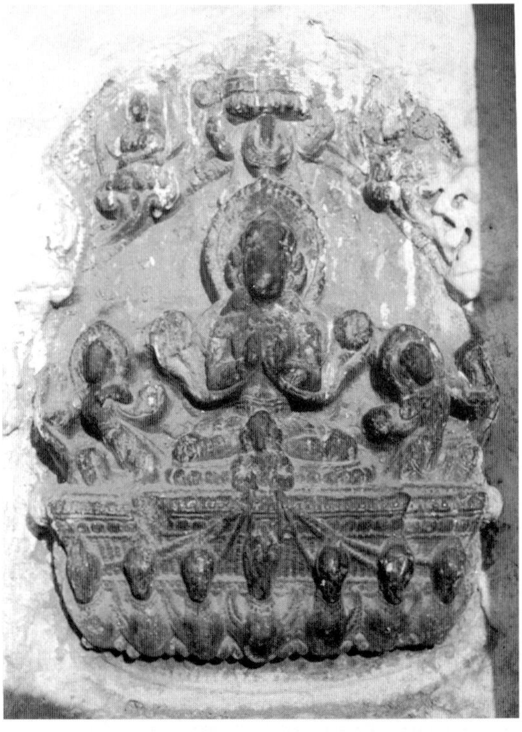

Pl. 17.4. *Sūryamaṇḍala* (S4), Kāṭhmāṇḍu, Tebahal, Photo: Mevissen 2003.

Pl. 17.5. *Sūryamaṇḍala* (S5), Bhaktapur, Tilamādhava temple, Photo: Mevissen 2003.

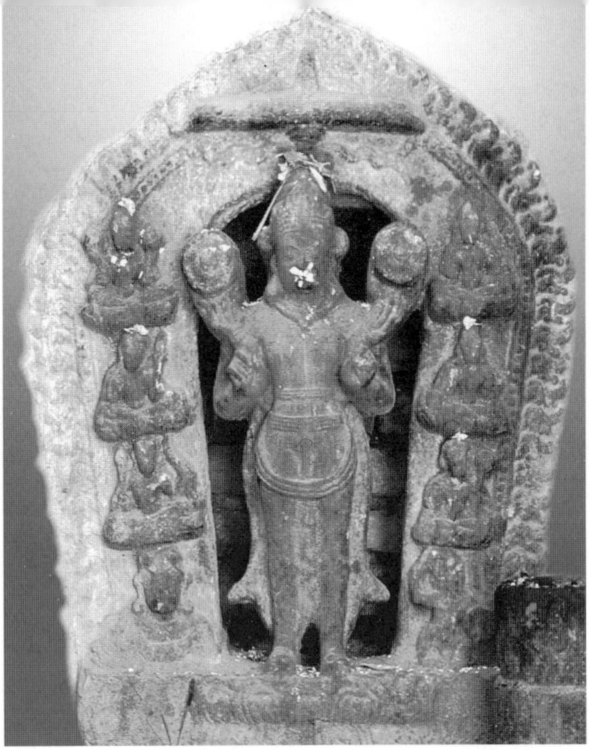

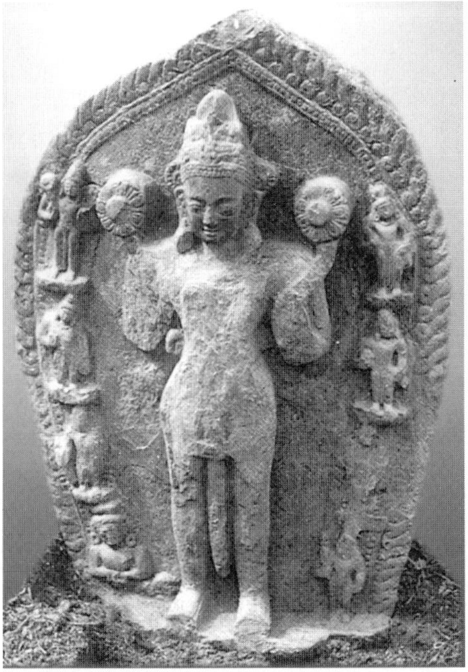

Pl. 17.6. *Sūryamaṇḍala* (S6), Bhaktapur, Bhelukhel, after: Bangdel 1995.

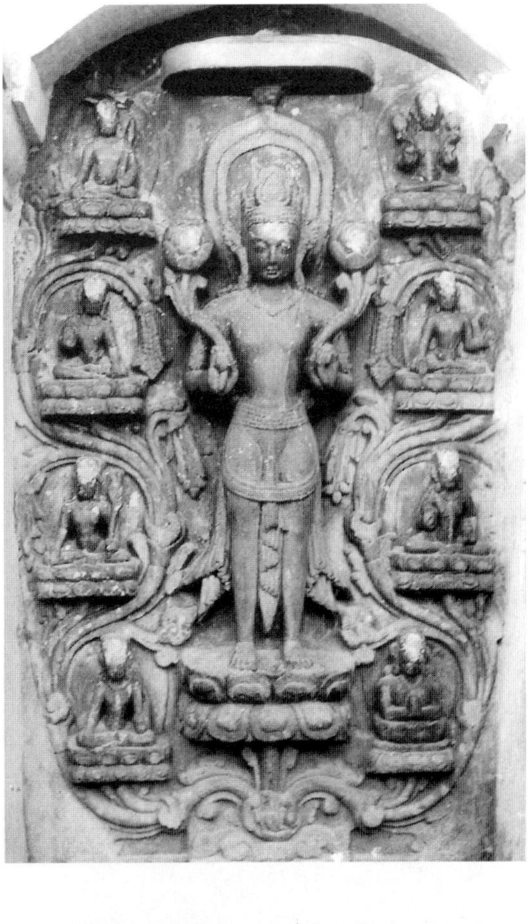

Pl. 17.7. *Sūryamaṇḍala* (S7), Bhaktapur, after: Srivastava 2000.

Pl. 17.8. *Sūryamaṇḍala* (S8), Stolen from Pharping, after: Bangdel 1989.

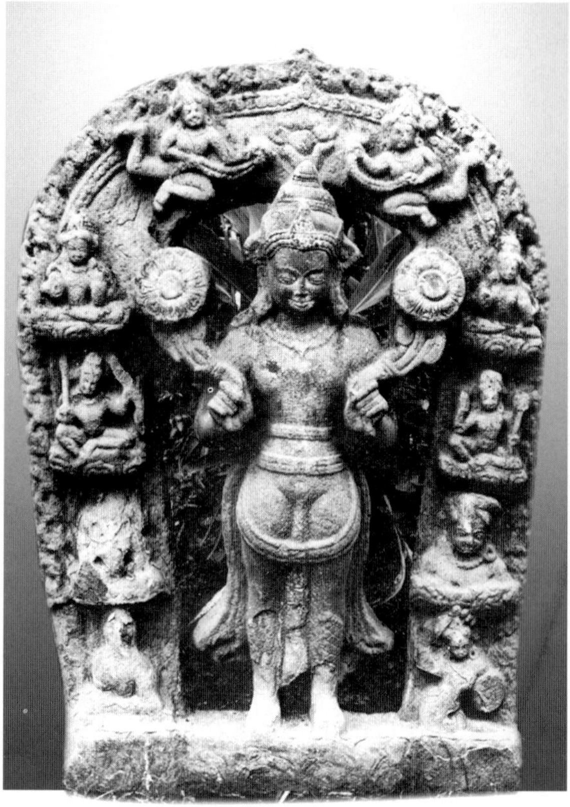

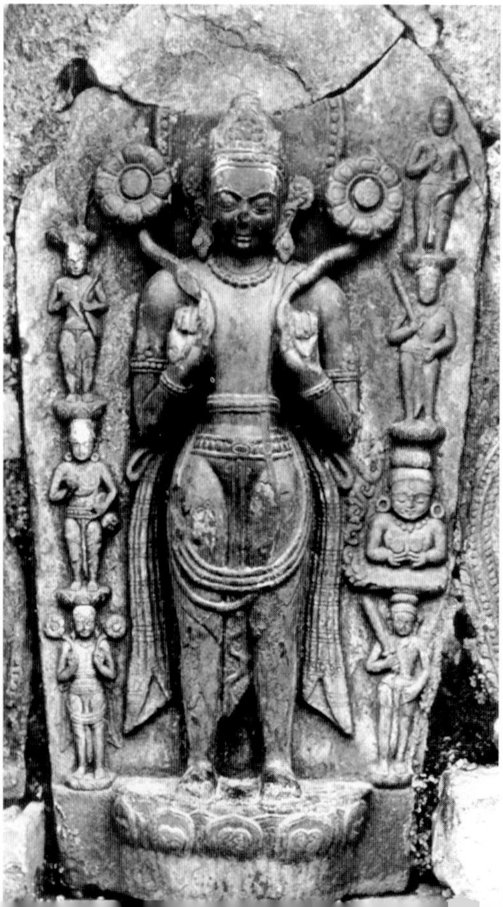

Pl. 17.9. *Sūryamaṇḍala* (S9), Stolen from Panauti, after: Bangdel 1989.

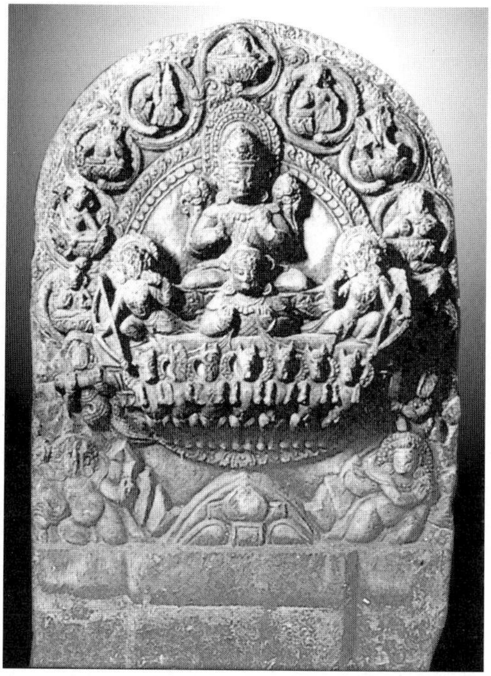

Pl. 17.10. *Sūryamaṇḍala* (S10), Bhaktapur, National Art Gallery, after: Bangdel 1995.

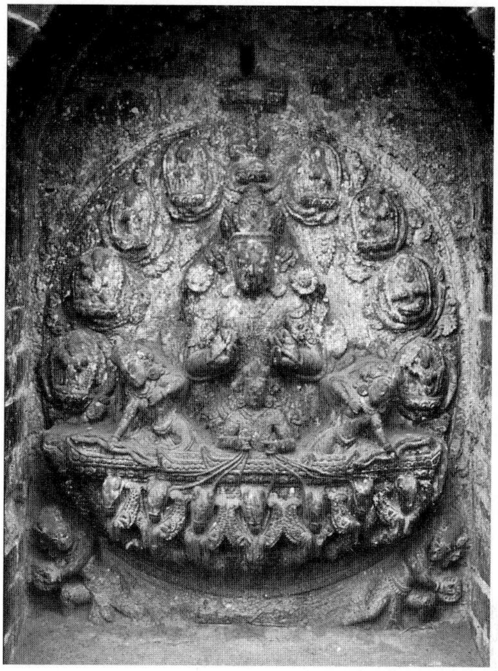

Pl. 17.11. *Sūryamaṇḍala* (S11), Panauti, Indreśvara temple, Photo: Mevissen 2003.

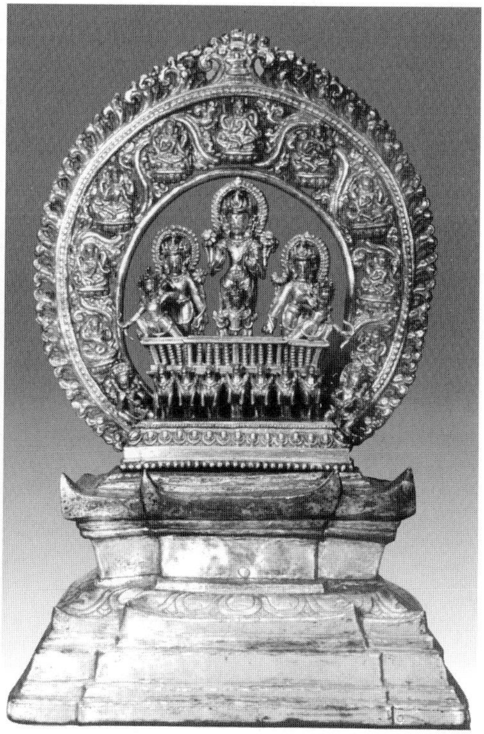

Pl. 17.12. *Sūryamaṇḍala* (S12), Private Collection, after: Alsop 1986.

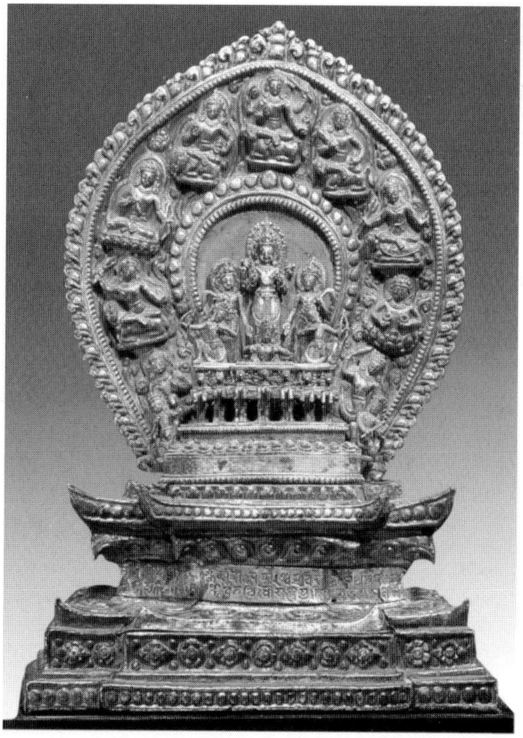

Pl. 17.13. *Sūryamaṇḍala* (S13), Present location unknown, after: Sotheby's New York 1999.

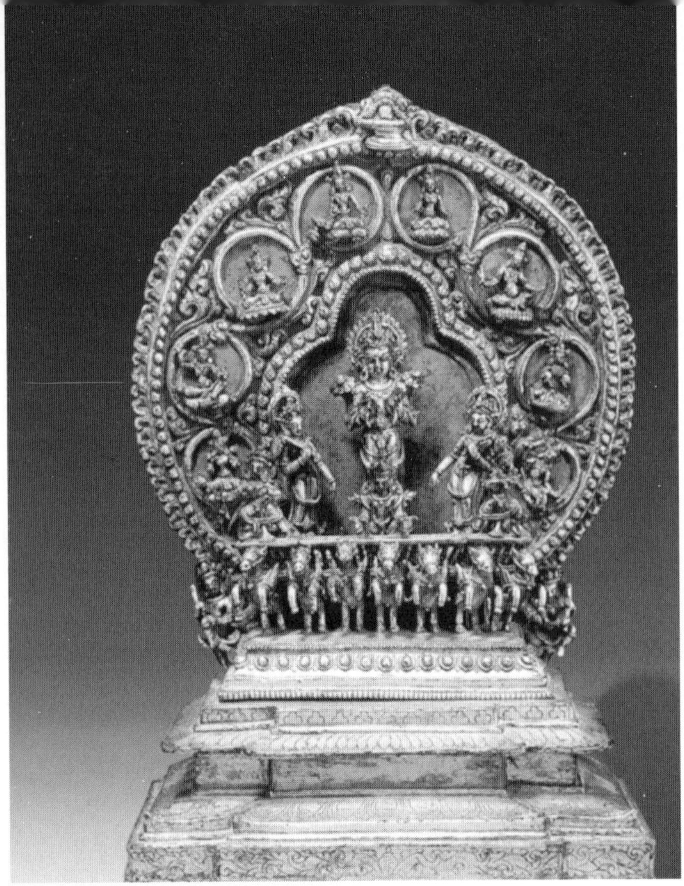

Pl. 17.14. *Sūryamaṇḍala* (S14), Present location unknown, after: Sotheby's new York 1994.

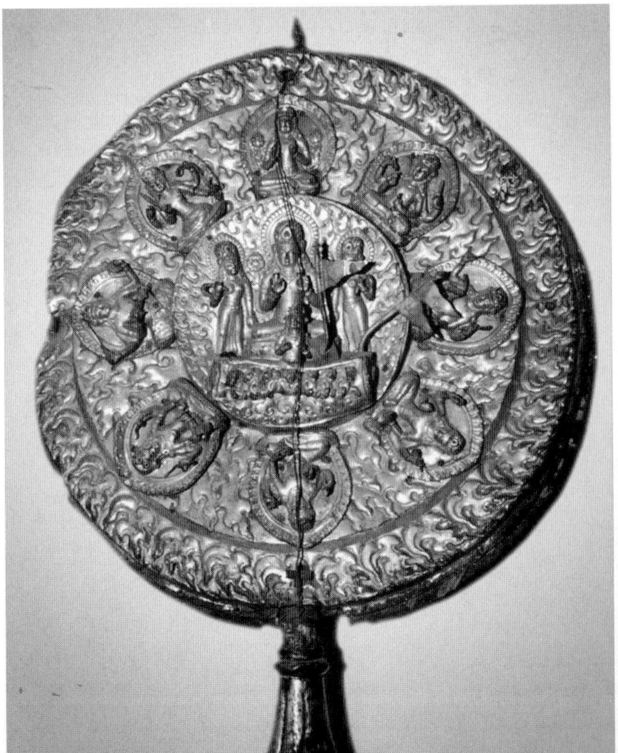

Pl. 17.15. *Sūryamaṇḍala* (S15), Kāṭhmāṇḍu, National Museum, Photo: Mevissen 2003.

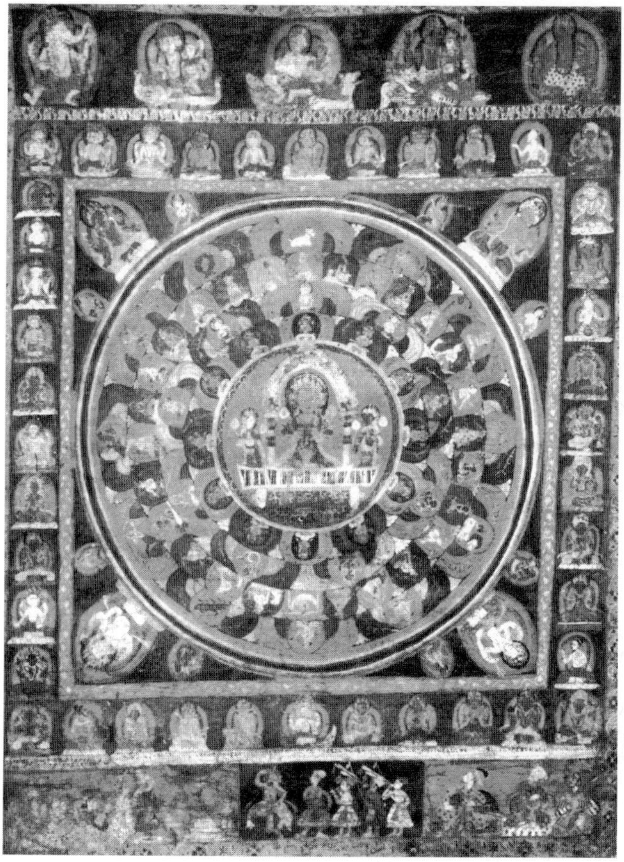

Pl. 17.16. *Sūryamaṇḍala* (S18), Berlin, Museum of Indian Art, Photo: I. Papadopoulos.

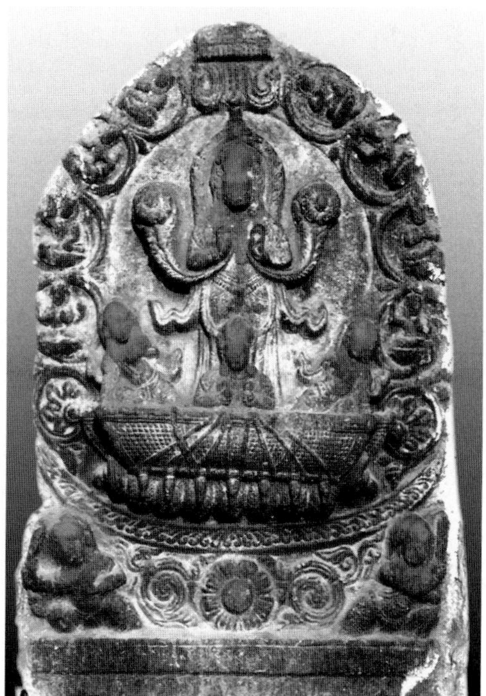

Pl. 17.17. *Candramaṇḍala* (C1), Kāṭhmāṇḍu, Tebahal, Photo: Mevissen 2003.

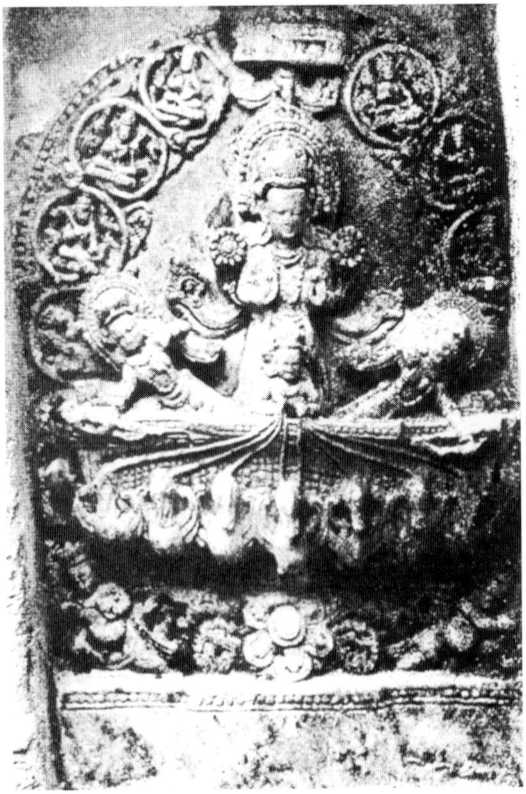

Pl. 17.18. *Candramaṇḍala* (C2), Patan, Kumbheśvara temple, after: Banerji 1972.

Pl. 17.19. *Candramaṇḍala* (C3), Patan Museum, Photo: Mevissen 2003.

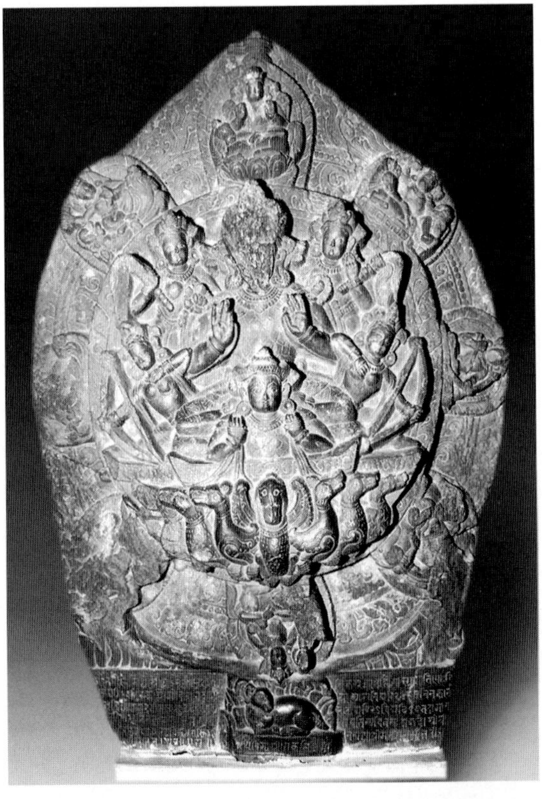

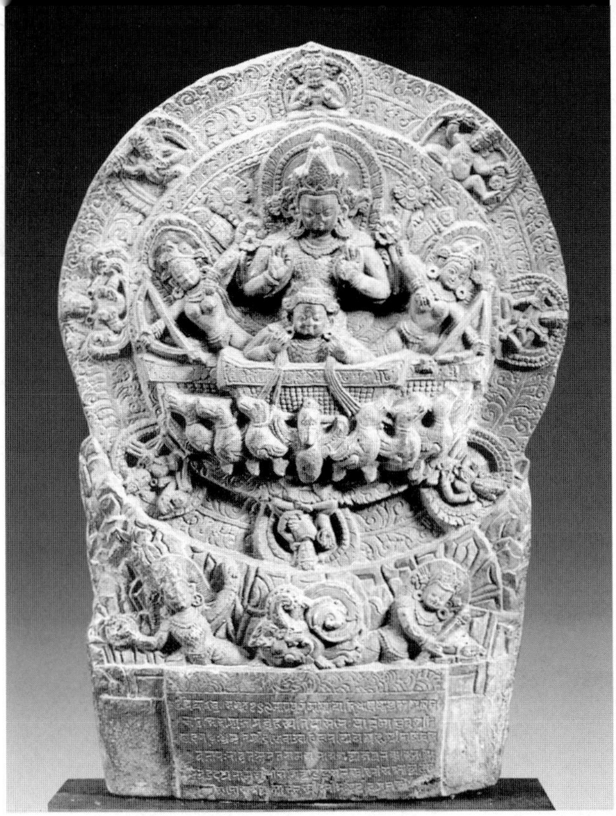

Pl. 17.20. *Candramaṇḍala* (C4),
Present location unknown,
after: Sotheby's London 1987.

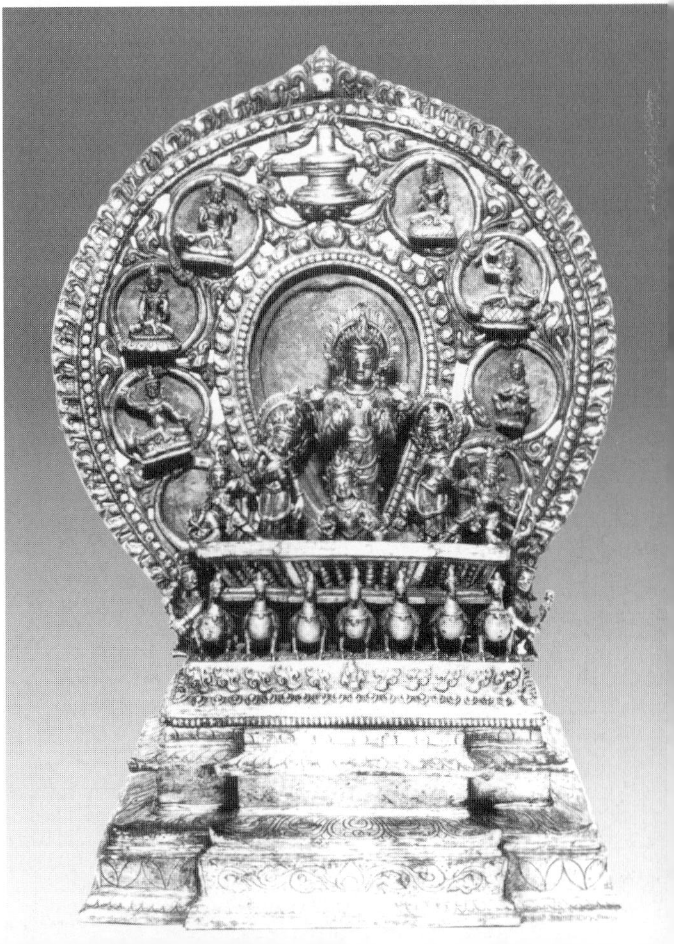

Pl. 17.21. *Candramaṇḍala* (C5),
Present location unknown,
after: Sotheby's London 1977.

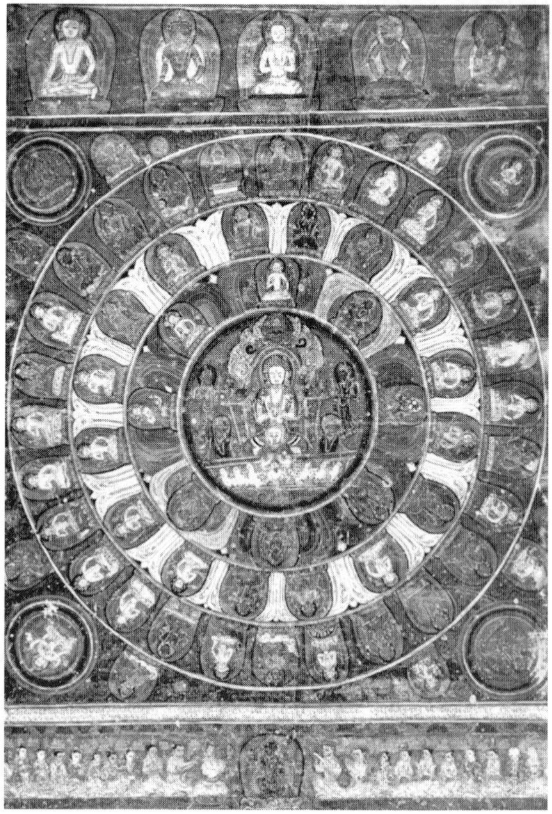

Pl. 17.22. *Candramaṇḍala* (C12), Present location unknown, after: Lauf 1972.

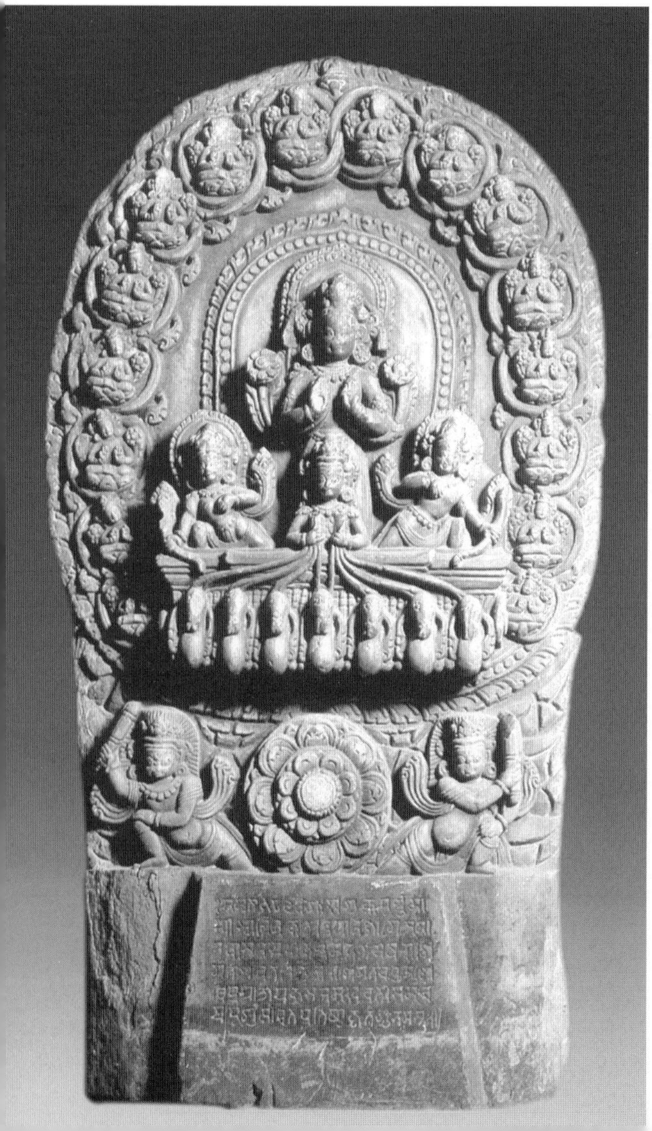

Pl. 17.23. *Candramaṇḍala* (C15), Bhaktapur, National Art Gallery, after: Bangdel 1987.

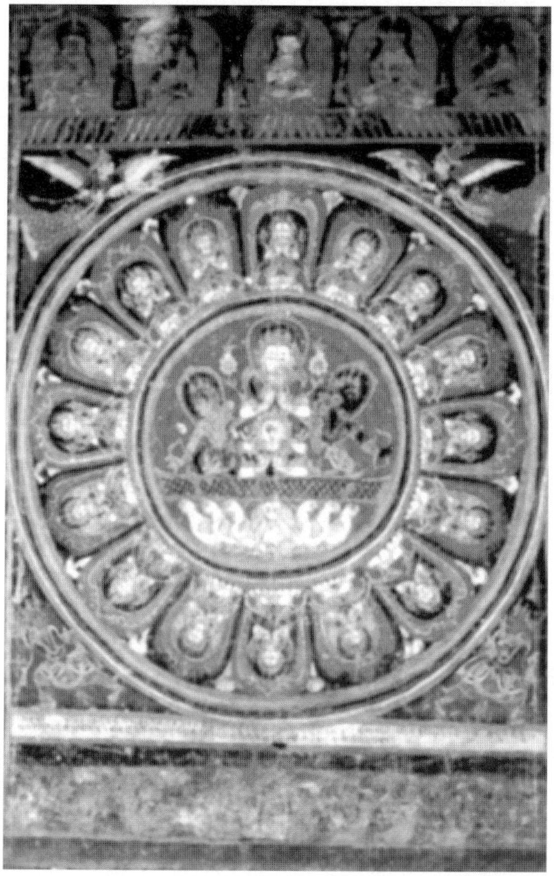

Pl. 17.24. *Candramaṇḍala* (C18), Present location unknown, after: Sotheby's New York 1997.

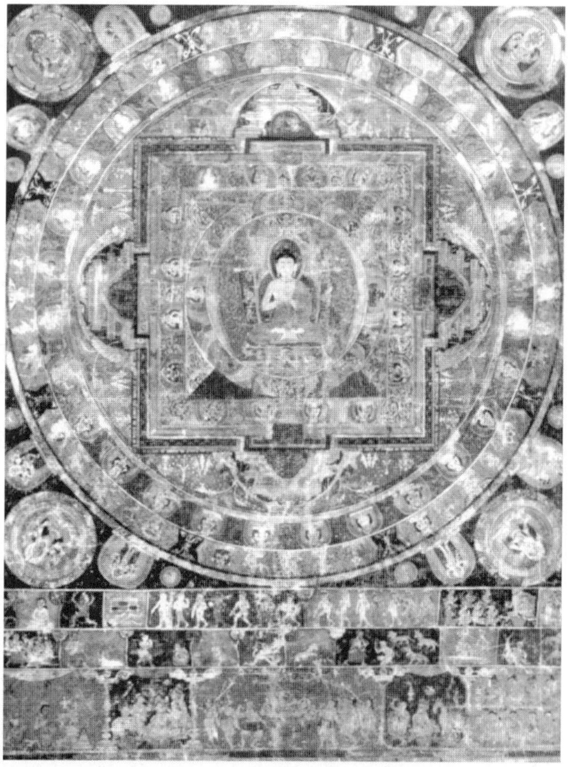

Pl. 17.25. *Buddhamaṇḍala* (B2), Present location unknown, after: Sotheby's London 1979.

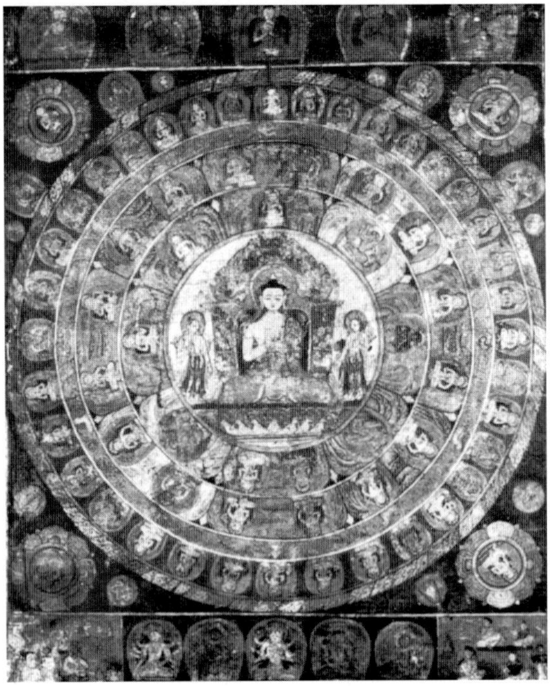

Pl. 17.26. *Buddhamaṇḍala* (B3), Present location unknown, after: Uhlig 1976.

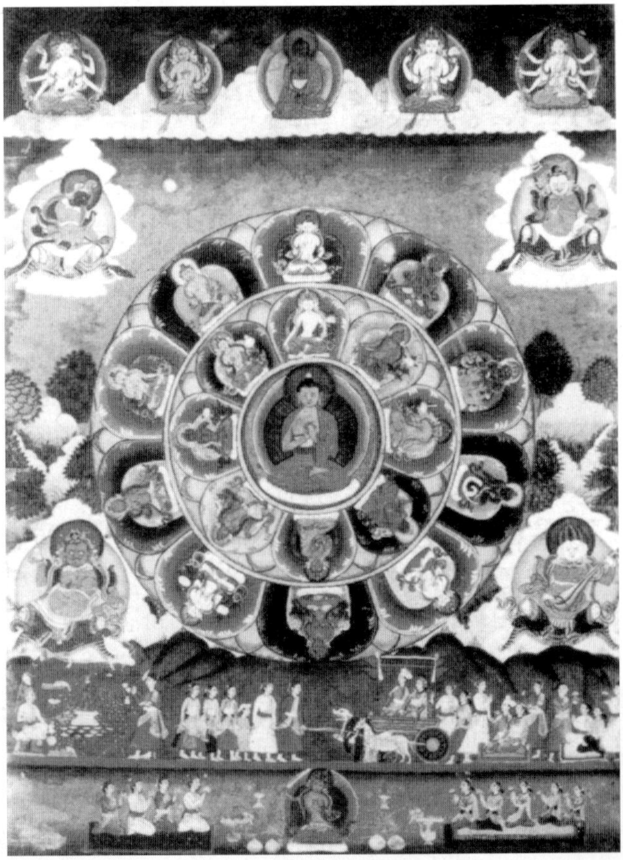

Pl. 17.27. *Buddhamaṇḍala* (B4), Present location unknown, after: Sotheby's London 1980.

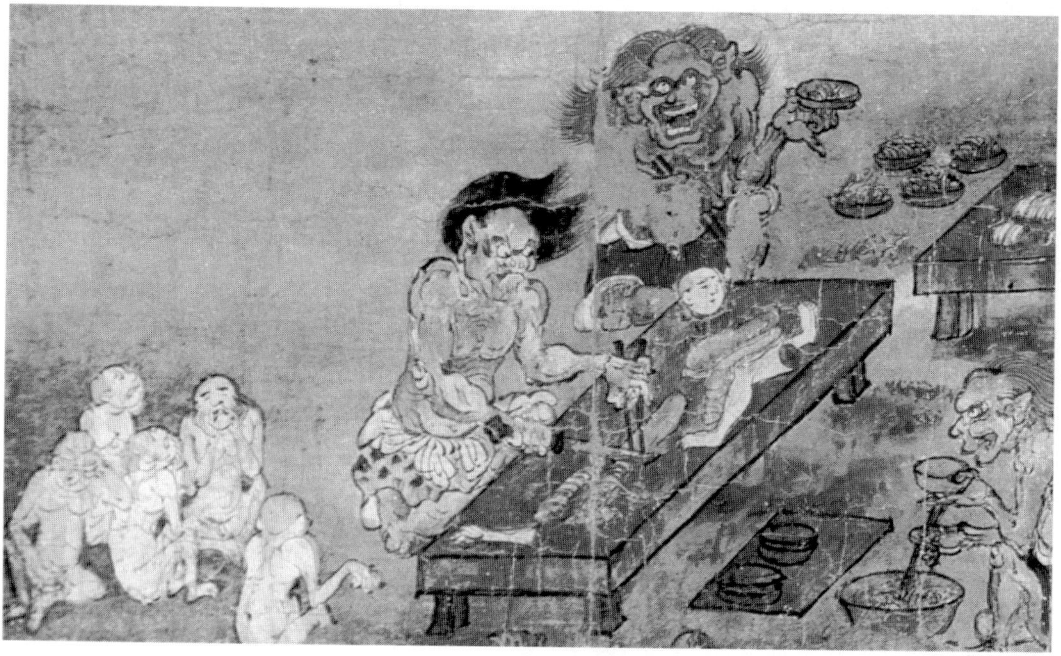

Pl. 18.1. *Rākṣasa* cooks (detail of the Maseda scroll vol. 1, fragment 6; Private Collection)

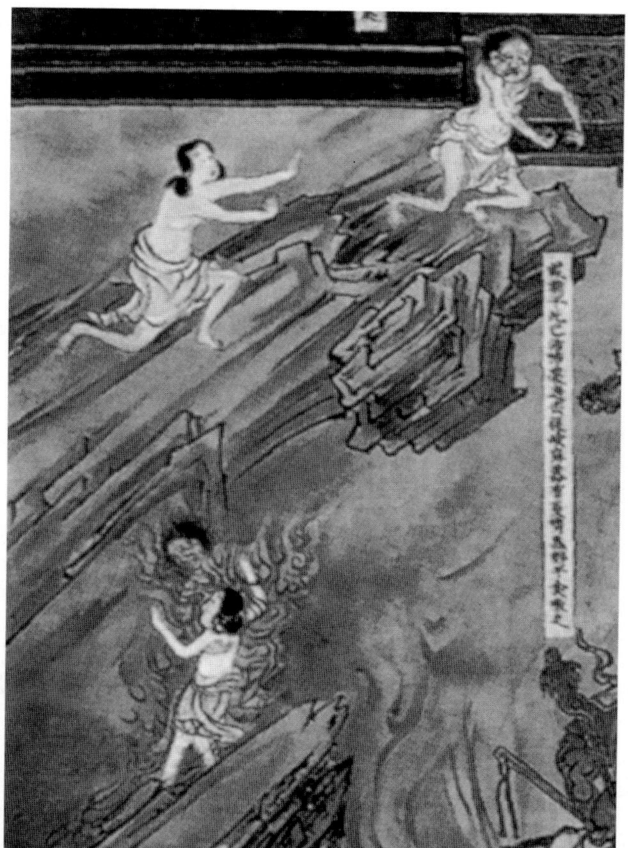

Pl. 18.2. Embracement by an iron image (detail of the Paintings of the Six *gati*s of the Shōju Raigō Temple, scroll 2)

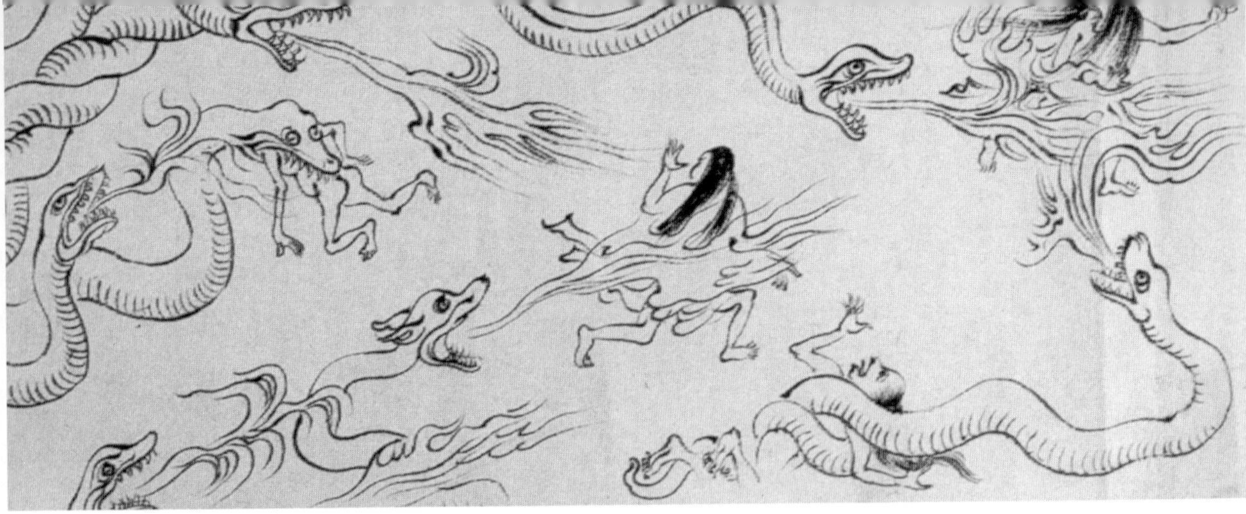

Pl. 18.3. Arrows (detail of the De Inferni Libelli, Copy vol. 3, fragment 3; Tokyo National Museum)

Pl. 18.4. Snakes (detail of the De Inferni Libelli, Copy vol. 4, fragment 1; Tokyo National Museum)

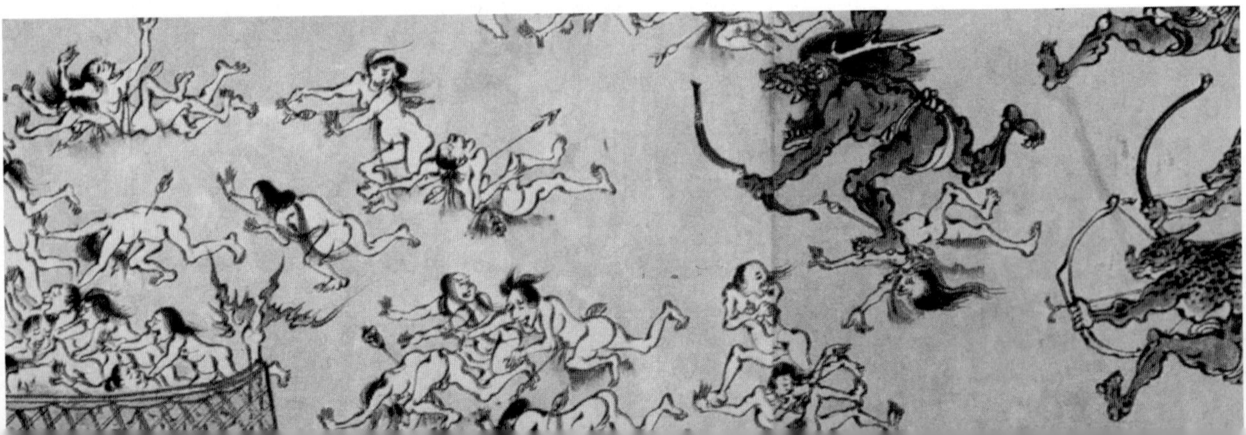

List of Contributors

Dr. Yogendra Singh
Director
Acharya Narendra Dev International
Research Institute of Buddhist Studies
Vipin Khand, Gomti Nagar
Lucknow - 226 010

Dr. Amar Singh
MM - 260, Sector - D, Aliganj Scheme
Lucknow - 226 024

Prof. K.K. Thaplyal
B 1-18/1, Sector K, Aliganj
Lucknow - 226 020

Dr. S.D. Trivedi
B 1/7, Sector G, Aliganj
Lucknow - 226 020.

Dr. G.B. Deglurkar
901, Purushottam Apartments
Street-1, Bhandarkar Road
Deccan Gymkhana
Pune - 411 008.

Dr. Preeti Trivedi
36, Bajaj Nagar
Nagpur - 440 001

Dr. H.C. Das
4918, Tankapani Road,
Buvaneswar - 751014
Orissa

Dr. R. Nagaswamy
11, 22 Cross Street
Besant Nagar
Chennai - 600 090
Email: nagaswamy@xlweb.com

Prof. S.B. Singh
8/152, Indira Nagar
Lucknow - 226 016

Dr. N.P. Joshi
CK-1/13, Patani Tola
Bhonsla Mandir, Bhonsla Ghat
Varanasi - 221 001

Dr. T.K. Biswas
Joint Director
Bharat Kala Bhavan
B.H.U.
Varanasi - 221 005
Email: bharatkala@sify.com

Prof. Kamal Giri
D 51/45, Daya Dham, Suraj Kund
Varanasi - 221 010

Prof. M.N.P. Tiwari
D 51/164-B, Suraj Kund
Varanasi - 221 010

Prof. R.C. Sharma
Hon. Director/Ācārya
Jñāna-Pravāha
Centre for Cultural Studies
South of Samne Ghat
Varanasi - 221 005

Sri Ajay Srivastava & Dr. Niharika
Archaeological Survey of India
Archaeological Museum
Sarnath, Varanasi - 221 007

Dr. Gouriswar Bhattacharya
Zillestrasse 113
10585 Berlin (Germany)
Email: indology@zedat.fu-berlin.de

Dr. Gerd J.R. Mevissen
Erasmus 17
Free University
10553 Berlin (Germary)
Email: gerdmevissen@hotmail.com

Dr. Falk Reitz
Dept. of Indian Art History
Free University
Berlin (Germany)
Email: rishab@zedat.fu-berlin.de

Prof. Enamul Haque
The International Centre for Study of Bengal Art
House 32-E, Road 17A, Banani
Dhaka 1213 (Bangladesh)

Prof. C. Willemen
Belgian Royal Academy Sciences
PB 656
8400 Oostende (Belgium)

Prof. Ineke Van Put
Belgian Royal Academy Sciences
PB 656
8400 Oostende (Belgium)

Index